T0340019

# U.S. Freight Rail Economics and Policy

The passage of the Staggers Rail Act in 1980 brought a renaissance to the freight rail industry. In the decade following, economists documented the effects of the Act on a variety of important economic metrics including prices, costs, and productivity. Over the succeeding years, and with the return of the industry to more stable footing, attention to the industry by economists faded. The lack of attention, however, has not been due to a dearth of ongoing economic and policy issues that continue to confront the industry.

In this volume, we begin to rectify this inattention. Rather than retread older analyses or provide yet another look at the consequences of Staggers, we assemble a collection of 10 chapters in four sections that collectively provide fresh and up-to-date analyses of the economic issues and policy challenges the industry faces: the first section sets the context through foundational discussion of freight rail, the second section highlights the role of freight rail in an increasingly interrelated economy, the third section examines industry structure and scope in freight rail, and the fourth section assesses current regulatory challenges that confront freight rail. This book will be of great value to researchers, academics, policymakers, and students interested in the fields of freight rail economics and policy, transportation, business history, and regulatory economics.

**Jeffrey T. Macher** is a Professor of Strategy, Economics, and Public Policy in the McDonough School of Business at Georgetown University, USA.

**John W. Mayo** is the Elsa Carlson McDonough Professor of Business Administration and a Professor of Economics, Business, and Public Policy in the McDonough School of Business at Georgetown University, USA.

# Routledge Studies in Transport Analysis

*For a complete list of titles in this series, please visit* www.routledge.com/
Routledge-Studies-in-Transport-Analysis/book-series/RSTA

# U.S. Freight Rail Economics and Policy

Are We on the Right Track?

Edited by Jeffrey T. Macher and
John W. Mayo

Routledge
Taylor & Francis Group

LONDON AND NEW YORK

First published 2019 by Routledge

2 Park Square, Milton Park, Abingdon, Oxon, OX14 4RN
605 Third Avenue, New York, NY 10017

*Routledge is an imprint of the Taylor & Francis Group, an informa business*

First issued in paperback 2020

Copyright © 2019 Taylor & Francis

The right of Jeffrey T. Macher and John W. Mayo to be identified as the authors of the editorial material, and of the authors for their individual chapters, has been asserted in accordance with sections 77 and 78 of the Copyright, Designs and Patents Act 1988.

All rights reserved. No part of this book may be reprinted or reproduced or utilised in any form or by any electronic, mechanical, or other means, now known or hereafter invented, including photocopying and recording, or in any information storage or retrieval system, without permission in writing from the publishers.

Notice:
Product or corporate names may be trademarks or registered trademarks, and are used only for identification and explanation without intent to infringe.

*Library of Congress Cataloging-in-Publication Data*
A catalog record for this book has been requested

ISBN: 978-0-367-14283-4 (hbk)
ISBN: 978-0-367-78646-5 (pbk)

Typeset in Sabon
by Apex CoVantage, LLC

# Contents

SECTION III
## The Structure of the Rail Industry

SECTION IV
## Railroads and Post-Staggers Regulation

# Preface

In 1980, the American freight rail industry lay at an inflection point. The prior decades had witnessed the financial and physical deterioration of the industry, while the future—catalyzed by the passage of the Staggers Rail Act—would bring a renaissance to the industry. Both the dire financial condition of the industry and the subsequent economic turnaround created an almost ideal setting for economists to analyze the causes of the deterioration and the emergent consequences of the Staggers Act. Indeed, in the decade following the passage of Staggers Act, economists documented its effects on a variety of important economic metrics including prices, costs, and productivity. Over the years, and with the return of the industry to more stable footing, attention to the industry by economists faded. The lack of attention, however, has not been due to a dearth of ongoing economic and policy issues that have continued to confront the industry.

In this volume, we begin to rectify this inattention. Rather than retread older analyses or provide yet another look at the consequences of Staggers, we assemble a collection of 10 chapters by a variety of economists (and even a lawyer!) who together provide fresh and up-to-date analyses of the economic issues and policy challenges the industry faces as it heads into the third decade of the new century. The first section of the volume includes two chapters that provide foundational discussion that permit economists, industry practitioners, and policymakers alike to understand both the policy evolution since the passage of Staggers and the economic foundations for policymaking going forward.

The second section of the volume consists of three chapters that highlight the role of the freight rail industry in an increasingly interrelated economy. These chapters, in particular, examine interrelationships involving railroads that are spatial in nature or occur across industries. Identifying and understanding these specific interrelationships are crucial for understanding the role of the rail industry in the U.S. economy and how policy might best evolve in this interrelated context.

The third section of the volume includes two chapters that address the fundamental economics of industry structure in freight rail. Here, industry issues around both the horizontal and the vertical scope are examined. Given the centrality of industry structure to economic performance, these chapters offer a new and important lens for assessing the industry.

The final section of the volume turns to assessments of regulatory challenges that confront the industry moving forward. This section consists of three chapters that address a number of "hot button" issues facing the industry, including the law and economics of "revenue adequacy," open access, and the incentive consequences of potential profit regulation.

For our part, it has been a pleasure to work with the outstanding contributors to this volume who have patiently tolerated our nudging (and sometimes outright pushing) on substantive aspects of their chapters as well as numerous smaller edits that have (we hope) enhanced the quality of the volume. We are also grateful to our publisher, Routledge, for making the process as seamless as possible. Finally, we are very grateful to the Georgetown Center for Business and Public Policy at Georgetown University's McDonough School of Business for hosting three annual colloquia on the economics and regulation of the freight rail industry. These colloquia provided opportunities to develop and vet the primary research that has become the core of this volume.

We hope that you enjoy reading the book as much as we have enjoyed producing it!

*Jeffrey T. Macher and John W. Mayo, Editors*

# Section I

# Foundations

# 1 The Evolution of the Post-Staggers Rail Industry and Rail Policy

*Mark Burton and Paul Hitchcock*

The rehabilitation of the North American railroad industry that followed regulatory reform has been referred to as a *renaissance.*[1] The policies embodied in the Staggers Rail Act of 1980, as well as other reform legislation, were the product of urgent compromise and were vigorously implemented by market-oriented reformers. This combination offered new opportunity to an industry on the verge of collapse. For their part, the railroads and their customers embraced the reforms by changing their business practices and by rapidly investing in the new facilities and equipment necessary to the consequent rebirth. It is a story that is often told and rightly celebrated.

Not surprisingly, a great deal has been written about the legislative reforms that led to the physical and fiscal industry recovery.[2] However, the nature of specific reform-related regulatory actions and how market participants responded to those actions have been less studied. Further, only recently have scholars begun to consider how implementing the Staggers Act has also changed the institutions that oversee railroads. Ultimately, it is all these factors—the nature of changed regulations, how they were applied, the behaviors they induced, and the evolved characteristics of the regulatory bodies—that explain current rail industry conditions and what might be necessary and possible going forward.

Against this backdrop, this introduction to the current volume attempts a slightly more holistic depiction of the past three and one-half decades of railroad industry oversight and performance. More important, we explore how the last 37 years of policy experience should guide future railroad policy.

## "The Most Successful Legislation Ever"

In 1995, as Congress prepared to terminate the Interstate Commerce Commission (ICC) and transfer remaining regulatory responsibilities to the newly created Surface Transportation Board (STB), the Senate Commerce Committee concluded, "The Staggers Act is considered the most successful rail transportation legislation ever produced, resulting in the restoration of financial health to the rail industry."[3] This unequivocal praise, although perhaps justified, neither reflected the 15-year struggle necessary to implement the 1980 legislation, nor anticipated the policy battles that would take place in the 20th century's waning years and thereafter. While in 1995, the Staggers Act was widely considered successful, the reforms it engendered were the result of torturous exertions over myriad legal and economic issues. Moreover, as later chapters will demonstrate, many of these issues have never been fully resolved.

The Staggers Act's most effective elements can be grouped into three areas: (1) provisions that promoted rate-making flexibility by allowing a significant amount of traffic to be excluded from oversight, (2) provisions providing for continued shipper protections and the regulatory redress of excessive rates, and (3) components that guide the rail industry structure through the oversight of mergers, abandonments, and branch-line sales.[4] While not always the case, the statute's language often signaled legislative intent without supplying implementation details. Instead, developing, vetting, and introducing numerous new standards and procedures was generally left to the ICC.

## Reducing the Regulatory Reach

In recent years, roughly 60% of railroad traffic has moved under rates that are not subject to direct regulatory oversight.[5] This reduced regulatory reach is the result of two legal elements that were introduced prior to Staggers but which were significantly strengthened by the 1980 statute. Specifically, Staggers expanded regulators' authority to exempt specific classes of traffic from rate oversight and, for the first time, the Act made it legal for carriers and shippers to enter into confidential contracts which are also exempt from regulatory intervention.

Congress had given the ICC authority to exempt "matters relating to a common carrier by railroad" in Section 207 of the Railroad Revitalization and Regulatory Reform (4R) Act of 1976. And the agency had used that authority to exempt trailer-on-flatcar and container-on-flatcar traffic.[6] Nonetheless, the sitting commissioners in the late 1970s were, at best, hesitant to use their exemption authority. Staggers lowered the standard for issuing exemptions, and the Commissioners appointed under the Reagan administration were more aggressive in their use.

Reasoning that boxcar traffic faces sufficient competition from trucks, the Commission exempted this traffic from regulatory oversight. Many other exemptions followed.[7] The most significant of these exempted specific commodities. On the basis of these decisions, the carriers could quickly adjust rates without fear that these changes would be investigated or suspended.[8]

Individual customers could receive individual rates without concern that a rate reduction for one would be immediately sought by all. The long-standing anti-rebate provisions of the Elkins Act, which made it a crime to charge a shipper less than the published tariff rate, could now be avoided by filing a request to exempt the refund from regulation.

As might be expected, exemptions were never fully favored by shippers. Accordingly, in 2010, the STB began to revisit the need for and appropriateness of continued exemptions.[9] In the years that followed, the STB developed little empirical evidence on the matter. Nonetheless, in 2016, the STB proposed eliminating commodity exemptions for four commodity groups.[10] To date, the STB has acted no further on this proposal.

Tailoring individual rates and service characteristics to specific demand conditions without regulatory oversight was also promoted by Staggers' provisions on contracting. The ICC had, to a degree, begun to sanction contracts in 1978, but contract terms could not be kept confidential.[11] Therefore, contracts were seldom used. This changed dramatically under Staggers.

As with exemptions, the methods used by the ICC to apply Staggers were as responsible for the growth in contracting as the statute itself. Staggers' language is relatively vague regarding which contract terms can be made confidential and which terms must be publicly reported. However, the ICC, responding to the desires of both carriers and most shippers, adopted rules that maximized confidentiality. This did not go without legal challenge, but the Commission was unrelenting in its defense of confidentiality. In addition to its support of confidentiality, the ICC promoted contracting by adopting rules that allow contract rates to be applied without delay and by reducing, then virtually eliminating, contract reporting requirements.[12]

There are, at least, two facets of railroad service contracts that affect rate regulation. First, the STB has no oversight powers for contract rates. By voluntarily entering into contracts, shippers relinquish any rights to rate relief. Further, the STB is not empowered to adjudicate non-rate disputes that arise under contracts. Instead, contract issues must be addressed through state or federal district courts. Of less importance, as will be further discussed, shippers who contract for one segment of a multi-segment movement may jeopardize their ability to invoke rate protections on related, non-contracted legs of the same movement.

It is easy to focus on the regulatory impacts of contracts, but the economic advantages are far more important. With contracts, a shipper could now offer volume commitments to a railroad in exchange for lower rates. With volume commitments available, railroads could make investment decisions with heretofore unimaginable confidence. A shipper could agree to acquire freight cars, and the railroad could make a contractually binding commitment to use them. Shippers could make multiyear budget decisions knowing that rates would not increase. Railroads could offer competitive rate and service packages to induce a customer to locate at a particular site, or to expand an existing facility. These abilities for carriers and customers to tailor commercial arrangements to their reciprocal needs underpinned a railroad marketing revolution based on practices that had previously been illegal.[13]

While the welfare implications of contracting are unarguably positive, their impact on observed rail rates is less clear. Contract shipments typically move at rates that are lower than those available through common carriage. However, the shipment characteristics are also different, so that it is difficult to isolate the extent to which contracts affect the costs incurred by shippers. Moreover, contracts often include performance clauses or volume guarantees that are not evident in observed rates.[14]

## Residual Shipper Protections

While Staggers promoted rail pricing flexibility, it did not abandon shipper protections or the policy objective that rail rates remain "reasonable" for shippers who have limited transportation alternatives. Instead, the Act mandates what has emerged as a three-step process through which shippers can challenge rail rates and potentially achieve relief through regulatory intervention. Under this process:

1.  A shipper must first show that the challenged rate exceeds a revenue-to-variable cost (R/VC) threshold of 180%. If this condition is not met, the complaint will not proceed, but a rate that exceeds the threshold is not to be treated as proof of carrier market dominance.
2.  If the challenged rate exceeds the prescribed R/VC of 180%, shippers are given the chance to further demonstrate that the incumbent carrier is market dominant within what was originally intended as a qualitative hearing process.[15]
3.  Finally, if the demonstration of market dominance is successful, the rates are adjudicated to evaluate their reasonableness.

The 4R Act, which predates Staggers by four years, required that the ICC define and implement a method for determining the presence of railroad "market dominance." Early standards emerged in 1978. However, Staggers redefined market dominance, so that its consideration first rests exclusively on the observed R/VC ratio. Complaints based on challenged rates that fall below the prescribed threshold are dismissed. Initially set at 160%, this threshold has effectively been 180% since 1984. The implication is that any rate that is less than 180% of a movement's average variable cost is sufficiently competitive in appearance to avoid regulatory attention, but a rate that is 180% or greater than the movement's average variable cost may be, at least, suspect in its reasonableness.[16]

The second step summarized earlier requires a definitive qualitative assessment as to the issue of market dominance. Neither Staggers nor the federal code it modified provides any real guidance regarding the specific course or content of this evaluation. The law simply states that "market dominance' means an absence of effective competition from other rail carriers or modes of transportation for the transportation to which a rate applies."[17] Making this definition operational has been the responsibility of first the ICC and later the STB. A relatively recent decision by the latter summarizes current practice.

> The Board determines whether there are any feasible transportation alternatives that are sufficient to constrain the railroad's rates to competitive levels, considering both intramodal competition –competition from other railroads – and intermodal competition –competition from other modes of transportation such as trucks, transload arrangements, barges, or pipelines. Even where feasible transportation alternatives are shown to exist, those alternatives may not provide "effective competition." Effective competition for a firm providing a good or service means that there must be pressures on that firm to perform up to standards and at reasonable prices, or lose desirable business.[18]

Notably missing is any reference to product or geographic substitutes. In a traditional antitrust setting, an early and always critical part of market assessment involves defining the relevant market on the basis of the availability and substitutability of alternative goods or services.[19] Typically, this includes both product and geographic dimensions. Thus, in the case of a rail-served market, the market definition process might consider rail and non-rail transportation alternatives evaluated over both current and alternative origin-destination pairs. And it might also include the substitution of an alternative commodity if the transportation options for that alternative are different from those available for movement of the commodity in question.

Staggers does not directly address the issue of product or geographic substitutes. However, the ICC, in 1981, included four specific substitutes within its qualitative evaluation of market dominance: (1) intramodal (other rail) transportation substitutes, (2) intermodal (other modal) substitutes, (3) geographic substitutes in the form of alternative origins or destinations, and (4) product substitutes that might afford different transportation alternatives.[20] Thus, in its market dominance standard, the ICC adopted a position that was consistent with economic practice in other settings. However, the ICC's position on geographic and product substitutes was reversed in a 1998 STB decision that is further discussed *infra*.

Just as rates that exceed the 180% R/VC threshold are necessary, but not sufficient proof of market dominance, a finding of market dominance is not sufficient proof that the challenged rates are unreasonable. More simply, a judgment that a railroad has market power is not proof that it has exercised it inappropriately. Accordingly, the last step in a rate challenge is to show that the rates charged by the market dominant carrier are unreasonable. Further, although both the 4R and Staggers Acts specify a threshold R/VC against which rail rates can be evaluated in establishing market dominance, neither statute provides guidance regarding rate reasonableness.[21] Instead, this task has been left exclusively to the ICC and the STB.

After at least one aborted attempt to develop reasonableness criteria, the ICC, in 1983, announced its intent to establish principles to be applied to coal movements and which were subsequently applied to most cases in which market dominance had been established.[22] These standards are embodied within a construct known as Constrained Market Pricing (CMP). CMP is a hybrid combination of Ramsey pricing and policies tied to the mechanics of contestable markets. Because the CMP methodology dominated residual rail regulation for two decades and retains a prominent role under current oversight, it warrants careful consideration here.

To begin, the efficient production of railroad services requires the shared use of common network elements that impose costs that often cannot be "attributed" or made incremental to specific freight services. These common costs, in combination with seemingly inexhaustible economies of density, lead to a situation in which marginal (or incremental) cost pricing fails to generate sufficient railroad revenues and in which the would-be revenue shortfalls cannot be recovered by assigning easily justified higher rates for some or all of the subject railroad traffic.

In a classic regulatory setting, this problem might be addressed by applying *Ramsey* or *quasi-optimal* pricing. However, in a railroad setting, this would be impossibly complex. Accordingly, CMP allows railroads to freely discriminate in setting rates among customers so long as two conditions are met. First, under the Coal Rate Guidelines decision, overall firm revenues cannot consistently exceed total costs, including a fair and necessary return on capital. This so-called revenue adequacy constraint is highly controversial and has been challenged by the rail industry as neither consistent with the statute nor sound economic policy, as discussed *infra*. Second, individual rates cannot exceed levels that are consistent with competitive outcomes. The determination of this second threshold or ceiling is based on the stand-alone cost (SAC) of providing the specific service(s) in question.

The concept of SAC was introduced to most economists by Gerald Faulhaber's seminal 1975 work on regulatory cross-subsidies. However, in the current context, SAC is made relevant by its key role within the theory of contestable markets.[23] In its 1985 decision, the ICC finalized four criteria that have come to define CMP as applied to rail rate reasonableness:

1.  The stipulation that CMP is available only to railroads with revenues that are inadequate on the basis of the ICC's application of Staggers' definition.

2. CMP is available only to railroads that are efficiently managed as evidenced by their operating practices, investment decisions, and pricing.
3. SACs are to serve as a regulatory guidepost. In the words of the court decision upholding CMP, "If a complaining shipper pays no more than the cost of providing service tailored to its need, it is benefiting from the economics resulting from shared facilities, whereas if it is paying more than that cost the shipper may be subsidizing service from which it derives no benefit."[24]
4. If shippers can demonstrate a probable disruption to their business, CMP rates are to be phased in over time.

The first condition reflects the ICC's interpretation of Staggers' intent that largely went unchallenged until very recently. However, in the event that one or more carriers are, at some point, judged to be revenue adequate and, thereby, limited in some way in their right to engage in differential pricing, the lawfulness of this interpretation is sure to quickly be revisited.

As noted, CMP was ultimately adopted by the ICC as the reasonableness criteria for nearly all rail rate cases, not just those pertaining to coal. These standards were eventually reviewed, upheld, and occasionally modified through a variety of additional ICC dockets and judicial proceedings. Still, the fundamental rate challenge process developed by the Commission in 1983 changed little for more than a decade.

## Facilitating Structural Change

Over the first three-quarters of the 20th century, the ICC had come to control nearly every aspect of railroad commerce. While unintentional, the results of this colossal oversight nearly had been disastrous. The regulatory reforms that culminated in the Staggers Act created the statutory basis for the industry's recovery. However, as noted earlier, these legislative reforms were equaled in importance by the willingness of Reagan-era ICC appointees to embrace reform's intent. Accordingly, although the Commission worked to replace direct rate oversight with market mechanics, it simultaneously acted to loosen other regulatory constraints that had made it difficult for railroads to adapt to changing economic conditions. Both the 4R Act and Staggers streamlined the administrative treatment of abandonments and railroad consolidations and, by the early 1980s, the ICC was attentive to both goals.[25]

Improving the abandonment process was, perhaps, the easier task. Beginning in the early 1970s, public sector attempts to cope with the Penn Central and related eastern railroad bankruptcies helped policymakers to understand that railroads had been forced to maintain and operate far too many low-density route-miles. Accordingly, network "rationalizations" through various means had emerged as an essential policy element prior to Staggers.[26] The 1980 Act further accelerated administrative schedules for proposed abandonments or line sales and bolstered trends that led to more of both throughout the 1980s.[27] As Figure 1.1 illustrates, whether through abandonment or line sale, U.S. Class I railroads reduced network route-miles by nearly 43% (184,000 to 106,000) between 1976 and 1996.[28]

Eliminating unprofitable trackage was an important way to reduce costs. A second means toward the same end was to eliminate interchange through mergers. This strategy was evident in the late 1970s but surged after the passage of Staggers. What is important, as Wilner (1997) notes, is that consolidation also facilitated the use of confidential contracts discussed earlier.

Depending on how one counts, in January 1981, there were roughly 20 surviving Class I railroads, including the two largest Canadian railroads and their U.S. subsidiaries.[29] Twenty years later, in 2001, there were seven. The consolidations that reduced the number of Class I carriers by two-thirds came in two groupings—the first wave in the immediate wake of Staggers and a second (and, for now, final) round of consolidations in the mid- to late 1990s.[30]

The Staggers Act made no fundamental changes to the law pertaining to railroad mergers, but the same economic pressures that led Congress to enact reforms were simultaneously leading railroad management to seek consolidations. By early 1980, the ICC had approved the merger of the St. Louis-San Francisco into Burlington Northern, and five months later approved the merger of the Chessie System and the Seaboard System. This

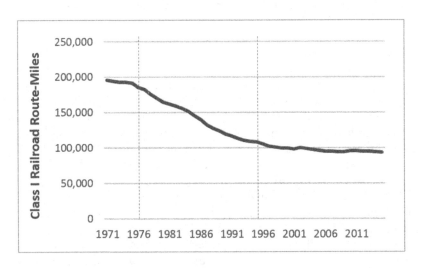

*Figure 1.1* Class I Railroad Route-Miles

latter transaction led the Norfolk and Western (prime competitor with the Chessie) and Southern Railway (prime competitor of the Seaboard) to seek and obtain merger authority. At about the same time, Union Pacific gobbled up the Missouri Pacific, the Western Pacific, and eventually the Missouri-Kansas-Texas.

The market-oriented ICC did have a significant role in approving (or disapproving) mergers. One of its most noteworthy actions was its 1981 decision to eliminate the so-called DT&I conditions.[31] For decades, merging railroads had been required to maintain rates, routes, and divisions with connecting carriers, without favoritism to their new merger partner. Thus, the merged carriers could not effectively capture many merger-related efficiencies.

The competitive pressures bolstered by the Staggers Act led to an early round of post-Staggers mergers. However, this proved to be only a precursor to a later wave of railroad mega-consolidations. These are summarized *infra*.

## Railroads, Shippers, and Traffic: 1980–1995

In 2018, finding a rail industry veteran who will admit to doubts about regulatory reform is more difficult than finding an aging hippie who will admit to *not* having been at Woodstock. But in 1981, doubts abounded. In particular, there was tremendous variation in expectations about deregulation's likely impact on rail rates, corresponding traffic volumes, contracting, and continued service availability.[32]

As noted earlier, the newly unleashed competitive pressures forced railroads to act quickly to reduce costs through network rationalizations and mergers, but these were only two of the more visible strategies for reducing costs. Cost-cutting was pursued across every aspect of operations. For example, the railroads tackled outdated labor agreements, reducing typical train crews from five to three members. This yielded the added benefit of enabling them to eliminate cabooses from most trains.[33] They rapidly replaced section track labor with mechanized system gangs and computerized most clerical functions, again, with the result of reducing labor costs.

As costs were reduced, railroads combined the resulting savings with new pricing flexibility to significantly alter rail rate structures. In aggregate, rates for nearly every commodity group fell, often both in real and in nominal terms. Nonetheless, the ability to tailor rates to reflect specific demand characteristics meant that rates for some shippers fell faster and further than the rates charged to others.[34]

On the output side, quality of service improved, new products were introduced, and traffic increased.[35] There was significant investment on both sides of rail freight markets. Railroads invested heavily in infrastructure. Shippers matched this investment and accelerated the acquisition of equipment. Perhaps the only faction that did not see clear gains was rail labor. As productivity increased, employment fell and, at the same time, the wage premiums that had long distinguished rail workers from similarly skilled labor in other industries were eroded.[36]

## The House of Morgan

The decade of the 1990s was a watershed period for the railroad industry and for rail industry oversight. In addition to a second wave of mergers, the 1990s witnessed the sale and division of Conrail, the abolition of the ICC and its replacement with the STB, and a host of key regulatory decisions, including the bottleneck cases, the exclusion of geographic and product substitutes, and the introduction of SAC alternatives. Very nearly all of this occurred under the leadership of Linda Morgan, who was sworn in as an ICC Commissioner in 1994, served as the ICC's last Chairman, and was the STB's first Chairman, all before retiring from the Board in 2003.

Merger activity had continued through the 1980s and early 1990s, but 1995 began a series of mergers that would ultimately culminate in an unprecedented governmentally imposed moratorium. In 1995, Union Pacific (UP) completed its acquisition of Chicago and Northwestern. The Burlington Northern (BN) completed its merger with Santa Fe (SF) the same year. Soon after, UP announced its acquisition of the last large road remaining in the west, the Southern Pacific (SP). This series of mergers left only two dominant carriers west of the Mississippi.

Geography suggested further consolidation in the east as well, where Conrail appeared to be the most likely target. However, neither CSX nor Norfolk Southern could allow the other to unilaterally capture the Conrail prize. Thus, the story of how the two competitors came to jointly acquire and then divide Conrail is as brutal as it fascinating.[37] Suffice it to say that the result of that transaction was a Canadian-like balance that left two mega-Class I railroads in the east and two in the west.

The BNSF merger, UP's acquisition of SP, and the Conrail transaction each suffered from highly disruptive implementations. Thus, when Canadian National (CN) and BNSF, in late December 1999, announced plans to merge, the Morgan-led STB acted quickly. Fearing that the proposed BNSF-CN consolidation would trigger a series of responsive mergers involving the other five remaining Class I carriers, the Board declared that new merger rules were needed in the face of what would likely be the end state of large railroad consolidations in North America.[38] To afford itself time to consider and adopt new rules, the STB imposed a 15-month moratorium on merger proceedings, thereby suspending all major merger activity.

The new merger rules are extensive and require the proponents to carry a substantially heavier burden, including proposing conditions for approval that would increase rather than preserve customers' competitive options.[39] Indeed, the STB's firm action left the industry with a structural equilibrium that has changed little in nearly two decades.

A large share of the STB's first years was consumed by what have come to be known as the *bottleneck* cases. The duration and complexity of these cases illustrate the extent to which precedent, unforeseen legal ambiguities, and complicated economics can wholly entangle well-intended regulatory reforms.

Historically, when vying for traffic with connecting carriers, railroads have sought the longest possible share of the total shipment mileage (the long-haul). *Ceteris paribus*, doing so yields the maximum economic rents. From a regulatory perspective, governing statutes and their application have protected the originating carrier's right to dominate in this tug-of-war, although exceptions have grown over the decades.[40] On the other hand, shippers, with little sympathy for individual railroads, have always sought to develop as many routing choices as possible. Moreover, breaking up the long-haul has been a frequent goal.[41] In the early 1950s the Supreme Court grappled with efforts to circumvent the statutory protections of the carriers' long-hauls, in the *Northern Pacific* and *Thompson* decisions.[42] The net result was a long-standing principle that the originating carrier could maximize its long-haul and could not be forced to interchange to another carrier at some point that would deprive it of that privilege.

The origin carrier's right to the long-haul went unchallenged for many years. But, with the post-Staggers emphasis on competition, in the late 1990s, several electric utilities sought to secure a decision that would provide the option of dictating interchange points that might require one carrier to surrender part of its long-haul to another. The test case in this regard was *Central Power & Light Co. v. Southern Pac. Transp. Co.*,[43] better known as *Bottleneck I*.

The complaining shipper began by characterizing the segment of rail service with no alternative route as a "bottleneck segment."[44] To provide a balance to what it perceived as the bottleneck carrier's excessive market power, the shipper sought to have the STB (1) establish a new obligation on the part of the bottleneck carrier to offer a separate service at a separate rate to the nearest interchange point, and (2) order the connecting carrier to also offer a separate rate to the interchange point with the bottleneck carrier. The commercial result, the shipper argued, would enable it to compare the bottleneck carrier's long-haul rate with the combined rates of the connecting carrier and the rate over the bottleneck segment. It would also enable the shipper to bring a stand-alone cost case challenging only the rate over the bottleneck segment.

Ultimately, the STB made several important rulings:

- A carrier is not required to establish an interchange (and a rate to it) simply upon request.

- Section 10705(a) assures the carrier of its right to its long-haul unless the STB makes certain findings related to the inefficiency or excessive length of the route.
- A shipper that is dissatisfied with the railroad's response to a request for a short-haul rate must look to the STB's existing competitive access rules.
- A shipper who obtains a contract for transportation with a non-bottleneck carrier to an interchange with the bottleneck segment might be able to demonstrate a set of service terms providing benefits, advantages, and projected efficiencies that would make the proposed service over the bottleneck segment more economically efficient than that offered over the bottleneck carrier's long-haul route. If so, that might warrant relief.

The last of these findings directly pits the contracting opportunities extended under Staggers against the historical long-haul precedent and rate-making flexibility inherent in the ICC's development of CMP.

One shipper seized upon this latter point and sought reconsideration and clarification (*Bottleneck II*).[45] It asked the STB to rule that, where a shipper obtains a rail transportation contract for a non-bottleneck segment, the bottleneck carrier must provide service over less than its long-haul and quote a challengeable common carrier rate to the point of interchange with the other carrier. The shippers were partially successful.

The Board ruled in *Bottleneck II* that, (1) where the bottleneck carrier does *not* serve the origin, and (2) when the shipper has entered into a contract with the origin carrier that calls for service to a particular interchange with the bottleneck carrier, then (3) the bottleneck carrier must offer service and a separate rate over its segment of the through route. But where the bottleneck carrier serves the origin, its statutory right to its long-haul is superior to that of the other carrier, and a contract between the shipper and the non-bottleneck carrier cannot divest the bottleneck carrier of its rights. In short, the Board "split the baby"—a practice it has often repeated—particularly under Morgan.

During the same period while the STB was wrestling with the bottleneck cases, it was also reconsidering the relevance of geographic and product substitutes in the adjudication of rate cases. Early in 1998, at Congress's request, the STB opened an *ex parte* proceeding exploring access and other competitive issues.[46] Within the course of that proceeding, the matter of geographic and product substitutes as determinants of market dominance surfaced as a major shipper concern. Accordingly, later in 1998, the Board solicited comments on the question of substitutes and subsequently decided to "eliminate from the market dominance determinations evidence of product and/or geographic competition."[47] This decision unleashed a succession of legal challenges by the railroads, but the 1998 STB ruling was upheld in 2002 and 2009.[48]

The STB's explanation of its decision did not disparage the economic relevance of non-transportation substitutes. Instead, the Board's actions were aimed at expediting the rate adjudication process, reducing its own regulatory burden and, perhaps, dampening the railroads' ability to exercise pricing power.[49] The Board wrote:

> We believe that the limited impact on the rail industry from this decision is far outweighed by the chilling effect that inclusion of product and geographic competition can have on the filing of valid rate complaints by captive shippers and on the resolution of rate complaints in a timely manner. And we also believe that negating this chilling effect will further level the playing field between railroads and shippers to the extent that disputes will be resolved in the private sector.[50]

The STB further contended that, in the face of truly effective geographic or product substitutes, shippers would not have an incentive to pursue costly rate challenges.[51] Their decision states:[52]

> Many shippers acknowledge that product and/or geographic competition can effectively constrain a railroad's rates, especially when such competition provides a direct transportation alternative. However, in such circumstances, AAR agrees that rate complaints are unlikely to be filed with the Board, because rate litigation is a costly, time-consuming and thus an ineffective means of obtaining competitive rates when actual competitive options give shippers negotiating leverage.

Finally, the Board suggested that its decision to disallow geographic and product substitutes in the determination of market dominance added no procedural burden to the defendant railroad given the STB's practice of combining that determination with its evaluation of rate reasonableness. The Board wrote:[53]

> [H]aving to defend the reasonableness of the rate in cases where product and geographic competition arguably could be found to effectively constrain the rate level imposes no additional burden on the railroads, because under our present procedures we generally do not bifurcate rate cases into separate evidentiary phases for the market dominance and rate reasonableness issues. Therefore, a carrier is generally required to fully defend the reasonableness of its rate before we make the market dominance determination.

Ignoring some competitive forces in the interest of administrative efficiency was one agency-initiated step. Another has been the increased regulatory importance of the R/VCs that are used as regulatory gate-keepers, which reinforces the need to periodically reexamine both the derivation and uses of these values and other similarly derived benchmark measures.

By all accounts, pursuit of a rate complaint under the CMP process is expensive and time consuming, with costs measured in millions of dollars and procedural durations measured in years.[54] Accordingly, from the time of CMP's introduction in 1983, shipper organizations had encouraged the ICC to develop a simplified analytical process that could be used in rate challenges with smaller potential awards.[55] Finally, the task of doing so was specifically mandated by Congress in the ICC Termination Act of 1995 (ICCTA).[56] Congress directed the new STB to complete that rulemaking within a year, which the new agency did in 1996.[57] The result was The Three-Benchmark method for evaluating rate reasonableness in relatively small rate cases.

From its inception, shippers were unsatisfied with the original form of the Three-Benchmark standard; in the first several years after adoption, only three cases were brought under these so-called simplified guidelines. In response, in April 2003 and July 2004, the STB held hearings to examine why the process had not been used more.[58] The results prompted changes by the Board in 2007.[59] The current iteration of the Three-Benchmark standard uses a variety of revenue to variable cost ratios (R/VCs) that are relatively easy to calculate and compares them to the revenue to variable cost ratio of the challenged movement.[60]

The first of the three benchmarks is referred to as the $R/VC_{>180}$ benchmark. Excluding all traffic with an R/VC less than or equal to 180%, this benchmark is calculated as the average R/VC for all the carrier's traffic with an R/VC greater than 180%. In a sense, it can be thought of as the average markup across regulated traffic for the defendant carrier.

The second of the three benchmarks is the Revenue Shortfall Allocation Method (RSAM), which calculates an R/VC ratio that the defendant carrier would have to earn on all its traffic above the 180 R/VC jurisdictional threshold in order to cover all of its costs including its cost of capital.[61] Rather than reflecting actual outcomes, the RSAM is better thought of as a target value that is consistent with adequate revenues.

The third of the three benchmarks is the most complicated. As stated by the Board:

> The third benchmark is revenue-to-variable cost comparison (R/$VC_{COMP}$). This benchmark is used to compare the markup on the challenged traffic to the average markup assessed on other potentially captive traffic involving the same or a similar commodity with similar transportation characteristics. The $R/VC_{COMP}$ ratio for appropriate comparison traffic is computed using traffic data from the rail industry Waybill Sample and applying the Board's Uniform Rail Costing System.[62]

Explaining the logic behind this benchmark is curious. The Board writes:

> The R/VC$_{COMP}$ benchmark evidence can be supplemented, where appropriate, with specific evidence as to why the markup on the traffic at issue *should* be higher or lower than that of the comparison traffic. We believe this imperfect approach is far preferable to abandoning any effort to take demand-based differential pricing into account in a simplified analysis.
>
> (emphasis added)

To calculate R/VC$_{COMP}$, the complainant shipper and the defendant railroad are required to propose a group of traffic that each contends is "comparable" and to calculate the R/VC ratio for their respective proposed comparable groups. The agency then selects one or the other traffic group for its final computation.

The three benchmarks are combined formulaically to set a cap on the allowable R/VC of the challenged movement, although the agency has left open the possibility that either or both parties could persuade it to depart from the formulaic result by presenting "other relevant factors." The cap is a straightforward calculation.

Each R/VC in the comparison group is adjusted to reflect the relative revenue needs of the defendant carrier through the use of an adjustment factor, Fa, defined as:

$$Fa = \frac{RSAM}{R/VC_{>180}}$$

Each R/VC$_{COMP}$ is multiplied by Fa and the mean value is then calculated. Mean R/VC$_{COMP}$ and its corresponding standard deviation, s, are determined. Finally, the process involves the calculation of a confidence interval around Mean R/VC$_{COMP}$. The upper bound of this confidence interval is then used as a limit against which the issue rate's R/VC is compared. Specifically, this limit equals:

$$Mean \; R/VC_{COMP} + t_{n-1} \left[ \frac{\sigma}{(n-1)^{1/2}} \right]$$

If the challenged rate exceeds the limit, the shipper is awarded refunds and a prescription for the future.

To date, there has been but little experience with the Three-Benchmark formulaic process. In a series of three cases brought simultaneously, the shipper challenged seven different railroad movements. In one, the STB found that the carrier did not have market dominance and dismissed the complaint, thus upholding the rate. In the six remaining challenged movements, the agency awarded reduced rates. However, before the matter became administratively final, the railroad and customer settled all issues between them.[63] Despite that apparent shipper success, only two further cases have been brought invoking the Three-Benchmark standard. One resulted in a shipper win, and the other in a settlement.

In the same decision that modified the Three-Benchmark standard in 2007, the STB created a new simplified standard that attempts to mimic a stand-alone cost analysis using the defendant's system average costs for the alternative hypothetical competitor. This "simplified stand-alone cost" procedure is commonly referred to as SSAC.

Conceptually, this approach tests whether the complaining shipper is cross-subsidizing other shippers rather than whether there are avoidable inefficiencies in the defendant's network or its operations. It imposes restrictions on what evidence must be used. Examples include the following:

- Evidence must be based on the existing railroad configuration and facilities.
- Evidence must be based on all traffic that actually moved over the selected portions of the defendant's rail network.
- Parties must use the system average costs to calculate the operating to calculate operating expenses for the stand-alone railroad.

This relieves the complaining shipper of the heavy expense of "building" the stand-alone railroad with selected cost data. In using SSAC, the complainant must design the stand-alone railroad within the defendant's existing rail network, but this had already become the norm in all stand-alone cases.[64] Since its adoption in 2007, only one case has been brought under the SSAC standard, and it settled prior to an STB ruling. All in all, the Three-Benchmark and SSAC procedures have been little used since the first Three-Benchmark rules were adopted in 1996.

Despite the STB's efforts to tighten time schedules in SAC cases, create simplified standards, increase the duration of rate prescriptions in simplified cases, and raise the recovery limits in simplified cases, the shipper community continues to seek faster, cheaper, and more certain outcomes. The STB again addressed these concerns in 2013, increasing the "small claims court" limit on Three-Benchmark cases from $2 million to $4 million and removing any limit on recovery under SSAC.[65] No additional simplified cases have been filed since then.

## Railroads, Shippers, and Traffic: 1996–Present

Sustaining the renaissance through the early decades of the 21st century has proven difficult, and further gains of any sort have come more slowly. Many of the headwinds the industry has faced have been beyond its control. Examples include the 2007–2009 recession, the reduced domestic and global demands for coal, volatile petroleum prices, and the federal mandate for the development and deployment of Positive Train Control (PTC). At the same time, the becalmed state of the industry also seems to reflect strategies that favor higher unit revenues over traffic growth.

Figure 1.2 compares nominal Class I rail traffic (revenue tons) with inflation-adjusted U.S. GDP since ICCTA. Traffic volumes have remained flat (1.42% growth), whereas the economy has grown significantly (55.67% growth).[66] Again, part of the post-recession stagnation is explained by the decline in coal traffic. Coal tonnage peaked in 2008 at 879 million tons and by 2015 had fallen more than 27% to 638 million tons. Still, Figure 1.2 also illustrates what total rail traffic might have looked like had coal volumes continued to grow and this counterfactual representation suggests that lost coal traffic is only part of the post-recession railroad story.[67]

Figure 1.3 provides industry-wide, inflation-adjusted revenues per ton-mile for a variety of commodities. While 2015 rates compare favorably to pre-Staggers prices, the downward trend in real rates ended around 2003 and, on average, carrier charges have increased measurably since that time. In a world where demand curves are assumed to slope down, it is hard not to link the paucity of railroad traffic growth with carrier pricing.

To an extent, the higher real rail rates observed since the early 2000s probably reflect increased carrier costs. By 2003, excess network capacity had long been exhausted and fuel prices were high during the new century's first decade. On the other hand, industry critics suggest that the

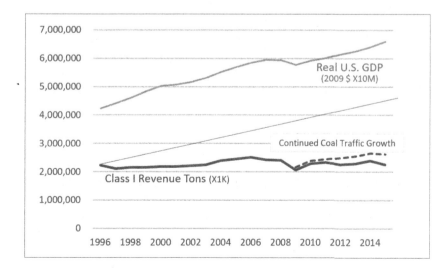

*Figure 1.2* Rail Traffic and Real U.S. GDP Growth

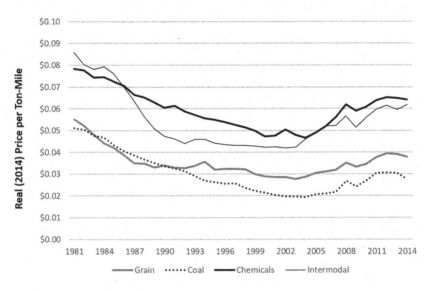

*Figure 1.3* Inflation-Adjusted Railroad Rates

higher rates reflect pricing strategies that were made possible by mergers. Further inference regarding railroad pricing and growth strategies is beyond the scope of our current text. Suffice it to say, however, that there is little or no evidence of excessive profits and there is ample evidence of unabated and strong network investments by each of the seven surviving Class I carriers.

As further discussed *infra*, most railroads continue to be judged as revenue inadequate by the STB. At the same time, since 1980, freight railroads have invested more than $660 billion on capital expenditures and maintenance expenses related to locomotives, freight cars, track, bridges, tunnels, and other infrastructure and equipment. Thus, it appears the railroad industry is directing a significant share of its earnings to renewed and expanded capacity.

## Rail Industry Oversight in the New Millennium

The merger moratorium and the STB's exclusion of product and geographic substitutes were the last major decisions in the Linda Morgan era and, so far, they are the most visible regulatory changes of the 21st century. By outward appearance and with only a few exceptions, the economic regulation of railroads has changed little in the intervening years. However, this apparent calm is misleading. What to an outsider might look quiet is really the turbulent result of two sides pushing hard against each other in opposite directions. The result is a stalemate that has sometimes postponed, but not necessarily informed, decisions on pivotal regulatory issues.

At the core of the various policy scuffles that have arisen in the past 15 years, there is a single fundamental dispute. Shippers feel that the railroad industry is physically and financially robust, so that the rate-making flexibility and attendant revenues afforded under CMP are no longer necessary or appropriate. Instead, they encourage policies that facilitate rate cases, engender more intramodal competition, and recapture economic profits. The railroad position is very different. Railroads contend that, although visibly stronger, the industry is still vulnerable, particularly on a forward-looking basis, so that the more aggressive rate oversight or the introduction of additional competition through regulatory fiat would geld revenues, choke investment, and perhaps ultimately return the industry to a state of near collapse.

Placed in the context of these strongly held and wholly dichotomous outlooks, specific actions by shippers and railroads are easier to understand. For example, a 2006 shipper proposal to substitute the Capital Asset Pricing Model (CAPM) in place of the Discounted Cash Flow Model (DCFM) in the STB's calculation of the cost of equity led to a brutal, two-year battle that, to the outside world, must have seemed inexplicable.[68] Initially, the STB decided in favor of the CAPM substitution, but on further consideration, opted to once again "split the baby" by averaging the results of CAPM and a multistage DCFM in its annual equity cost calculation.[69]

The finance literature points to advantages and disadvantages in each method and the same literature reveals no academic consensus on which is best, but the underlying beliefs and strategies of shippers and railroads made their positions predictable.[70] At the time, economic conditions and expectation were such that CAPM produced consistently lower estimates of the equity costs than the DCFM. Thus, shipper interests favored CAPM, whereas the railroads tirelessly defended the DCFM.[71]

The capital cost issue is an important element in the larger matter of railroad revenue adequacy which may, in fact, be the most important of all issues.[72] Each year, the STB directs a comparison of each railroad's cost of capital to its corresponding return on investment (ROI). If the ROI exceeds the cost of capital, then the railroad is judged as revenue adequate for that year. While seemingly innocuous in its origins, the matter of revenue adequacy has become a pivotal element in a number of current policy debates.

As a concept, revenue adequacy was first introduced, without effect, in the 4R Act and it also appears in Staggers.[73] However, the Coal Rate Guidelines added considerable potential significance to the measure's annual calculation by conditioning CMP's availability on revenue *inadequacy*.[74] And finally, revenue adequacy and its derivatives are basic components in the Three-Benchmark alternative to SAC cases discussed *supra*.[75] Given the rise in this revenue adequacy's importance, there are three questions that demand regulatory, (probably) judicial, and (possibly) legislative attention.

First, do the underlying statutes encourage or even authorize the use of revenue adequacy as a component of regulatory standards, or was it simply intended as a benchmark? Second, as an empirical device, is the current measure of revenue adequacy sufficient to support the many roles it now plays and, if not, how can it be improved? Finally, from a policy perspective, if the railroads are ever deemed to be revenue adequate, will that require a reformation of CMP that regulates railroad profits? These issues are teed-up for clarification, if not yet ripe for adjudication, in the STB's *Ex Parte 722, Railroad Revenue Adequacy* proceeding.[76]

The governing statute refers to revenue adequacy in two places. First, the National Rail Transportation Policy states that federal policy is "to promote a safe and efficient rail transportation system by allowing rail carriers to earn adequate revenues as determined by the Board."[77] Next, the section giving the Board the authority to prescribe maximum rates, states:

> The Board shall maintain and revise as necessary standards and procedures for establishing revenue levels for rail carriers . . . that are adequate, under honest, economical, and efficient management for the infrastructure and investment needed to meet the present and future demand for rail services and, to cover total operating expenses, including depreciation and obsolescence, plus a reasonable and economic profit or return (or both) on capital employed in the business. The Board shall make an adequate and continuing effort to assist those carriers in attaining revenue levels prescribed under this paragraph.[78]

The railroads maintain that, if Congress had intended to cap railroad revenues, it would not have described such a fundamental policy decision so obliquely. On the other hand, shippers point out that, in the 1985 Coal Rate Guidelines, the ICC included revenue adequacy as a condition. The ICC's order stated:

> [The] revenue adequacy standard represents a reasonable level of profitability for a healthy carrier. It fairly rewards the rail company's investors and assures shippers that the carrier will be able to meet their service needs for the long term. Carriers do not need greater revenues than this standard permits, and we believe that, in a regulated setting, they are not entitled to any higher revenues. Therefore, the logical first constraint on a carrier's pricing is that its rates not be designed to earn greater revenues than needed to achieve and maintain this "revenue adequacy" level.[79]

In essence, the ICC appears to have said that if a railroad ever reaches revenue adequacy, the pricing flexibility inherent in CMP will no longer be available to it. Interestingly, no legal challenge was brought in response to this language, so that whether the pricing flexibility fostered by CMP can be conditioned on revenue *inadequacy* was never judicially tested.

As part of an academic treatment of revenue adequacy, Macher et al. focus on a different issue. They write, "The phrase itself (revenue adequacy) provokes the natural question, *adequate for what?*"[80] Congress answered this question in part in the Surface Transportation Board Reauthorization Act of 2015, which states that revenues must be adequate to provide "for the infrastructure and investment needed to meet the present and *future* demand for rail services." Still, although this language speaks to the level of revenues the STB might find "adequate," it sheds little light on the regulatory debate over the agency's authority.

In a 2018 rate case decision, the STB had to address a shipper's argument that the defendant railroad was revenue adequate—despite having been found revenue inadequate in each of the preceding 28 years.[81] The Board was unpersuaded by the evidence introduced; thus, it appears it will resolve the legal and policy issues surrounding this subject within a rulemaking rather than through individual cases. For the STB, this is an important departure from a historical tendency to form regulatory policy on a case-by-case basis.[82]

The issue of revenue adequacy is fundamental to a second major policy matter currently before the Board, the matter of mandatory, noncooperative network access. While the Staggers Act generally reduced regulatory intervention, in the case of network access, it expanded the ICC's authority by adding the power to prescribe reciprocal switching arrangements when "practicable and in the public interest or where necessary to provide competitive rail service."[83]

In response, as it worked to implement Staggers, the ICC adopted a set of competitive access regulations (CARs) to guide the application of this new authority.[84] These regulations were the outgrowth of railroad-shipper negotiations that proposed a set of rules to implement section 11102 and were adopted with very little modification by the agency.

Central to the CARs was this definition of when a request for mandated switching would be considered:

> [A] switching arrangement shall be established under [the statute], if the Commission determines: (1) That the prescription or establishment (A) is necessary to remedy or prevent an act that is contrary to the competition policies of 49 U.S.C. § 10101a or is otherwise anticompetitive and (B) otherwise satisfies the criteria of [the statute] . . . 49 C.F.R. § 1144.5(a).

The application of this anticompetitive act prerequisite to a switching order was tested in the now-famous *Midtec* case.[85] In rejecting a shipper's request for reciprocal switching, the ICC held that it was not enough that the shipper would likely secure a lower rate if a second carrier in effect had "access" to the plant, nor was it enough that the shipper's competitors often had access to two rail carriers. Similarly, although inadequate service would have been at least an indicator of abuse of monopoly power, the customer could make no showing of abuse.

Since the so-called *Midtec* standard was sustained by the D.C. Circuit in 1988, few cases have been brought under the competitive access regulations and no shipper has prevailed. The shippers maintain that it is impossible to obtain relief under the rules because the anticompetitive standard is too high to meet.

Accordingly, in 2014, the National Industrial Traffic League (NITL) filed a petition in which it urged the agency to abandon the Midtec standard and rewrite the CARs to make it easier for a shipper to obtain a switching order. At its core, the NITL proposal called for the STB to order switching by a sole serving Class I carrier if (1) the railroad faces no effective intermodal or intramodal competition and (2) there is or could be a "working interchange" within 3 miles of the petitioning shipper's facility. Under this proposal, there would no longer be a need to demonstrate any competitive abuse.

In response to the NITL petition, the STB opened a new proceeding, EP 711 (Sub-No. 1) *Reciprocal Switching* in which it proposed its own version of competitive access.[86] Under the STB proposal, "The Board may require rail carriers to enter into reciprocal switching agreements, where it finds such agreements to be *practicable and in the public interest*, or where such agreements are *necessary to provide competitive rail service*."[87]

In its proposal, the Board made one very substantial change from the NITL tender. By eliminating the specific quantifiable criteria of the NITL proposal, the STB converted the proposed across-the-board right into a case-by-case award. Under the Board proposal, switching would not be automatically available on demand, but rather would require a formal proceeding. It appears this course is intended to limit the use of enforced switching and, thereby, the effects of any access-related ills. In this regard, Vice Chairman Miller expressed the hope that:

> [T]he Board will rarely be called upon to impose the reciprocal switching remedy, but instead, that whatever final rules we adopt will merely provide a bit more incentive for carriers to ensure that their customers' needs are being met in those instances where that is not the case.[88]

Whether access is easily obtained or must be won on a case-by-case basis, any STB action that liberalizes the availability of network access raises myriad economic questions that are made all the more complex by the network setting in which rail freight services are produced and consumed. If nothing else, there is certainly the possibility of service disruptions as a result of forcing traffic onto infrastructure that may be ill-suited to more volume, additional train movements, and consequential changes in operating plans. How these disruptions would be resolved and who would face the cost of doing so has rarely been explored.

The STB can probably impose more liberal network access without additional statutory authority, and it can certainly clarify revenue adequacy issues and revisit categorical rate exemptions under current law. There are, however, those who advocate more sweeping changes that cannot be imposed without new statutory authority.

As conclusions to its 2015 report on modernizing railroad regulation, a National Academies of Science (NAS) committee of economists made recommendations that would fully abandon the regulatory regime established under the Staggers Act and replace it with a rail price control mechanism that is clearly more sympathetic to shippers.[89]

Among the NAS recommendations, four would unquestionably require statutory action:

1. Repeal the 180% revenue-to-variable-cost formula and direct USDOT to develop rate benchmarking methods that would replace revenue-to-cost relationships in screening rates for eligibility to be challenged.
2. Replace STB rate reasonableness hearings with standardless arbitration procedures that would quickly set a rate deemed eligible for challenge because it substantially exceeded rate benchmarks.
3. End annual revenue adequacy determinations and, instead, require periodic assessments of industry-wide economic and competitive conditions.
4. Transfer merger review authority to the antitrust agencies and apply customary antitrust principles rather than a public interest standard.

A thorough analysis of these proposed actions is far beyond the scope of this introduction. Suffice it to say, however, that for Congress to abandon the regulatory structure established under Staggers in favor of any such sweeping change would require a demonstration that there are substantial economy-wide advantages to be gained in exchange for the costs (and risks) that any regulatory overhaul would necessarily impose. To date, there have been no such demonstrations, nor do we know of plans to undertake them. In this light, it is highly unlikely that sweeping legislative change is imminent.

Meanwhile, we are left with an equilibrium where the fundamental tension between carriers and shippers is unresolved and where regulators face unremitting pressure to resolve that tension. The presence of large common costs necessarily drives a wedge between some railroad rates and the underlying costs that are incremental to specific transportation services. Shippers who derive the greatest value from rail transport (as

evidenced by the higher rates they are willing and able to pay) are predictably embittered by being forced to bear a larger than average share of
those common costs to ensure railroad solvency.

On the other hand, the railroads worry that any policy that arbitrarily
constrains individual rates in order to limit individual contributions to
common costs, will result in aggregated railroad revenues that are entirely
*inadequate*. In this event, they warn, available capital will find better
uses in non-railroad investments precisely at a time when private railroad
spending is critical to North America's future freight mobility.

Finally, although CMP is largely supported by sound economics, it
has been painfully difficult to apply. Moreover, the simplified standards
adopted in the interest of fairness, lower litigation costs, and expediency
have found little favor with either railroads or rail shippers, even as they
move further and further from an acceptable economic basis.

With all this unhappiness noted, we are prepared to conclude that
*none* of it matters. Economic efficiency implies nothing about the hap-
piness of market participants. To the contrary, tension and even bitter-
ness are essential forces that keep markets informed and motivate the
search for and development of market alternatives. The only salient
question is whether public oversight of the transactions in which railroad services are bought and sold can be altered in a way that improves
the economic efficiency of those transactions. To date, there is no evidence such advances are possible, but it is good and necessary that we
keep looking.

## Notes

1. Anthony B. Hatch is generally credited with coining the phrase "Railroad
   Renaissance" in the mid-1990s. See Traffic World (Nov. 16, 2008) www.joc.
   com/railroad-renaissance-proven-true_20081116.html.
2. *See, e.g.,* Winston (2005) or Caves et al. (2010).
3. *See* Comm. on Commerce, Sci. and Transp., 104th Cong., Rep. on S. 1396 3
   (1995).
4. Title II treated rates, rate appeals, confidential contracting, and railroad
   mergers. Title IV contained new provisions regarding line abandonments.
   *See* Staggers Rail Act of 1980, Pub. L. No. 96–448, S. 1946.
5. *See* Macher, Mayo and Pinkowitz (2014).
6. Improvement of TOFC/COFC Regulation, 364 I.C.C. 731 (1981), aff'd in
   relevant part sub nom; *American Trucking Ass'ns v. ICC*, 656 F.2d 1115 (5th
   Cir. 1981).
7. For a full list of exempt commodities, as well as exemptions for boxcar and
   intermodal shipments, *see* 49 C.F.R. § 1039.
8. Suspension meant that the change could not go into effect, pending an investigation and determination that the new rate or practice was lawful; if merely
   investigated, the rate went into effect but the carrier was required to "keep
   account" of the difference so as to be prepared to promptly refund to the
   shipper any charges ultimately found to be unlawful.
9. *See* Review of Commodity, Boxcar, and TOFC/COFC Exemptions, EP 704
   (Sub-No. 1) (STB served Mar. 28, 2016).

10. *Id.*
11. *See* Macher, Mayo and Pinkowitz (2014).
12. *See* Sidman (2003).
13. The Elkins Act penalties were not limited to cash refunds. Even small benefits could run afoul of the law.
14. Interestingly, in an early assessment of contracting's effects, Meyer and Tye suggest that shippers may have been disadvantaged in negotiations because they had made irreversible investments based on expectations of continued regulation. *See* John R. Meyer and William B. Tye (1988).
15. While originally treated as a qualitative issue, the STB has increasingly moved toward quantitative determinants of market dominance.
16. In rate adjudications, shipment costs are estimated through the application of the Uniform Rail Costing System (URCS), developed by the ICC and retained by the STB. The URCS construct has received considerable criticism. *See, e.g.*, "Modernizing Freight Rail Regulation," National Academy of Science, Transportation Research Board Special Report 318, June 2015.
17. 49 U.S.C. § 10707(a).
18. *See M & G Polymers USA, LLC v. CSX Transp., Inc.*, NOR 42123, p. 2 (STB served Dec. 7, 2012).
19. For a thorough discussion of market definition, *see* U.S. Department of Justice Horizontal Merger Guidelines (2010) www.justice.gov/atr/horizontal-merger-guidelines-08192010.
20. *See* Market Dominance and Consideration of Product Competition, 365 I.C.C. 118 (1981); Rail Market Dominance 365 I.C.C. 116 (1981). With this noted, the 1981 ICC decision represented a reversal from an earlier position.
21. Staggers sometimes makes distinctions between the standard of reasonableness applied to existing rates versus the reasonableness of rail rate increases. Generally, however, these are treated similarly. In both cases, the statute directs the ICC to consider the revenue needs of the carrier, but to also "prevent [a] carrier with adequate revenues from realizing excessive profits on the traffic involved." Staggers also directs the ICC to consider "the carrier's mix of rail traffic to determine whether one commodity is paying an unreasonable share of the carrier's overall revenues." *Id.*
22. *See* Coal Rate Standards—Nationwide, EP 347 (Sub-No. 1) (STB served Feb. 24, 1983). An only slightly different variant of these standards was later applied to rates for the movement on non-coal commodities. *See* Rate Guidelines—Non-Coal Proceedings, EP 347 (Sub-No. 2) (STB served Dec. 1996).
23. The theory of contestable markets was introduced and described at length by Baumol et al. (1982). However, its most extensive application to issues of economic regulation is found in Baumol and Sidak (1995).
24. This decision provides useful descriptions of all four criteria. *See Consol. Rail Corp. v. United States*, 812 F.2d 1444 (3d Cir. 1987).
25. *See* Wilner (1997).
26. Abandonments are treated in Title VIII of the Railroad Rehabilitation and Regulatory Reform Act of 1976, Pub L. 94–210, S. 2718. Further changes appear in Title IV of the Staggers Rail Act of 1980, Pub. L. No. 96–448, S. 1946.
27. Staggers also included a new statutory provision that, under certain circumstances, compels an incumbent carrier to sell an unprofitable route segment to a qualified buyer rather than abandon it. Though not popular with carriers, the ICC's willingness to embrace and enforce the Feeder Railroad Development Program sent a clear signal that network rationalization through abandonment would not necessarily be sanctioned if there were (are) viable alternatives that preserve railroad network access.

28. U.S. Class I railroads are line haul freight railroads with operating revenue of $457.91 million or more. The U.S. Class I railroads in 2017 are BNSF Railway, CSX Transportation, Grand Trunk Corporation, Kansas City Southern Railway, Norfolk Southern Combined Railroad Subsidiaries, Soo Line Railroad, and Union Pacific Railroad. Two Canadian railroads, Canadian National and Canadian Pacific, have enough revenue that they would be U.S. Class I railroads if they were U.S. companies. Both companies also own railroad systems in the United States that, by themselves, qualify to be Class I railroads. Grand Trunk Corporation consists of almost all of CN's U.S. operations. Soo Line Corporation consists of almost all of Canadian Pacific's U.S. operations. Source: Association of American Railroads.
29. Exact counts depend on the treatment of joint ownership, financial control, and other forms of quasi-consolidation.
30. While the number of Class I carriers has dwindled, the number of short lines and regional railroads has grown precipitously from roughly 200 in 1980 to more than 550.
31. Railroad Consolidation Procedures, General Policy Statement, EP 282 (Sub-No. 6) 363 I.C.C. 784 (1981).
32. These variations were thoroughly chronicled in the industry press. *See, e.g., Deregulation Clouds '81 Traffic Picture*, RAILWAY AGE, Dec. 29, 1980, at 46.
33. In 1978, Class I railroads owned 12,992 cabooses. By 1988, this number had fallen to 5,795. And in 1998, only 1,349 cabooses remained. As with many of the cost-reducing activities undertaken in the wake of Staggers, the ability to eliminate cabooses and reduce train crew size was not a direct result of regulatory reform. Rather, this ability required the renegotiation of labor contracts and, in some cases, changes to state laws. However, it was the competition fostered by the Staggers Act that motivated these actions.
34. *See* Burton (1993) or Wilson (1994).
35. *See, e.g.,* Grimm et al. (1986), Rose (1988) and Muller (1989).
36. *See* McFarland (1989) or Talley, Schwarz-Miller and Belzer (1998).
37. *See, e.g.,* Wilner (1997).
38. Public Views on Major Rail Consolidations, EP 582 (STB served Mar. 16, 2006).
39. Often ignored in the policy debates over railroad market power is the long-standing ICC/STB policy of preserving two-carrier service for customers that would otherwise go from two serving railroads to just one (so-called 2-to-1 situations). Thus, if customer X were served by railroad A and railroad B, and the two railroads proposed to merge, the ICC long required that railroad C be given an ability to serve customer X as a condition to merger approval.
40. The current statute is 49 U.S.C. § 10705(a)(2) (2018).
41. The reader's attention is directed to the phrase *ceteris paribus*, for all things are seldom equal. Consider, for example, an eastern carrier that is the sole originating railroad, but which must interchange to one of two western railroads, each of which serves the destination. While the western railroads may have longer hauls, the eastern railroad will be able to command a share of the through rate out of proportion to its mileage. Still, the general principle of the long-haul holds true over millions upon millions of movements every year, as the shippers' enthusiasm for changing the rules demonstrates.
42. *Thompson v. United States*, 343 U.S. 549 (1952); *United States v. Great N. Ry.*, 343 U.S. 562 (1952).
43. No. 41242, 1996 STB LEXIS 358 STB 1996.
44. In the STB's words, "[a] bottleneck segment is the portion of a rail movement for which no alternative rail route is available." *Cent. Power & Light Co. v. S. Pac. Transp. Co.*, FD No. 41242, at 1 (Dec. 27, 1996). Good advocacy often begins with an astute choice of terminology.

45. *Cent. Power & Light Co. v. S. Pac. Transp. Co.*, No. 41242, 1997 STB LEXIS 91 (STB 1997).
46. *See* Review of Rail Access and Competition Issues, EP 575 (STB served Feb. 20, 1998).
47. *See* Market Dominance Determination—Product and Geographic Competition, EP 627 (STB served Dec. 21, 1998).
48. While the topics of geographic and product substitutes are still relevant in terms of economic import, legal challenges to the STB's decision appear to have concluded with the D.C. Court of Appeals decision rendered in 2009. *See CSX Transp., Inc. v. S.T.B.*, 568 F.3d 236 (D.C. Cir. 2009).
49. A less generous observer could be forgiven for suspecting that this decision was yet again a Morgan-style split of the baby in the face of extensive pressure to act.
50. *See* Market Dominance Determination—Product and Geographic Competition, EP 627, p. 2 (STB served Dec. 21, 1998).
51. *Id.* at 9.
52. *Id.*
53. *Id.* at 12–13.
54. In defense of the agency's process, though, it should be remembered that the outcome of a major case can shift hundreds of millions of dollars in economic rents between the parties over the prescription period. Commercial litigation with similar sums at stake rarely proceeds to a decision with anything like the speed of an STB rate case.
55. *Supra* note 19.
56. *Supra* note 31, § 102.
57. Rate Guidelines—Non-Coal Proceedings, 1 S.T.B. 1004 (1996).
58. Rail Rate Challenges in Small Cases, EP 646 (STB served June 29, 2004); Rail Rate Challenges in Small Cases, EP 646 (STB served Mar. 26, 2003).
59. Simplified Standards for Rail Rate Cases, EP 636 (Sub-No. 1) (STB served Sept. 5, 2007).
60. A detailed discussion of the simplified standard is beyond the scope of this introduction. For a comprehensive description of the Three-Benchmark standard and critique of its economic foundation, *see* Burton (2015).
61. This is calculated annually by the agency, thus relieving the complaining party of the need to develop that number itself.
62. Simplified Standards for Rail Rate Cases—2010 RSAM and $R/VC_{>180}$ Calculations, EP 689, p. 2 (Sub-No. 3) (STB served Feb. 24, 2012).
63. *See E.I. Dupont De Nemours & Co. v. CSX Transp., Inc.*, No. 42099 (STB served Sept. 1, 2009).
64. If the complainant limits the configuration of the stand-alone railroad to the defendant's existing footprint, the STB allows it to ignore any environmental permitting costs and delays that would otherwise have to be considered.
65. Rate Regulation Reforms, EP 715 (STB served July 18, 2013).
66. Data are from the Surface Transportation Board's annual R-1 statistics and are reproduced by the Association of American Railroads in its annual *Analysis of Class I Railroads*.
67. Coal traffic peaked in 2008. To simulate the continued growth of coal, the 2008 coal volume was grown at 1.8 percent, the average annual growth rate between 1996 and 2008, and the resulting values were substituted for the actual coal volumes observed in the 2009–2015 data.
68. *See* Methodology to be Employed in Determining the R.R. Industry's Cost of Capital, EP 664 (STB served Jan. 17, 2008).
69. *Id.*; Use of a Multi-Stage Discounted Cash Flow Model in Determining the Railroad Industry's Cost of Capital, EP 664 (Sub-No. 1) (STB served Jan. 28, 2009).

70. In actuality, neither model is intended for the calculation of capital costs. Instead, both were developed for firm valuation. However, because the cost of capital is a parameter in both models, it can be isolated and solved for if other parameter values are known (or assumed).
71. These positions represent a reversal for both railroads and shippers of positions voiced only a decade earlier.
72. The annual determination of revenue adequacy rests on the estimated costs of capital, but it is equally influenced by the carriers' ROI. The ROI calculations have also been a source of controversy. Specifically, railroads argue that the replacement cost of an efficient capital stock is more appropriate than the depreciated historical values currently used as the basis for ROI calculations. From an economic vantage, their case is unassailable. However, the STB, its predecessor, the ICC, and the Government Accountability Office (GAO) have each concluded that replacing depreciated book values with replacement costs is simply too difficult to implement. *See* Association of American Railroads—Petition Regarding Methodology for Determining Railroad Revenue Adequacy, EP 679 (STB served Oct. 24, 2008).
73. *See* the Railroad Rehabilitation and Regulatory Reform Act of 1976, Pub L. 94–210, S. 2718. and the Staggers Rail Act of 1980, Pub. L. No. 96–448, S. 1946.
74. The court was not asked to review the revenue adequacy aspects of the ICC's decision – likely because revenue adequacy seemed to be out of reach to the rail industry in the 1980s.
75. Coal Rate Guidelines at 534–537.
76. Railroad Revenue Adequacy, EP 722 (STB served April 2, 2014).
77. 49 U.S.C. § 10101(3) (2018).
78. 49 U.S.C. § 10704(a)(2).
79. *See* Surface Transportation Board Reauthorization Act of 2015, S. 808, 114th Cong. § 16 (2015).
80. *See* Macher, Mayo and Pinkowitz (2014).
81. *Consumers Energy Co. v. CSX Transp.*, STB Docket NOR 42142 (Jan. 11, 2018).
82. Stone (1991) is particularly critical of the case-by-case approach often used by the ICC to develop transportation policy.
83. The statute uses the term "reciprocal switching"—a puzzling expression for a regulatory outcome that is wholly one sided. It is almost certainly a holdover from much earlier industry usage wherein two railroads operating in a city would agree to pick up and deliver traffic for each other.
84. 49 C.F.R. § 1144.
85. *Midtec Paper Co. v. Chicago and N.W. Transp. Co. (Midtec II)*, No. 39021 (ICC served Dec. 15, 1996), *aff'd, Midtec Paper Co. v. United States*, 857 F.2d 1487(D.C. Cir. 1988). In *Midtec I*, the ICC had rejected the customer's switching petition and the customer appealed. But while the appeal was pending, the ICC adopted its CARs, and the case was remanded by the court without a decision. *See Midtec Paper Co. v. Chicago and N.W. Transp. Co. (Midtec I)*, 1 I.C.C.2d 362 (1985).
86. Petition for Rulemaking to Adopt Revised Competitive Access Rules, EP 711, *decision consolidated with* Reciprocal Switching, EP 711 (Sub-No. 1) (STB served July 25, 2016).
87. 49 U.S.C. § 11102(c)(1). Emphasis added.
88. EP 711 at 33 (Miller, Vice Chairman concurring).
89. For a further discussion of the NAS recommendations, *see* Burton (2015).

# References

Baumol, William, John Panzar, and Robert Willig. 1982. *Contestable Markets and the Theory of Market Structure.* New York: Harcourt Brace Jovanovich, Inc.

Baumol, William and J. Gregory Sidak. 1995. *Transmission Pricing and Stranded Costs in the Electric Power Industry.* Washington, DC: AEI Press.

Burton, Mark L. 1993. "Railroad Deregulation, Carrier Behavior, and Shipper Response: A Disaggregated Analysis." *Journal of Regulatory Economics* 5(4): 417–434.

Burton, Mark L. 2015. "Existing Railroad Oversight and Proposed Policy Change: An Application of 'Results-Based Regulation'." *Transportation Law Journal* 42(2): 153–192.

Caves, Douglas W., Laurits R. Christensen, and Joseph A. Swanson. 2010. "The Staggers Act, 30 Years Later." *Regulation* 33(4): 28–31.

Grimm, Curtis M., Robert G. Harris, and Kenneth G. Smith. 1986. "The Impact of Rail Regulatory Reform on Rates, Service Quality, and Management Performance: A Shipper Perspective." *Logistics and Transportation Review* 22(3).

Macher, Jeffrey T. and John W. Mayo. 2018. "The Evolution of Contracting." Working paper, McDonough School of Business, Georgetown University, Washington, DC.

Macher, Jeffrey T., John W. Mayo, and Lee F. Pinkowitz. 2014. "Revenue Adequacy: The Good, the Bad and the Ugly." *Transportation Law Journal* 41(2): 85–128.

McFarland, Henry. 1989. "The Effects of United States Railroad Deregulation on Shippers, Labor, and Capital." *Journal of Regulatory Economics* 1(3): 259–270.

Meyer, John R. and William B. Tye. 1988. "Toward Achieving Workable Competition in Industries Undergoing a Transition to Deregulation: A Contractual Equilibrium Approach." *Yale Journal on Regulation* 5(2): 273–297.

Muller, Gerhardt. 1989. *Intermodal Freight Transportation,* 2nd Ed. Washington, DC: Eno Foundation.

Rose, Nancy L. 1988. "An Economic Assessment of Surface Freight Transportation Deregulation." Working Paper, Sloan School of Management, Massachusetts Institute of Technology, Boston.

Sidman, Mark H. 2003. *Transportation Contracts: Small Railroad Perspective.* Newport, RI: Association of Transportation Law Professionals. www.transportcounsel.com/wp-content/uploads/2012/12/Transportation-Contract-HandoutFive.pdf

Stone, Richard. 1991. *The Interstate Commerce Commission and the Railroad Industry: A History of Regulatory Policy,* Westport, CT: Prager.

Talley, Wayne K., Anne V. Schwarz-Miller, and Michael Belzer. 1998. "Railroad Deregulation and Union Labor Earnings." In: Peoples, J. (eds.), *Regulatory Reform and Labor Markets.* Recent Economic Thought Series. New York: Springer, Dordrecht.

Wilner, Frank N. 1997. *Railroad Mergers: History, Analysis, Insight.* Nebraska: Simmons-Boardman Books.

Wilson, Wesley W. 1994. "Market-Specific Effects of Rail Deregulation." *Journal of wIndustrial Economics* 42(1): 1–22.

Winston, Clifford. 2005. "The Success of the Staggers Rail Act of 1980." *AEI-Brookings Joint Center for Regulatory Studies.* www.brookings.edu/wp-content/uploads/2016/06/10_railact_winston.pdf (accessed August 7, 2018).

# 2 Economic Foundations for 21st Century Freight Rail Rate Regulation*

*John W. Mayo and Robert D. Willig*

## Introduction

The Staggers Rail Act of 1980 made a substantial break from an almost century-old policy of pervasively regulating the prices for freight rail services provided in the United States. In particular, rather than regulators establishing prices, Staggers permits shippers and railroads to voluntarily negotiate rates, terms, and conditions, with regulation providing a fallback if negotiation fails or is too onerous for what is at stake on the shipment. While largely deregulating the rate-setting process, the statute requires that rates be "reasonable" in the event of a complaint filed by a shipper and where a railroad is found to be market dominant—a requirement that necessitates that regulators determine a method for assessing whether a given rate or set of rates is, in fact, reasonable.

In the wake of the passage of Staggers, the Interstate Commerce Commission (ICC) [now the Surface Transportation Board (STB)] established the method for determining whether a rate is "reasonable," in which case the rate is allowed to stand, or whether the rate is unreasonable and must be reduced. The system, known as Constrained Market Pricing (CMP), was established largely on a bedrock of economic theory and has been in place now for almost 35 years. Yet, absent a refresher, the passage of time creates the prospect that the economic foundations of CMP will fade. The purpose of this chapter is to provide that refresher. Along the way, we seek to reestablish the fundamental economic appeal of CMP, reflect on criticisms and alternatives that have been proffered, and offer refinements for rail regulation moving forward.

The chapter is organized as follows. We begin in the next section with a short tutorial on the fundamental economic characteristics of the rail industry. These characteristics necessarily have shaped, and will continue to shape, the consequent policy framework for the industry. Next, we turn to a discussion of the modern economic policy dictates of CMP. Our penultimate section discusses some of the criticisms of, and alternatives to, CMP that have surfaced. Finally, we close with a discussion of opportunities for and challenges to freight rail regulation looking forward.

## Foundations: The Economic Characteristics
## of the Freight Rail Industry

In 2020, the (de)regulatory framework established by the passage of the Staggers Act will be 40 years old. As amply documented elsewhere, the Staggers Act and the light-touch regulatory decisions adopted first by the ICC and later by the STB have proven strikingly successful.[1] Prices today are lower than they were in 1980, output has expanded dramatically, innovation has flourished, and private sector investment has grown to tens of billions of dollars per year. Yet, despite these striking aggregate statistics, certain characteristics of the industry make it a natural target for government intervention. First, there are substantial economies of scale in the provision of some rail services, whether along particular routes or for specific types of freight, which result from the heavy fixed costs associated with rail infrastructure and operations. To transport even small amounts of freight, a railroad must generally incur substantial costs of track, right-of-way, locomotive power, crew, and certain facilities-costs that do not rise proportionately with traffic volume. In such cases, costs per ton of freight fall as traffic volume increases, and rail services are most economically supplied by a single carrier. Some rail services, in other words, are natural monopolies, inasmuch as other modes of transport such as trucks and barges are not close substitutes and supply by two or more rail carriers involves an unnecessary increase in the resources employed in the transport process.

While economies of scale and scope are endemic to freight railroad technology, a railroad may well have far less price-setting discretion than a textbook monopolist. A rail carrier's ability to control price for a shipment or shipments will depend on whether its services are shielded from competition by barriers to entry from within the industry narrowly conceived (freight rail services) and from competitive alternatives from its relevant market broadly conceived (transportation services on the same or substitute route, including practically feasible trucking and barge services). In the railroad industry, extensive capital sums must be sunk in way and structures and in a variety of ancillary facilities in order to create new rail lines. These sunk costs generally suffice to deter the entry of new rail lines. Despite these barriers, however, rival services and rival sources of supply (including trucks, barges, and alternative rail routes) may impose effective competitive constraints upon many, if not most, rail activities.

Another pertinent feature of the railroad industry is that there are substantial economies of scope which result from the common costs of rail operations. Outlays on rails, ties, rights-of-way, yard facilities, locomotives, and train crews are among the many common costs of rail operations incurred in carrying a variety of types of freight between a variety of origins and destinations. These costs confer economies of scope on carriers offering a multiplicity of transportation services: a carrier that provides an array of services can do so at a lower total cost than a set of carriers producing each service separately.

In the presence of substantial economies of scale and scope, there remain cases where competition is weak. The resulting monopoly power is the basic justification for regulation of rail rates and defines the basic task with which regulation must grapple. Ironically, it is these same features of the industry that render the industry particularly difficult to regulate in the public interest. In particular, the presence of substantial economies of scale and scope in the rail industry creates a number of problems for government regulation. Perhaps the most troubling is the fact that for purposes of assessing the reasonableness of a set of prices it is impossible to allocate, in any nonarbitrary way, a share of fixed and common costs to any one of a railroad's many activities. There is simply no way to subdivide those costs in a mechanical fashion that is unique and has any foundation in economic logic. The significance of this problem is much magnified by the fact that a substantial share of total railroad costs is fixed and common. In addition, if the regulator attempts to force rates to equal marginal costs, overall revenues will endemically fall short of overall costs. For rail systems that are characterized by scale and scope economies, rates must generally lie above the costs economically attributable to individual services if the firm's revenues are to cover its total costs.

The prevalence of common costs and the financial infeasibility of marginal-cost pricing rule out any sensible mechanical or formula-based procedure for regulatory determination of rail rates. In particular, compensatory rates cannot be determined by the regulator on the basis of cost data alone since the financial viability of any price depends also on the quantity of rail services customers are willing to buy at that price. Rational determination of prices must be based on both cost and demand conditions. But that, in turn, precludes the use of a price-setting formula since no formula can possibly capture the subtleties of demand behavior. For instance, demand varies from one prospective customer to another and among services, demands for various services respond differently to changes in the applicable prices and to market and general economic conditions, and demand is affected by heterogeneous competitive conditions.

Another relevant feature of the rail industry is that the supply of some services involves elements of monopoly power while the supply of other services is subject to strong competitive pressures. This creates real challenges for government regulation since, in the presence of economies of scope, it can be highly inefficient to separate the competitive and monopolistic services and have them provided by different suppliers. Alternatively, attempts to comprehensively regulate the portfolio of both competitive and monopolistic services offered by the rail carrier are likely to introduce substantial disincentives for innovative behavior.[2] Even if regulators attempt to narrow the scope of regulation to only noncompetitive services, distortions are likely to arise.[3] In particular, regulating the services over which a supplier has monopoly power may interfere with the efficient supply of competitive services. It is also important to avoid inducing anti-competitive behavior in the supply of the competitive services, such as cross-subsidies which permit underpricing of the competitive services at the expense of the customers of the other services.[4]

Finally, the efficient supply of most rail services requires cooperative behavior on the part of many firms. Rail transportation often involves interline service, with individual shipments traversing the tracks of more than one railroad. Similarly, more than one railroad is often involved in reloading and employing empty cars returning from deliveries. Other efficient cooperative arrangements involve the use of terminal, switching, and yard facilities. The challenge is to determine when it is appropriate to regulate cooperative relationships. Should railroads be free to negotiate agreements over responsibilities and the division of revenues? What if a railroad owns facilities that are indispensable for moving certain shipments?

## The Economic Determination of "Reasonable" Rates in the Rail Industry

Faced with the various dilemmas posed by the fundamental economic characteristics of the freight rail industry, regulators are tasked with the job of establishing a method to protect shippers from exploitation of railroad monopoly power, where that exists, without distorting the otherwise efficient and competitive operations of railroads where there is no such monopoly power. In the corresponding legal and regulatory parlance, regulators are tasked with establishing a method by which a rate or set of rates can be determined to be "reasonable" or "unreasonable." Arguably, the presence of choice and competition, available to most but not all customers, is a powerful driver of reasonable rates. In recognition of this, the regulator's posture in developing its rate regulation methodology in the post-Staggers era has been to focus on a set of "captive customers" that may be subject to the exercise of substantial monopoly power.[5] For these customers, the challenge is to establish a methodology to reveal, and constrain, unreasonable prices without creating excessive social losses from a large set of potentially unintended consequences, including (1) extending the coverage of regulation to services in which customer choice and competition provide adequate customer protections and incentives for efficient contracts resulting from bilateral negotiations, (2) misincentives in the amount and placement of rail investments, (3) disincentives to entrepreneurship and productivity advances, (4) pricing that creates unnecessary suppression of the outputs of the carriers and their customers, and (5) regulatory impediments to railroads' earning enough revenues to financially sustain themselves and to invest efficiently.

In pursuit of these objectives, several basic and salient tenets emerge from economic theory. In particular, economic theory indicates that two policy options, although alluring, should be avoided assiduously. First, the model of perfect competition is not a reliable foundation for establishing the reasonableness of freight rail rates. In this model, the free interplay of competition among existing firms and the process of free entry and exit of firms will lead to an industry equilibrium in which prices stabilize at levels that are equal to representative firms' marginal costs. These prices have the attractive feature that they are consistent with allocative efficiency, and are therefore often referred to as first-best prices. Accordingly, it is tempting to use this model as a benchmark to declare that "reasonable" rates are equal to the firm's marginal costs. The allure of this benchmark should fade, however, once it is recalled that the rail industry is subject to considerable economies of scale and scope. Indeed, "reasonable" prices set equal to a firm's marginal costs will fail to allow the firm to recover its total costs, with the result of firm bankruptcy and a failure of supply. In short, such prices are not a reasonable standard for "reasonable" rates in the rail industry.

Second, benchmarks of "reasonable" rates that derive from the allocation of fixed costs across services and customers demonstrably produce inefficient and distortionary rates. This point has been forcefully and repeatedly made over the past 40 years, so we will not belabor the full-blown arguments here other than to underscore the unambiguous conclusion from professionally accepted economic theory that any attempt to ensure that a rail carrier is made financially solvent through the use of allocations of unattributable joint and common costs that are independent of shippers' demands and willingness to pay will lead to gross economic inefficiencies.[6]

Fortunately, economic theory not only rules out inappropriate regulatory methods, but also can conversely provide a foundation upon which to develop a sound 21st century regulatory framework for the freight rail industry. That is, relevant and sound economic principles for adjudicating the "reasonableness" of rail rates do exist. To see this, first note that while cost calculations or estimations alone do not provide a sound economic benchmark for pricing, the combination of demand-side principles and cost principles offered from established economic theory can provide a foundation for guideposts and upper bounds on economically efficient and financially sustainable rates, characteristics that appropriately provide economic content to the rubric of "reasonable rates."

From the demand side, because economies of scale and scope are pervasive in the rail industry, prices set equal to the rail carriers' marginal cost of providing transportation will fail to be compensatory for the firm. The question that arises in this circumstance is how might rates be adjusted above the marginal costs of providing the range of services sufficiently for coverage of the total costs of service, inclusive of common and fixed and all capital costs, while minimizing output distortions and losses to consumer surplus?

This problem (in a slightly different context) was addressed by Frank Ramsey in 1927, and the features of its solutions have stood the test of time since then.[7] The answer, he demonstrates, is to raise prices on particular services above their respective incremental costs so that the resulting margins are inversely proportional to the price elasticities of demand for those services. The resulting set of rates (now referred to as *Ramsey prices*) allow a multiproduct firm to remain economically viable while minimizing the damage to consumers, and society more generally, from output reduction associated with the price elevations above marginal costs.

The logic of this inverse elasticity rule is straightforward. The elasticity of demand provides a quantitative interpretation of the traditional concept of value of service, which has played an important role in public utility pricing. Consumers who place relatively high value on a service will have demands for it that are relatively inelastic, and vice versa. If a rise in the price of a service would lead to no significant reduction in quantity demanded (that is, if demand is inelastic), then the service must be worth at least the higher price to its consumers (i.e., the value of the service must be high). Conversely, if a rise in the price of a service would lead consumers to curtail their demand substantially (i.e., if demand is quite elastic), then the service must be worth little more to its consumers than the original price (i.e., the value of the service must be low).

In view of this correspondence between value of service and demand elasticity, the inverse elasticity rule associated with Ramsey pricing can be restated in terms of a familiar and long-used principle in railroad pricing. Services with relatively high values to their customers should contribute relatively large net revenues to aid in the recovery of unattributable fixed and common costs. Conversely, services with relatively low values to their customers should contribute relatively small net revenues to aid in the recovery of unattributable fixed and common costs. All factors that influence a rail carrier's elasticities of demand are relevant for the carrier's Ramsey prices. These factors may include the value of the commodity shipped, the urgency with which the shipment is to be made, the extent of intermodal, intramodal, and interport competition, and the substitutability of other commodities for the one shipped at its destination.

Under Ramsey pricing, the burden for recovering the firm's unattributable joint and common costs are borne by those customers who, when faced with the prospect of higher prices, would reveal through their continued patronage of the rail carrier that the specific shipment (or group of shipments) is of sufficiently high value that they will continue to be purchased despite the higher prices. While it may seem uncomfortable that higher prices are being set for customers whose circumstances dictate that they must continue to purchase despite higher prices or have no other transport options, the alternative of collecting the necessary revenues from customers who will halt their patronage in the face of higher prices is not feasible. Moreover, those customers who would halt their patronage reveal a lower value for such shipments—a basis for providing them with lower prices. Collectively, by permitting the firm to establish Ramsey prices, economic efficiency is promoted by providing the firm with revenues required to recover its total costs, while minimizing the necessary output reductions that occur as a consequence of prices that exceed their marginal cost. In short, in situations in which purely allocatively efficient (marginal cost) pricing is infeasible, Ramsey pricing provides an economically efficient set of rates.[8]

As a matter of formal economic theory, Ramsey prices are economically efficient, as they maximize consumer and social real income (i.e., social welfare in terms of consumers' utility or consumer and producer surplus), subject to the stipulation that the prices generate revenues sufficient to cover the total costs of production, under the condition of increasing returns to scale that make marginal cost pricing financial insufficient. It is important to recognize that while the formal treatment of Ramsey pricing is illuminating economic theory, it is not usually treated as the source of quantitative formulas to set actual market prices. Precise estimates of the needed elasticities of demand are rarely available, and they are apt to change in the market faster than they can be reliably reestimated. Consequently, the theory of Ramsey pricing is generally regarded as more of a source of conceptual guidance for the conduct of regulation than as a source of real-time quantification for prices.

The practical realities of the demand for freight rail services, however, provide private market incentives for rail carriers to negotiate efficient arrangements with substantial demanders of their services, in the absence of regulatory micro management. In particular, customers and their corresponding demands for rail services are substantially heterogeneous in nature. In such situations, suppliers exercise market judgment, learn from experience, negotiate with customers, try out pilot experiments, and generally grope their way through decentralized decision-making to determine compensation based on both costs and volumes and values of service. The result, achieved through the voluntary interaction of the sellers of rail services and buyers of rail services, is the proliferation of individual tailored contracts.[9] The contracts are apt to charge differential prices to different customers in reaction to the heterogeneous values that shippers experience from the particular services offered by their suppliers. It can also be expected that the individual contracts will include heterogeneous non-price terms that respond to particular needs of the customers, including, for example, assurances of deliveries' timeliness, reliability, and adaptability to the customer's dynamic circumstances.

With such individually tailored contracts, customers with relatively low values, but values that still exceed the supplier's marginal costs of production, are beneficially served at relatively low prices that lie between their values and the marginal costs of serving them. These customers receive positive net value from their purchases equal to the difference between their value of consumption and the price they pay, and the supplier receives a contribution to its profitability equal to the difference between that price and its marginal cost. Prices to other customers who experience greater value from their consumption are apt efficiently to provide relatively greater margins above marginal costs to the supplier.

In addition, it can be expected that the individual deals will include individuated volume discounts whose quantity break points and degrees of discount will themselves be heterogeneous. As a matter of economic logic and formal theory, mutually beneficial volume discounts are always a feasible addition to uniform pricing that is above marginal costs.[10] To see this, imagine as a simple example that without a volume discount, the customer's price is $10/unit, the marginal cost of production is $7/unit, and the customer's demand is 9,000 units. Then the supplier could offer the volume discount deal under which the first 9,000 units carry the price of $10/unit and any additional units are available at the price of just $8/unit. The customer may be stimulated to purchase more than 9,000 units under this deal, to the customer's benefit, while the additional volume earns additional contribution to the supplier's profits with the still positive markup of $1 above marginal cost.

Thus, it is plain that a volume discount deal exists that is mutually beneficial, and it should also be noted that the details of such a volume discount are individual to the customer—since the effective volume break points and the depth of the discounts depend on the customer's level of demand and on the customer's price elasticity of demand. Such individuated volume discounts are not only consistent with workable competition, but they are also necessary reactions to the forces of any such competition. An incumbent who did not make heterogeneous deals with its heterogeneous sizable customers, including individuated terms and volume discounts, would find its business diverted by active rivals or entrants who would make those mutually beneficial deals in a sufficiently competitive or contestable market.

Note too that while there may be a superficial equity appeal to a set of rates that are all elevated uniformly above marginal costs, the market's Ramsey-like prices improve economic efficiency and raise total output and real social incomes relative to uniform markups. In particular, customer demands with value greater than marginal cost but less than the needed average markup above marginal cost are excluded by such average-markup pricing. This, in and of itself, represents an inefficient loss of social real income (social welfare) since the lost utilization of the product would have been beneficial to the customer by more than its marginal cost of supply. Further, the loss of this demand means less sales volume and thus a higher average markup above marginal cost is needed to cover total cost from the remaining volume of sales whose customers must pay more. Moreover, the consequent higher prices likely exclude more customer demands with values that exceed marginal costs but that are not sufficient to bear the higher prices, causing additional loss of social welfare and additional loss of volume with yet further negative consequences. In sharp contrast, setting prices with relatively small markups above marginal costs to customers with relatively low value demands allows those demands to be met with net benefits to social welfare and with positive contributions to total costs that allow other customers to pay less toward the recovery of total costs than they would have to if that volume were not gainfully transacted. Customers with relatively high value demands must be charged prices with relatively high markups above marginal costs in order to complete the recovery of the total cost of supply.

In sum, even though regulators are generally unable to determine specific Ramsey prices and efficient volume discounts for the market, Ramsey-like price schedules, referred to in the rail industry as "differential pricing," emerge organically in the market as a consequence of private market negotiations of rail carriers and shippers. The crucial learning for policy is that it is unnecessary and generally counterproductive for regulation to attempt to force pricing through fully allocated costs, uniform markups, or even quantified application of Ramsey pricing formulae. Instead, it is necessary to understand that differential price schedules, that reflect values of service and volume considerations, achieved as part of the buyer-seller interaction process, have the potential to promote the same efficiency results as Ramsey pricing.[11]

While negotiations between a rail carrier and a shipper with enough business to warrant them have the strong potential to achieve efficient Ramsey-like results, such a salutary outcome is more assured if any substantial inbalance in the bargaining power of the parties is counterbalanced by a regulated "reasonable" fall-back. If the rail carrier is market dominant so that the shipper is "captive" in that its logistics have no practical alternative to rail services, its bargaining position may be far out of balance inasmuch as the carrier's serving assets have other gainful uses while the shipper's assets may lose much of their value without reasonable rail service. In such circumstances, absent some regulatory restraint, short-sighted exploitation of monopoly power could lead to the carrier inequitably and inefficiently extracting much of the value of the shipper's business, with resulting repression of investment and long-term business prospects. In so doing, the carrier would likely be charging the shipper more than its long-run costs of serving the shipper, thereby bolstering its overall profits or cross-subsidizing other shippers with better logistical alternatives.

Under such circumstances of a market dominant rail carrier and a captive shipper, the existence of a well-designed "reasonable" regulated fall-back for a complaining shipper has two critical functions. First, it can offer the shipper a way out of what might otherwise become a punishing and at least long-run highly inefficient position of facing excessive pricing. Second, the known option of a well-designed regulatory "reasonable" fall-back for the captive shipper upon complaint will influence its negotiations with its market dominant carrier. The regulated fall-back available to the shipper can mitigate or eliminate what would otherwise be the substantial inbalance in the negotiating parties' bargaining strengths. The expectations about the effects of the well-designed regulatory fall-back can create a de facto protective bound to the outcome of the negotiations, without weakening the ability of the negotiations to reflect efficiently the character of the shipper's demands and needs as well as the costs to the carrier of supplying them. Thus, a well-designed regulatory fall-back for the pricing offered to a complaining captive shipper by a market dominant rail carrier can create appropriate protection against long-run inefficiently excessive rates, and by so doing can facilitate and stimulate negotiations to efficient contracts that are even better for the shipper than the regulatory fall-back.

What economic properties of a regulatory fall-back of "reasonable" rates would qualify it as "well-designed" to play the key roles of providing appropriate protection to a captive shipper while promoting long-run efficiency of outcomes, whether it actually becomes the operative price or rather the de facto bound on the outcome of efficient negotiations? Four, in particular, emerge:

1. The fall-back should protect captive shippers from pricing that would provide cross-subsidies to other shippers or that would itself yield supra-competitive overall profits for the rail carrier.
2. The fall-back should protect the long-run sustainability of a socially efficient shipper—that is, a shipper whose business could cover its long-run costs including the long-run costs of its needed transportation logistics.
3. The fall-back should avoid creating misincentives for the rail carrier subject to regulation, unlike caps on prices that are related to expended costs that consequently promote overspending and unlike fully allocated cost pricing that discourages serving shippers with under-average willingness-to-pay.
4. The fall-back should be consistent with Ramsey pricing in that generally (idiosyncratic exceptions aside) it would not confine pricing to below the level that would be part of the welfare optimal set of prices that provide coverage of the carrier's total costs (including a competitive return on capital).

The standard for regulatory "reasonable" rates that has the requisite economic properties is based on stand-alone cost—the cost that would be incurred by a hypothetical efficient *de novo* rail carrier to provide the service or services at issue. Formally, consider a customer or group of customers purchasing a set $T$ of services with quantities given by the vector $y_T$ from among a possibly larger set of $N$ services offered by the supplier in quantities given by the vector $y_N$. The *stand-alone cost* of serving the customer (or group of customers) is the total cost that would be incurred by an efficient supplier of $y_T$ were it to produce only those services without simultaneously producing any other services or additional quantities of any services included in $T$.[12] Under the standard for regulatory "reasonable" rates based on stand-alone cost, or the "stand-alone cost test," the prices a customer is asked to pay are "unreasonable" if the revenues they generate from the customer exceed the stand-alone costs of the services the customer is to be provided.

Where the provision of the services a customer employs is implemented more efficiently in combination with the services purchased by a group of other customers, then the applicable and more protective form of the stand-alone cost test could aggregate those services and compare the total payments of the entire group of customers with the stand-alone costs of the totality of the services purchased by the group. Equivalently, the revenue paid by a particular customer is to be compared with the customer's net stand-alone cost: the stand-alone cost of provision of the group's total services, less the total revenues paid at contemporaneous prices by the other customers in the group. If the revenues paid by the total group exceed the stand-alone cost of the production of the group's total services, or equivalently if the particular complaining customer pays revenue in excess of its net stand-alone cost, then at least some of the prices involved are shown to be "unreasonable."[13] In short, under this standard of rate reasonableness, no buyer or group of buyers should be required to pay more for their purchases than the stand-alone cost of those purchases. Prices necessitating customer payments in excess of the services' stand-alone costs can be said to be "unreasonable."[14]

In accordance with the first of the aforementioned properties of a well-designed regulatory fall-back, passing the stand-alone cost test implies the absence of cross-subsidization.[15] Any customer who receives a set of services for no greater expenditures than their associated stand-alone cost is not harmed relative to the alternative of self-supply (or supply by a third party producing only those services), and is thus not paying extra to support other customers by means of cross-subsidies. Indeed, to the extent that the payments are less than the associated stand-alone costs, the customer derives pecuniary benefits that come from being part of the rail carrier's larger customer pool and the associated economies of scale and scope from serving that customer group. Cross-subsidies are properly of public policy concern because they generally lead to a misallocation of resources by encouraging inefficient investment by the recipients and repressed investment by the donors. Cross-subsidies may be of special concern to shippers because they are perceived to be unfair.[16] It has been shown that if all services and combinations of services satisfy the stand-alone cost test (i.e., they are not the source of cross-subsidies), then in the presence of zero economic profits (i.e., no monopoly profits overall), all services and combinations of services will also provide revenues that exceed their associated incremental costs (i.e., they are not the recipient of cross-subsidies).[17]

The stand-alone cost test also exhibits the second of the aforementioned properties of a well-designed regulatory fall-back. Absent regulatory protection, a captive shipper could be charged so much for its needed rail services that it would be unable to sustain itself financially over the long run, even if it could survive in the short run by neglecting maintenance, efficient replacement, and monetizing depreciation of its sunk capital assets. Long-run economic welfare would be harmed by this outcome if the shipper's business could cover its total social costs of long-run operation, including the costs of provision of its needed rail services, but it is facing the commercial exigency of paying more for those services than their long-run cost to the carrier. Thus, the regulatory cap of stand-alone costs on the captive shipper's obligations to pay for its market dominant rail services protects the shipper and long-run social welfare from excessive rail rates impelling the contraction of beneficial economic activity.

The third property of well-designed regulatory fall-backs is satisfied since the stand-alone cost is the cost of service by an efficient hypothetical entrant that offers alternatives to the shippers at issue, rather than determined by any of the costs actually incurred by the regulated railroad. Consequently, under the system of stand-alone cost rate ceilings, a railroad has no incentive to pad or otherwise increase its expenditures for the purpose of relaxing a regulatory constraint. Further, the ceilings and their calculation apply only to services over which the railroad has monopoly power, so they do not diminish the railroad's incentives to pursue aggressively additional traffic and other new business opportunities.

That the stand-alone cost test satisfies the fourth aforementioned property of a well-designed regulatory fall-back follows from its intrinsic connection to the economic theory of contestable markets. By their theoretical definition, contestable markets are driven by the competitive forces that arise from the threats of diversion of incumbents' business to potential entrants. In a perfectly contestable market, firms not already active are capable of entering into the production and sale of any quantities of any of the market's products or services by making use of the generally available technology and inputs, and thus incurring efficient economic total costs of that production. Such potential entrants evaluate the profitability of their entry into the market by comparing these costs with their potential revenues from diverting sales of the incumbent firm or firms at prices just below those charged to the incumbent customers. The potential entrants into a perfectly contestable market are assumed to face no entry barriers (unlike rail carriers facing substantial economic entry barriers), and this is the primary reason why contestability is a benchmark model of workable competition rather than a generally accurate description of real markets.[18]

In contestable markets, no customer or group of customers would agree to pay more to a supplier for their services than it would cost to produce them efficiently in the long run on their own, or than it would cost a competing entrant to implement their supply. In other words, the competition from the potential entrants characteristic of the contestable market benchmark would drive reductions in incumbents' prices by the threat of stand-alone supply at stand-alone costs of each of the services and combinations of services. Thus, equilibrium outcomes in perfectly contestable markets necessarily pass the stand-alone cost test.[19] The stand-alone cost test imposes the same constraints, discipline, and ceilings on customers' prices that the market would impose if the incumbent supplier were subject to robust competition from potential entrants with efficient technology and inputs and facing no barriers to entry.[20] In short, the stand-alone cost test provides the same protections to shippers that they would be afforded by effective competition in contestable markets.

The relationship between contestable markets and stand-alone costs underlies the consistency between the stand-alone cost test and Ramsey pricing that constitutes the aforementioned fourth economic property of a well-designed regulatory fall-back for reasonable rates. The so-called weak invisible hand theorem demonstrates that the Ramsey prices for a multiproduct natural monopolist are consistent with equilibrium in perfectly contestable markets.[21] This implies that Ramsey prices pass the stand-alone cost test, since this test is one of the necessary conditions for equilibrium in perfectly contestable markets. Accordingly, the stand-alone cost test does not confine prices away from their Ramsey optimal levels.

In summary, then, we have shown that the stand-alone cost test can serve as the well-designed standard for a regulatory fall-back mechanism to protect complaining captive shippers against unreasonable rates by a market dominant rail carrier. It is well designed in that it satisfies the economic properties delineated earlier: protecting shippers against providing cross-subsidies, protecting long-run efficient shippers from rates that would drive them from the market, promoting incentives for rail carriers to be cost efficient and to market aggressively, and maintaining consistency with optimal differential (Ramsey) pricing.

As a simple illustrative example of the application of stand-alone costs to pricing analysis, consider an incumbent whose services to customers A and B make use of common facilities with long-run recurring costs of 10, specialized facilities used only to serve A with recurring cost of 6 and specialized facilities used only to serve B with recurring cost of 9. The stand-alone cost of service to A is 16 (10 + 6) because the common facilities would be needed for that production even in the absence of service to B, along with the specialized facilities that are employed only to serve A.[22] Similarly, the stand-alone cost of service to B is 19 (10 + 9) because the common facilities would be needed for that production even in the absence of service to A, along with the specialized facilities that are employed only to serve B. The total recurring cost is 25 (10 + 6 + 9), which is significantly less than the sum of the stand-alone costs of A and B. This is a reflection of the firm's economies of scope, which means that joint production of the services is more efficient than the total cost of producing them all separately.[23]

Now suppose the incumbent charged prices that generated revenues of 18 from the services provided to A and 7 from the services provided to B. These prices could not hold sustainably in a contestable market since an entrant could produce service to A for its stand-alone cost of 16 and divert that business from the incumbent who was charging 18 for it.[24] Alternatively, suppose the incumbent charged prices that generated revenues of 14 from the services provided to A and 16 from the services provided to B. Then these levels of revenues are below the stand-alone costs of 16 for just A and the stand-alone costs of 19 for just B, so that in contestable markets an entrant would not be able to profitably divert the incumbent's business of just A nor that of just B. However, an entrant would be motivated to divert the business of both A and B since the incumbent's revenues from that group of services are 30 (14 + 16) while the stand-alone costs for the services of A and B together are just 25.

This same example provides an illustration of the benefits of demand-based pricing (as per Ramsey pricing), the economic dangers of pricing based on fully allocated costs, irrespective of customers' demands, and the connections to stand-alone cost limits on pricing. Suppose the value of the services to A is a flow of benefits of 9 and the flow of benefits to B is 18. Since the incremental costs of service to A are 6 and the incremental costs of service to B are 9,[25] it might seem under some accounting principles that the equitable prices to A and B would raise revenues of 10 from A and 15 from B. These prices are both the same percentage above incremental costs (67%) that is needed to boost the total of the incremental costs (15 = 6 + 9) to the level of the total cost of 25. Another common accounting principle might exercise "fully allocated costs," or "fully distributed costs," by dividing up the common costs of 10 in accordance with relative use, for example, equally, to derive revenue targets of 11 (6 + ½ of 10) and 14 (9 + ½ of 10) for A and B, respectively.[26]

The pricing methods based on seemingly equitable accounting principles that neglect customers' individual values of service lead to dramatic economic harms for this market. Customer A does not experience sufficient value from its services to warrant paying the revenues of either 10 or 11 derived from the accounting principles. Then, with customer A out of the market, and making no contribution to the needed costs, customer B with the much higher level of value of service of 18 must face its own stand-alone cost of 19, which exceeds its willingness-to-pay. The result is no service at all, and an incumbent impelled to price this way will soon be out of business.

In sharp contrast, Ramsey prices generating revenues of 8 from A and 17 from B are socially optimal here, because they leave both customers with benefits from their services that are greater than their payments, and they cover the total costs of service effected jointly with the available economies of scope. This is an illustration of how demand-based pricing, or more formal Ramsey prices, maximizes the use of the common facilities and the net benefits to consumers, while still providing financial sustainability to the efficient enterprise doing the production. And, here, the optimal prices for social welfare are fully consistent with the workable competition provided by perfectly contestable markets. The revenues from the optimal prices do not exceed the stand-alone costs of A, of B, and of A and B taken together.

## The Suitability of the Economic Theory of CMP Going Forward

The lessons from economic theory for regulation of freight railroads that have been recounted earlier underlaid the formulation and acceptance by the ICC in the early 1980s of the regulatory system termed "Constrained Market Pricing (CMP)."[27] In particular, CMP embraces individualistic contracting between shippers and rail carriers, the railroads' ability to utilize differential pricing across customers (consistent with Ramsey pricing), and the rights of shippers to complain that they are captive to a market dominant rail carrier and thereby obtain protection against excessive pricing through the regulatory application of a stand-alone cost (SAC) test. The history of the U.S. freight railroad industry shows a dramatically successful industry turnaround resulting from the adoption of the CMP regulatory system as replacement for a previous disastrously counterproductive form of regulation, under the stimulus of the passage of the Staggers Act in 1980.[28] The complexity of that turnaround is concisely summarized by the data on the large U.S. freight railroads displayed in Figure 2.1. The figure shows that shortly after 1980, productivity began a new period of steep elevation, average prices began a long period of decline, revenues declined by far less than price and costs, and volume of service began an increasing trend.

Nonetheless, in recent years, criticisms of CMP have emerged. They alternatively include charges that (1) while the economic theory behind CMP is relevant, as a practical matter, stand-alone cost is too cumbersome and complex to serve as a practical test of rate reasonableness; and (2) the economic theory underpinning the determination of the upper bound of reasonable rates is itself flawed.

We focus here on the second of these claims, noting only on the former that (1) the 35 years of experience with rate cases utilizing SAC should permit the regulators to establish precedents in the application of practical considerations that can very much streamline the set of relevant issues in

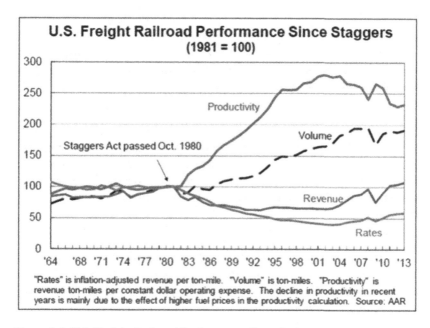

**U.S. Freight Railroad Performance Since Staggers**
**(1981 = 100)**

Productivity

Staggers Act passed Oct. 1980

Volume

Revenue

Rates

'64   '68  '71  '74  '77  '80  '83  '86  '89  '92  '95  '98  '01  '04  '07  '10  '13

"Rates" is inflation-adjusted revenue per ton-mile. "Volume" is ton-miles. "Productivity" is revenue ton-miles per constant dollar operating expense. The decline in productivity in recent years is mainly due to the effect of higher fuel prices in the productivity calculation. Source: AAR

*Figure 2.1* U.S. Freight Railroad Performance Since Staggers

actual cases; (2) in recognition of the complexity of the original specification of the SAC test, the STB has developed the Simplified SAC method for adjudicating cases in practice;[29] and (3) it is unsurprising and not unusual that important regulatory decisions are complex and require extensive procedural and substantive records to establish the congruence of public policy decisions with economic theory.

At the more conceptual level, a criticism has arisen that alleges that the SAC test is unyoked from the concept of fairness. That is, it is alleged that the stand-alone cost test does not provide a test of the unfair treatment of a customer, and therefore is not a sound measure of "reasonable" rates as required by statute. This charge, however, is inconsistent with at least one coherent definition of fairness. Specifically, the fundamental linkage between the stand-alone cost test and fairness was laid out clearly by Professor Baumol in his book *Superfairness*.[30] He pointed out that the conventional equity consideration in price regulation historically centered on the concept of compensatory pricing. In particular, fairness would seem to require that each customer and customer group should pay at least the incremental cost of serving them; that is, customers' prices should be compensatory. Rather than focusing on the inequity brought about by the recipients of uncompensatory prices, however, Professor Baumol enunciated the complementary thought that "the object of an intercustomer fairness calculation is presumably to protect the interests of . . . the potential *payers* who would be the victims of unfairness, rather than to inhibit the flow of benefits to the potential recipients of any subsidy."[31]

This reframing focuses on the fundamental unfairness of firm pricing that would extract more than reasonably required from a customer or customer group. This is precisely the stand-alone cost test. When prices violate the stand-alone cost test for a customer, that customer is inequitably and unreasonably required to provide to the railroad more revenues than would be necessary for the customer to efficiently self-supply the services. In this context, the customer (group) is required to unfairly cross-subsidize other customers.[32] Conversely, when prices satisfy the stand-alone cost test, the focal set of services demonstrably share in the economies of scale and scope afforded by a continuing relationship with the railroad at existing prices.

Another criticism has arisen from the observation that both Ramsey pricing and the theory of contestable markets are developed in a context where the firm earns zero economic profit, whereas freight railroads in the United States may earn more than that. However, it has been a reasonable judgment that the vast majority of rail shipments in the United States are, in fact, subject to the presence of competitive alternatives,[33] so that the working assumption of zero economic profit is generally tenable. Moreover, as a practical matter, detailed empirical analyses of the profitability of railroads in the United States reveal virtually no evidence of extraordinary profitability, indicating that market conditions have to a rough approximation produced results consistent with the underlying theories.[34]

Yet another criticism is also centered on the salient economic theory's seeming reliance on zero economic profits. Specifically, when positive economic profits exist, the economic equivalence of a stand-alone cost tests and incremental cost tests is severed. It is argued that this result renders the stand-alone cost test inapplicable.[35] But while the uncoupling of the equivalence of the stand-alone cost test and an incremental cost test does occur with positive economic profits, it is easy to see that, if anything, the presence of such profits makes the case for the stand-alone cost test even more compelling.

To see this, initially suppose that profit ($\pi$) is zero. A violation of the stand-alone cost test for a subset of focal services $T$ offered by a railroad providing the services $N$ requires that:

$$\sum_{i \in T} p_i y_i > C(y_T), \tag{1}$$

where $p_i$ is the price of service $i$, $y_i$ is the output of service $i$, and $C(y_T)$ is the cost of providing the relevant set of services in $T$. With zero economic profit, we know that:

$$\sum_{i \in N} p_i y_i = C(y_N), \tag{2}$$

where $N$ is the set of all services provided by the railroad.

Subtracting (1) from (2) yields:

$$\sum_{i \in N-T} p_i y_i < C(y_N) - C(y_T) \equiv IC_{N-T} \tag{3}$$

Note that $C(y_N) - C(y_T)$ is the incremental cost ($IC_{N-T}$) of providing the $N - T$ services. Thus, (3) reveals that when the zero profits assumption holds, the stand-alone cost test is equivalent to an incremental cost test. That is, violations of the stand-alone cost test for a focal set of services necessarily indicates the presence of non-focal services that fail to cover their incremental costs (i.e., they are non-compensatory). From a policy perspective, this would seem to make the application of the stand-alone cost test especially attractive because violations of stand-alone cost indicate not only that a group of customers is harmed by having revenues extracted from them that are greater than the costs of providing the service them-selves, but also that these funds are used to cross-subsidize other customers whose rates are set below the incremental costs of supplying them.

But now consider the application of the stand-alone cost test when economic profits are positive. We can rewrite (2) to include a positive profit $\pi > 0$:

$$\sum_{i \in N} p_i y_i = C(y_N) + \pi \tag{4}$$

Now, subtracting (1) from (4) yields:

$$\sum_{i \in N-T} p_i y_i < C(y_N) - C(y_T) + \pi \tag{5}$$

Here, although (1) still implies that more revenue is extracted from the focal services than the competitive benchmark provided by their associated stand-alone costs, (5) shows that the revenue from non-focal services $(N - T)$ may or may not fail an incremental cost test.

Rearranging (5) yields:

$$\sum_{i \in N-T} p_i y_i - \left[ C(y_N) - C(y_T) \right] < \pi. \tag{6}$$

The left-hand side of (6) is the excess of incremental revenues from the non-focal services above the associated incremental costs of providing those services. In the event that the pricing of the non-focal services is compensatory (i.e., the left-hand side of (6) is positive), then we see that the contribution of these services is less than the total level of monopoly profit earned by the supplier. In such cases, violations of the stand-alone cost test with positive total profits indicate that focal services are contributing to those monopoly profits. This condition would appear to strengthen the case for the application of the stand-alone cost test as in this event the pricing of focal services is sufficiently high to not only violate the stand-alone cost test, but additionally are a source of monopoly profits.

Alternatively, suppose that the left-hand side of (6) is negative so that the non-focal services fail to cover their incremental costs. This condition indicates the presence of intra-customer cross-subsidies, with non-focal services benefiting from these transfers while customers of focal services are payers of the cross-subsidy flows, and in addition fund the firm's total positive economic profits. In this situation, the logic is only enhanced for interpreting the failure of the stand-alone cost test as indicating unreasonably excessive rates. In sum, the merits of the stand-alone cost test are robust to the presence of positive profits, were that situation to arise. Another criticism of the application of the stand-alone cost test has been that it is developed within the context of contestable markets theory even though the provision of freight rail services does not comport with the underlying free-entry assumptions of a perfectly contestable market. Specifically, there is no doubt that there are high barriers impeding the entry of new rail carriers due to their need to sink substantial capital costs for rail infrastructure as well as their need to somehow assemble needed rights of way. However, this seeming incongruity is in no way a reason to doubt the validity of applying the lessons from contestable market theory to the formulation of applicable regulatory standards. In fact, if the industry were contestable, there would be no rationale for the application of regulation to it since the forces of competition from rivals and potential entrants would enforce reasonable and efficient pricing.

But, here, the theory is not intended to describe the industry actually as perfectly contestable. Rather it is used to evoke the counterfactual: what would be the properties of prices in the rail industry were the industry subject to the competitive forces present in perfectly contestable markets? The theory reveals that in such markets, competition would yield prices consistent with stand-alone cost tests, and thereby protect shippers from excessive pricing. Thus, the stand-alone cost test emerges not as a consequence of the actual presence of contestable market conditions in the rail industry but rather as the standard that would guide regulation to offer captive shippers the same protection from excessive pricing that they would experience from workable competition in actually contestable markets.

While the CMP approach described herein and employed by rail regulators has largely adhered to sound principles of economics, several alternative approaches to separating "reasonable" from "unreasonable" rates have been suggested in recent years. One of the most threatening of these alternatives is that standard rate-of-return regulation will be applied to rail carriers, perhaps due to interpretations of the statutory language that requires rail revenues to be "adequate."[36] Determination of the reasonableness of rail rates based on the measured profitability of the carrier, in terms of its expended costs and its book of capital assets, systematically generates market distortions and misincentives for the firm's decision-making. Indeed, a comprehensive literature review of economic research papers studying regulation indicates that the effects of such profit-based regulation generally included

(1) limited incentives for innovation and cost reduction; (2) over-capitalisation; (3) high costs of regulation; (4) excessive risks imposed on customers; (5) cost shifting; (6) inappropriate levels of diversification and innovation; (7) inefficient choice of operating technology; and (8) insufficient pricing flexibility in the presence of competitive pressures.[37]

More specifically with respect to the rail industry, it has been shown that comprehensively regulating the earnings of railroads would introduce substantial disincentives to innovation.[38] Moreover, attempts to target earnings regulation to only a subset of rail services, say those that are thought to be contributing to positive economic profits, are also fraught with economic distortions.[39]

However, in this regard, it is significant to note that the stand-alone cost test can validly be applied to the traffic of large groups of shippers that could, in concept, approach the totality of a carrier's operations, or its operations within one of its regions. Such a test would compare the shippers' total expenditures for their services, which are essentially the total revenues of the carrier, to the total costs of an efficient hypothetical entrant providing those services. This is a test of the profitability of that entrant and not a test of the profitability of the actual carrier based on its expended costs and booked capital stock. Here, the notion of a regulatory constraint based on "revenue adequacy" is properly interpreted as whether actual prices generate more than adequate revenues to cover the stand-alone costs of the analyzed services, no matter how extensive they are. Since the stand-alone costs are long-run replacement costs, inclusive of competitive costs of capital, and independent of the actual expenditures of the carrier, such appropriate considerations of adequate revenues avoid most of the distortionary and repressive effects of standard rate-of-return regulation.

Another suggestion for determining rate reasonableness has been to simply establish a cap on the ratio of revenues to variable costs.[40] Such a cap is devoid of any economically grounded benchmark. Consequently, any such cap would necessarily be arbitrarily chosen with the result that "reasonable" rates would be distinguished from "unreasonable" rates by the arbitrary judgment of the regulatory body at the time that a set of challenged rates were adjudicated. Most important, in the absence of an economically grounded benchmark (such as stand-alone costs), this proposal would satisfy none of the properties delineated earlier for a well-designed regulatory fall-back: it would not protect against cross-subsidization, it would not promote long-run efficiency in shippers' operations, it would engender misincentives inasmuch as carriers' conduct would influence the allowed ratio, and it would diminish overall consumer welfare by impeding Ramsey pricing.

Recently, a proposal has arisen to replace the existing rate reasonable-ness methodology utilized by the STB with an arbitration procedure.[41] This approach would rely on independent arbitrators to adjudicate the reasonableness of rates based on a final-offer arbitration method, as is used in the Canadian rail industry. The principal motivation for and appeal of the proposal is that it would substantially simplify the rate reasonableness adjudication process. "Reasonable" rates would be chosen by the arbitrator after "a brief hearing" with restricted opportunities to appeal arbitration rulings.[42] The Canadian model of arbitration is, how-ever, completely confidential to the parties and therefore provides no basis for knowing what standards are used by the arbitrator to decide which among the alternative rates proffered are "reasonable." The absence of transparent standards that are demonstrably consistent with economic principles creates the distinct possibility of arbitrary arbitration outcomes. Of course, there can be no confidence that the arbitration decisions would be consistent with the principles of well-designed regulatory fall-backs. The resulting uncertainty and pricing consequences are likely to be detri-mental to both shippers and railroads.

Thus, although the goal of regulatory expedience is laudable, it is doubt-ful that the gains from implementing an expedited arbitration mechanism for determining the reasonableness of rates is worth the corollary sacri-fices that would occur to transparency, economic standards and expert adjudication embedded in the current system. But that is not to deny the possibility of other procedural innovations that could accomplish far greater speed and access to smaller shippers than today's regulatory procedures, without substantial sacrifice of the reliability of principled outcomes.

## Conclusions

No regulatory mechanism is perfect either in theory or in practice. Conse-quently, periodic reviews of prevailing regulatory systems are warranted. In this chapter, we have reviewed the economic underpinnings of the core elements of regulation used by freight rail regulators in the United States since the mid-1980s. We find that permitting individualized contracting, differential pricing by rail carriers (with the attendant Ramsey-like fea-tures), and availability of a regulatory fall-back based on stand-alone cost tests for captive complaining shippers constitutes an economically sensible and attractive basis upon which to regulate freight rail prices in the 21st century. This system has both powerful efficiency and equity features. Moreover, during the post-Staggers period in which this light-touch regulatory structure has been in place, numerous economic characteristics of the freight rail industry have much improved, including prices, output, investment, safety, and innovation. It may be possible to further improve the performance of this regulatory system with attention to procedural innovations to speed, simplify, and lower the costs of the needed adjudication, but the impulse for such worthwhile ends to undermine the principled operation of CMP regulation must be resisted.

## Notes

* We dedicate this chapter to the memory of William J. Baumol, who was the inspiration and co-author of its better thoughts, as well as a prime intellectual mover behind the creation and adoption of modern regulation of freight railroad services.
1. *See* Mayo (2015) and the references cited therein.
2. *See* Mayo and Sappington (2016), reprinted as Chapter 10 in this volume.
3. *Id.*
4. Brennan (1990).
5. "Captive customers" are defined by the STB to be those customers facing a set of rates and associated revenue (R) that exceed the variable cost (VC) of supply by eighty percent (i.e., R/VC > 180), or for whom it is determined that no viable substitute for the focal rail carrier's services exists. For a more detailed description, *see* Mayo and Sappington (2016).
6. *See* our simple example, *infra*, as well as numerous articles, including Braeutigam (1980), Baumol and Willig (1983), Sweeney (1982), Baumol et al. (1987), Davidoff and Hermalin (2004), and Mayo and Sappington (2016).
7. Ramsey (1927). A clear restatement of Ramsey's seminal contribution which was set in the context of optimal taxation, making it applicable to pricing of a regulated firm is found in Baumol and Bradford (1970).
8. This result is widely known across both the economics profession and within the rail policy community. *See, e.g.,* Baumol and Bradford (1970), Baumol and Willig (1983), Sherman (1989), Braeutigam (1989), Train (1991), and Kaserman and Mayo (1995). Within the rail policy community, the appeal to Ramsey pricing in the post-Staggers era was acknowledged by policymakers as early as 1985. *See Coal Rate Guidelines, Nationwide,* Interstate Commerce Commission, August 8, 1985.
9. For a detailed discussion of the emergence and proliferation of such individual contracts in the U.S. freight rail industry, *see* Macher and Mayo (2018).
10. *See* Willig (1978).
11. For a rigorous treatment and demonstration, *see* Baumol et al. (1977).
12. Properly calculated stand-alone costs are determined from a long-run, forward-looking perspective. This follows since they represent the costs that a new entrant into the relevant market would bear, with no preset rigidities and with the ability to choose the current best available technology and the most efficient inputs. The capital expenditures that the entry plan requires must be seen as engendering capital costs, including competitive rates of return on capital investment that are comparable to those earned by firms outside the industry that experience equivalent levels of risk. Recognition that these costs must be expected to be covered by revenues if there is to be entry is necessary

for the entrant to compete successfully in competitive capital markets for the financing it needs initially and over its life span. For more background on the economic theory of stand-alone costs, *see* Willig (1979).

13. Here, the prices charged to the specific complaining captive shipper are shown to be unreasonable under this standard if the associated revenues exceed the shipper's net stand-alone cost and if the payments made by the other shippers in the group do not exceed the stand-alone costs of their total services (excluding the services provided to the complaining shipper).

14. Clearly, the stand-alone cost is unnecessary and inappropriate where there is competition. In a competitive market, the price offered by competitors will set a market ceiling. However, for any shippers that are truly captive, which is to say that the rail carrier faces no effective direct, indirect, or potential competition for their freight, the stand-alone cost provides an economically rational ceiling.

15. *See* Faulhaber (1975) for early recognition and explanation of the relationships between cross-subsidization and stand-alone costs.

16. Note that if payments of one group of shippers help make up for smaller margins in payments by another, the first group might well believe it is being forced to cross-subsidize the second. Yet mere payment of a relatively higher rate is not evidence of a cross-subsidy where fixed and common costs must be covered. Rather, a cross-subsidy in an economic sense can occur only if a shipper (or a group of shippers) pays more than the total cost of serving it alone. If no shipper pays more than that amount, differences in their rates simply reflect differing contributions to the common costs of the system, not cross-subsidies.

17. Faulhaber (1975).

18. For the most complete original treatment, *see* Baumol et al. (1982); and for discussion of the role of contestable markets as a benchmark for regulation, *see* Baumol and Willig (1986).

19. This result is most thoroughly and rigorously documented in Baumol et al. (1982).

20. It is economically efficient that the workable competition of contestable markets constrains incumbents' prices with levels of the forward-looking long-run economic costs that comprise stand-alone costs rather than any backward-looking historic costs or accounting conventions that may have their appropriate uses but that do not play a role in shaping the outcomes of competition.

21. *See* Baumol et al. (1977). The assumptions needed to establish this result include "normal" demands and cost conditions that in essence result from a balance between economies of scale and economies of scope.

22. Of course, those common costs might be efficiently reduced if they were to serve only A without B, and this would somewhat complicate the example without changing its lessons.

23. Panzar and Willig (1981).

24. Another reflection of this unsustainability is that the revenue from services to B of 7 is less than the incremental cost of 9 of producing those services for B.

25. These are the costs of the specialized facilities needed only to support the services of one of the customers.

26. *See* R. Braeutigam, op. cit., for explanation of the general economic harms from such methods for pricing the outputs of a firm with pervasive economies of scale and scope.

27. Indeed, the ICC specifically identified two economic concepts as foundational for CMP: differential pricing and contestable markets. *See Coal Rate Guidelines, Nationwide*, Interstate Commerce Commission, August 8, 1985.

28. Indeed, the Staggers Act was so successful that the Senate Commerce Committee declared that it "is considered the most successful rail transportation legislation ever produced, resulting in the restoration of financial health to the rail industry." Senate Report No. 104–176 (1995). Economic studies have similarly found that the policy environment post-Staggers precipitated numerous positive economic improvements in the industry. *See, e.g.,* McFarland (1989), Barnekov and Kleit (1990), Burton (1993), Ellig (2002), Winston (2005), Gaskins (2008), Caves et al. (2010), McCullough and Thompson (2013), and Macher et al. (2014).

29. A key simplifying assumption of the simplified stand-alone cost is its reliance on existing infrastructure along the route used for transporting the traffic that is subject to complaint. In contrast, a full stand-alone cost case allows the complainant to design an operating plan that shows how an efficient railroad would serve the focal traffic and to determine the optimal network configuration. *See Rate Guidelines—Non-Coal Proceedings*, Surface Transportation Board, December 27, 1996.

30. Baumol (1986, p. 120).

31. *Id.* Emphasis added.

32. Braeutigam (1989) describes fair rates as those that are free from cross-subsidies. He further observes that "the idea behind the (stand-alone cost) test is that if the revenues generated by [the focal] services exceed the cost of providing those services alone, then users of the services . . . are subsidizing users of other services" (p. 1339).

33. For example, as noted in the introductory language of the Staggers Act "most transportation within the United States is competitive." Public Law 96–448, Findings, Sec. 2 (3).

34. *See* Macher et al. (2019), Chapter 8 in this volume.

35. *See, e.g.,* Faulhaber (2005) asserting that when positive economic profits exist, stand-alone cost tests are "not helpful." (p. 446).

36. For an extended discussion, *see* Macher et al. (2014).

37. Sappington (2002, p. 240).

38. Mayo and Sappington (2016), reprinted in this volume.

39. *Id.*

40. Pittman (2010).

41. Transportation Research Board (2015, pp. 107–119).

42. *Id.*, p. 212.

# References

Barnekov, Christopher C. and Andrew N. Kleit. 1990. "The Efficiency Effects of Railroad Deregulation in the United States." *International Journal of Transport Economics* 17 (1): 21–36.

Baumol, William J. 1986. *Superfairness: Applications and Theory.* MIT Press, Cambridge, MA.

Baumol, William J., Elizabeth E. Bailey and Robert D. Willig. 1977. "Weak Invisible Hand Theorems on the Sustainability of Multiproduct Natural Monopoly." *American Economic Review* 67 (3): 350–365.

Baumol, William J. and David F. Bradford. 1970. "Optimal Departures from Marginal Cost Pricing." *American Economic Review* 60: 265–283.

Baumol, William J., Michael F. Koehn and Robert D. Willig. 1987. "How Arbitrary Is 'Arbitrary'?: Or, Toward the Deserved Demise of Full Cost Allocation." *Public Utilities Fortnightly* 120 (5): 16–21.

Baumol, William J., John C. Panzar and Robert D. Willig. 1982. *Contestable Markets and the Theory of Industry Structure.* Harcourt Brace Jovanovich, New York.

Baumol, William J. and Robert D. Willig. 1983. "Pricing Issues in the Deregulation of Railroad Rates." In *Economic Analysis of Regulated Markets.* Jörg Fingsinger, Ed. Macmillan Press, London.

Baumol, William J. and Robert D. Willig. 1986. "Contestability: Developments since the Book." *Oxford Economic Papers,* New Series 38, Supplement: Strategic Behaviour and Industrial Competition: 9–36.

Braeutigam, Ronald R. 1980. "An Analysis of Fully Distributed Cost Pricing in Regulated Industries." *The Bell Journal of Economics* 11 (1): 182–196. https://doi.org/10.2307/3003407.

Braeutigam, Ronald R. 1989. "Optimal Policies for Natural Monopolies." In *Handbook of Industrial Organization,* Volume 2. Richard Schmalensee and Robert D. Willig, Eds. North Holland, Amsterdam.

Brennan, Timothy J. 1990. "Cross-Subsidization and Cost Misallocation by Regulated Monopolists." *Journal of Regulatory Economics* 2 (1): 37–51. https://doi.org/10.1007/BF00139361.

Burton, Mark L. 1993. "Railroad Deregulation, Carrier Behavior, and Shipper Response: A Disaggregated Analysis." *Journal of Regulatory Economics* 5 (4): 417–434.

Caves, Douglas W., Laurits R. Christensen and Joseph A. Swanson. 2010. "The Staggers Act, 30 Years Later." *Regulation* 33 (4): 28–31.

Davidoff, Thomas and Ben E. Hermalin. 2004. "The Parable of Red Pens and Blues." Lecture Notes for 201a, University of California, Berkeley.

Ellig, Jerry. 2002. "Railroad Deregulation and Consumer Welfare." *Journal of Regulatory Economics* 21 (2): 143–167.

Faulhaber, Gerald R. 1975. "Cross-Subsidization: Pricing in Public Enterprises." *American Economic Review* 65 (5): 966–977.

Faulhaber, Gerald R. 2005. "Cross-Subsidy Analysis with More Than Two Services." *Journal of Competition Law and Economics* 1 (3): 441–448.

Gaskins, Darius W. 2008. "Regulation of Freight Railroads in the Modern Era: 1970–2010." *Review of Network Economics* 7 (4): 561–572.

Kaserman, David L. and John W. Mayo. 1995. *Government and Business: The Economics of Antitrust and Regulation.* Dryden Press, Ft. Worth, TX.

Macher, Jeffrey T. and John W. Mayo. 2018. "The Evolution of Contracting." Working paper. Georgetown University, Washington, DC.

Macher, Jeffrey T., John W. Mayo and Lee F. Pinkowitz. 2014. "Revenue Adequacy: The Good, the Bad and the Ugly." *Transportation Law Journal* 41 (2): 85–127. http://search.ebscohost.com/login.aspx?direct=true&AuthType=ip,uid&db=ofm&AN=102647998&site=ehost-live&scope=site.

Macher, Jeffrey T., John W. Mayo and Lee F. Pinkowitz. 2019. "The Law and Economics of Revenue Adequacy." In *U.S. Freight Rail Economics and Policy: Are We on the Right Track?* Jeffrey T. Macher and John W. Mayo, Eds. Routledge, New York.

Mayo, John W. 2015. "Statement before the House Subcommittee on Railroads, Pipelines and Hazardous Materials." Hearings on "The 35th Anniversary of the Staggers Rail Act: Railroad Deregulation Past, Present and Future." May 13. https://cbpp.georgetown.edu/sites/default/files/Anniversary_Staggers_House_Railroad_John_MayoJohn-20150513.pdf

Mayo, John W. and David E. M. Sappington. 2016. "Regulation in a 'Deregulated' Industry: Railroads in the Post-Staggers Era." *Review of Industrial Organization* 49 (2): 203–227. https://doi.org/10.1007/s11151-016-9524-1.

McCullough, Gerard J. and Louis S. Thompson. 2013. "A Further Look at the Staggers Act: Mining the Available Data." *Research in Transportation Business and Management* 6: 3–10.

McFarland, Henry. 1989. "The Effects of United States Railroad Deregulation on Shippers, Labor, and Capital." *Journal of Regulatory Economics* 1 (3): 259–270.

Panzar, John C. and Robert D. Willig. 1981. "Economies of Scope." *American Economic Review* 72 (2): 268–272.

Pittman, Russell. 2010. "Against the Stand-Alone-Cost Test in U.S. Freight Rail Regulation." *Journal of Regulatory Economics* 38 (3): 313–326. https://doi.org/10.1007/s11149-010-9130-3.

Ramsey, Frank P. 1927. "Contribution to the Theory of Taxation."*Economic Journal* 37 (1): 47–61.

Sappington, D. E. M. 2002. "Price Regulation." In *Handbook of Telecommunications Economics*, Volume 1. Martin E. Cave, Sumit K. Majumdar and Ingo Vogelsang, Eds. North Holland, Amsterdam.

Sherman, Roger. 1989. *The Regulation of Natural Monopoly.* Cambridge University Press, Cambridge.

Sweeney, George. 1982. "Welfare Implications of Fully Distributed Cost Pricing Applied to Partially Regulated Firms." *American Economic Review* 71 (3): 437–447. https://doi.org/10.2307/3003471.

Train, Kenneth E. 1991. *Optimal Regulation: The Economic Theory of Natural Monopoly.* MIT Press, Cambridge, MA.

Transportation Research Board. 2015. *Modernizing Freight Rail Regulation.* Special Report 318. The National Academies of Sciences, Engineering, Medicine.

Willig, Robert D. 1978. "Pareto Superior Nonlinear Outlay Schedules." *Bell Journal of Economics* 9 (1): 56–69.

Willig, Robert D. 1979. "Multiproduct Technology and Market Structure." *American Economic Review* 69 (2): 346–351.

Winston, Clifford. 2005. "The Success of the Staggers Rail Act of 1980." *AEI-Brookings Joint Center for Regulatory Studies,* Washington, DC.

# Section II
# Railroads in an Increasingly Interrelated Economy

# 3 International Trade and the Demand for U.S. Rail Services

*Ferdinando Monte*

International economic integration creates links between local outcomes and economic conditions in potentially very distant places; in so doing, it affects the demand of shipment services within a country. The strength and direction of these links are shaped by many factors, including locations' comparative advantage, input-output linkages, and the level of integration in local labor markets. In this chapter, we explore the significance of international trade for rail shipments; we further demonstrate how recent advances in the spatial economics literature can be used to infer changes in the demand of shipment services among U.S. counties following any change in local or global economic conditions.

## Introduction

Can an increase in productivity in Vietnam change the demand of rail services between Chicago, IL, and Boston, MA? The answer to this and similar questions hinges certainly on the patterns of sectoral specialization of Vietnam and of different regions in the United States. Further, it is also a function of the degree of international integration among the United States and Vietnam and of those countries with other trade partners. Perhaps more subtly, it might also depend on the degree of integration between different U.S. local labor markets and the degree of spatial frictions among U.S. locations.

As the world grows more integrated, these considerations become more relevant for policymakers, infrastructure planners, and practitioners alike. Policymakers, for example, may be interested in the degree of economic integration between areas in the country; infrastructure planners need to know the demand imposed on competing modes of transportation, like highways and waterways; practitioners want to anticipate trends in transportation demand to make appropriate business decisions.

This chapter has two broad parts. In the first (Sections 2 and 3), it presents some basic facts about international integration, and it shows evidence on the significance of international transactions for the demand of internal shipments by rail. In the second (Sections 4 and 5), it presents in a non-technical way recent advances in quantitative spatial economics that allow an answer to this class of questions, and it illustrates a possible application quantitatively.

This chapter starts by characterizing the degree to which economies have become more integrated over time. The ability of moving goods and information over space creates economic linkages between production and consumption activities in a particular country's area and local economic conditions in other, potentially distant, places.

The local consequences of these spatial linkages are shaped and potentially amplified by two orders of considerations. First, the current transportation network and the degree of spatial integration between a country's locations help to determine where the adjustment to a shock occurs and how much of the impact is on quantities versus prices. Second, countries and regions tend to be specialized in sectors in which they have a comparative advantage, and the production of a good in general uses inputs from different sectors: hence, different regions may interact via input-output linkages even if their firms do not compete head-to-head in the same sectors.

The ability to track the propagation of a change in the international environment down to the local level is significant for the demand of transportation services, in general, and of rail services, in particular: to the extent that a shock implies equilibrium changes in international and/or internal trade flows, it also implies changes in the demand for transportation. Hence, spatial economic models provide a natural starting point to think about our opening question.

We present the main mechanisms behind one such model in Section 4. This model represents the world economy with its spatial frictions, input-output linkages, and product market interactions; the U.S. economy has a finer level of detail, and accounts for products and labor market interactions among 3,000 counties. After a brief description of the sources used to quantify this model, we use it to explore the quantitative consequences of a simple counterfactual exercise: an increase in bilateral tariffs in the Chemical sector between the United States and the European Union (E.U.). In particular, we describe the change in the demand of shipment services for chemical products both with the European Union and across U.S. counties; further, we show how demand for shipment services of a related product, Rubbers and Plastic, is also influenced across U.S. counties.

While this simple exercise is certainly suggestive of the potential of a general equilibrium approach, some caveats on the limitations of these current results, both broadly and for the rail sector specifically, are in order. The chapter concludes with such discussion.

## International and Internal Integration: Motivating Facts

International flows of goods and services have become steadily more significant in the last decades. A simple and commonly used measure of the world's international integration looks at the total value of exports by any country in the world, divided by the total world Gross Domestic Product (GDP). The light gray line in Figure 3.1 shows that, by this measure, the world recorded 12¢ of exports for every dollar of income produced in the year 1960; by 2016, this number grew to around 29¢.[1] The United States experienced comparable increases. For individual countries, a better measure of integration divides the total value of imports plus exports by the country's GDP. For the United States (see black line in Figure 3.1), this measure of integration goes from around 9¢ of international trade per dollar of GDP in the year 1960 to around 27¢ in 2016.[2]

While this level of international integration is not totally unprecedented, its nature is unique in many dimensions.[3] An aspect that is particularly relevant for our purposes is that today, rather than being shipped just once, goods (in the form of intermediate inputs) may cross national borders multiple times before the final product reaches its consumer. The term "global value chains," coordinated production processes that stretch across multiple countries and potentially involve several firms, has become part of everyday parlance in the business and academic community.[4] Timmer et al. (2014), for example, finds that for 85% of the value chain they examine, the share of foreign value added incorporated in products at their final consumption country has increased: the average share has grown from 28% in 1995 to 34% to 2008. This increase indicates that production is increasingly fragmented. When value chains stretch across multiple countries (or even multiple regions), a constant value of final goods' trade tends to generate larger demand for shipment services of intermediate inputs.

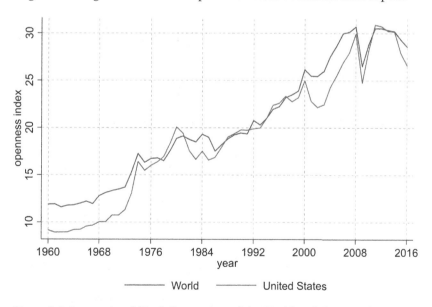

*Figure 3.1* International Trade Integration of the World and the United States

Note: See main text for the definition of these indices.

Multiple reasons account for this growing integration. Several rounds of the World Trade Organization negotiations and the arrival of new members have laid out the basis for a remarkable fall in tariffs; this has been complemented by several bilateral and regional trade agreements that have further reduced man-made trade impediments. The scope for spatial coordination among firms has further improved because technological improvements have made communication and shipping cheaper. Whatever the reason, economic events in potentially distant places are now much more likely to affect economic conditions in any given country.

Goods move not only internationally, but also within the boundaries of a country. A useful data source for this type of information is the Commodity Flow Survey (CFS). The CFS, produced every five years since 1993, is a survey produced jointly by Bureau of Transportation Statistics (BTS) and the Census Bureau at the U.S. Department of Commerce. The survey is the primary source of national and state-level data on domestic freight shipments. Data are collected via questionnaires to selected establishments as a part of the Economic Census. Among others, information is gathered on shipment value, weight, commodity type, destination (or gateway for export shipment), and mode of transportation (and export mode for export shipments).

Internal shipments for the United States are, indeed, much more significant than international ones. In 2012, the last year for which these data are available from the CFS, for each dollar of U.S. GDP, the economy recorded about 86¢ of internal shipments of goods. This value has fluctuated between 76 and 86¢ since 1993, the first year available.[5] The CFS also provides information on the average distance of one ton of internal shipments, which has increased from around 250 miles in 1993 to around 300 miles in 2012, signaling that the U.S. economy has become more spatially integrated.[6]

The fact that the United States is spatially integrated implies, together with growing international linkages, that events in distant places of the world can affect to a significant extent specific local areas in particular. Because of growing international spatial linkages, for example, some cities in the United States are directly impacted by increases in productivity in China when those cities produce similar goods (Autor et al., 2013). Moreover, because of deep internal spatial linkages, other cities in the United States are also potentially impacted in an indirect way: for example, they may experience a reduction in demand of products supplied to locations negatively affected by Chinese competition.

Changes in the spatial patterns of production and consumption of goods and services in a country have, quite naturally, consequences for the demand of shipment services between any two places within that country. In this sense, the demand for transportation services within a country is increasingly exposed to changes in international conditions: in particular, to understand changes in demand for rail services in modern economies, it is important to account for economic linkages that extend beyond the national boundaries.

In the rest of this chapter, we take a closer look at the relation between spatial integration and demand for transportation services in general, and rail services in particular. We first provide direct evidence on the significant interaction between rail services and international trade. We then show how one can leverage recent advances in quantitative spatial modeling to explore the consequences of changes in the international environment on internal demand for transportation services.

## Rail and U.S. International Integration

We have argued earlier that international integration impacts the demand of shipping services in a country. A portion of this demand is embedded in internal shipments that are part of domestic value chains, and hence are hard to measure: the next sections in this chapter use economic theory to shed more light on it. On the other hand, transportation services in general, and rail services in particular, are also demanded for export from a U.S. port of exit toward a foreign country, and for shipments between the factory or warehouse gates and U.S. ports of entry/exit. While import shipments from U.S. ports of entry are not recorded separately, the Commodity Flow Survey measures directly those two sources of demand of the export side. We summarize them here.[7]

In the last 15 years of available data (from 1997 to 2012), rail transportation from U.S. ports of exit toward foreign countries has accounted for a steady 3%–4% of the total value of U.S. exports of goods.[8] Shipment demand for export activities has then increased by 55% in terms of goods' values, roughly in the same proportion as total real value exported over the same 15 years, for the industries covered by the CFS. This growth essentially has been split equally between Mexico and Canada.

The share of tons exported via rail increased slightly from around 8% in 1997 to around 10% in 2012, which amounts to a growth of around 60% of tons shipped in the same amount of time. About four-fifths of this growth in tons is accounted for by increased shipments to Mexico.

Merchandise must reach a port of exit before being exported. The demand for these internal shipment services is then directly connected to the level of international integration and is directly measured in the Commodity Flow Survey. Table 3.1 reports select statistics on these flows. Panel I shows that the overall value of goods shipped to a U.S. port of exit for export purposes increased by about 50% in real terms over 15 years. Since rail transportation captures around 6%–7% of those shipments, there has been a roughly 50% increase in the value-based demand of single-mode shipment services from 1997 to 2007. Intermodal shipments (Table 3.1 reports rail and truck, but similar patterns are found for rail and water when the data are available) are capturing an increasing share of value: overall, the share of value shipped where rail services are involved grows from around 10% in 1997 to around 12% in 2012.

Panels II and III report corresponding statistics for tons and ton-miles moved. As typical for shipments in general, rails are involved in heavier-than-average and longer-than-average shipments. The share of intermodal shipments is increasing on these measures as well. By and large, a direct consequence of growing international engagement has been growing demand for rail internal shipments across all measures.

A comparison of these patterns with data on all internal shipments yields additional insights. We report information corresponding to Table 3.1, now for all U.S. shipments, in Table 3.2. Data for internal shipments are

*Table 3.1* Export Shipment Characteristics by Domestic Mode of Transportation

| Year | | 1997 | 2002 | 2007 | 2012 |
|---|---|---|---|---|---|
| **Panel I: Dollar Value (million USD)** | | | | | |
| Levels | Rail | 51,580 | 38,196 | 73,091 | 80,743 |
| | Rail & Truck | 26,048 | 17,856 | 57,450 | 66,543 |
| | All Shipments | 807,686 | 794,271 | 1,017,728 | 1,212,394 |
| Shares of All Shipments | Rail | 6.4% | 4.8% | 7.2% | 6.7% |
| | Rail & Truck | 3.2% | 2.2% | 5.6% | 5.5% |
| | Rail (combined) | 9.6% | 7.1% | 12.8% | 12.1% |
| **Panel II: Tons (thousand)** | | | | | |
| Levels | Rail | 125,004 | 114,042 | 132,541 | 169,631 |
| | Rail & Truck | 8,433 | 9,366 | 26,263 | 41,846 |
| | All Shipments | 445,324 | 487,473 | 479,578 | 564,520 |
| Shares of All Shipments | Rail | 28.1% | 23.4% | 27.6% | 30.0% |
| | Rail & Truck | 1.9% | 1.9% | 5.5% | 7.4% |
| | Rail (combined) | 30.0% | 25.3% | 33.1% | 37.5% |
| **Panel III: Ton-miles (million)** | | | | | |
| Levels | Rail | 79,012 | 78,035 | 74,474 | 114,698 |
| | Rail & Truck | 9,666 | 9,760 | 34,741 | 21,763 |
| | All Shipments | 183,712 | 207,534 | 230,154 | 274,934 |
| Shares of All Shipments | Rail | 43.0% | 37.6% | 32.4% | 41.7% |
| | Rail & Truck | 5.3% | 4.7% | 15.1% | 7.9% |
| | Rail (combined) | 48.3% | 42.3% | 47.5% | 49.6% |

Note: This table shows select statistics on shipments originating in the United States and delivering merchandise to a U.S. port of exit for export, by mode of transportation. "All shipments" refers to all shipments for final export. Dollar values are converted into year 2017 real terms using the U.S. implied GDP deflator from the Bureau of Economic Analysis. Raw data come from the 2002–2012 Export Summary Report of the Commodity Flow Survey.

*Table 3.2* Overall Shipment Characteristics by Domestic Mode of Transportation

| Year | 1993 | 1997 | 2002 | 2007 | 2012 |
|---|---|---|---|---|---|
| ***Panel I: Value (million USD)*** | | | | | |
| Levels | | | | | |
| Rail | 388,380 | 464,707 | 414,641 | 508,533 | 509,965 |
| Rail & Truck | 130,429 | 110,052 | 93,268 | 218,188 | 242,368 |
| All Shipments | 9,178,072 | 10,095,819 | 11,199,770 | 13,615,640 | 14,932,486 |
| Shares of All Shipments | | | | | |
| Rail | 4.2% | 4.6% | 3.7% | 3.7% | 3.4% |
| Rail & Truck | 1.4% | 1.1% | 0.8% | 1.6% | 1.6% |
| Rail (combined) | 5.7% | 5.7% | 4.5% | 5.3% | 5.0% |
| ***Panel II: Tons (thousand)*** | | | | | |
| Levels | | | | | |
| Rail | 1,544,148 | 1,549,817 | 1,873,884 | 1,861,307 | 1,628,537 |
| Rail & Truck | 40,624 | 54,246 | 42,984 | 225,589 | 213,814 |
| All Shipments | 9,688,493 | 11,089,733 | 11,667,919 | 12,543,425 | 11,299,409 |
| Shares of All Shipments | | | | | |
| Rail | 15.9% | 14.0% | 16.1% | 14.8% | 14.4% |
| Rail & Truck | 0.4% | 0.5% | 0.4% | 1.8% | 1.9% |
| Rail (combined) | 16.4% | 14.5% | 16.4% | 16.6% | 16.3% |
| ***Panel III: Ton-miles (million)*** | | | | | |
| Levels | | | | | |
| Rail | 942,561 | 1,022,547 | 1,261,612 | 1,344,040 | 1,211,481 |
| Rail & Truck | 37,675 | 55,561 | 45,525 | 196,772 | 169,524 |
| All Shipments | 2,420,915 | 2,661,363 | 3,137,898 | 3,344,658 | 2,969,506 |
| Shares of All Shipments | | | | | |
| Rail | 38.9% | 38.4% | 40.2% | 40.2% | 40.8% |
| Rail & Truck | 1.6% | 2.1% | 1.5% | 5.9% | 5.7% |
| Rail (combined) | 40.5% | 40.5% | 41.7% | 46.1% | 46.5% |

Note: This table shows select statistics on shipments originating and terminating within the United States by mode of transportation. Dollar values are converted into year 2017 real terms using the U.S. implied GDP deflator from the Bureau of Economic Analysis. Raw data come from the 1997, 2007, and 2012 United States Summary Reports of the Commodity Flow Survey.

available starting 1993, rather than 1997. The general trend over time is for rail shipment services to account for a slightly declining share of value shipped, a roughly constant share of tons, but a growing share of ton-miles.

Overall, rail shipment services are relatively more important for exports than for all shipments: shares of export-oriented shipments services in value and tons are always above the corresponding share for all shipments (Panels I and II). Hence, rail services are relatively important for export activities.

On the other hand, export activities are important for the rail industry. Comparing the first row of Panel I across the Tables 3.1 and 3.2, we find that exports account for a growing share of the overall value shipped via rail, which goes from around 11% in 1997 to around 16% in 2012. Similar patterns are observed for tons (from 8% to 10%), and ton-miles (from 7.7% to 9.5%) shipped.

Taken together, these statistics indicate a significant interaction between rail services and the international engagement of the United States. However, the consequences of international trade on internal transportation services run much deeper, once its indirect effects on the internal geography of production and consumption are considered. To clarify this impact, one needs a quantitative model of the economy that both accounts for international linkages between countries and allows for a fine enough spatial detail within the country. We describe such a model in the next section.

## A Quantitative Model for Internal Shipments

The primary data presented so far are useful to characterize the interrelation between international economic conditions and demand for transportation services, but the data come with limitations. A first limitation we have observed is that we lose track of import shipments once they cross the U.S. border. A second, and perhaps more significant, limitation is that the demand of internal shipments is indirectly affected by international (and intra-national) conditions via the impact that any change, or "shock" in economic parlance, has on local economic conditions. To track the influence that a given local or international shock has on the demand of shipment services, one needs to have a model that accounts for the main spatial and sectoral linkages that characterize modern economic activity.

In this section, we present a verbal description of a quantitative model that accounts for international and local interactions in a consistent way. This model (Monte, 2018) builds on the seminal contribution by Eaton and Kortum (2002) and the large quantitative literature that followed.

The quantitative theory we draw upon models the world economy as a series of "locations": Three thousand one hundred and eight U.S. counties and 38 foreign countries composing about 95% of the world GDP and a residual "Rest of the World." Locations will be indexed alternatively with $d$ or $i$. The model accounts for 29 separate sectors, 15 manufacturing and 14 non-manufacturing, covering the whole economy of each country. Sectors will be indexed alternatively by the letter $s$ or $k$.

The model incorporates two main types of markets: labor markets (possibly local, when considering U.S. counties) and product markets. Labor markets within the United States are connected via spatial linkages in the form of commuting—residents of a county choosing where to work according to the wage offered, commuting costs, and possibly individual idiosyncratic preferences. We assume, however, that workers cannot live in a country and work in another. Product markets are connected via spatial linkages (e.g., firms producing in a place choose the origin location for their inputs) and input-output linkages (e.g., firms producing in a sector use inputs from several other sectors). A general feature of spatial relationships is that economic activity (e.g., expenditure flows or commuting flows) declines with the distance between two locations. This feature, "gravity," is present in our model both in labor and goods market.

In the remainder of this section, we provide a non-technical discussion of these links; we then briefly describe the general equilibrium interactions that these links entail and provide an overview of the data sources used to calibrate the model to the world economy. The theory assumes full employment and hence it is useful to compare the long-run consequences of a shock.

In the section that follows, we will then illustrate how these recent advances in quantitative spatial models can be used to track the consequences of a particular shock on the demand for transportation services.

*Local Labor Supply*

When looking at a country as a whole, labor markets have a fairly simple characterization: the labor supplied by people in a country must be equal to the labor demanded by all firms in the economy at the equilibrium wage. If one wants to attempt a quantification of the consequences of a trade shock at a micro-geographical scale, however, it is important to recognize that people live and work in potentially different places: this is because while labor supply at country-level is fixed, labor supply at U.S. county level depends on the prevailing wages of neighboring counties as well.[9]

Considering labor market interactions is necessary because labor costs are a significant determinant of firms' unit costs of production: if a shock impacts one county, its effects can spill over to firms in neighboring counties simply via commuting linkages. Suppose, for example, that labor demand in County 1 increases: wages there grow, everything else equal. Some local residents who are working in a different county, call it County 2, are then induced to switch and find a higher paying job in County 1. As they do so, labor supply to County 1 increases, thus dampening the initial increase in wages; however, labor supply to County 2 falls, thus increasing the wage in that county as well. The importance of commuting for local labor markets is not only a theoretical conjecture: for example, Monte et al. (2018) find that the openness of a county to commuting is a fundamental determinant of the elasticity of local employment to local shocks; further, Monte (2018) finds that the share of a county's residents working in the same county falls when that county is exposed to increases in import penetration from China.

The model we use here incorporates these commuting linkages among U.S. counties. In particular, given a set of wages across the United States, labor supply to a county $i$ can be written as

$$Workers_i = \sum_d \lambda_{d,i} \times Residents_d$$

that is, the labor supply to county $i$, $Workers_i$, is the sum over all residences $d$ of how many people live there, $Residents_d$, times the fraction of those residents that choose to work in county $i$, $\lambda_{d,i}$. This fraction is itself a function of the wages of all the counties that residents of $d$ are close enough to reach. Note that commuting patterns also contribute to determine total local income[10] of residents in a county $d$, and hence, local expenditure:

$$Income_d = Residents_d \times \sum_i \lambda_{d,i} \times wage_i$$

Labor supply has to be equal to labor demand in each U.S. county and in all countries of the world for the economy to be in equilibrium. Labor demand arises from production activities of the firms, which, in turn, depends on consumers' expenditure across sectors and over space. We now turn to the description of these two remaining pieces.

### Local Labor Demand and Trade Linkages

Labor demand in a location $d$ (be it a country or a U.S. county) arises from firms who are located there and active in any sector $s$. Since labor is an input, its demand is derived from the products that firms sell: hence, to get at labor demand, we need to understand local firms' revenues. The revenues of location $i$'s firms active in sector $s$ are given by

$$Revenues_i^s = \sum_d \pi_{d,i}^s \times Expenditure_d^s$$

The term $Expenditure_d^s$ is location $d$'s total market size: the total expenditure that consumers and firms in this location devote to sector $s$. This expenditure depends on consumers' income—as described earlier—and on the demand for sector $s$ intermediate inputs of all firms active in location $d$, whatever their sector of activity. We will describe the expenditure term in more detail in the next subsection.

The term $\pi_{d,i}^s$ represents the market share that firms active in location $i$ and sector $s$ are able to capture, out of the total expenditure of location $d$ in the same sector. Three aspects impact such market share. First, the market share is impacted by local unit costs of production, $c_i^s$. Firms in sector $s$ use labor and bundles of intermediate inputs from all sectors in the economy.[11] Local conditions that raise equilibrium input costs, like higher wages, reduce the market share.

Second, the market share is impacted by bilateral transportation costs and other spatial frictions. For manufacturing sectors, gravity in international and internal trade is a well-recognized empirical regularity (see, e.g., Hillberry and Hummels, 2007, for internal U.S. trade and Disdier and Head, 2008, for international trade): trade flows decrease in space because of transportation costs, other costs possibly associated with distance and, internationally, tariff and non-tariff barriers. For non-manufacturing sectors, Agarwal et al. (2018) find steep decays of consumers' expenditure with space, and in general very limited consumer mobility. The model captures the impact of these frictions both by accounting for the measured impact of spatial frictions and by assuming that services cannot be purchased from counties farther than 120 kilometers.[12] When bilateral spatial frictions are stronger, the market share falls.

Third, the market share of firms located in $i$ depends on the strength of the competition that these producers face when selling to consumers and firms in $d$. The strength of competition depends on what other options purchasers located in $d$ have available. Those options are better (and hence, competition is tougher) when the unit costs of other potential providers, $c_j^s$, are low, and especially so when those providers are close by, or face low spatial frictions. Note that these two conditions are, indeed, the first two determinants of market share we have described earlier, just applied to firm $i$'s competitors. When competition is strong, everything else equal the market share of $i$'s producers falls.

For given expenditures and market shares, firms located in $i$ and active in $s$ derive their revenues as described earlier. In turn, this implies production needs to serve all markets, and hence, labor demand arising from sector $s$. The total labor demand in location $i$ is then simply the sum of sectoral labor demands over all sectors active in location $i$.

The last term left to describe is the expenditure by sector and location. We turn to this task in the next subsection.

### Expenditure and the Role of Input-Output Linkages

We denote the demand of sector $s$ output in location $d$ with *Expenditure*$_d^s$. This demand comes from two sources—consumers and firms—and is described by

$$Expenditure_d^s = \alpha_d^s \times Income_d + \sum_k \gamma_d^{k(s)} \times Revenues_d^k$$

The first term on the right-hand side of this equation is consumer demand. This term is intuitive to understand. The model assumes that each consumer spends a constant share $\alpha_d^s$ of its income on a given sector $s$, and hence, total consumer demand for sector $s$ goods is simply $\alpha_d^s \times Income_d$; we recall, however, that the income of residents in $d$ depends on the commuting choices of those residents, and this provides a spatial link between local labor market conditions and consumer demand.

The second term in the equation represents the demand of sector $s$ products for production purposes of all firms located in $d$ (irrespective of their sector $k$ of activity). For example, services of the sector $s$ "Renting of Machines and Equipment and Other Business Activities" (henceforth "Renting of M&E") are consumed by sector $k$ "Mining and Quarrying" (henceforth "Mining"), by sector $k$ "Chemicals and Chemical Products" (henceforth "Chemicals"), and potentially all other sectors. As for aforementioned labor, this sector $s$ is an input, and hence, its demand is understood only as a function of total output of those firms which use this input. The total output of firms located in $d$ and producing in sector $k$, $Revenues_d^k$, has been described earlier. The term $\gamma_d^{k(s)}$ refers to the share of sector $k$ revenues that fall on inputs from sector $s$. This share may depend on where the firms are located, $d$, and is essentially a representation of the production function of these firms. To follow on the earlier example, the Mining sector spends about 20% of its total intermediate purchases on Renting of M&E; the same share for Chemicals is around 15%.[13] If we sum up the demand of firms active in $d$ over all sectors $k$, we obtain the total demand of firms for intermediate inputs of the Chemicals sector.

Note that the unit cost of firms active in sector $k$ and location $d$, $c_d^k$, is affected by the price of all sectors at a rate given by the coefficients $\gamma_d^{k(s)}$ of the production function. The fact that firms active in a sector $k$ and location $d$ use inputs from potentially all sectors generates what are called input-output linkages. These linkages provide a further mechanism through which shocks that first impact a particular sector-location may propagate to other sector-locations. For example, if the cost of Renting of M&E grows in a particular location, this affects firms in the Mining sectors more than those in the Chemicals sectors. Since the final unit cost $c_d^k$ contributes to determine market shares, sales of firms located in $d$ will fall everywhere. As those firms' market shares fall, market shares of firms in other locations grow, and so input demand in other locations—and across all sectors, not only in Renting of M&E—also grows. The model accounts jointly for these spatial and input-output linkages.

In the remaining subsection, we briefly describe how all market outcomes are made consistent with each other and the data sources used to calibrate the model. The following section shows, then, how one can use this model to describe the impact of a trade shock on the demand of shipment services across any two locations and for any sectors, accounting for labor and product markets linkages.

*Equilibrium and Data Sources for Calibration*

For the model to be internally consistent, all agents need to maximize their objective functions and all markets need to clear. Consumer optimization is implicit in the optimal job location and the income shares devoted to each sector; firms' optimization is implicit in the derivation of market shares and in the demand of different sectoral inputs. When markets are in equilibrium, labor (or sectoral inputs) demand is equal to labor (or sectoral input) supply in each location (U.S. county or country), and the expenditure of firms and consumers on each input is consistent with the revenues and market shares of all firms in any location of the world. In the calibration of the model, we have also allowed for the overall level of trade deficits in the data to be replicated in the initial equilibrium.

To make quantitative statements, the model needs to be simulated, and all the parameters of the model need to have numerical values. The model is calibrated for the world economy around the year 2000. Information on the production function of different countries and sector comes from the World Input-Output Database (WIOD) (Timmer et al., 2015). This data source provides, for each industry-country, its composition of expenditure on all other industry-country pairs; hence, it gives information jointly on international trade flows and the purchasing sectors from which such flows arise. WIOD also provides information on the final consumption shares of expenditure across different sectors. For the United States, this information is integrated by the County Business Pattern 1997 and 2002, the U.S. Economic Census of 1997 and 2002, and the Bureau of Economic Analysis' regional accounts. To recover bilateral spatial frictions, we use international trade flows from WIOD and U.S. internal trade flows from the Commodity Flow Survey. International spatial frictions are estimated making use of international flows and standard controls like distance, country contiguity, regional trade agreements in force, and several others from the Centre d'Études Prospectives et d'Informations Internationales. Internal spatial frictions are estimated complementing the Commodity Flow Survey with information on trade flows by U.S. Port of Entry/Exit from Schott (2008). Note also that since import and export flows from any U.S. county to any other U.S. county or to a foreign country are not in the data, they need to be estimated. Other parameters are taken from standard values in the literature. For a detailed description of the calibration process, see again Monte (2018).

## A Tariff War on Chemicals

In recent months, international trade policy has regained centrality in economic policy debates. The U.S. Government has moved toward a more active use of tools—whether or not directly sanctioned within the World Trade Organization framework—that can impact international trade flows directly; U.S. trade partners have responded, or threatened to respond, to those policies with countervailing measures. While the full effects of any precise episode is beyond the scope of the present chapter, these circumstances do provide an opportunity to illustrate the potential of this model to speak to the demand of shipment services in the United States.

In this section, we describe the results of a simulation that increases by 5% spatial frictions between any U.S. county and the European Union, in either direction, in the "Chemicals and Chemical Products" sector (again, simply "Chemicals" in what follows). We can think of this exercise as investigating the consequences of an increase in bilateral tariffs in the sector and will refer to this interpretation ahead. This experiment is interesting because the European Union and the United States are quite well integrated: the share of the European Union in U.S. imports and exports of Chemicals was about 75% and 42% in the year 2000, respectively. Moreover, "Chemicals and Chemical products" as a sector has accounted for around 10% of total ton-miles shipped by Class I railroads in the last two decades.

The contemporaneous increase in bilateral tariffs raises the cost of E.U. Chemicals for U.S. purchasers, and the cost of U.S. chemicals for E.U. purchasers, by 5%. In our parameterization, the elasticity of trade flows to costs is around −1.2 for Chemicals, which would imply a drop in bilateral flows of around 6% each way. Because the United States is running a deficit in this sector, however, imports would fall more than exports in dollar value, thus generating a trade surplus. In equilibrium, trade balance must be restored. In the simulations, we see that U.S. imports from the European Union fall, but imports of Chemicals from other countries rise slightly; on the other hand, exports of Chemicals fall toward the European Union and also, slightly, toward all the other partners, to restore trade balance. Overall imports and exports of Chemicals fall by around 1%–2%, since international trade flows are diverted toward other countries.

An immediate implication of the drop in imports from the European Union is that the demand of shipment services of chemical products from the European Union to U.S. counties also falls. This demand is, however, not uniformly distributed across the United States. Our model can be used to investigate where this demand falls the most, by looking at where those imports drop the greatest in dollar value. Figure 3.2 shows a map of U.S. counties, with darkest gray implying the strongest drop. White counties are those with negligible changes in the value of shipments from the European Union. The largest reduction in shipment demand are, quite naturally, occurring where countries in the European Union were (estimated to) export most initially. Integrating these changes with knowledge of the typical ports of entry for Chemical products from the European Union would allow to compute drop in demands along specific railroad routes.

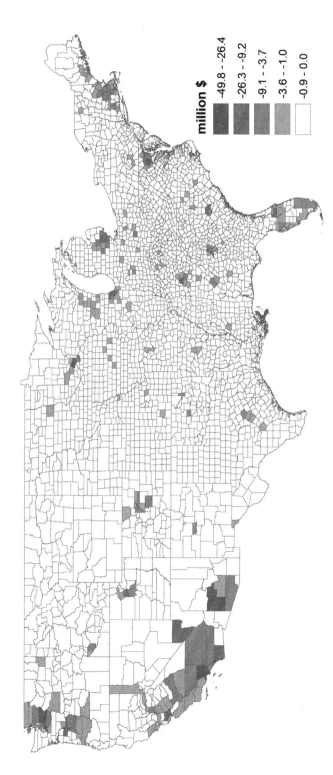

*Figure 3.2* Drop in Shipment Demand of Chemicals From the European Union

Our discussion earlier suggested that if the price of an input increases from a particular origin, spatial linkages will reshuffle market shares toward other producers. In this exercise, since tariffs of the European Union toward the United States also increase, U.S. producers export less; however, these firms do produce and ship more to the domestic market: these forces reorient the internal demand of Chemical shipments for any given origin, away from the ports of exit, and toward other U.S. counties. In Figure 3.3, we map out the change in *internal* shipments of chemical products from each county toward any other county in the United States (excluding itself, obviously); this is also the change in demand for internal transportation of chemical products from a particular county.

Figure 3.3 shows that regions like the Texas Gulf Coast and the New Jersey-New York-Connecticut area are among the ones most impacted by this episode; some counties in the Bay area and in Illinois also significantly increase shipments toward other U.S. counties.[14] In principle, one could dig even deeper and identify for each selling county the composition of destinations where the change in shipments come from: the model delivers bilateral changes in the flow of goods for any pair of locations.

We conclude this exercise with a note about input-output relations. We have said that a single shock can propagate over space and sectors because of the input composition of different sectors. For the United States, producers in the Chemicals sector spend about 4% of their intermediate purchases on "Rubber and Plastics" (henceforth, "Rubber"). It is then natural to expect that in counties where total *supply* of Chemicals grows the most, total *demand* of Rubber for production purposes also rises the most. Since Rubber can in principle be purchased from producers located anywhere, the bilateral increase in Chemicals tariffs also affects observed shipments of Rubber products toward any county producing Chemicals. Figure 3.4 shows the relation between changes in these two quantities across U.S. locations: each dot in the figure represents a U.S. county. The x-axis records the change in total production of Chemicals in a county (in million dollars), irrespective of the destination location. The y-axis shows the change in the deliveries of Rubber to the same county from other U.S. counties; this is also the change in the demand of shipments services for Rubber products to any county induced by the bilateral tariffs on Chemicals.

In counties where the bilateral tariff changes imply a larger increase in Chemical output, demand of Rubber and Plastics products grows more. Since these products are shipped from other locations, a tariff on Chemicals implies a spatial reorganization of the demand for Rubber transportation services. Note also that for some counties, inward shipments of Rubber can fall. A plausible explanation again points to input-output linkages: the increase in tariffs, raising the price of Chemicals, reduces the demand of products that use Chemicals (say, Pulp, Paper, and Printing and Publishing). As the output of these other industries falls, demand

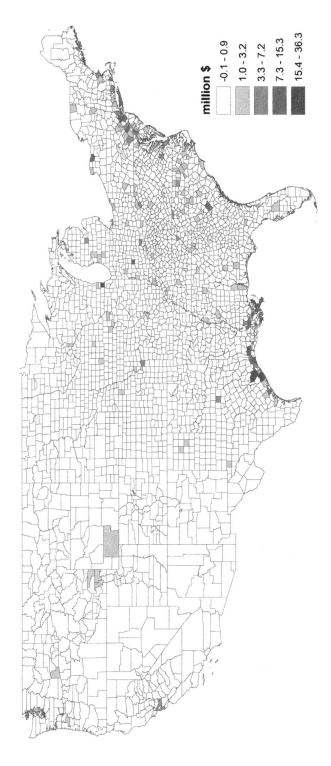

million $

-0.1 - 0.9

1.0 - 3.2

3.3 - 7.2

7.3 - 15.3

15.4 - 36.3

*Figure 3.3* Change in Demand of Internal Shipments of Chemicals, by Origin

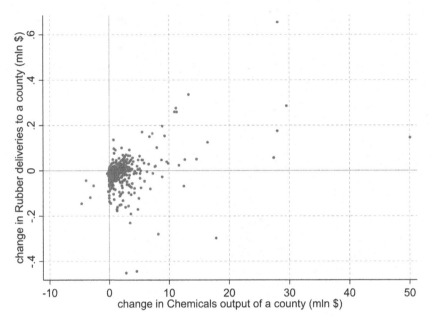

*Figure 3.4* The Impact of Chemical Tariffs on Internal Shipments of Rubber

for all their inputs—including Rubber—also shrinks. In counties where the output of Chemicals does not grow enough, the latter force tends to dominate and inward shipments of Rubber fall.

## Conclusions

As economic integration between countries proceeds, the demand for internal transportation services is likely to be increasingly impacted by changes in international conditions. In this chapter, we have illustrated how recent advances in quantitative spatial economics can be used to infer, for example, the consequences of a tariff shock on the demand of transportation services of different products within the United States.

While the model described here is used for a particular exercise, it is important to note that it carries with it the potential for greater applicability and some limitations. For instance, the same model can be used to simulate the impact of changes in productivity in particular locations and sectors or improvements in transportation technology that changes commuting costs or internal freight costs.

At the same time, although accounting for input-output and spatial linkages at product and labor market level is certainly useful, these tools have ample margins for improvements, and the magnitudes in our exercise should be taken more as indications rather than actual predictions. As an example, tariffs usually generate government revenues: we have ignored the redistribution of these receipts into the economy. More important for our purposes here, incorporating a more realistic transportation network could be valuable in providing an even finer spatial detail. Finally, the extent to which demand for transportation services explicitly translates into demand for rail services has been left out of the analysis: in this sense, the model presented here is still only a necessary (but not sufficient) stepping stone for the demand of any transportation mode.

As the state of knowledge progresses, the explicit magnitudes of the consequences of this exercise may change while the intuitions will become more refined.

## Notes

1. *See* World Bank: World Bank and OECD National Accounts, retrieved at www.data.worldbank.org.
2. *See* World Bank, *ibid.*
3. For a broader discussion, *see, e.g.,* Baldwin and Martin (1999).
4. *See* Baldwin (2016) for a recent discussion of causes and consequences of global value chains. The Global Value Chains Center at Duke University provides a wealth of resources on the topic.
5. *See* Commodity Flow Survey, U.S. Department of Transportation, 1993, 1997, 2002, 2007, 2012.
6. To compute this measure, one divides the total ton-miles shipped within the country by the total tons; both measures are available in the Commodity Flow Survey since 1993.
7. Except where noted, all data in this section come from the 1997–2012 Export Summary Reports and United States Reports of the Commodity Flow Survey.
8. A note of caution is required in relating these statistics to official U.S. exports, since the industry coverage of the Commodity Flow Survey does not exactly match statistics on merchandise trade by the Department of Commerce.
9. In principle, labor supply varies as a function of economic conditions also via other channels like labor force participation. Here we abstract from these aspects.
10. To keep exposition simple, we will talk only about labor income. The actual model used in the simulations also includes payments to local "land and structures," or capital income.
11. As indicated earlier, we omit capital in this description. The model used for our simulations also allows for "land and structures," or capital, in the production function of firms.
12. Monte et al. (2018) show that the relation between commuting flows and distance has a structural break around such distance.
13. Multiplying these shares by the correspondent share of intermediates into total output gives us the $\gamma_d^{k(s)}$.
14. This reallocation of demand toward domestic producers is not frictionless. The search for new firms and the writing of new supply and transportation contracts may absorb significant resources and time. These processes are not accounted for in our exercise.

## References

Agarwal, Sumit, J. Bradford Jensen, and Ferdinando Monte (2018). "The Geography of Consumption," mimeograph, Georgetown University.

Autor, David, David Dorn, and Gordon H. Hanson (2013). "The China Syndrome: Local Labor Market Effects of Import Competition in the United States," *American Economic Review*, Vol. 103:6, pp. 2121–2168.

Baldwin, Richard (2016). *The Great Convergence*, Cambridge, MA: Harvard University Press.

Baldwin, Richard, and Philippe Martin (1999). "Two Waves of Globalisation: Superficial Similarities, Fundamental Differences," R. Baldwin and P. Martin, NBER working paper 6904.

Disdier, Anne-Célia, and Keith Head (2008). "The Puzzling Persistence of the Distance Effect on Bilateral Trade," *Review of Economics and Statistics*, Vol. 90:1, pp. 37–48.

Eaton, Jonathan, and Samuel S. Kortum (2002). "Technology, Geography, and Trade," *Econometrica*, Vol 70:5, pp. 1741–1779.

Hillberry, Russell, and David Hummels (2007). "Trade Responses to Geographic Frictions: A Decomposition Using Micro-Data," *European Economic Review*, Vol. 52:3, pp. 527–550.

Monte, Ferdinando (2018). "The Local Incidence of Trade Shocks," mimeograph, Georgetown University.

Monte, Ferdinando, Stephen Redding, and Esteban Rossi-Hansberg (2018). "Commuting, Migration and Local Employment Elasticities," forthcoming, American Economic Review.

Schott, Peter (2008). "The Relative Sophistication of Chinese Exports," *Economic Policy*, Vol. 23:53, pp. 6–49.

Timmer, Marcel P., Erik Dietzenbacher, Bart Los, Robert Stehrer, and Gaaitzen J. de Vries (2015). "An Illustrated User Guide to the World Input: Output Database: The Case of Global Automotive Production," *Review of International Economics*, Vol. 23:3, pp. 575–605.

Timmer, Marcel P., Abdul A. Erumban, Bart Los, Robert Stehrer, and Gaaitzen J. de Vries (2014). "Slicing Up Global Value Chains," *Journal of Economic Perspectives*, Vol. 20:2, pp. 99–118.

# 4 Accounting for External Costs in Freight Transport
## Eight Policy Options

*David Austin*

## Introduction

Freight transport plays a role of increasing importance to the U.S. economy. Ton-miles of surface freight by truck and rail have more than doubled since 1980 and are projected to grow almost 50% over the next three decades (USDOT, 2017a, 2017b). That intensifying use of the nation's freight transport infrastructure has been accompanied by rising external costs. Going beyond the expected roadway depreciation and congestion, freight transport also constitutes a growing share of the nation's emissions. For example, heavy trucks now contribute 23% of greenhouse-gas emissions from transport, up from 15% in 1990 (the rail share is 2.5%, up from 2%) (EPA, 2017a). Heavy trucks are also the fastest-growing transport source of $NO_x$ emissions in the United States (EPA, 2017b).

Economic efficiency requires that external costs be borne by those responsible for them. But existing taxes and fees reflect only a small fraction of external costs and, in particular, do not reflect the relative cost differences associated with alternative shipment modes. The result is that shippers have little incentive to take those taxes and fees into account when choosing between truck and rail. The external costs associated with shipping by truck differ substantially from the external costs to ship by rail. The per ton-mile external costs of pavement damage, traffic congestion, and accidents are an estimated 10 to 15 times higher for trucks than for rail, even after accounting for differences in current taxes. For emissions of carbon dioxide ($CO_2$) and local pollutants, damages from truck transport are about three times greater per ton-mile. As a result, market shares for truck versus rail, and total freight shipping, diverge from socially optimal values.[1]

This chapter simulates several kinds of freight taxes for internalizing those costs. Among the key predictions from the simulations is that a ton-mile tax equal to average external damages would cause around 3% of truck ton-miles to shift to rail while reducing total tons shipped by around 0.7% to 0.8%. Those effects would, in combination, reduce fuel consumption by more than 600 million gallons every year and reduce external costs by around $2 billion per year. That particular tax would raise around $70 billion per year in revenue; another policy option examined in this chapter would have roughly similar effects at a much lower cost to shippers.

Such predictions are meant to be of use to analysts and policymakers interested in mode choices made by shippers (how much freight would shift from road to rail if a tax based on external costs were imposed?), fiscal policy (how much revenue might be produced by different federal tax policy options?), or social consequences of freight transport (what is the expected value of benefits—reductions in accidents, pavement damage, emissions, traffic congestion—from those policy options?). The options examined in this chapter include a weight-distance tax reflecting all external costs, a distance-only tax, several types of fees on shipping containers, and a pair of extensions of existing taxes—on diesel fuel and on truck tires—that would be easier to administer than the other options but that would only partially internalize costs.

Federal policymaking has begun to address inefficiencies in freight transport but remains at an early stage. The Fixing America's Surface Transportation (FAST) Act of 2015 calls for formulation of a national freight policy. (Some state and local jurisdictions already have policies toward freight—primarily road-use taxes—to mitigate costs and to finance freight infrastructure.) Federal fuel taxes, including those paid by freight trucks, supply revenue for highway construction and maintenance. But the taxes on gasoline and diesel fuel have not increased since 1993. Compared with current federal policy—including taxes on diesel fuel and several types of taxes and fees on heavy trucks—the simulated policies could provide a better price signal of freight transport demand to inform decisions about infrastructure spending and boost economic efficiency.

An increase in infrastructure spending may be necessary to arrest degradation in transportation system performance, from declining pavement quality (USDOT, 2016) to rising congestion (Texas Transportation Institute [TTI], 2015; Association of American Railroads, 2007). But by internalizing external costs, the policy options discussed in this chapter would encourage more efficient use of the transport system, reducing the amount of spending that would be needed to achieve a given level of performance for that system.

The chapter is organized as follows: it begins with a description of the external costs of freight transport and the policy context in which the simulation is conducted. Next, it presents the simulation model, the data used in the simulations, and the eight policy options to be examined in the simulations. After that, it goes through the results and analyzes sensitivity to changes in key parameters. The chapter concludes by recapitulating and discussing key findings.

## External Costs of Freight Transport

Nearly all of the external costs of freight transport fall in one of five categories: pavement damage, traffic congestion, accident risk, emissions of local pollutants (PM and $NO_x$, or particulate matter and nitrogen oxides), and emissions of carbon dioxide. On average, rail has much lower external costs per ton-mile than trucking. That is particularly true for pavement damage and traffic congestion: trains operate on private, railroad-owned track and—except at grade crossings—thus cause little traffic congestion or damage to public roads. Emissions damages, in large part because of rail's greater fuel efficiency, are only about one-fourth as great for rail as for trucking. Freight trains get about 475 ton-miles per gallon versus approximately 150 ton-MPG for trucks (TTI, 2012).[2] For both modes, the greatest external cost (per ton-mile) is accident risk (see Table 4.1).

GAO (2011) concludes that rail poses a much lower risk of uncompensated accidental damage to third parties (per ton-mile, net of insurance premiums) because trucks operate on shared highways and may lack passive safety controls that trains are required to have. GAO's assessment predates the recent rise in rail transport of crude oil, including a number of costly derailments. But expected damages per ton-mile from those derailments may not be very high when averaged over the many accident-free ton-miles of what are very heavy shipments of crude oil. Such shipments, in addition, still represent only a small share of total rail traffic (see Figure 4.1).

Where GAO (2011) is my source for road-use damages, for PM and $NO_x$ emissions, I use median estimates from Matthews et al. (2001).[3]

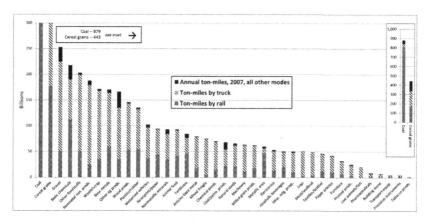

*Figure 4.1* Annual Freight Transport, by Type and Mode, 2007 (Billions of ton-miles)

(GAO's estimates for PM and $NO_x$ are five to seven times higher than the median estimates from the literature, and predate EPA regulations that have reduced emissions from truck engines.) GAO did not estimate damages from $CO_2$ emissions; for those damages, I rely on estimates (for a 3% social discount rate) from the U.S. Interagency Working Group on Social Cost of Carbon (IWGSCC).[4]

Net of existing taxes, the costs in Table 4.1, combined, average about 20% and 11%, respectively, of average shipping costs for truck and rail.[5] I net out existing taxes because they internalize some social costs. In the simulations, policy responses are determined by the relative size of cost increase (due to the policy) for one mode versus the other. Responses vary by distance, location, and type of freight.

The costs in Table 4.1 are given as ranges of values, in terms of cents per ton-mile. Except for $CO_2$ damages, I treat the ranges as uniform probability distributions, from which the simulation model draws its values. For $CO_2$, the model draws from IWGSCC's empirical frequencies, which are represented in Table 4.1 by the 5th-, 50th-, and 95th-percentile values of those empirical estimates. Values toward the middle of the range for $CO_2$ have much higher selection probabilities.

In reality, most of the external costs relate only indirectly to ton-miles. Accidents and traffic congestion are more closely related to miles, and emissions relate to fuel use. Although pavement damage is directly related to ton-miles, it varies by the attributes of a particular road.

*Table 4.1* Unpriced External Costs (2014 cents per ton-mile)

| Type of Cost | Truck Costs* | Rail Costs* |
| --- | --- | --- |
| Accident Risk | 0.85–2.28 | 0.11–0.25 |
| Pavement Damage | 0.74–0.96 | 0.05–0.06 |
| Emissions: PM and $NO_x$ | 0.59–0.80 | 0.13–0.24 |
| Traffic Congestion | 0.42–0.90 | 0–0.03 |
| Emissions: $CO_2$† | 0.02–0.22–0.92 | 0.007–0.05–0.24 |
| Total | 2.62–5.86 | 0.30–0.82 |

Sources: GAO (2011), except:

for PM and $NO_x$, H. Scott Matthews, Chris Hendrickson, and Arpad Horvath, "External Costs of Air Emissions From Transportation," *Journal of Infrastructure Systems* (March 2001), pp. 13–17, www.cmu.edu/gdi/docs/external-costs.pdf (46 KB);

for $CO_2$, U.S. Interagency Working Group on Social Cost of Carbon (IWGSCC), *Technical Update of the Social Cost of Carbon for Regulatory Impact Analysis Under Executive Order 12866* (November 2013).

\* Costs deflated using chained PCE price index. Conversion into cents per ton-mile terms is based on the average fuel consumption rates given in the text.
† $CO_2$ values here are the 5th-,50th-, and 95th-percentile values from IWGSCC's distribution of estimate for 2020 using a 3% discount rate.

## Policy Context

Various federal, state, and local policies have influenced baseline ton-miles shipped and mode choices. Those federal and state-level policies are described briefly ahead. It is against those baseline policies that the effects in the policy simulations are measured.

### Federal Programs

The construction of the Interstate Highway System, starting in 1956, was crucial to the development of long-haul trucking as an alternative to rail. Federal spending on the National Highway System, most prominently including the Interstate highways, was $45 billion in 2014, primarily for construction and maintenance.

The Highway Trust Fund (HTF), from which those expenditures came, is funded mostly from motor-fuel tax revenues, although since 2008, Congress has transferred about $65 billion to the HTF from the Treasury's general fund and other sources. In 2018, 24% of HTF revenues were projected to come from the federal excise tax on diesel fuel (about nine-tenths of that was from freight trucks), at a rate of 24.4¢/gallon. Another 13% or so came from federal excise taxes on freight trucks, tires, and trailers and from the annual heavy-vehicle use tax.[6] Railroads are currently exempt from the federal tax on diesel fuel, except for 0.1¢/gallon for the Leaking Underground Storage Tank Trust Fund.[7]

The trucking industry's share of the tax payments into the HTF exceeds its share of miles traveled on the National Highway System (around 14% on rural roads and 9% overall).[8] But heavy trucks are also responsible for a disproportionate share of costs for highway maintenance and repair (Federal Highway Administration [FHWA] 2000a). In its most recent cost allocation study, FHWA concluded that heavy trucks pay substantially less than their full share of federal highway costs (FHWA, 2000b).

Federal aid to rail is an order of magnitude smaller than to highways, even net of fuel taxes (CBO, 2014). The Federal Railroad Administration has issued roughly $2 billion in loans, some of which have gone to freight railroads, out of a total authority of up to $35 billion in direct loans and loan guarantees for railroad infrastructure and refinancing of associated debt. The Moving Ahead for Progress in the 21st Century Act authorized $0.22 billion of annual federal spending to improve rail-highway grade crossings. Until the end of 2013, short-line railroads were eligible for federal tax credits of 50% of qualified track-maintenance expenditures, up to $3,500 per track mile.

The Department of Transportation's TIGER (Transportation Investment Generating Economic Recovery) grant program has since 2009 distributed more than $100 million to freight rail infrastructure and other transportation projects. In 2013, rail-related TIGER grants from $1.8 million to

$14.4 million aided rail improvements in several states. TIGER grants also went to projects to improve intermodal freight handling at several seaports and at the Oklahoma City Intermodal Transportation Hub.

### State and Local Programs

Every state imposes its own tax on diesel fuel, ranging from 11.8¢/gallon in Alaska to 64.2¢/gallon in Pennsylvania and averaging about 30¢/gallon (American Petroleum Institute, 2017). Several states also impose a vehicle-miles-traveled (VMT) tax on heavy trucks. In Kentucky and New Mexico, the tax rates are 2.85¢ and 4.378¢ per mile, respectively, for trucks with gross weight ratings above 60,000 or 78,000 lbs. New York has gradu-ated rates ranging from 0.84¢ to 5¢ per mile depending on a truck's rated capacity and whether it is loaded or empty (TRB, 2012). Illinois now gives truck owners the option of paying a graduated VMT tax in lieu of a flat fee: for trucks whose gross weight will exceed 77,000 lbs., the rate is 27.5¢ per mile versus an annual fee of $2,790 (Illinois General Assembly, 2018).

Finally, Oregon's graduated rates are based on a truck's loaded weight (and axle configuration) and range from 6.23¢ to over 20¢ per mile and are in lieu of a diesel fuel tax on heavy trucks (Oregon DOT, 2018). Oregon does not tax the actual ton-miles of each shipment: its per-mile tax rates apply to a truck's maximum *intended* gross operating weight, which truck operators must declare annually in a filing with Oregon DOT. (The same tax rate applies whether the truck is driven at that maximum declared weight or empty.) Thus, Oregon's approach has attributes of both of the central policies in my analysis: like a weight-distance tax, the Oregon truck tax has different rates for different (declared) weights; like a distance tax, the Oregon tax applies the same rate to a given vehicle regardless of how its gross weight changes from one trip to the next.

In past years, other states have adopted, then repealed, VMT taxes of their own. According to the Transportation Research Board, "collection expense, compliance costs imposed on carriers, legal challenges, and con-cerns over the impact on state economic development and competitive-ness" were behind the repeals (Transportation Research Board, 2012, pp. 50–51). Several states, Oregon and California prominent among them, are conducting pilot studies of automated tax assessment and col-lection technologies (Oregon DOT, 2017; California STA, 2017).

Beyond state taxes, certain shipping ports impose fees on container freight to finance the construction of local freight infrastructure or to reduce congestion and emissions. Examples include the Ports of Los Angeles and Long Beach, which assess a "traffic mitigation fee" of about $63 per 40-foot container or equivalent (FEU, for "40-foot equivalent unit") for truck access to the ports' container-loading facilities and around $49 per loaded, waterborne FEU for rail access to the Alameda Corridor[9] (PierPass, 2018; ACTA, 2018). The Ports of New York and New Jersey impose a container fee of $63.06 to finance the ports' container-handling facility.[10] And the Port of Tacoma charges railroads $20 per container for infrastructure improvements in Washington's FAST (Freight Action Strategy for Seattle-Tacoma) Corridor.

## Modeling the Effects of Policy Changes

The purpose of the policy simulations is to predict how changes in various taxes on overland freight transport would affect mode choice. This work fits into a literature extending back to when Congress began considering legislation to deregulate the trucking and rail industries.

### *Previous Research*

In the 1970s, with policymakers considering legislation that would eventually become the Staggers Rail Act and the Motor Carrier Act (both becoming law in 1980), researchers began to analyze how shippers' choices between truck and rail are affected by changes in relative prices. Empirical studies tended to find that although deregulation could induce substantial shifts in some markets, many others would experience only small effects due to shippers' being strongly committed in those markets to one mode over the other (Levin, 1978; Oum, 1979; Winston, 1981).

The past two decades have seen researchers attempting a number of advances in empirical freight-choice modeling. For example, Picard and Gaudry (1998) found that a logit model can better explain freight mode choice after a nonlinear transformation of its independent variables. Rich et al. (2009) developed a weighted logit approach to freight mode-choice modeling, for the purpose of estimating transport demand elasticities of shipping cost and of travel time. In a similar vein, Samimi et al. (2011) developed a binary choice model that identifies shipping cost as a central factor motivating shippers who choose rail, with delivery time more important to shippers choosing to ship by truck.

Over the same span of time, researchers and policymakers have increasingly looked to policies encouraging mode switching as a way to reduce emissions, noise, and traffic congestion—and to help finance related infrastructure spending. Much empirical research in this area, including my own, has been informed by Forkenbrock's (1999, 2001) estimates of external costs in freight transport. Bontekoning et al. (2004) examined intermodal transport—and the price differentials that would draw shippers from truck to rail—as a way to reduce highway congestion and increase safety. A considerable literature has been developed by state Transportation Departments interested in using externality taxes, public investments in rail capacity, or the subsidized use of "excess" rail capacity as a way to encourage such mode switching (Florida DOT, 2002; Virginia DOT, 2004; Interstate-95 Corridor Coalition, 2009; USDOE, 2013).

One study in particular, using European data, found results similar to those I present in this chapter: that study estimates that external-cost pricing would raise the cost to ship by truck by 8% to 25%, inducing a shift of 2% to 8% of road ton-miles to rail (CE Delft/TRT, 2011). As with the results I will present in this chapter, those ranges reflect variation in baseline shipping costs. But—unlike with my analysis—they do not also reflect uncertainties in the underlying parameter values. That study also differs from mine in that its European fuel prices, road tolls, highway and rail networks, shipping distances, intermodal capacities, and flow of goods from seaport to points inland do not always match up very closely with the U.S. equivalents in my data. Even so, both studies suggest that mode choice responds to incentives, but that the response will be measured because truck and rail are not perfect substitutes and shippers may strongly prefer trucking to rail in certain markets.

### Simulation Model

As in those studies, I use mode-choice elasticities to simulate the effects of freight external-cost taxes and fees on mode choice. Values for shipping rates (prices) and external costs are drawn, at each iteration of my simulation model, from underlying probability distributions, then taxes based on the external costs are applied to those rates. In response to the increase in costs, shippers send slightly less freight overall and shift somewhat toward the mode whose prices have gone up less in percentage terms—usually rail.

Total demand for transport of a commodity is derived from a policy's effects on its end sales as a delivered good. The model calculates that as $(\eta_i \times T_i \times C_{i,j})$, where $\eta_i$ is the own-price elasticity of demand for commodity type $i$, $T_i$ is the average share of transport costs in the total cost of production and distribution for that type of commodity, and $C_{i,j}$ is the percentage change—due to the policy—in the cost to ship that type of commodity between origin-destination pair $j$, including any changes to drayage (truck delivery) costs over the final miles of a rail shipment.[11] For most commodities and origin-destination pairs, $(\eta_i \times T_i \times C_{i,j})$ works out—for the policies that I simulate—to a reduction of less than 1% in total ton-miles over both modes.

The effect on mode choice is typically more substantial. The model calculates the percentage of ton-miles that switches modes, for each commodity type and origin-destination pair, as

$$\exp(\varepsilon_{r,d} \times \ln[(1 + C_d)/(1 + C_r)]) \approx R_c \times \varepsilon_{r,d},$$

where $\varepsilon_{r,d}$ is the cross-price elasticity of the "receiving" mode ($r$) (usually rail) with respect to the "donating" mode ($d$) (usually truck) for that type of commodity and $R_c$ is the relative change in total shipping costs. (I have suppressed the *i, j* subscripts.) The expression in ln[·] is the percentage increase in the total cost to ship a commodity on a route by the donating mode relative to the receiving mode, with $C_d$ and $C_r$ their absolute percentage increases. So, for example, if truck shipping costs increased by 10% relative to rail (for commodity *i* on route *j*) and their cross-price elasticity was 0.5, then rail ton-miles in that market would increase by exp(0.5 × ln[1.1]) = 1.049, or 4.9%. Truck ton-miles would decrease by the *number* of ton-miles corresponding to rail's gain.[12]

The mode-choice elasticities in the simulation model assume that the demand for bulk-commodity and raw materials transport is inelastic and the demand for finished goods transport is elastic—in some cases, very elastic (Transportation Research Board, 1997). For example, a 10% relative increase in truck shipping costs for "bulk farm products" would increase rail shipping of those commodities by 0.2% to 0.3%, whereas for coal and other "bulk, all else" commodities, the shift would be 1.4% to 1.9%. For furniture, by contrast, rail ton-miles of furniture shipping would increase by 40% to 47%. Truck and rail evidently compete intensely for finished goods business.

Graphically, the new transport prices and quantities reflect an outward shift in own demand due to the (policy-induced) increase in the other mode's prices, as well as an upward shift in own supply due the tax wedge between the prices now paid by shippers and the prices now received by carriers (see Figure 4.2).

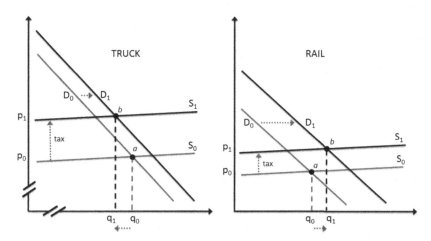

*Figure 4.2* Effect of External-Cost Taxes on Demand for Freight Transport

Notes: Pre-policy prices and quantities are given by $(p_0, q_0)$ and post-policy values by $(p_1, q_1)$.

In each panel, the shift in demand from $D_0$ to $D_1$ is in reaction to the increase in the cost to ship by the other mode. For instance, in the "TRUCK" panel, the demand curve shifts out because of the increase in *rail* shipping costs, which causes shippers to demand more trucking services at any given price. The same logic applies to the "RAIL" panel. In both panels, points "a" and "b" indicate the market equilibria before and, respectively, after a tax is imposed.

The figure shows rail ton-miles increasing and truck ton-miles decreasing after a freight transport tax is applied. The ton-mile responses differ because the truck tax is sufficiently greater than the rail tax and shippers' mode choices are sufficiently cross-price-elastic. Higher prices to shippers also cause a slight decrease in total shipping as well.

Because of increasing congestion on the highway and freight rail networks, I assume that both trucking and rail have somewhat upward-sloping supply curves (FHWA, 2008). The trucking industry can add trucks and drivers more quickly and at lower cost than railroads can add locomotives and trained engineers (and although railcars can be added to some existing trains, others already operate at maximum capacity), but has begun noting, in effect, that it faces an upward-sloping labor supply curve.[13]

With upward-sloping transport supply curves, neither type of carrier would fully pass along a freight tax to their customers. Thus, I assume for both modes a tax pass-through rate of between 90% and 100%, consistent with slightly upward-sloping supply curves.[14] For each iteration, pass-through rates for each transport mode are selected independently from a uniform density function.

The model also draws several other parameter values from probability distributions. In addition to prices, external costs, and pass-through rates, it selects values for elasticities of demand and mode choice, transport cost shares, drayage distances, lift costs (for placing shipping containers on vehicles), rail route circuity, and payload capacities.[15] The assumed randomness reflects, in all cases, a combination of likely variation in true values under varying circumstances and statistical uncertainty in the available estimates of those values. In most cases, the model draws values from uniform distributions defined over the relevant range. Values for drayage costs and $CO_2$ emissions are drawn from distributions that put more weight on midrange values.

## Data

The unit of observation in the model is annual ton-miles for each origin/destination/commodity, by transport mode and in total. Origin-destination pairs are states, excluding Alaska and Hawai'i but including the District of Columbia. The data include 39 types of commodities. Flows of commodities from, say, California to Tennessee are counted separately from those from Tennessee to California. Thus, there are up to 78 observations per state pair (not all commodities are transported between all state pairs). In all, the data comprise nearly 76,000 observations.

They come from FAF, the Freight Analysis Framework (FHWA, 2010). FAF reports one-year total estimated freight flows within the United States, by origin, destination, commodity, and mode, based primarily on the Commodity Flow Survey of 2007 (USDOT, 2010). My analysis estimates expected outcomes for 2007 if the simulated policies had been in place far enough in advance for shippers to re-optimize their logistics.

FAF publishes new data every five years. At time of writing, data for 2012 are available—although they were only published a year after I began work on this project—but the 2017 data are not. One advantage of using 2007 data is that they were not affected by the recession of 2008 and 2009, as the 2012 data likely are. In estimating tax revenues and other outputs, my analysis does not attempt to project how conditions might change in future years. The release of the 2017 data will, however, be an occasion to update the analysis and to observe how freight transport has evolved.

## Policy Options

I examine three sets of options for accounting for external costs in freight transport. The first would impose external-cost taxes on all overland freight shipments, based on the weight and/or the distance of each shipment or on the amount of fuel used. The second would impose taxes on containerized shipments, reflecting interest by some interest groups in a potentially dedicated source of revenue for funding intermodal freight facilities. Finally, I consider an option to increase and expand the scope of the excise tax on truck tires.

The options are as follows:

- Taxes on all freight shipments, based on weight, distance, or fuel consumption

    1. An average-external-cost tax: a weight-and-distance tax plus a fuel tax
    2. A tax on vehicle miles traveled plus a fuel tax: shipment weight not taxed
    3. A tax on vehicle miles traveled only
    4. A fuel tax only

- Taxes or fees on containerized shipments only (i.e., on intermodal freight)

    5. An average-external-cost tax on weight, distance, and fuel consumption
    6. A rising fee for increasing transport distance "bands" or ranges of miles
    7. A uniform fee on overland container shipments regardless of distance

- Taxes on truck tires

    8. An excise tax on truck tires and retreads

The simulations will show that among the first set of options, the VMT tax—Option 3—has effects rather like those of Option 1 while collecting about $25 billion *less* from freight carriers. Although the other differences all favor Option 1—its effects are closest to optimal among these policy options because it more accurately reflects the external costs—policymakers might weigh those differences against the lower tax burden of Option 3.

Putting aside the distortions from taxing only one type of transport, the three intermodal Options (5–7) show that unintended consequences can be created by seemingly small variations in policy design. Taking the intermodal weight-distance tax (Option 5) as a basis of comparison (like Option 1, its all-transport counterpart), the distance fee (Option 6, which for illustrative purposes is based on mile ranges, not actual VMT) has consistently larger effects. By contrast, the uniform fee (Option 7) has both larger and smaller effects. As I will discuss, those differences depend on the empirical distribution of truck versus rail intermodal shipping distances.

The increased tax on new truck tires (Option 8), discussed from time to time by policymakers in Congress, although quite small—it collects only a small fraction of the tax revenue the other options collect—has disproportionately large effects because it falls much more on trucking than on rail. It does affect rail because many rail trips include one or two segments of truck drayage.

I list the options, within each set, in declining order of both fidelity to the targeted externalities and presumed administrative costs. For instance, in the first set, Option 1 would probably be the most costly to administer, but it would also target all of the external costs from all trucks and trains—Option 2 would also—and more accurately than other options because it alone accounts for payload weight.

I do not know the administrative costs, but I suggest that a weight-distance tax would probably cost the most to administer because it requires the most information. A distance-only tax would be less costly, but it would still require a record of travel for every tax-paying unit. (My administrative-cost ranking of the three container options has a similar logic.) By contrast the excise taxes on fuel and truck tires would rely on collection systems already in place, and which simply involve applying a tax rate at each sale to the number of units sold.

Table 4.2 presents the tax rates for each option, net of existing taxes. Because existing taxes are higher for trucking than for rail, the rates in Table 4.2 do not fully reflect the 8:1 ratio of average truck:rail external costs in Table 4.1. The rates in Table 4.2 have an average ratio about 6:1.

The rates and fees in the table were calculated before the simulations were run and were held constant at the values given in Table 4.2. Those values are the averages of 10,000 independent draws from each external cost's assumed probability distribution. This analysis, then, assesses the

*Table 4.2* Policy Options (2014 dollars)

| Option | Average Tax Rates (To be added to existing taxes)[a] | |
|---|---|---|
| | Truck | Railcar |
| **Taxes on Taxes on All Freight Shipments** | | |
| 1. Weight-Distance Tax & Fuel Tax[b] | 3.1¢ per ton-mile (2.3¢/ton-mile + $1.50/gal) | 0.5¢ per ton-mile (0.3¢/ton-mile + $1.50/gal) |
| 2. VMT Tax & Fuel Tax[b] | 30¢ per mile + $1.50 per gallon | 12¢ per mile + $1.50 per gallon |
| 3. VMT Tax Only | 30¢ per mile | 12¢ per mile |
| 4. Fuel Tax Only[b] | $1.50 per gallon | $1.50 per gallon |
| **Taxes or Fees on Container Transport** | | |
| 5. Intermodal Container Tax[c] (weight-distance tax & fuel tax) | 3.1¢ per ton-mile | 0.5¢ per ton-mile |
| 6. Rising Container Fee (based on ranges of distances) | $140–$1,597[d] | $27–$309[d] |
| 7. Uniform Container Fee (for shipment anywhere in the United States) | $286 per container | $138 per container |
| **Taxes on Truck Tires** | | |
| 8. Excise Tax on Truck Tires | 1.5¢ per mile equivalent[e] | not applicable |

a. Simulated policies are net of highway tolls and taxes on diesel fuel and new tires, and rail's contribution to the Leaking Underground Storage Tank (LUST) Trust Fund. *See* GAO (2011).

b. The simulated tax on emissions is actually assessed on ton-miles (at rates averaging 0.92¢ and 0.24¢ for truck and rail, respectively). Based on average fuel consumption, those rates imply a fuel tax of about $1.50 per gallon.

c. Drayage portion of rail journey assessed at higher truck rate. For options 6 and 7, rail rate reflects average external costs of drayage.

d. See Table 4.3 for fee schedule.

e. Truck tire rate assumes 18 wheels per truck; 5,000-lb. rated capacity per tire (giving 90,000 lbs. total weight-bearing capacity); and 530,000 mile tire life with retreading and with new tires lasting 130k, 340k, and 530k miles as trailer, drive, and steering tires, respectively, with any remaining miles being on retreads. *(Personal communication, Knight Transportation.)* Most steer tires actually require a 6,000-lb. rating.

effects of constant tax rates and fees chosen in the absence of certainty about true costs in different possible states of the world. That mirrors the circumstances under which actual policymaking typically occurs.

### Options 1–4

These options would tax all overland freight shipments.

### Taxes on Weight, Distance, and Fuel

Option 1 would address all five of the external costs in Table 4.1: pavement damage, traffic congestion, and accident risk (each addressed by the weight-distance tax) and emissions of PM, $NO_x$, and carbon dioxide (addressed by the fuel tax). It is not a perfect instrument because it targets averages. (Actual damages vary by time of day, season, weather, pavement type, cargo, terrain, population exposures, and other factors.) But it is the most accurate and comprehensive of the options that I simulate.

Option 1 would also require the most information, suggesting that it would be the most costly to administer. As technologies for on-board weighing become more widespread—including the possibility to record real-time weights at each axle—and their costs come down, Option 1 will become more feasible and less costly (Transport & Environment, 2013).

### Tax on Vehicle Miles Traveled

The simulated VMT tax targets roadway external costs—pavement damage, accident risk, and traffic congestion—not emissions. The tax rates I simulate—30¢ per (laden) mile for trucks versus 12¢ for railcars—are much less divergent than the underlying roadway damages. For example, expected truck accident damages are almost nine times greater (per ton-mile) than for rail. But truck payloads are smaller, so truck transport also involves fewer *ton*-miles per mile. Thus expected accident damages per *mile* are much less than nine times greater for truck than for rail.

Relative to Option 1, a VMT tax—Option 2 if combined with a fuel tax, or Option 3 by itself—would create incentives for shippers to batch shipments into fewer, heavier payloads. That could be socially costly because pavement damage increases exponentially with axle weight. Maximum weight restrictions on trucks—which can occasionally be exceeded with permission—limit somewhat the potential for additional damage. But a VMT tax could necessitate greater expenditures on enforcement of those weight limits.

The simulated VMT tax—like the weight-distance tax in Option 1—does not apply to unladen miles, which are not reported in the data. Instead, the external costs that would be predicted for the empty miles are prorated.[16] A policy that taxed all miles, rather than just laden miles, would increase carriers' incentives to minimize empty returns. But the difference compared to a tax only on laden miles would likely be small, as carriers already have strong cost incentives to minimize empty return miles.

## Tax on Diesel Fuel

The simulated fuel tax—Option 4 as a stand-alone policy, or a part of Options 1 and 2—reflects external costs from PM, $NO_x$, and $CO_2$. Those costs are estimated to be about $1.50 per gallon of diesel fuel, on average, regardless of mode. Existing truck fuel taxes average 54.4¢ per gallon, including state taxes (API, 2017). The simulations convert the $1.50 tax rate into assessments of 0.92¢ (trucks) or 0.24¢ (railcars) per ton-mile, based on estimated average fuel efficiency.[17] The tax would be added to the existing federal tax on diesel fuel.

Administrative costs would be lowest for the diesel fuel tax (and the tax on truck tires, Option 8) because point-of-sale collections are already in place for those taxes, and they require no delivery-dependent information. The trade-off is that fuel taxes only indirectly target most external costs. The exception is carbon dioxide damages, because the carbon content of fuels is known, and no current on-board technology reduces those emissions.

## Options 5–7

These options would tax only overland shipments of containerized (intermodal) freight.

## Container Taxes or Fees

On economic grounds it is hard to defend imposing a tax or fee on just one type of freight shipment. I include Options 5–7 because some jurisdictions employ container fees for incentive purposes or to fund freight infrastructure projects, and new fees are proposed from time to time.[18] Option 5 applies a weight-distance-fuel tax to intermodal shipments only. Option 6 is like a VMT tax except rather than assessing actual miles, it applies a fixed fee to all shipments falling within a given range of miles. The rates are calibrated so that the option generates about the same revenue as Option 5.[19] Finally, Option 7 is a uniform fee for any distance, also calibrated to match the revenue that Option 5 would generate.

Table 4.3 reports the fee schedule for Option 6. For trucks, the fees range from $140 to nearly $1,600; for rail, from $27 to $309. For Option 7, the fees are a uniform $286 for trucks and $138 for rail. For context, the federal Harbor Maintenance Tax averaged about $109 per imported 40-foot container in 2012 (Federal Maritime Commission, 2012).

For trucks, the uniform fee is relatively low compared with external costs, which would average around $500 for a trucked container, for a trip

*Table 4.3* Distance-Range Container Fee Schedule (2014 dollars)

| Mode | Distance | | | | |
|---|---|---|---|---|---|
| | 0–500 Miles | 500–1,000 Miles | 1,000–2,000 Miles | 2,000–3,000 Miles | >3,000 Miles |
| Truck | 140 | 394 | 728 | 1,237 | 1,597 |
| Rail | 27 | 75 | 140 | 239 | 309 |

of average distance.[20] The fee is relatively low because aggregate external costs for trucks could be allocated over many more trips than for rail, in no small part because of trucking's dominance in short-haul markets.

Because the taxes and fees of Options 5–7 would apply only to inter-modal freight, they would create incentives for shippers to remove cargo from containers before overland shipment. But the fees are probably too small relative to the cost savings from containerization to make that worthwhile for many shippers.

### Option 8

#### Truck Tire Tax

New truck tires are currently taxed by the federal government at 0.945¢ for every pound of rated weight-bearing capacity over 3,500 lbs. Federal policymakers have considered a tenth-of-a-cent increase in that tax, to 1.045¢.[21] There is no federal tax on retreaded tires.

Option 8 would increase the tax on new truck tires by 0.5¢—to 1.445¢—and would apply the tax to retreads as well. Although that would be a much bigger increase than that considered by Congress, the tax would still reflect only a small share of the highway-related external costs from freight trucks (pavement damage, traffic congestion, and accident risk).

On average, if truck tires last 530,000 miles including retread miles (one expert's estimate), the incremental cost of this option would be around 1.5¢ per mile (for an 18-wheel truck) compared with current policy.[22] That would amount to $8,135 per truck every 530,000 miles: $75 more per new tire plus $217.50 per retread. For the median truck payload of about 16 tons, that translates into a median tax rate of less than 0.1¢ per ton-mile. For comparison, the Weight-Distance-Fuel tax rate of Option 1 is 3.1¢ per ton-mile for trucks.

Introducing a tax on retreaded tires could discourage retreading to the point where trucking companies would discard old tires before the end of their service life. Some analysts assert that retreads are less safe than new tires, although others contend that they are equally safe (Washington State DOT, 2009).

# Simulations

I simulated each policy option 1,000 times, with new random values chosen anew in each iteration for rates charged by carriers, mode-choice elasticities, freight lift costs, drayage trip lengths, rail route circuity (rail routes tend to be less direct), tax pass-through rate to shippers, average payload sizes, and mode fuel efficiencies.[23]

I also draw new values for external costs in every iteration—the resulting randomness capturing policymakers' uncertainty about true costs. As previously noted, the tax rates in the simulations do not change.

I highlight key findings with a focus on the weight-distance-fuel tax (Option 1). That enables me to treat the other policy options much more briefly, via contrasts with the weight-distance-fuel tax.

## Option 1: Effects on Transport

Among all eight options, Option 1 (column 1 in Tables 4.4–4.6), most accurately addresses external costs. But it is also potentially the most costly to administer because it requires the most information about each shipment. I find that a tax just on VMT (Option 3) can produce similar outcomes—albeit with too much mode-shifting—for less administrative cost.

In my simulations, Option 1 increases shipping costs by about 18% by truck and about 12% by rail (see Table 4.4). Since shipping costs typically amount to around 4% of a good's final price, the tax adds about 0.6% to final prices on average.[24] That causes a decline in total shipping of about 0.7%, since the demand for shipping is derived from the demand for the shipped goods.

The tax has much greater effects on mode choice, varying by commodity and route. On average the tax causes trucking costs to rise by about 6% *relative to rail*, which shifts about 3% of truck ton-miles to rail. Including the slight market contraction, truck ton-miles fall by 4% in total. (Rail ton-miles increase by 3%.)[25] In *tons*, only 0.5% of trucked freight shifts to rail, the difference indicating that most mode shifting occurs on longer routes. That is consistent with trucks' strong competitive advantage on shorter routes, with lower costs and faster service than rail.

On the basis of typical payloads, Option 1 would eliminate around 2.9 million highway truck trips per year and increase the number of trips by railcar (which carry more cargo) by around 0.7 million.[26] (My analysis does not consider the amount of time the nation's freight rail network might need to develop adequate capacity to absorb such an increase in demand.)

## Effects on External Costs, Fuel Use, and Tax Revenues

In Table 4.5, the weight-distance-fuel tax reduces fuel consumption by 2.6%, or roughly 600 million gallons per year, due to mode shifting and

*Table 4.4* Effects of Policy Options on Transport in 2007

| Policies Concerning: | Truck and Rail Transport | | | | Container Freight* | | | Trucks Only |
|---|---|---|---|---|---|---|---|---|
| Policy: OUTCOME | Option 1: Wgt/Dist. & Fuel Taxes | Option 2: VMT & Fuel Taxes | Option 3: VMT Tax Only | Option 4: Fuel Tax Only | Option 5: Wgt/Dist Container Tax | Option 6: Distance-Range Container Fee | Option 7: Uniform Container Fee | Option 8: Tire Tax |
| Avg. Shipping Cost Increase, Rail (%) | 12.1 | 15.9 | 10.1 | 5.9 | 10.5 | 10.5 | 10.5 | 0.1 |
| Avg. Shipping Cost Increase, Truck (%) | 17.9 | 18.4 | 11.9 | 6.3 | 15.7 | 15.7 | 15.7 | 0.9 |
| *Market Contraction* | | | | | | | | |
| Reduction, Total Tons Shipped (%) | -0.7 | -0.7 | -0.4 | -0.3 | -0.04 | -0.1 | -0.2 | -0.03 |
| *Mode Choice* | | | | | | | | |
| Reduction, Ton-Miles, Truck (%) | -4.0 | -4.6 | -4.3 | -1.1 | -1.0 | -1.3 | -0.8 | -0.7 |
| Increase, Ton-Miles, Rail (%) | 3.0 | 3.7 | 4.1 | 0.7 | 0.9 | 1.3 | 0.7 | 0.7 |
| Shift, Ton-Miles: Truck to RR (%) | 3.1 | 3.8 | 3.7 | 0.8 | 0.8 | 1.1 | 0.6 | 0.6 |
| *Shift, Tonnage: Truck to RR (%)* | 0.5 | 0.6 | 0.5 | 0.1 | 0.1 | 0.2 | 0.2 | 0.1 |
| *Mode Choice (level effects)* | | | | | | | | |
| Net Shift, Ton-miles, Truck to RR (bn) | 61 | 73 | 73 | 16 | 16 | 22 | 12 | 12 |
| Reduction, Truck Trips (000) | -2,899 | -3,189 | -2,578 | -847 | -631 | -1,327 | -1,986 | -351 |
| Increase, Railcar Trips (000) | 686 | 885 | 829 | 149 | 356 | 631 | 663 | 135 |

Notes: 1,000 iterations per policy; standard errors not reported.

* = Cost increases for container policies apply only to intermodal freight

Table 4.5 Effects of Policy Options on External Costs, Fuel Use, and Revenues in 2007

| Policies Concerning: | Truck and Rail Transport | | | | Container Freight | | | Trucks Only |
|---|---|---|---|---|---|---|---|---|
| Policy: OUTCOME | Option 1: Wgt/Dist. & Fuel Taxes | Option 2: VMT & Fuel Taxes | Option 3: VMT Tax Only | Option 4: Fuel Tax Only | Option 5: Wgt/Dist Container Tax | Option 6: Distance-Range Container Fee | Option 7: Uniform Container Fee | Option 8: Tire Tax |
| *Percentage Effects* | | | | | | | | |
| Change, Social Costs (%) | −2.9 | −3.3 | −3.0 | −0.8 | −0.7 | −0.9 | −0.6 | −0.5 |
| Fuel Savings (%) | 2.6 | 2.9 | 2.6 | 0.8 | 0.6 | 0.8 | 0.5 | 0.4 |
| *Level Effects* | | | | | | | | |
| Fuel Savings (millions of gal.) | 602 | 676 | 611 | 173 | 136 | 181 | 119 | 91 |
| Change, External Costs (billions of 2014 $) | −2.0 | −2.3 | −2.1 | −0.6 | −0.5 | −0.6 | −0.4 | −0.3 |
| Tax Revenue (billions of 2014 $) | 69 | 70 | 43 | 26 | 13 | 16 | 28 | 4 |

Note: 1,000 iterations per policy; standard errors not reported.

market contraction. Projected annual revenue from the tax, in 2007 data, is $69 billion.[27] By comparison, tax revenue credited to the HTF in 2017 totaled around $41 billion, mostly from fuel-tax revenues. (CBO, 2017). Option 1 reduces external costs by around $2 billion per year.

### Variations by Type of Freight

Carriers charge different rates for different types of transport, and demand elasticities and shippers' propensities to switch modes vary by commodity. As a result, Option 1 causes rail ton-miles to increase in every type of freight transport except bulk (see Table 4.6). Bulk freight is different because rail rates are relatively low for bulk transport (so the tax causes a larger percentage increase in shipping costs), mode-shifting propensities are lower (bulk payloads are heavy and the rail hopper cars that carry bulk-freight offer economies over truck hopper trailers), and rail stands to gain less new bulk-freight business from trucking because has a relatively large share of that business to begin with. Under Option 1, rail loses slightly more bulk-freight business through market contraction than it gains from mode shifting.

By contrast, rail *intermodal* experiences a large gain from trucking under Option 1, with a nearly 10% increase in railcar trips. That is because rail rates tend to be higher for intermodal transport (so the tax is a smaller share of the cost of shipping), mode-switching propensities are higher (naturally so, as "intermodal" implies), and demand elasticities are higher for the finished goods that intermodal containers tend to carry, so shippers are more sensitive to transport costs. Rail also has a relatively smaller share of intermodal ton-miles in the data, so any given shift from trucking represents a larger percentage increase in rail business.[28] Rail intermodal also experiences less market contraction due to the tax because intermodal freight such as furniture, electronics, machinery, and textiles often has a high value-to-weight ratio. So shipping costs for intermodal goods tend to be just a small share of the goods' prices.

### Comparing Option 1 to Other Policy Options

### Options 2–4: VMT and Fuel Taxes

In contrast with Option 1, the VMT tax of Options 2 and 3 does not require information about shipping weight. But by imposing the same tax rate on all shipments regardless of weight, a VMT tax, in effect, creates a cross-subsidy from lighter shipments to heavier ones.[29] As a result, more lightweight freight—and less heavy freight—switches to rail compared with Option 1. The effect of Option 2—a VMT tax plus an increase in the fuel tax—is to shift an additional 12 billion ton-miles from truck to rail, or nearly 20% more than under Option 1. It also eliminates about

Table 4.6 Effects of Policy Options on Mode Choice by Type of Freight in 2007

| Policies Concerning: | Truck and Rail Transport | | | | Container Freight | | | Trucks Only |
|---|---|---|---|---|---|---|---|---|
| Policy: OUTCOME | Option 1: Wgt/Dist. & Fuel Taxes | Option 2: VMT & Fuel Taxes | Option 3: VMT Tax Only | Option 4: Fuel Tax Only | Option 5: Wgt/Dist Container Tax | Option 6: Distance-Range Container Fee | Option 7: Uniform Container Fee | Option 8: Tire Tax |
| *Carload/Truckload Freight* | | | | | | | | |
| % Reduction, Truck Trips | -1.1 | -1.1 | -0.9 | -0.3 | 0 | 0 | 0 | -0.1 |
| % Increase, Railcar Trips | 7.4 | 7.2 | 6.9 | 1.7 | 0 | 0 | 0 | 1.1 |
| *Bulk Freight* | | | | | | | | |
| % Reduction, Truck Trips | -1.6 | -1.6 | -1.0 | -0.6 | 0 | 0 | 0 | -0.1 |
| % Increase, Railcar Trips | -0.1 | 0 | 0.2 | -0.1 | 0 | 0 | 0 | 0.1 |
| *Intermodal Freight* | | | | | | | | |
| % Reduction, Truck Trips | -1.6 | -2.2 | -1.9 | -0.4 | -1.6 | -5.1 | -3.4 | -0.3 |
| % Increase, Railcar Trips | 9.6 | 15.1 | 13.9 | 2.0 | 9.6 | 17.9 | 17.0 | 2.3 |
| *Automobile Transport* | | | | | | | | |
| % Reduction, Truck Trips | -1.6 | -1.7 | -1.2 | -0.5 | 0 | 0 | 0 | -0.1 |
| % Increase, Railcar Trips | 3.4 | 2.6 | 2.0 | 1.0 | 0 | 0 | 0 | 0.4 |

Note: 1,000 iterations per policy; standard errors not reported.

10% more truck trips than Option 1 does, and reduces fuel consumption by an additional 4%.

Because Option 1 presents shippers with the best approximation of their actual external costs, the additional impacts that Option 2 has imply that it would produce smaller social gains (though it would save on administrative costs). The cross-subsidy created by the VMT tax affects rail more than trucking because rail payloads vary more by weight.[30] Option 2, the combination VMT-and-fuel tax, raises rail shipping costs by an average of 16% (versus 12% for Option 1).

The incremental effects of that combined tax are small (and sometimes negative) compared with those of the VMT tax by itself (Option 3). That is because the fuel tax (Option 4) only modestly alters the effect that the VMT tax has by itself on relative increases in shipping costs. The VMT tax achieves outcomes closer (in most, but not all, ways) to those of Option 1 than to those of Option 2 (the combination tax) while costing shippers around one-third less in tax payments.

### Options 5–7: Container Taxes or Fees

Carriers' intermodal rates are slightly higher than their average rates for other types of freight.[31] Thus, the weight-distance-fuel tax on container shipments (Option 5) and the fee based on ranges of distances (Option 6) have smaller effects on container freight than the analogous Options 1 and 2 have on all freight. In my analysis data set, container freight accounts for around one-tenth of tons shipped, but the market contraction due to Option 5 is only around one-twentieth as big, at 0.04%, as the same effect for Option 1. But Option 5 produces more mode-switching, a net shift of 19 billion ton-miles to rail, or nearly 30% of the amount from Option 1 though only 14% of total ton-miles are container freight. That is consistent with intermodal freight being designed to switch modes easily.

The uniform container fee, Option 7, although less costly to administer, causes five times more market exit and nearly three times more of a reduction in truck trips than Option 5's weight-distance-fuel tax on containers. The uniform fee also collects more than twice the tax revenue while achieving less of a reduction in external costs. It shifts 30% fewer ton-miles to rail than Option 5 while eliminating almost three times more truck trips. Option 7 would be particularly burdensome on shorter truck trips, which would effectively be cross-subsidizing longer trips under this option.

The results for the distance-range fee, Option 6, show that using distance information can improve greatly upon a uniform fee. But a cross-subsidy from shorter to longer trips still exists within each distance range and, as a result, Option 6 eliminates twice as many truck trips as Option 5 and shifts 20% more ton-miles to rail. Basing the fee on actual VMT rather than on ranges of distances traveled would require no additional information but would eliminate that cross-subsidy and produce results more like those of Option 5.

### Option 8: Truck Tire Tax

As simulated, the tire tax increases truck shipping costs by less than 1% in the 2007 data. Because it does not apply to rail—except for the truck drayage segments of many rail trips—the tax has a disproportionate effect on mode choice, inducing a shift three times greater—as a proportion of its effect on shipping costs—than Option 1. In the simulations, the tax on new and retreaded truck tires shifts 12 billion ton-miles to rail, over one-sixth as much as from Option 1 despite being a much smaller tax—the equivalent of 0.1¢ per ton-mile versus 3.1¢ per ton-mile for Option 1. The tax would cost shippers $4 billion per year (in 2014 dollars) versus $68 billion for Option 1.

## Sensitivity Tests

The simulation approach provides a way of estimating a likely range of effects of changes in policy without necessarily having data on past policy changes. It also requires modelers to make explicit their assumptions about uncertainty and functional relationships. But among the *limitations* of the approach is that there is no formal way to validate the outputs of a simulation model.

In the absence of the formal hypothesis testing framework that validates fitted statistical models, the simulation modeler would make a case for validity by varying the model's parameter assumptions to see how sensitive the model's predictions are to those assumptions. Here, I re-simulate the benchmark weight-distance-fuel tax (Option 1) while systematically varying in turn each key model parameter.

I find that my main results are relatively insensitive to even large changes in the values of those parameters. Table 4.7 reports the sensitivity results in order of influence. Each test is reported as an average over 1,000 simulations.

### Uncertainty

The second column of Table 4.7, "Likely Range," shows how the model's main predictions vary over the original simulations reported in the previous section. The so-called likely range is the central two-thirds of the predicted outcomes in those simulations. For instance, the first two rows of Table 4.7 show that in two-thirds of the simulations, the Option 1 tax rate on trucked freight differed from true (unobserved) external costs by somewhere between 5% and 29%, and the rail rate differed by 4% to

28% from true external costs for rail. On average, as reported in the first column, the truck tax differed from its targeted external costs by almost 17%, or about half a cent per ton-mile. For the rail tax, being off by 16% from its targeted costs means about 0.08¢ per ton-mile on average.

The "likely range" in Table 4.7 reflects uncertainty about parameter values only, not about future freight volumes. If the model were making projections about future demand for freight transport, the likely ranges would expand accordingly.

### Tests of the Most Influential Parameters

I present the sensitivity tests in Table 4.7 in order of influence, as approximated by the number of outcomes (rows in Table 4.7) that are pushed out of the "likely range" when I change the assumed value of a parameter (columns in Table 4.7).

### Test 1: Double the Railroad Accident Risk

The range of rail accident risks assumed in the simulations predates the rise in rail transport of crude oil from North Dakota's Bakken Formation and Alberta's Athabasca oil sands. There have been several large and, in some cases, deadly rail accidents involving those shipments. As a conservative test of how my results would change if those accidents were accounted for in the model's rail accident risk, I double the assumed risk to a range of 0.22¢ to 0.5¢ per ton-mile. (It is unlikely that the true accident risk has doubled.)

Test 1 shows that with a higher rail tax (to reflect the higher accident risk), about 40% fewer ton-miles would shift from truck to rail under the Option 1 policy, or 1.9% (down from 3.1%). Fuel savings would decline by a similar amount.

### Tests 2 and 3: Alternate Cross-Elasticities of Mode Choice

The research literature offers two very different sets of cross-price elasticities for truck versus rail. For my main analysis, I used the much more variable elasticities estimated by Jones et al. (1990) (as cited in Transportation Research Board, 1997). Its estimates range from around 0 to 7, clustering around 0.5 for bulk freight and around 4 for finished goods. Bulk-freight shippers—especially of coal, cereal grains, or gravel—tend to depend relatively heavily on one transport mode, whereas finished goods tend to be shipped intermodally.

In Test 2, I examine the influence of those elasticity estimates, some of which are very high for some types of freight. For this test, I compress all elasticity values between 1 and 7 into a tighter range from 1 to 2.5. That has about the same effect on the shift from truck to rail as does Test

Table 4.7 Sensitivity Analyses

| Policy Effect: | Wgt-Dist Tax (Avg Result) | Likely Range† | Test 1 Double RR Accident Risk | Test 2 Trim High Elasticities | Test 3 Alternate Elasticities | Test 4 No Dray or Lift Costs | Test 5 Full Truck Pass-through | Test 6 Truck Rates × 0.95 | Test 7 Truck Rates × 1.05 |
|---|---|---|---|---|---|---|---|---|---|
| Avg Pct Diff. (Truck Tax vs. External Cost) | 16.9 | 4.6–29.0 | 16.6 | 17.4 | 16.9 | 16.5 | 16.5 | 17.2 | 15.6 |
| Avg Pct Diff. (RR Tax vs. External Cost) | 16.0 | 3.6–27.9 | 15.3 | 15.3 | 15.7 | 14.9 | 16.1 | 16.9 | 15.3 |
| Change, External Costs (%) | -2.9 | (-2.7)—(-3.1) | -1.9 | -2.1 | -2.5 | -3.3 | -3.3 | -3.2 | -2.6 |
| Fuel Savings (%) | 2.6 | 2.4–2.8 | 1.9 | 1.9 | 2.2 | 2.9 | 2.9 | 2.8 | 2.3 |
| Tax Revenue (billions of 2014 $) | 68.6 | 68.3–69.0 | 72.9 | 69.2 | 68.9 | 68.3 | 68.3 | 68.4 | 68.8 |
| Shift, Ton-miles: Truck to RR (%) | 3.1 | 3.0–3.3 | 1.9 | 1.9 | 2.5 | 3.6 | 3.6 | 3.5 | 2.8 |
| Market Contraction, Tot. Tons Shipped (%) | -0.7 | (-0.7)—(-0.8) | -0.8 | -0.7 | -0.7 | -1.0 | -0.8 | -0.8 | -0.7 |
| Reduction, Truck Trips (millions) | -2.9 | (-2.8)—(-3.0) | -2.3 | -2.3 | -2.8 | -4.4 | -3.2 | -3.1 | -2.7 |
| Increase, Railcar Trips (millions) | 0.7 | 0.65–0.72 | 0.4 | 0.3 | 0.4 | 0.9 | 0.8 | 0.8 | 0.6 |
| % Reduction, Truck Trips (truckload) | -1.1 | (-1.0)—(-1.1) | -0.8 | -0.8 | -0.9 | -1.7 | -1.2 | -1.1 | -1.0 |
| % Increase, Railcar Trips (carload) | 7.4 | 7.1–7.7 | 4.7 | 4.2 | 4.8 | 10.2 | 8.4 | 8.2 | 6.7 |
| % Reduction, Truck Trips (bulk) | -1.6 | (-1.5)—(-1.6) | -1.6 | -1.6 | -2.8 | -1.6 | -1.7 | -1.7 | -1.5 |
| % Change, Railcar Trips (bulk) | -0.1 | (-0.1)—(-0.1) | -0.3 | -0.1 | 3.2 | -0.1 | -0.1 | -0.1 | -0.1 |
| % Reduction, Truck Trips (intermodal) | -1.6 | (-1.5)—(-1.7) | -1.1 | -1.0 | -0.9 | -2.3 | -1.8 | -1.8 | -1.5 |
| % Increase, Railcar Trips (intermodal) | 9.6 | 9.1–10.1 | 5.3 | 4.3 | 3.8 | 12.8 | 11.3 | 10.8 | 8.5 |
| % Reduction, Truck Trips (auto transport) | -1.6 | (-1.5)—(-1.7) | -1.5 | -1.6 | -3.9 | -1.6 | -1.7 | -1.7 | -1.5 |
| % Increase, Railcar Trips (auto transport) | 3.4 | 3.0–3.9 | 2.9 | 3.4 | 15.3 | 3.5 | 3.7 | 3.7 | 3.2 |

Note:

† = In 1,000 iterations of the simulation model, two-thirds of the model's predictions lay within this range.

1 (doubling the rail accident risk)—in both tests about 40% less freight shifts to rail, well outside the "likely range." In both tests, rail becomes a less attractive alternative (more prone to accidents or less substitutable for trucking), but that does not alter my overall conclusions.

In Test 3, I switch from the Jones et al. (1990) elasticities to those of Abdelwahab (1998), which have a much narrower range, just 0.9 to 1.6. With those estimates in place, the simulations predict a much greater shift of bulk and automotive freight from truck to rail, because the alternate elasticities are bigger than those of Jones et al. for those types of freight. Likewise, the simulations predict a much *smaller* shift of intermodal and truckload/carload freight. Overall, with the alternate elasticities, the aggregate predicted shift toward rail is smaller and slightly outside the "likely range."

### Test 4: No Drayage or Lift Costs

In the main analysis, I assign the costs of truck drayage (delivery of rail payloads from railhead to final destination) to rail (intermodal and carload freight only).[32] I apply the cost of a lift (crane-assisted loading and unloading of a shipping container) to intermodal freight for both modes.

For Test 4, I considered several variations of drayage and lift costs (for my baseline assumptions see endnote 32): that (1) the costs for drayage and lift are zero; (2) drayage occurs at both origin and destination, not just the latter; and (3) drayage and lift costs apply only to intermodal freight, not carload freight. Of those variations, the first one made the biggest difference, and I report it here as Test 4.

With no drayage or lift costs, the Option 1 weight-distance tax would have a smaller average effect on rail shipping costs (because now there are no drayage movements to tax) and a *larger* effect on truck costs (in my model, lifts are not taxed because they are not movements, so assuming lift costs are zero reduces total transport costs for both modes and makes the tax a larger percentage increase in the remaining costs. That affects trucking more than rail because the truck tax rate is higher). In Test 4, the model predicts a larger shift toward rail (3.6%, up from 3.1% in the main analysis), greater market contraction (1%, up from 0.7%), and thus a greater reduction in external costs. However, most of the predictions lie closer to the "likely range" than do those of Tests 1–3 (excepting market contraction and reduction in truck trips).

### Test 5: Full Truck Pass-Through

In this test, trucks become slightly less competitive because they now pass along the full Option 1 tax to their customers. That increases the shift to rail, the amount of market contraction, the reduction in external costs, and the amount of fuel savings. Most of the new values lie slightly outside the "likely range" but do not change my conclusions.

*Tests 6 and 7: Truck Rates*

Truck shipping rates (prices) are proprietary and not easily acquired. Instead of actual rates, then, I use predicted values from FHWA's *Intermodal Transportation and Inventory Costing* model (FHWA, 2016). Like the rail rates in my model—which come from the Surface Transportation Board—the FHWA predicted truck rates vary by commodity and distance.[33] I calibrate them so that they reflect average truck revenue per ton-mile from the National Transportation Statistics (USDOT, 2017c).

If true truck rates are higher than the estimates that my model uses, then shippers value trucking services more than my model assumes, and my simulations overstate the shift to rail. To test the sensitivity of those predictions to the assumed truck rates, I raise (Test 6) and lower (Test 7) the truck rates by 5%. With higher (lower) rates, the weight-distance tax represents a smaller (larger) increase in truck shipping costs. In Test 6, the shift to rail, therefore, decreases—and in Test 7, it *increases*—in both cases, by more than 10%, lying just outside the "likely range." The same is true of many of the model's predictions in these two tests, which leaves my basic conclusions intact.

## Conclusions and Discussion

This chapter has compared the likely effects of a weight-distance tax on overland freight transport to effects of several less-well-targeted freight taxes that would, however, be less costly to administer. The *optimal* tax on the freight transport externalities that I examine here—pavement damage, traffic congestion, uncompensated accident risk, and emissions of greenhouse gases and local criteria pollutants—would depend not only on weight and distance but also on location (to capture variation in pavement strength, average traffic conditions, and population exposures to local pollutants) and time of day (to capture variation in traffic density). But, barring the costly development and adoption of technologies accurately to measure those factors and apply a corresponding tax rate, a weight-distance tax might be the optimal *feasible* tax on freight transport.

Even so, I find that the benefits of the weight-distance tax—the most information intensive and costly of the policies I analyze—can be *approximated* by a less costly VMT tax. And the performance of the VMT tax could be improved by an approach like Oregon's—with per-mile tax rates that depend on a truck's declared weight (the maximum gross weight at which its operator intends to drive that truck over the next year) and axle configuration. Verification of each declaration would add to the cost of administering the tax, but with weight-dependent rates, such a tax could achieve some of the efficiency gains of a weight-distance tax relative to a VMT tax while avoiding the cost of administering a tax on the actual weight and distance of each shipment. And technological advances like the development of axle strain gauges that can measure and communicate payload weights in real time could bring down the cost of administering a weight-distance tax.

One important caveat is that external costs are not known with certainty. Thus, it is possible for policymakers inadvertently to choose tax rates that exceed true external costs. In that case, too much mode-switching and market contraction will occur. The findings here show, however, that the rates would have to be far above actual external costs before consumer losses offset the social gains from these policies.

For illustrative purposes, I also examine several narrower taxes on specific subsets of freight transport. I find that, for the current tax on truck tires, increasing those tax rates and broadening the tax base would affect mode choice out of proportion to the costs of those changes, saving fuel and reducing emissions. But the tire tax does not target external costs and, by including retreads, creates some incentive to delay tire replacements. I also examine a variety of container fees, which are relatively effective at encouraging mode shifting but could distort shippers' freight packaging decisions. (The substantial cost advantages of containerization would limit the size of that distortion.)

If shippers and consumers paid no other taxes, then setting freight transport taxes equal to external costs would be efficient, because that would fully internalize the external costs of shipping. In practice, however, the taxes would compound the costs associated with existing taxes on individual and corporate income. So the incremental cost to the economy would be higher than the tax rates themselves suggest. If the tax revenues were used in ways that did not offset that compounding effect—for example, if they were distributed to all U.S. residents on an equal lump-sum basis—the economically efficient tax rates would probably be lower than external costs. Alternatively, to the extent that lawmakers used the revenues in ways that offset the taxes' negative effects on real (inflation-adjusted) wages, investment, and output, the efficient rates of the taxes would be closer to—or perhaps even greater than—external costs (CBO, 2013, pp. 17–18).

Carriers can be expected to respond to these policies in ways not captured by my analysis. They could adopt cleaner technologies to reduce emissions, add tankers or railcars with increased resistance to spills, develop new accident-avoidance technologies, or add truck axles to reduce pavement damage. Thus, my findings should be considered medium-run responses that would take some time to develop and that would eventually be partly neutralized by technology adoptions and other strategic responses.

## Notes

1. The modes also differ by various measures of service quality, such as speed of delivery. But the value of those private benefits is reflected in transport prices.
2. Rail estimate applies to locomotives hauling double-stacked containers.

3. GAO (2011) estimates very high damages from PM and NOx emissions, in part because the engine data on which they are based predate current EPA standards. *See* Austin (2015).

4. Results provided to me by EPA as an empirical distribution of results from 15,000 runs of a variety of climate simulation models. *See* Figure 1 in IWG-SCC (2016). Note that GAO (2011) excludes $CO_2$ emissions.

5. On the basis of available estimates, truck and rail charges average about 15.6¢ and 5.1¢ per ton-mile, respectively, across service types and distances. *See* Austin (2015), Table A-4.

6. CBO, "The Budget and Economic Outlook: 2018 to 2028," www.cbo.gov/publication/53651.

7. FHWA, "Fuel Sales and Taxes: Exemptions," www.fhwa.dot.gov/motorfuel/sales_taxes_exemptions.htm.

8. Author's calculations based on FHWA, *Highway Statistics 2013*, Table VM-1.

9. The Alameda Corridor connects the Ports to the national rail system near downtown Los Angeles and includes a 10-mile, triple-tracked railway trench that avoids more than 200 grade crossings.

10. Millennium Marine Rail, *ExpressRail Elizabeth Terminal Schedule* (September 17, 2013), www.millenniummarinerail.com.

11. *See* Austin (2015) Table A-5 for mode-choice elasticities by type of commodity. (The types are groups of commodities designated by the researchers who estimated the elasticities.)

12. The model does not allow gains to exceed the donating mode's total ton-miles, so that new ton-miles are not "created" when the receiving mode has a much larger market share than the donating mode.

13. *See, e.g.,* "Trucking Industry Struggles with Growing Driver Shortage," *NPR* (January 9, 2018). www.npr.org/2018/01/09/576752327/trucking-industry-struggles-with-growing-driver-shortage.

14. For sensitivity-testing purposes, I repeat the simulations assuming a 100% pass-through rate for trucking firms, reflecting its more competitive structure than that of the rail industry, including more national firms and many independent carriers. I report those results in the section on sensitivity tests.

15. For parameter values, *see* appendix to Austin (2015).

16. I predict external costs based on the weight of empty tractor-trailers and railcars and prorate assuming 19% average unladen miles for each mode. (Federal Railroad Administration, 2009, Exhibit 4–7, p. 69).

17. Fuel efficiency is estimated at 150 ton-miles per gallon for freight trucks and about 475 ton-miles per gallon for rail (for locomotives hauling double-stacked containers) (TTI, 2012, pp. 5–6).

18. In 2017, California's South Coast Air Quality Management District proposed fees of $35 per 20-foot equivalent (TEU) to help fund the adoption of low- and zero-emissions drayage trucks, port cargo-handling equipment, or incentives for cleaner ships and locomotives operating in the Los Angeles-Long Beach port complex (SCAQMD, 2017).

19. The calibration reduces the fees on truck transport by 7% and increases rail fees by 24%, relative to fees based on zone midpoint distances. The difference reflects differences in average trip lengths and carrier rate structures.

20. For the same distance, rail external costs would average around $100 for intermodal.

21. Senate Committee on Finance, *Energy, Natural Resources, and Infrastructure Subcommittee* (April 25, 2013).

22. *See* note 'e' of Table 4.2 for source of that calculation.

23. For information on my distributional assumptions for these parameters, *see* appendix to Austin (2015).
24. Austin (2015), Table A-6.
25. Excluding Wyoming coal, which is shipped almost exclusively by rail, the increase in rail ton-miles is 5%.
26. For average payloads by commodity, *see* Austin (2015), Table A-8.
27. Net external costs could be further affected by the uses to which that revenue would be put, such as financing infrastructure investments or reducing other distortionary taxes. Implications of revenue use are beyond the scope of my analysis.
28. *See* Austin (2015), Table A-5 for mode-choice elasticities and Table A-1 for ton-mile market shares.
29. I calibrate the VMT tax rates to produce about the same revenue as the weight-distance tax, making the VMT tax into essentially an "average weight"-distance tax.
30. Because most railcar payloads average either below 30 tons or above 70 tons (*see* Austin (2015), Table A-8), the distortion relative to Option 1 could be limited by imposing a higher VMT tax rate on railcars that can accommodate the heavier payloads.
31. Austin (2015), Table A-4.
32. The model draws drayage costs from a triangular distribution with a range of $50 to $500 per trip and a peak at $150 (TRB, 2007). It assumes lift costs are uniformly distributed over a range of $50 to $150 (Barton et al., 1999; Resor and Blaze, 2004).
33. *See* Austin (2015), Table A-4.

# References

Abdelwahab, Walid M. 1998. "Elasticities of Mode Choice Probabilities and Market Elasticities of Demand: Evidence from a Simultaneous Mode Choice/Shipment-Size Freight Transport Model." *Transportation Research Part E: Logistics and Transportation Review* 34 (4): 257–266.

Alameda Corridor Transportation Authority. 2018. "ACTA Rate History." Accessed 22 May 2018. www.acta.org/gen/ACTARate%20History.pdf.

American Petroleum Institute (API). 2017. "State Motor Fuel Taxes." Accessed 2 August 2018. www.api.org/oil-and-natural-gas/consumer-information/motor-fuel-taxes.

Association of American Railroads. 2007. "The National Rail Freight Infrastructure Capacity and Investment Study." Prepared by Cambridge Systematics (September). Accessed 2 August 2018. expresslanes.codot.gov/programs/transitandrail/resource-materials-new/AARStudy.pdf.

Austin, David H. 2015. "Pricing Freight Transport to Account for External Costs." Congressional Budget Office Working Paper 2015–03.

Barton, James E., Cecil Selness, R. John Anderson, Donna Lindberg, and Norman Foster. 1999. "Developing a Proposal for a Multi-User Intermodal Freight Terminal as a Public-Private Partnership: Lessons Learned about Public and Private Perspectives, Timing, and Roles." *Transportation Research Record* 1659: 145–151.

Bontekoning, Yvonne M., Cathy Macharis, and J.J. Trip. 2004. "Is a New Applied Transportation Research Field Emerging? A Review of Intermodal Rail-Truck Freight Transport Literature." *Transportation Research Part A* 38: 1–34.

California State Transportation Agency (STA). 2017. "California Road Charge Pilot Program Final Report." (December). Accessed 2 August 2018. www.dot. ca.gov/road_charge/resources/final-report/docs/final.pdf.

CE Delft/TRT. 2011. "Potential of Modal Shift to Rail Transport." (March). Accessed 2 August 2018. www.cer.be/sites/default/files/publication/2189_ Modal_shift_study_final.pdf.

Congressional Budget Office. 2013. "Effects of a Carbon Tax on the Economy and the Environment." (May). Accessed 2 August 2018. www.cbo.gov/ publication/44223.

Congressional Budget Office. 2014. "The Highway Trust Fund and the Treatment of Surface Transportation Programs in the Federal Budget." (June). Accessed 2 August 2018. www.cbo.gov/publication/45416.

Congressional Budget Office. 2017. "An Update to the Budget and Economic Outlook: 2017 to 2027." (June). Accessed 2 August 2018. www.cbo.gov/ publication/52801.

Environmental Protection Agency (EPA). 2017a. "Inventory of US Greenhouse Gas Emissions and Sinks, 1990–2015." (Table 2–13), EPA 430-P-17–001.

EPA. 2017b. "Why Freight Matters to Supply-Chain Sustainability." Accessed 22 May 2018. www.epa.gov/smartway/why-freight-matters-supply-chain-sustainability.

Federal Highway Administration (FHWA). 2000a. "1997 Federal Highway Cost Allocation Study Final Report." Accessed 2 August 2018. www.fhwa.dot.gov/ policy/hcas/final/.

FHWA. 2000b. "Addendum to the 1997 Federal Highway Cost Allocation Study Final Report." (May). Accessed 2 August 2018. www.fhwa.dot.gov/policy/ hcas/addendum.cfm.

FHWA. 2008. "Freight Story 2008." Accessed 22 May 2018. ops.fhwa.dot.gov/ freight/freight_analysis/freight_story/fs2008.pdf.

FHWA. 2010. "Freight Analysis Framework 3 User Guide." Accessed 2 August 2018. ops.fhwa.dot.gov/freight/freight_analysis/faf/faf3/userguide/index.htm.

FHWA. 2016. "Intermodal Transportation and Inventory Costing Model State Tool (ITIC-ST)." Accessed 22 May 2018. www.fhwa.dot.gov/policy/otps/ 061012/iticst_info.htm.

Federal Maritime Commission. 2012. "Study of U.S. Inland Containerized Cargo Moving through Canadian and Mexican Seaports." (July). Accessed 2 August 2018. www.fmc.gov/assets/1/News/Study_of_US_Inland_Containerized_ Cargo_Moving_Through_Canadian_and_Mexican_Seaports_Final.pdf.

Federal Railroad Administration. 2009. "Final Report: Comparative Evaluation of Rail and Truck Fuel Efficiency on Competitive Corridors." Accessed 2 August 2018. www.fra.dot.gov/Elib/Document/2925

Florida DOT. 2002. "The Response of Railroad and Truck Freight Shipments to Optimal Excess Capacity Subsidies and Externality Taxes." (September). Accessed 22 May 2018. www.bebr.ufl.edu/sites/default/files/Research%20 Reports/rail_freight_subsidy_report_0.pdf.

Forkenbrock, David J. 1999. "External Costs of Intercity Truck Freight Transportation." *Transportation Research Part A* 33: 505–526.

Forkenbrock, David J. 2001. "Comparison of External Costs of Rail and Truck Freight Transportation." *Transportation Research Part A* 35: 321–337.

Government Accountability Office (GAO). 2011. "Surface Freight Transportation: A Comparison of the Costs of Road, Rail, and Waterways Freight Shipments That Are Not Passed on to Consumers." GAO-11-134.

I-95 Corridor Coalition. 2009. "Mid-Atlantic Rail Operations Phase II Study." Prepared by Cambridge Systematics (December). Accessed 2 August 2018. i95coalition.org/wp-content/uploads/2015/02/MAROps_Phase_II_Final_Report.pdf?66d0ea.

Illinois General Assembly. 2018. "625 ILCS 5, Ch. 3, Art. VIII." (Sections 3–815 and 3–818).

Levin, Richard C. 1978. "Allocation in Surface Freight Transportation: Does Rate Regulation Matter?" *Bell Journal of Economics* 9: 18–45.

Matthews, H. Scott, Chris Hendrickson, and Arpad Horvath. 2001. "External Costs of Air Emissions from Transportation." *Journal of Infrastructure Systems* 7 (1): 13–17.

Oregon DOT. 2017. "Oregon's Road Usage Charge: The OReGO Program Final Report." (April). Accessed 2 August 2018. www.oregon.gov/ODOT/Programs/RUF/IP-Road%20Usage%20Evaluation%20Book%20WEB_4-26.pdf.

Oregon DOT. 2018. "Mileage Tax Rates." (January) Accessed 2 August 2018. www.oregon.gov/ODOT/Forms/Motcarr/9928-2018.pdf.

Oum, Tae Hoon. 1979. "A Cross Sectional Study of Freight Transport Demand and Rail-Truck Competition in Canada." *Bell Journal of Economics* 10: 463–482.

Picard, Guy, and Marc Gaudry. 1998. "Exploration of a Box-Cox Logit Model of Intercity Freight Mode Choice." *Transportation Research Part E: Logistics and Transportation Review* 34 (1): 1–12.

PierPass. 2018. "PierPASS to Adopt Appointment System and Flat Fee." (April). Accessed 22 May 2018. www.pierpass-tmf.org/Documents/2018-04-16%20PierPASS%202.0%20Press%20Release.pdf.

Resor, Randolph, and James Blaze. 2004. "Short-Haul Rail Intermodal: Can It Compete with Trucks?" *Transportation Research Record* 1873: 45–52.

Rich, Jeppe, P. Michael Holmblad, and Christian Hansen. 2009. "A Weighted Logit Freight Mode-Choice Model." *Transportation Research Part E: Logistics and Transportation Review* 45 (6): 1006–1019.

Samimi, Amir, Kazuya Kawamura, and Abolfazl Mohammadian. 2011. "A Behavioral Analysis of Freight Mode Choice Decisions." *Transportation Planning and Technology* 34 (8): 857–869.

South Coast Air Quality Management District. 2017. "SCAQMD Air Quality Management Plan." Accessed 22 May 2018. docketpublic.energy.ca.gov/PublicDocuments/17-IEPR-10/TN220060_20170706T102143_SCAQMD__Air_Quality_Management_Plan_AQMP.pdf.

Texas Transportation Institute (TTI). 2012. "A Modal Comparison of Domestic Freight Transportation Effects on the General Public, 2001–2009." (February). Accessed 2 August 2018. www.nationalwaterwaysfoundation.org/study/FinalReportTTI.pdf.

Transportation Research Board (TRB). 1997. "A Guidebook for Forecasting Freight Transportation Demand" (*citing J. Jones, F. Nix, and C. Schwier, The Impact of Changes in Road User Charges on Canadian Railways*, prepared for Transport Canada, September 1990, Table 4.2). NCHRP Report 388, National

Academy Press. Accessed 2 August 2018. onlinepubs.trb.org/Onlinepubs/nchrp/nchrp_rpt_388.pdf.

Transport & Environment. 2013. "Study on Heavy-Vehicle On-Board Weighing." (December). Accessed 2 August 2018. www.transportenvironment.org/sites/te/files/publications/2014%2001%20RappTrans_Weight%20sensors%20report.pdf.

TRB. 2007. *Rail Freight Solutions to Roadway Congestion*, National Cooperative Freight Research Program, Report 586, pg. G-81. Washington, DC: National Academy Press.

TRB. 2012. *Dedicated Revenue Mechanisms for Freight Transport Investment*, National Cooperative Freight Research Program, Report 15, Washington, DC: National Academy Press.

TTI. 2015. "2015 Urban Mobility Scorecard." (August). Accessed 2 August 2018. static.tti.tamu.edu/tti.tamu.edu/documents/mobility-scorecard-2015.pdf.

U.S. Department of Energy (USDOE). 2013. "Freight Transportation Modal Shares: Scenarios for a Low-Carbon Future." Prepared by Cambridge Systematics and National Renewable Energy Laboratory, Washington, DC. DOE/GO-102013–3705. Accessed 2 August 2018. www.nrel.gov/docs/fy13osti/55636.pdf.

U.S. Department of Transportation (USDOT). 2010. "2007 Commodity Flow Survey." Accessed 2 August 2018. www.census.gov/prod/2010pubs/ec07tcf-us.pdf.

USDOT. 2016. "2015 Status of the Nation's Highways, Bridges, and Transit: Conditions and Performance." (December). Accessed 2 August 2018. www.fhwa.dot.gov/policy/2015cpr/.

USDOT. 2017a. "National Transportation Statistics." Table 1–50: *U.S. Ton-Miles of Freight*. Accessed 2 August 2018. www.bts.gov/archive/publications/national_transportation_statistics/table_01_50.

USDOT. 2017b. "Freight Shipments Projected to Continue to Grow." Bureau of Transportation Statistics (August). Accessed 22 May 2018. www.transportation.gov/connections/freight-shipments-projected-continue-grow.

USDOT. 2017c. "National Transportation Statistics." Table 3–21: *Average Freight Revenue per Ton-Mile*. Accessed 2 August 2018. www.bts.gov/archive/publications/national_transportation_statistics/table_03_21.

U.S. Interagency Working Group on Social Cost of Carbon (IWGSCC). 2016. "Technical Update of the Social Cost of Carbon for Regulatory Impact Analysis under Executive Order 12866." (August). Accessed 2 August 2018. www.epa.gov/sites/production/files/2016-12/documents/sc_co2_tsd_august_2016.pdf.

Virginia DOT. 2004. "Freight Diversion and Forecast Report." Accessed 22 May 2018. www.virginiadot.org/projects/resources/freight.pdf.

Washington State DOT. 2009. "Retreaded Tire Use and Safety: Synthesis." (September). Accessed 22 May 2018. pdfs.semanticscholar.org/6589/d8022fc6dda23c06bdddf5da7872445da730.pdf.

Winston, Clifford. 1981. "A Disaggregate Model of the Demand for Intercity Freight Transportation." *Econometrica* 49 (4): 981–1006.

# 5 Price Effects in Truck-Competitive Railroad Markets

*Gerard J. McCullough
and Ishay Hadash*

## Introduction

This chapter updates the results of a classic study of the 1972 U.S. freight market published by Ann Friedlaender and Richard Spady in the *Review of Economics and Statistics* journal in August 1980.[1] That study provided a macro-level perspective on the earlier freight market by focusing on transportation decisions in key manufacturing sectors—food, wood products, paper, chemicals, automobiles, and so on. In the Friedlaender and Spady (FS) analysis, shipper decisions were modeled using a translog (TL) cost function whose arguments included shipper outputs, their quasi-fixed stocks of capital and material inputs, labor prices, and generalized prices of truck and rail freight transportation. From the cost function, FS derived input demands and own-price and cross-price elasticities for rail and truck freight services for a cross section of manufacturers in the 1972 Economic Census.

The updated analysis presented here applies the same basic method to data from the 1997, 2002, and 2007 Economic Census reports and Commodity Flow Surveys (CFS). The new elasticity projections are consistent with those reported by FS but are significantly larger in absolute value. The results illustrate the dramatic extent to which changes in technology and regulation have enabled railroads to compete with trucking firms in higher value markets that they did not serve effectively in 1972. Though the projected changes in relative transport rates are fairly small, the market share effects—the diversions of freight from rail to truck or truck to rail—are significant. Projected impacts on highway users, railroad shippers, and railroad stockholders from even modest changes in the relative prices of these transportation modes could also be significant.

The underlying assumption of the FS analysis is that freight shippers are private sector firms whose decisions can be modeled using cost analysis. The specification that FS use to represent shipper costs is the TL cost function, a generalization of the Cobb-Douglas cost function often used in applied economic analysis because of its ability to represent the cost characteristics of industries whose technologies are complex. FS apply Shepherd's lemma to derive demand equations which specify how the *shares* of freight carried by each mode will respond to changes in truck and rail prices and labor prices as well.

Movement data for the FS study are from a cross section of 96 three-digit Standard Transportation Commodity Code (STCC) manufacturing industries reported in the 1972 Census of Transportation. Non-transportation data on the 96 industries were from the Economic Census (Annual Survey of Manufactures) for 1972. The STCC categories used by FS corresponded directly to the Standard Industrial Classification (SIC) categories used in the Economic Census at that time.

FS use the parameter results from the input demand function to calculate a set of industry-specific own-price and cross-price demand elasticities for railroad and truck freight services. These are summarized in Table 5.1.

The *own-price elasticities* for rail and truck are estimates of the direct effect that a percentage increase (or decrease) in a mode's generalized price would have on the amount of traffic shipped by that mode. The expected sign of these elasticities is negative, and the own-price elasticities estimated by FS meet this basic criterion. The *cross-price elasticities* for rail and truck are estimates of the direct effect that a percentage increase in the competing mode's generalized price would have on the amount of traffic shipped by rail or truck. The expected sign for these elasticities is positive. The cross-price elasticities estimated by FS are quite small, though, and some have the wrong sign. The rail-truck cross-price elasticities for 1972 show that even if trucks were to significantly increase their prices—or railroads lower their prices—in key manufacturing markets there would be little or no change in modal shares.

*Table 5.1* Friedlaender Spady Price Elasticities of Demand for Freight Service

| Industry | Rail Own-Price | Truck Own-Price | Truck-Rail Cross-Price | Rail-Truck Cross-Price |
|---|---|---|---|---|
| Food Products | −2.583 | −1.001 | 0.004 | −0.023 |
| Wood Products | −1.971 | −1.547 | −0.129 | −0.050 |
| Paper & Rubber | −1.847 | −1.054 | 0.003 | 0.007 |
| Stone, Clay, & Glass | −1.681 | −1.031 | 0.016 | 0.025 |
| Iron & Steel | −2.542 | −1.083 | −0.013 | −0.053 |
| Fabricated Metal | −2.164 | −1.364 | −0.099 | −0.059 |
| Nonelectrical Machinery | −2.271 | −1.085 | −0.010 | −0.032 |
| Electrical Machinery | −3.547 | −1.230 | −0.061 | −0.151 |

## Generalized McFadden Cost Model

In the updated analysis presented here, the 1972 data that FS used are replaced by a multiyear set of combined industry-level observations from the Economic Census reports and the CFS for 1997, 2002, and 2007. For a technical reason described below, the TL cost function is replaced by a Generalized McFadden (GM) cost function. This function is also derived from the Cobb-Douglas and has the same flexible characteristics as the TL.

The function, proposed by Diewert (1987), can be written as follows,

$$C(w, y, F) = \sum_i \alpha_i w_i + 0.5 \sum_i \sum_j \beta_{ij} \left( {w_i w_j} \middle/ {w_k} \right) + \sum_i \gamma_i w_i y$$
$$+ \sum_i \sum_h \delta_{ih} w_i F_h + \sum_h \pi_h F_h y \tag{1}$$

where $y$ is a single output, $w_k$ is a price that serves as numeraire, $F_h$ is the set of fixed factors, and $\alpha$, $\beta$, $\gamma$, $\delta$, and $\pi$ are parameter vectors. Use of $w_k$ as a numeraire is a technical device which ensures that the cost function is homogeneous of degree one in input prices—consistent with microeconomic theory.

Application of Shepherd's Lemma gives a vector of input demands for rail and truck freight services. Each element has the following form,

$$\frac{\partial C}{\partial w_{it}} = x_{it} = \alpha_i + \sum_j \beta_{ij} \left( {w_{jt}} \middle/ {w_{lt}} \right) + \gamma_i y_{it} + \sum_h \pi_h F_{ht} \tag{2}$$

where $x_{it}$ is the corresponding volume of truck or rail service demanded by each major industry in 1997, 2002, and 2007, $w_{it}$ is the price of truck or rail service, and $w_{lt}$ is the labor price which serves as numeraire. The quantity $y_{it}$ is the level of industry $i$'s output.in year $t$.

As in the FS paper, the full cost model includes four equations—demand equations for rail and truck transportation, and pricing equations for rail and truck. Letting the subscripts $R$ represent rail, $T$ truck, and $L$ labor, and letting $tx$ represent time (in years), $mx$ material stock (in dollars), and $kx$ capital stock (in dollars), the following equations (3) through (6) comprise the full set of equations that is estimated.

$$x_{Rt} = \alpha_R + \beta_{TR} \left( \frac{w_{Tt}}{W_{Lt}} \right) + \beta_{RR} \left( \frac{w_{Rt}}{W_{Lt}} \right) + \gamma_R y_{it} + \pi_{R\tau} tx$$
$$+ \pi_{Rm} mx_{it} + \pi_{Rk} kx_{it} + \varepsilon_1 \tag{3}$$

$$x_{Tt} = \alpha_T + \beta_{TT} \left( \frac{w_{Tt}}{W_{Lt}} \right) + \beta_{TR} \left( \frac{w_{Rt}}{W_{Lt}} \right) + \gamma_T y_{it} + \pi_{T\tau} tx + \pi_{Tm} mx_{it}$$
$$+ \pi_{Tk} kx_{it} + \varepsilon_2 \tag{4}$$

$$w_{Rt} = \theta_{R0} + \theta_{R1} LOH_{Rt} + \varepsilon_3 \tag{5}$$

$$w_{Tt} = \theta_{T0} + \theta_{T1} LOH_{Tt} + \varepsilon_4 \tag{6}$$

Equations (3) and (4) are the input demand equations for rail and truck. Equations (5) and (6) are pricing equations for the two modes. These follow FS in using average length of haul (LOH) for each industry sector and each mode in order to incorporate quality of service into the price measure. All four equations include additive disturbance terms.

The GM cost function addresses a missing data problem. The 1997, 2002, and 2007 Economic Census reports provide details on shipper output levels, expenditures for labor and other intermediate inputs, and material stock values and capital stock values. However, the public reports did not allow us to directly identify expenditure *shares* by mode. The demand functions for the TL model cannot be estimated without this (left-hand side) data. The GM input demand functions, on the other hand, can be estimated using the quantity of rail or truck freight service and these data are available in the CFS.

## Carrier-Shipper Data 1997–2007

The variables used in the current analysis along with their sources in the Economic Census, the CFS, the Bureau of Labor Statistics Producer Price Indices and Occupational Employment Statistics, and the Economic Report of the President are listed in Appendix Table 5.A1.

NAICS was adopted by the federal government in 1997 to replace the SIC system that FS used. It is now the standard classification system used in collecting and publishing data on business activity. The basic units of observation in the current study are industry sectors identified at the three-digit level of NAICS.[2] At the three-digit level, NAICS describes industry *sectors* such as Agricultural Products (111), Wood Products (321), Chemicals (325), and so on. Variables taken from NAICS include employment levels, payrolls, capital, and material stocks and values of shipments for each industry sector. The financial and operating data are combined with corresponding shipment data from the CFS using Standard Transportation Commodity Group (STCG) classifications. These were adopted by the federal government in 1997 to replace the STCC codes that FS used.

The FS analysis was restricted to manufacturing industries. This list was expanded in the current analysis to include Agricultural Products (NAICS 111) and Mining (NAICS 212). A number of STCG categories were not included because production data on the commodities whose movements were described in the CFS could not be precisely identified in the NAICS data. These included STCG 04 Animal Feed; STCG 05 Meat, Fish and Seafood; STCG 10–13 Stone Sand and other minerals; STCG 16 Crude petroleum; and STCG 37 Railroad Equipment and Aircraft.

To limit the effect of outliers, FS eliminated from their data any industry where the mode share of rail was less than 5% of ton-miles. That practice is followed in the current paper. The NAICS industries included in the estimation results are listed in Table 5.2.

Rail and truck rates for 1997, 2002, and 2007 are taken from the Bureau of Labor Statistics Producer Price Indices and Occupational Employment Statistics. The base period for the rail and truck price series is December 1996. As in FS, sector-specific labor prices were calculated by dividing annual payroll for each sector by the reported number of employees (multiplied by 2,000 to approximate hours worked). Monetary values were converted to real terms using the aggregate 1982 Producer Price Index. The data are summarized in Table 5.3.

*Table 5.2* NAICS Industries With STCG Source

| NAICS Code | Industry Description | STCG Source |
| --- | --- | --- |
| 111 | Agricultural Products | 02, 03 |
| 311 | Food Manufacturing | 06, 07 |
| 312 | Beverages & Tobacco | 08, 09 |
| 321 | Wood Product Manufacturing | 26 |
| 322 | Paper Manufacturing | 27, 28 |
| 324 | Petroleum & Coal Products | 17, 18, 19 |
| 325 | Chemical Manufacturing | 20, 21, 22, 23 |
| 326 | Plastic & Rubber Products | 24 |
| 327 | Nonmetallic Mineral Products | 31 |
| 331 | Primary Metal Manufacturing | 32 |
| 332 | Fabricated Metal Manufacturing | 33 |
| 333 | Machinery Manufacturing | 34 |
| 336 | Transportation Equipment | 36 |

*Table 5.3* Summary Statistics

| Variable | Mean | Standard Deviation |
| --- | --- | --- |
| Truck Ton-miles (billions) | 40.4 billion | 35.4 billion |
| Rail Ton-miles | 50.3 billion | 131.5 billion |
| Truck Rate Index | 114.89 | 11.14 |
| Rail Rate Index | 118.51 | 19.94 |
| Payroll | 75.6 million ($) | 21.6 million ($) |
| Years | 6.29 | 4.16 |
| Material Stock | 75.7 billion ($) | 72.7 billion ($) |
| Capital Stock | 102.6 billion ($) | 143.9 billion ($) |

## Econometric Results

From an econometric standpoint, it is important to note that the observations in equations (3) to (6) are contemporaneously correlated. For example, the first 13 observations in equations (3) and (5) represent industry demands and prices for *rail* services in 1997, and the first 13 observations in equations (4) and (6) represent demand and prices for *truck* services in the same year. This pattern is repeated in equations (3) through (6) for 2002 and 2007. The usual approach to estimating a set of contemporaneously correlated observations of this type is to use a seemingly unrelated regression estimator, but the price variables $w_R$ and $w_T$ appear as regressors in equations (3) and (4) and as dependent variables in equations (5) and (6). Simultaneous estimation of all four equations dictated the use of a full information maximum likelihood (FIML) estimator.

The system was estimated using the full information likelihood procedure in SAS© Version 9.2, and the parameter results from the FIML estimation are presented in Table 5.4.

All of the parameters have the expected signs and the key parameters are significant. The intercept terms for rail ($\alpha_R$) and truck ($\alpha_T$) are positive and significant. The larger value for truck reflects the fact that the highway mode starts with larger initial shares than rail in most commodity markets. The own-price parameters for rail ($\beta_{RR}$) and truck ($\beta_{TT}$) are both

*Table 5.4* Nonlinear FIML Parameter Estimates

| Parameter | Estimate | Standard Error | t Value |
|---|---|---|---|
| $\alpha_T$ | 3.66E + 11 | 4.10E + 10 | 8.92 |
| $\alpha_R$ | 1.31E + 11 | 1.95E + 10 | 6.71 |
| $\beta_{TT}$ | −1.18E + 13 | 4.38E + 12 | −2.7 |
| $\beta_{TR} (=\beta_{RT})$ | 1.37E + 13 | 4.39E + 12 | 3.13 |
| $\beta_{RR}$ | −1.86E + 13 | 4.61E + 12 | −4.04 |
| $\gamma_{TY}$ | 0.257666 | 0.167 | 1.54 |
| $\gamma_{RY}$ | −0.03605 | 0.1299 | −0.28 |
| $\theta_{T0}$ | 113.7303 | 1.7493 | 65.01 |
| $\theta_{T1}$ | 0.000791 | 0.000482 | 1.64 |
| $\Theta_{R0}$ | 117.084 | 3.1665 | 36.98 |
| $\theta_{R1}$ | −0.00053 | 0.00039 | −1.36 |
| $\pi_{RT}$ | −1.64E + 10 | 1.04E + 09 | −15.77 |
| $\pi_{RM}$ | 0.025472 | 0.1907 | 0.13 |
| $\pi_{RK}$ | 0.393097 | 0.0836 | 4.7 |
| $\pi_{TT}$ | −5.52E + 10 | 1.48E + 09 | −37.31 |
| $\pi_{TM}$ | −0.23155 | 0.2447 | −0.95 |
| $\pi_{TK}$ | −0.06819 | 0.1049 | −0.65 |

negative as expected and are significant at the 1% level. The cross-price parameter between rail and truck ($\beta_{TR} = \beta_{RT}$) is positive as expected and is also significant. This is the basis for concluding that there is now more effective general competition between truck and rail. In the FS estimation results, the cross-price parameter was not significant.[3] The cross-price elasticities presented below are commodity specific and provide more detail about the degree of competition in specific markets.

Turning to other key parameters, the control variables for time, $(\pi_{R\tau})$ and $(\pi_{T\tau})$, are negative and highly significant. This means that the derived demand curves for truck and rail have shifted downward over time—indicating that the relative amount of transportation resources that manufacturers consume has declined over time. Also, the slope parameters for rail length of haul $(\theta_{R1})$ and truck length of haul $(\theta_{T1})$ in equations (5) and (6) are both significant. The generalized price of truck is positively related to length of haul while the generalized price of rail is negatively related. This is consistent with the generally accepted view among freight market participants that rail service becomes more competitive as shipping distances increase.

## *Projected Elasticities*

The own-price elasticities of truck and rail and the cross-price elasticities for the two modes are point estimates calculated for each observation in the data set. Letting $w_{tl}$ represent the normalized price of truck $(w_t/w_l)$ and $w_{rl}$ represent the normalized price of rail $(w_r/w_l)$, the own-price elasticity for truck is as follows,

$$\varepsilon_{TT} = \frac{dxt}{dwtl}\frac{wtl}{xt} = \beta_{TT}\frac{wtl}{xt} \tag{7}$$

where $w_T$ and $x_T$ are the observed truck price and the observed truck ton-mileage for a particular NAICS industry in a particular year (1997, 2002, or 2007). The own-price elasticity for rail is calculated in similar fashion.

The cross-price elasticity of rail with respect to (normalized) truck price is

$$\varepsilon_{RT} = \frac{dxr}{dwtl}\frac{wtl}{xr} = \beta_{RT}\frac{wtl}{xr} \tag{8}$$

and the cross-price elasticity of truck with respect to (normalized) rail price is

$$\varepsilon_{TR} = \frac{dxt}{dwrl}\frac{wrl}{xt} = \beta_{RT}\frac{wrl}{xt} \tag{9}$$

The elasticities, reported in Table 5.5, are projected at the midpoint of the data. All have the expected signs, and all are generally consistent with the

*Table 5.5* Own-Price and Cross-Price Demand Elasticities

| NAICS | Description | Rail-Truck | Truck | Railroad | Truck-Rail |
|---|---|---|---|---|---|
| | | Cross-Price | Own-Price | Own-Price | Cross-Price |
| 311 | Food & Kindred Products | 1.849 | −0.879 | −2.191 | 1.008 |
| 321 | Wood Products | 4.222 | −1.601 | −5.003 | 1.837 |
| 322 | Paper | 1.117 | −1.103 | −1.323 | 1.265 |
| 324 | Petroleum & Coal Products | 1.117 | −0.908 | −1.323 | 1.042 |
| 325 | Chemicals[1] | 0.521 | −0.537 | −0.618 | 0.617 |
| 327 | Nonmetallic Mineral Products | 2.098 | −1.289 | −2.486 | 1.478 |
| 332 | Fabricated Metal Products | 1.644 | −0.930 | −1.948 | 1.068 |
| 336 | Transportation Equipment | 0.823 | −0.500 | −0.975 | 0.574 |

[1] This category includes finished chemicals in addition to bulk chemicals.

FS estimates reported in Table 5.1. The area where the newer elasticities are significantly different is the cross-price elasticities.

Setting aside the Wood Products elasticities, which reflect very large (and possibly erroneous) changes between the 2002 and 2007 rail ton-mile levels reported in the Commodity Flow Survey, all of the industries listed are sensitive to relative changes in modal prices. A 5% increase in the relevant truck rate would generate a 9.2% increase in rail food shipments, a 5.6% increase in rail paper shipments, or a 4.1% increase in rail automotive shipments.

The higher degree of price sensitivity in these recent results can be explained in three ways.

First, the FS results are based on a *cross section* while the current analysis is based on a *panel* of observations that spans a 10-year period. This gives shippers time to adjust their logistics systems to reflect the underlying economic characteristics of the two modes.

Second, the FS analysis (though it appeared in 1980) could not reflect the fact that railroads were deregulated by the Staggers Rail Act of 1980. Staggers gave railroads the ability to disinvest in markets where trucks had technological advantages, but it also enabled them to invest and to price aggressively in markets where they could compete. After deregulation railroads identified a number of "commonly important commodities" for both truck and rail where railroads were able to achieve good profit margins. These included Food and Kindred Products (NAICS 311), Paper (NAICS 322), and Transportation Equipment (NAICS 336).

Third, and perhaps most important, the 1972 data did not reflect the important role that intermodal containers now play in enabling railroads to compete with trucks. U.S. railroads began moving a significant number of containers in the 1960s, but the technology did not mature until the 1980s when dedicated double-stack container trains were introduced and railroads became essential components of international supply chains. The importance of containers can be seen clearly in data from the Commodity Flow Surveys. In the 1997 Commodity Flow Survey, intermodal shipments comprised 15.8% of rail-related food industry traffic, 10.3% of rail-related paper industry traffic, and 31.8% of rail-related automotive industry traffic. In the 2007 Commodity Flow Survey, the numbers were 25.1 for the food industry, 33.9 for the paper industry, and 47.8 for the automotive industry traffic.

## Diversion Effects

One policy-relevant application of these results is to project the longer-term effects that *reductions* in relative truck rates would have on the market for intercity freight movements. The likely causes of such reductions would be changes in truck technology, particularly those associated with a loosening of truck size and weight (TS&W) restrictions. The question here is: what effect would significant decreases in truck costs—leading presumably to reductions in truck rates—have on freight market shares? These effects are estimated by rearranging the first two expressions in equation (8) to isolate *dxr/xr*, the percent change in rail shipments. This equation is as follows:

$$\frac{dxr}{xr} = \varepsilon_{RT} \frac{dwtl}{wtl} \tag{10}$$

The projected market share values for a stipulated 10% *reduction* in relative truck rates are reported in Table 5.6. This reduction is consistent with the truck cost impacts projected by the U.S. Department of Transportation (DOT) Federal Highway Administration's *Comprehensive Truck Size & Weight Study* (2000). The study projected an 11.4% reduction in shipper costs for an "LCV Nationwide Scenario."[4]

Though the projected 10% reduction is fairly small, the losses of rail market share are significant. In several key markets—agriculture, food products, wood products, plastics, nonmetallic mineral products, and fabricated metal products—the loss is greater than or equal to 15%. The final column of Table 5.6 lists the change in the total market share for rail. The effect on the rail market is generally larger than the change in rail share of the total market because in most markets, railroads start with a smaller share. Projected losses in the key rail markets (as a

*Table 5.6* U.S. Freight Markets—NAICS Basis Impact of 10% Truck Rate Decrease

| NAICS | Description | Base Shares | | Price Effect | |
|---|---|---|---|---|---|
| | | Truck | Rail | Truck | Rail |
| 311 | Food & Kindred Products | 0.72 | 0.26 | 0.77 | 0.21 |
| 321 | Wood Products | 0.55 | 0.44 | 0.71 | 0.28 |
| 322 | Paper | 0.66 | 0.33 | 0.71 | 0.28 |
| 324 | Petroleum & Coal Products | 0.39 | 0.22 | 0.42 | 0.19 |
| 325 | Chemicals | 0.50 | 0.40 | 0.53 | 0.37 |
| 327 | Nonmetallic Mineral Products | 0.78 | 0.19 | 0.83 | 0.14 |
| 332 | Fabricated Metal Products | 0.85 | 0.13 | 0.88 | 0.10 |
| 336 | Transportation Equipment | 0.75 | 0.23 | 0.78 | 0.21 |

percent of rail total market) are 7.5% for chemical, 8% for transportation equipment, 15% for paper, 19% for food products, and 36% for wood products.

It is also possible to use this analysis to predict the effects that *increased* energy costs, highway congestion, and/or highway user fees might have on the relative demands for railroad freight service. The question here (also policy-relevant) is: what effect would significant increases in truck prices have on the levels of railroad freight traffic? Presumably, a significant increase in truck prices could have a direct effect on rail freight traffic by diverting shipments with rail alternatives off the highway system and onto the rail network.

To estimate these effects, we start again with equation (10). The percent change in rail traffic is a product of the cross-price elasticity and a stipulated increase in normalized truck prices. A 10% increase in truck prices generates the results reported in Table 5.7.

The gains in rail markets here are equally impressive. Projected increases in the key rail markets are 20% for chemicals, 22% for transportation equipment, 15% for paper, 23% for food products, and 29% for wood products.

There is an important *caveat* here that applies to the projections in Tables 5.6 and 5.7. The changes shown in these tables are based on changes of 10% in the normalized truck price (*wt/wl*). The GM estimation uses normalized prices in equations (3) and (4) as do the elasticity formulas in equations (7) through (10). This means that a hypothetical 10% increase in the normalized truck price would actually require a 10% incremental increase over whatever change would occur in the labor prices and rail prices.

*Table 5.7* U.S. Freight Markets—NAICS Basis Projected Impact of 10% Truck Rate Increase

| NAICS | Description | Base Shares | | Price Effect | |
|-------|-------------|-------|------|-------|------|
| | | Truck | Rail | Truck | Rail |
| 311 | Food & Kindred Products | 0.72 | 0.26 | 0.66 | 0.32 |
| 321 | Wood Products | 0.55 | 0.44 | 0.43 | 0.57 |
| 322 | Paper | 0.66 | 0.33 | 0.61 | 0.38 |
| 324 | Petroleum & Coal Products | 0.39 | 0.22 | 0.36 | 0.25 |
| 325 | Chemicals | 0.50 | 0.40 | 0.42 | 0.48 |
| 327 | Nonmetallic Mineral Products | 0.78 | 0.19 | 0.72 | 0.17 |
| 332 | Fabricated Metal Products | 0.85 | 0.13 | 0.82 | 0.13 |
| 336 | Transportation Equipment | 0.76 | 0.23 | 0.74 | 0.28 |

## Conclusion

The basic aim of this research was to provide an historical perspective on the changes that have occurred in railroad freight markets since deregulation. The changes that have taken place in the cost structure and profitability of U.S. freight railroads since passage of the Staggers Rail Act in 1980 have been extensively analyzed. Discussions continue over regulatory issues involving railroads and shippers of bulk commodities—coal, grain, and bulk chemicals. The idea here was to use Friedlaender and Spady's classic analysis of the derived demand for freight transportation in 1972 as an entry into the relationship between pre-Staggers railroads and shippers of higher-valued manufactured goods.

The primary finding of the update is that railroads now compete more effectively in markets where they were not able to compete in 1972. Of particular interest are the markets for Food and Kindred Products (NAICS 311), Paper (NAICS 322), and Transportation Equipment (NAICS 336). Data in the Commodity Flow Surveys for 1997, 2002, and 2007, which provide a basis for this study, show that the growth of intermodal containers has played a key role in freight railroads' abilities to compete in these markets.

The analysis also showed that a relatively small change in truck prices would be consequential for railroads. A 10% *decrease* in relative truck rates would generate a significant amount of diversion from high-valued rail markets onto the highway network. This, in turn, could put downward pressure on railroad maintenance spending and investment in the rail system. It would also put upward pressure on rates paid by bulk and intermodal shippers who remain on the rail system. The estimates provided here do not take into account the significant external affects that TS&W changes could have on the environment and on highway users.

These issues are addressed in companion Chapter 4 in this volume written by David Austin.

On the other hand, the direct effect of a 10% increase in relative truck rates would divert a significant amount of traffic off the highway network and onto the rail network. More dramatic increases in energy prices, congestion, or user fees—leading to higher relative differences in truck rates—could divert even more freight onto rail, especially if the differential changes in rates were accompanied by improvements in levels of rail service.

From a methodological standpoint, this chapter illustrates the feasibility and enduring value of the method that FS developed in 1980 to analyze the industry-level effects of changes in the freight market. Logit models present a relatively fixed assessment of freight demand that is shipment focused and market specific. The FS analysis is based on a more generalized economic framework in which shippers have the flexibility to choose across a range of productive inputs that includes truck and rail freight transportation along with labor inputs, and quasi-fixed stocks of materials and capital.

## Notes

1. Ann Friedlaender and Richard Spady, "A Derived Demand Function for Freight Transportation," *Review of Economics and Statistics*, 62:3, 1980, pp. 432–441.
2. NAICS classifications extend to six digits, but in order to relate NAICS economic data to shipment data in the Commodity Flow Survey, three-digit NAICS classifications are used.
3. FS, op. cit., Table 1, p. 437.
4. *CTS&W Summary Report*, Table 13, p. 38.

## References

Diewert, Walter E. and Terence J. Wales. 1987. "Flexible Functional Forms and Global Curvature Conditions." *Econometrica*, 55(1): 43–68.

Friedlaender, Ann F. and Richard H. Spady. 1980. "A Derived Demand Function for Freight Transportation." *Review of Economics and Statistics*, 62(3): 432–441.

U.S. Census Bureau. 1997, 2002, 2007. *Commodity Flow Survey*. Washington, DC: U.S. Department of Commerce.

U.S. Census Bureau. 1997, 2002, 2007. *Economic Census*. Washington, DC: U.S. Department of Commerce.

U.S. Department of Transportation. 2000. *Comprehensive Truck Size & Weight Study*. Washington, DC: U.S. Department of Transportation.

# Appendix

*Table 5.A1* Data and Sources

| Name | Explanation | Source |
|------|-------------|--------|
| Commodity | NAICS Industry | Standard NAICS Classification |
| Year | Calendar Year | |
| Trucktm | Truck Ton-miles | CFS (1997, 2002, 2007)—Column G |
| Truckp | Truck Price | BLS PPI Series PCU4841212 |
| Railtm | Rail Ton-miles | CFS (1997, 2002, 2007)—Column G |
| Railp | Rail Price | BLS PPI Series PCU4821111 |
| IM_TM | Intermodal Ton-miles | CFS (1997, 2002, 2007)—Column G |
| Employ | Number of Employees | Economic Census (1997, 2002, 2007) American Fact Finder Spreadsheet |
| Payroll | Annual Payroll | Economic Census (1997, 2002, 2007) American Fact Finder Spreadsheet |
| Mat | Materials | Economic Census (1997, 2002, 2007) American Fact Finder Spreadsheet |
| ASM_VOS | Value of Shipments | Economic Census (1997, 2002, 2007) American Fact Finder Spreadsheet |
| Cap_s | Capital Stock | Economic Census (1997, 2002, 2007) American Fact Finder Spreadsheet |
| PPI82 | 1982 Producer Price Index | Economic Report of President B-67 |

# Section III

# The Structure of the Rail Industry

# 6 Restructuring Rail Systems
## Implications for Network Quality and Welfare

*David Besanko*

## Introduction

Over the last three decades, many countries around the world have either privatized formerly state-owned railway systems (e.g., the United Kingdom), or they have significantly deregulated those systems (e.g., the United States). These initiatives have almost always involved an immediate or eventual restructuring of how those systems are organized. Policymakers have adopted two broad approaches to restructuring: horizontal separation (HS) and vertical separation (VS). HS involves what Pittman (2011) calls *systems competition*. Under this approach, a national-level rail system is divided up into several vertically integrated networks that are unregulated and establish rail rates through competition. VS, by contrast, involves what Pittman (2011) calls *components competition*. Under this model, services thought to be inherently competitive are "unbundled" from other activities in the vertical chain considered to be natural monopolies. In the case of rail, this is implemented by separating the management of "below-the-rail" network infrastructure (track, signals and communications, stations, yards, and intermodal facilities) from "above-the-rail" transportation services, with the former being entrusted to a monopoly from and the latter being provided by multiple operators who are given open access to the network. In most (though not all) implementations of VS, the access tariff charged by the monopoly network company is regulated, whereas transport rates are determined through competition among rail transport operators. Although several forms of VS exist—including where the network firm has a downstream subsidiary that competes with independent transport operators, a model Pittman (2005) refers to as *vertical access*—our focus here is on full separation in which the network firm cannot also provide transport services.

Freight rail service in the United States and Mexico offers quintessential examples of HS. In the United States, two vertically integrated Class I railroads (Norfolk Southern and CSX) compete with each other for traffic in the eastern part of the United States, whereas two other vertically integrated Class I railroads (BNSF and Union Pacific) compete in the western United States.[1] This structure was not *directly* created by U.S. policymakers; instead, it evolved over two decades. But this evolution was very much facilitated by policymakers, for example, through the system design choices embodied in the 3R Act of 1974, the deregulation of railway rates under the Staggers Act of 1980, and merger enforcement in the post-Staggers Act period (Gallamore and Meyer, 2014).

Mexico's freight rail system evolved more quickly toward HS.[2] Starting in the 1930s, Mexico's rail system was run by a state-owned enterprise Ferrocarriles Nacionales de Mexico (FNM), which was directed by the country's transport ministry, Secretaria de Comunicaciones y Transportes (SCT). FNM was restructured in 1995 by dividing it into three regional rail systems, each emanating from Mexico City. The assets associated with each of these systems were sold to three private sector companies that were granted 50-year concessions, giving them wide latitude to expand their systems by building new lines.[3] Like FNM, these regional rail systems were vertically integrated. Following privatization, the SCT maintained responsibility for oversight of the railroads, but those regulatory responsibilities were largely confined to adjudicating disputes among the concessionaires. In particular, SCT did not regulate prices which were instead set by the rail systems themselves. Though Mexico's freight railways serve different geographies and thus engage in only a limited measure of parallel competition, they still discipline each other on price through source competition.[4]

VS is widely used in other infrastructure industries—think of air service or cargo shipping, for example, where airports and seaports are separated from the transport services—but it is less common in rail, especially freight. The best examples of VS in freight service are found in Europe. In 1991, the European Union (E.U.) issued directive 91/440, which permitted independent rail companies to apply for operating access over railroads within E.U. countries. That and subsequent directives, such as the First Railway Package of 2001, put the European Union on a path toward an approach to railway restructuring that entailed separation of network management and transport operation, which, in turn, has led a number of European countries, including the United Kingdom, Netherlands, Sweden, and Denmark to adopt the VS model in freight operations. For example, in the 1993 Railways Act, Britain privatized its rail services, creating in the process a network firm, originally called Railtrack and now called Network Rail. Network Rail owns the rail infrastructure in the United Kingdom and is responsible for maintaining and dispatching trains over about 20,000 miles of track comprising eight different routes in England, Wales, and Scotland (National Audit Office, 2015). There are currently four freight rail operating companies: Direct Rail Services, Freightliner, GB Railfreight, and DB Cargo UK. These companies pay access charges to Network Rail, and these access charges (as well as general policies toward access) are regulated by the Office of Rail and Road. Access prices take the form of track usage charges and capacity charges, both of which vary based on mileage, weight, and type of freight. (Passenger train operators also pay a fixed annual fee that is independent of how much the operator uses the network.) In addition, freight and passenger train operators receive penalty payments from Network Rail if it cannot provide access to a train that is running on schedule (e.g., due to track or signaling problems), and train operators may pay penalties to Network Rail if their train blocks access to a line or station (e.g., due to a mechanical problem). About 27% of Network Rail's revenues in the early 2010s came from access charges paid by the independent freight and passenger train operating companies, with most of the rest coming from subsidies from the government (Office of Rail and Road, 2013).

Another example of VS is found in the Netherlands, where restructuring began in the late 1990s and was largely completed by 2002.[5] The entity responsible for infrastructure management is a state-owned enterprise ProRail. Eight independent freight rail operators compete over ProRail's tracks. However, one of these firms—DB Cargo, formerly the freight subsidiary of the state-owned railway that existed prior to reform—dominates the market with a market share that has remained well over 50% since restructuring. In contrast to the United Kingdom in which Network Rail's access charges are determined through a conventional regulatory process, access prices in the Netherlands are directly determined by ProRail. These prices are monitored by the Authority for Consumers and Markets (ACM), a division within the Netherlands' Competition Authority, whose primary role is to ensure nondiscriminatory access to the network.

We can see from these examples that while HS and VS each have a variety of possible implementations, the differences between the two as organizing principles for restructuring a country's railway sector are stark. HS relies on there being at least workable competition between railways systems to hold down transport rates, whereas VS relies on open access to the system breaking down entry barriers into the "above-the-rail" portion of the value chain and creating price competition among train operators. HS banks on the ability of vertical integration to achieve economies of scope between infrastructure management and transport operation, whereas VS relies on a combination regulation and negotiation between the rail network firm and transport operators to achieve the needed coordination that underlies these economies. Investment incentives under HS arises from the ability of the vertically integrated firms to achieve rates of return on investments in excess of the cost of capital, which, of course, depend on the price-cost margins that arise under competition between systems. By contrast, investment incentives under VS depend on the margin between access price and marginal cost realized by the network firm, which in many implementations of VS depends on the tariffs that emerge through the regulatory process.

In light of these differences, it is perhaps not surprising that is no consensus among policymakers and practitioners in the railway industry, nor among economists, on the optimal structure of a railway system (Drew, 2009). Academic research on optimal system structure is ambiguous, and the literature has discussed advantages and disadvantages of each model (Pittman, 2011).

An advantage of HS is that it maintains economies of scope between transportation operations and infrastructure management, thus enhancing technical efficiency and productivity as compared with vertical separation (Ivaldi and McCullough, 2008; Growitsch and Wetzel, 2009; Sánchez et al., 2008; Pittman, 2011). In addition, the HS model may be beneficial for attracting private investment capital (Pittman, 2011). On the other hand, HS compromises economies of system size (Bitzan, 2003; Pittman, 2011), and it might leave some rail customers with no competition (TERI, 2009).

An advantage of VS is that it is explicitly designed to foster competition among independent transport providers. Ideally, VS would offer nondiscriminatory access to the network by qualified operators and would prevent the infrastructure provider from discriminating in favor of any particular operator. The most optimistic version of this argument would be that VS creates the potential for a rail market to become perfectly competitive, or at least, perfectly contestable. A disadvantage of VS is that it elevates the transaction costs of negotiating and enforcing contracts between the network firm and transport operators (Nash, 2008). In addition, VS may result in higher operating costs, poorer performance, or a greater number of accidents due to foregone economies of vertical integration (Bitzan, 2003; Pittman, 2005) or to misalignment of incentives between the network firm and transport operators (Nash et al., 2014). There is evidence that VS increased operating costs in the European Union, with the largest increases for systems with the highest traffic densities and the highest proportion of freight traffic (Nash et al. 2014).

Though extremely informative, the existing literature leaves some fundamental questions unresolved. What are the implications of each approach for the quality of rail infrastructure? And under what conditions would we expect one approach to dominate the other with respect to consumer surplus and social welfare (i.e., consumer surplus plus producer surplus)? This chapter develops a conceptual framework for identifying the impact of HS and VS on network quality, consumer surplus, and social welfare. The framework is based on the theoretical analysis in Besanko and Cui (2016). It starts from the recognition that these two structures create different incentives for pricing rail transport services and for investing in network quality. We argue that there is strong reason to conclude that HS creates stronger incentives for investing in network quality than VS. These superior incentives for quality tend to give HS an advantage in generating higher levels of consumer and social welfare. We further argue, though, that there can be circumstances under which VS generates higher consumer and social welfare despite its disadvantage in encouraging investment in infrastructure quality. Broadly, the comparison between VS and HS often involves a trade-off: lower infrastructure quality but lower prices under VS and higher quality but higher prices under HS. If network quality is deemed to be particularly important, HS would usually be the preferred choice. Overall, the "best case" for HS from a social welfare perspective occurs when the existing state-owned railway can be divided into rail systems with just enough horizontal differentiation between them to lead to modest, but not cutthroat, competition. The best case for VS is when (1) consumers care primarily about price, and the regulator can ensure uniform service offerings by competing firms each of whom has open access to the entire network and (2) the system under HS would involve so few opportunities for parallel or source competition that price and quality rivalry between systems was very soft. We argue that achieving this best-case outcome would place strong demands on a country's regulatory capacity. Moreover, it might be inconsistent with the cost economics of freight rail service.

Though many countries have already restructured their freight rail networks over the last three decades, some have not. The most notable example of a country that has yet to undertake a major, market-oriented reorganization of its freight rail system is China. The framework developed in this chapter has implications for how China should undertake railway reform. In particular, our framework leads us to conclusions that are in accord with Pittman's (2004, 2011) analyses of options for Chinese railway restructuring: China would be best served by adopting HS as the organizing principle for a privatized rail system, with the independent rail systems being organized largely along geographic lines. We suggest that VS would be an inferior model because it would require a capacity for regulation that China currently does not have.

We organize this chapter in six additional sections. The second section develops the conceptual framework for thinking through the impact of HS and VS on market competition, incentives to invest in network quality, consumer welfare, and social welfare. The third section discusses the how cost and demand fundamentals shape market structure, conduct, and performance under HS and VS, and the fourth section explains how quality and pricing incentives under HS and VS differ and how these differences affect market performance. The fifth section uses the insights of the two preceding sections to identify circumstances under which one restructuring approach is likely to enjoy a comparative advantage over the other with respect to our three focal performance metrics. In the sixth section, we apply the conclusions in this section to provide insight into railway restructuring in China. The seventh section summarizes and concludes.

## Conceptual Framework

To build intuition about the economic implications of VS and HS, we use the conceptual framework summarized in Figure 6.1. The framework is grounded in the structure-conduct-performance paradigm from industrial economics, with the analysis of conduct and performance informed by the formal model of rail competition and regulation in Besanko and Cui (2016). Any framework necessarily abstracts from real-life complexity, but the advantage of ours, we believe, is that it focuses attention on the key considerations that would lead to different outcomes under VS and HS.

Under VS, a natural monopoly network firm is assumed to operate and maintain the rail infrastructure, and independent rail operating companies (ROCs) compete with each other in the downstream rail transport market. ROCs incur *transport costs*—for example, operating trains, maintaining motive power, and rolling stock—while the network firm incurs *network costs*—for example, maintaining roadbed and track and operating network facilities such as rail yards. (Thus, in what follows, *marginal transport cost* refers to the additional transport cost from an additional ton-mile of freight, and *marginal network cost* refers to the additional cost of network operations from an additional ton-mile of freight on the network.) The Besanko and Cui (2016) model does not endogenize the number of ROCs, but we argue ahead that it is unlikely the transport market under VS would be perfectly competitive or contestable. The ROCs are thus treated as oligopolistic price setters, offering services that buyers see as potentially differentiated. The access tariff that the ROCs pay to the network firm is assumed to be set by a regulator, as in the United Kingdom and many other countries that employ VS. Though a number of pricing mechanisms are used in practice, a common one is a two-part tariff consisting of a variable access charge based on how intensively a given ROC uses the system, plus a fixed charge that is independent of usage (Vidaud and de Tilière, 2010).[6] To best identify the potential for VS to serve the public interest, we think of the regulator as benevolently setting the access tariff to maximize social welfare.[7]

Under HS, several vertically integrated rail systems (VISs) own rail infrastructure and also provide transport services on their own networks. Consistent with observed practice, we assume that the move to HS results in the creation of only a few systems. As with VS, then, the systems under HS are assumed to engage in oligopolistic competition.

We envision the quality of the rail infrastructure as being determined by investments to enhance quality undertaken by the parties responsible for the network: the network firm under VS and the VISs under HS. Quality should be interpreted broadly. It includes characteristics of the railway that enhance the transport experience of end-customers (e.g., speed of shipment, reliability, safety). Network quality could, therefore, arise out of the level and nature of investments in "hard assets" such as signaling and communications systems, as well as from investments in track and yard capacity. It could also be influenced by decisions that determine network management and upkeep, such dispatching protocols and maintenance routines. In short, enhancing network quality includes increases in the amount of infrastructure capacity, its performance capabilities, and its sophistication.

The quality-enhancing investments in our framework should be interpreted as additions to quality that go beyond minimum quality standards mandated by a regulatory authority that can monitor compliance. Consistent with Laffont and Tirole (1993, Chapter 4) and Buehler et al. (2004), quality upgrades beyond minimum standards are assumed to be unverifiable, and thus regulatory authorities cannot dictate their levels under HS or VS. While some aspects of network quality may, indeed, be verifiable (e.g., the radii of track curves), other aspects of quality may be difficult to verify. For example, the level and nature of day-to-day maintenance of substructure, track, and communications systems carried out by the network operator is considered a critical determinant of rail network quality in both the short run and long run (European Commission, 2013), but it is typically carried out by local "on-the ground" personnel whose actions would be very costly, if not altogether infeasible, for a regulator to verify.

To think systematically about pricing and investment decisions, we conceptualize this conduct under VS as unfolding in three stages and under HS in two stages (see Figure 6.1). Under VS, the regulator commits to an access tariff. The network firm then chooses a level of investment to improve the quality of the network inherited from the state-owned system.

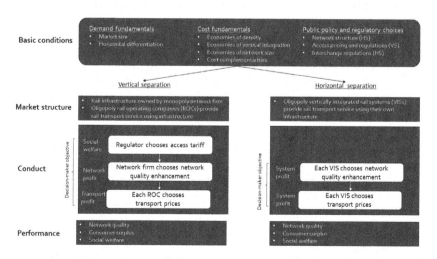

*Figure 6.1* Order of Decision-Making under VS and HS

It does so to maximize network profit—revenues from access tariffs minus costs of operating the network minus the investment costs incurred to enhance network quality. Finally, the ROCs, taking both quality and the access tariff as given, compete in the downstream rail transport market by setting transport rates to maximize transportation profits—revenues from transport services minus the cost of transport operations minus the cost of network access.

Under HS, each VIS is responsible for determining the quality of its own network through quality-enhancing investments. These investment decisions are made competitively and are aimed at maximizing overall system profit—revenues from transport services minus the cost of network operations and transport operations minus the investment cost incurred to enhance network quality. Given those investments, the VISs compete in the downstream transport market by setting transport prices.[8]

Imagining that the conduct of decision makers unfolds in stages is, to be sure, an abstraction, but it reflects an important difference between investment and pricing decisions. Transport prices are almost certainly more flexible than changes in infrastructure quality (Haucap and Klein, 2012), so it would be natural for transport operators to make pricing decisions taking infrastructure quality as given, whereas investment choices would be made with an eye toward how those choices subsequently affected prices. The assumption that under VS the regulator "moves first" resumes that the regulator can commit to an access tariff and will not, after the fact, engage in opportunistic behavior by changing the access tariff once the network firm has invested in network quality. This is a strong assumption, though not completely implausible. In the United Kingdom, for example, rail access charges are established for five-year periods, and they reflect efficiency targets that the Office of Rail and Road establishes during the mandatory review prior to the end of each five-year period.

It is important to emphasize that even though we endow the social welfare-maximizing regulator with strong commitment ability, this *does not* imply that the outcome under VS will be the first-best welfare optimum. The regulator directly controls neither the downstream transport prices nor the network firm's unverifiable quality investment. The best it can do is to use its ability to regulate the access tariff to indirectly affect these outcomes.

We will use the framework in Figure 6.1 to assess systematically how the choice of HS and VS affects consumer surplus and social welfare. These performance metrics are shaped by three distinct mechanisms, summarized in Figure 6.2:

- The direct effect of demand and cost fundamentals.
- The equilibrium effect of demand and cost fundamentals.
- The equilibrium effect of structural incentives for pricing and network quality.

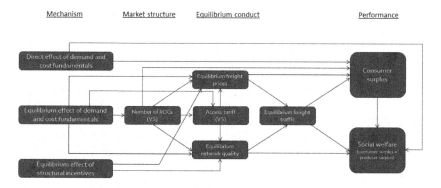

*Figure 6.2* Framework for Assessing How the Choice of HS and VS Affects Rail Market Conduct and Performance

Demand and cost fundamentals can have *direct effect* that could favor one restructuring approach over the other. For example, economies of vertical integration would imply that, all things equal, the total cost of transport operations plus infrastructure management should be lower under HS. Demand and cost fundamentals can also have *equilibrium effects*, on either conduct or the market structure that shapes conduct. For example, the two restructuring approaches will probably give rise to different substitution opportunities for shippers, affecting perceived differentiation between competing rail firms, and leading to different equilibrium conduct and performance. As another example, the cost economics of freight rail are likely to affect how many ROCs would compete in the transport market under VS, which affects equilibrium prices and network quality and, in turn, helps determine how VS performs relative to HS with respect to consumer surplus and social welfare. Finally, HS and VS will lead rail firms to internalize the effect of their pricing and investment decisions in ways that give rise to different *structural incentives*. Differences in structural incentives would lead to different equilibrium investment and pricing outcomes under HS and VS even if there were no differences in demand and cost fundamentals.

## An Example

To illustrate these points concretely, we present a stripped-down example based on the model in Besanko and Cui (2016). This example makes several simplifying assumptions:

- The structure of the transport market is the same under VS and HS: two ROCs under VS and two VISs under HS (referred to, in each case, as firms 1 and 2).

- Demand fundamentals are the same under VS and HS, and competing firms under both approaches face symmetric demand functions:

$$X_1\left(P_1,P_2,q_1,q_2\right)=1+2q_1-q_2-2P_1+P_2$$
$$X_2\left(P_1,P_2,q_1,q_2\right)=1-q_1+2q_2+P_1-2P_2$$

where $q_1$ and $q_2$ denote the investment in network quality enhancement by each firm, $P_1$ and $P_2$ denote freight prices, and $X_1$ and $X_2$ are the quantities of transport services demanded. These demand functions reflect that transport providers are differentiated from one another to a certain extent: if one operator raises its price, it does not lose all its business to the other operator, nor can an operator steal all its rival's business by undercutting its price. This example also assumes that a higher level of network quality increases traffic on the network that improves quality while decreasing traffic on the rival network.
- There are no fixed costs of transport operations, and total variable costs are a linear function of freight traffic. Thus, there are no economies of density.[9]
- The variable costs of network operations are zero. The total fixed cost of network operations for a VIS when its investment in network quality is $q$ is $f+\frac{1}{2}q^2$, whereas under VS, the total fixed cost of the network firm is $2f+q^2$, where $f$ is the baseline network cost with no quality enhancement. Thus, there are no economies of network size.
- The only difference between the two structures is that there are economies of vertical integration, so that for any given quantity $X$ of freight shipped over the system, total cost is lower under HS than under VS, that is, $\gamma_H X<\gamma_V X$, or equivalently, $\gamma_H<\gamma_V$, where the subscripts $_V$ and $_H$ refer to VS and HS.[10]

This example, as stripped down (and unrealistic) as it is, shows how HS and VS can give rise to dramatically different outcomes, and in so doing, it illustrates the three mechanisms in Figure 6.2. Table 6.1 shows the equilibrium prices, network qualities, quantities, and social welfare arising under VS and HS.[11]

- The last line of the table highlights the *direct effect* of economies of vertical integration. *If* prices, quantities, and network qualities were the same across HS and VS, HS would still have a higher social welfare because $\gamma_H<\gamma_V$.
- The expression for equilibrium price highlights the *equilibrium effect* of economies of vertical integration. By making marginal cost of transport under HS lower than it would be under VS, economies of vertical integration serve as a force for a lower equilibrium price

and a higher equilibrium quantity under HS, which, in turn, works to make consumer surplus and social welfare higher under HS.

- The difference in the expressions for network quality in the third row of the table are the result of differences in the equilibrium effect of *structural incentives in quality choice* across the two structures. In this example, these differences work to make network quality higher under HS than VS, which, in turn, contributes to equilibrium quantity, consumer surplus, and social welfare being higher under HS as well.
- The differences in the expressions for equilibrium prices also reflects differences across the two approaches in the equilibrium effect of *structural incentives for pricing*. If we "zero out" economies of vertical integration and economies of network size, and if we also imagine that quality is the same under HS and VS, that is, $q_H^* = q_v^*$, we see that equilibrium price under VS differs from that under HS. In this case, the regulator finds it optimal to set a variable access charge that is less than the marginal cost of access.[12] This "reverse" double marginalization works to lower the transport price under VS and increase quantity, working in turn to increase consumer surplus and social welfare.

*Table 6.1* Equilibrium Outcomes under Vertical and Horizontal Separation in a Simple Example

|  | HS | VS |
|---|---|---|
| Price | $P_H^* = \dfrac{1}{3}\left(1 + q_H^*\right) + \dfrac{2}{3}\gamma_H$ | $P_V^* = \dfrac{1}{3}\left(1 + q_V^*\right)$ $+ \dfrac{2}{3}\left(\gamma_V + c_V^*\right)$ |
| Network Quality Enhancement | $q_H^* = \dfrac{28\left(1 - \gamma_H\right)}{17}$ | $q_V^* = 0$ |
| Variable Access Charge | implicitly 0 | $c_V^* = -\dfrac{1}{2}\left(1 - \gamma_V\right)$ |
| Quantity | $X_H^* = \dfrac{30}{17}\left(1 - \gamma_H\right)$ | $X_V^* = 1 - \gamma_V$ |
| Consumer Surplus | $CS_H^* = \left(X_H^*\right)^2$ | $CS_V^* = \left(X_V^*\right)^2$ |
| Social Welfare | $SW_H^* = CS_H^* + 2\left(P_H^* - \gamma_H\right)$ $X_H^* - \left(q_H^*\right)^2 - 2f$ | $SW_V^* = CS_V^* + 2\left(P_V^* - \gamma_V\right)$ $X_V^* - \left(q_V^*\right)^2 - 2f$ |

Ultimately in this example, HS results in not only more network quality enhancement (as can be seen in Table 6.1) but also higher consumer surplus and social welfare, even when are no economies of vertical integration.[13] But the key point of the example is not that HS always dominates VS but rather that a comparison between the two approaches on our performance metrics reflects a set of cross-cutting factors whose effect are important to isolate in order to help clarify the circumstances under which one restructuring approach would perform better than the other on our metrics of interest.

## Basic Conditions

Let us now take a deeper look at the basic conditions that could shape differences in market structure, conduct, and performance under HS and VS. We begin with demand fundamentals that could have direct or equilibrium effect and then turn to cost fundamentals.

### Demand Fundamentals

#### Market Size

Restructuring a state-owned rail system is largely about organizing a system through which competition can unfold so that the restructured system delivers benefits to customers while allowing rail firms to cover operating costs and earn adequate returns on their investments. Sufficiently large market size makes investments in network quality more lucrative, either by VISs under HS or the network firm under VS. But in our framework market size *per se* does not create a comparative advantage for either HS and VS. It is a background force that effect the level of profitability of each approach but not their relative profitability.

#### Horizontal Differentiation

Our framework assumes that the ROCs under VS and the VISs under HS behave non-cooperatively, but this does not necessarily mean that profits will be competed away entirely. Prices and profits under oligopoly competition are shaped by the extent of market power firms enjoy. A key determinant of an oligopoly firm's market power is the horizontal differentiation between it and its rivals.

Horizontal differentiation is the degree to which consumers perceive the offers of competing sellers to be imperfect substitutes.[14] Horizontal differentiation in a market depends on the extent to which consumers' preferences for tangible or intangible elements of rival firms' offers are positively associated or in "disagreement." In rail, a key dimension of a carrier's offer to consumers is the geographic location of its rail lines and switching facilities in comparison to rival carriers. One shipper, who is located directly along railroad *A* but is farther away from railroad *B* will find railroad *A*'s offer more attractive than railroad *B*'s (barring any other significant differences in their offers).[15] Another shipper who is geographically closer to railroad *B* than *A* will have the reverse preferences. (Hence, they "disagree.") But geography is not the only factor that can lead to differences in how consumers evaluate rival offers. Another key dimension of rail carriers' offers in the extent to which they specialize in certain types of freight. A coal shipper might prefer a railroad with a specialty in coal shipping to one that occupies in a niche in container shipping because the former may have more hopper car capacity on hand at a moment's notice than the latter. A manufacturing firm or a large retailer that does large volumes of container shipping would probably have reverse preferences. Consumers can also have idiosyncratic preferences, seemingly unrelated to the tangible elements of firms' offers, that drive purchase decisions. One potential source of idiosyncratic preferences would be real or perceived switching costs that arise due to different consumers' histories with different carriers. For example, it may be easier to update shipping contracts with one's existing carrier than it would be to contract with a new supplier, making it worthwhile not to switch even in return for a somewhat lower price. Even if the tangible dimensions of the offers of competing rail carriers are evaluated in the same way by different shippers, the presence of idiosyncratic preferences can lead consumers to view seemingly identical rail services as imperfect substitutes.

To the extent that a market consists of many consumers who disagree about the geographic or product-based attractiveness of different rail carriers' offers, the market will consist of a relatively large number of "loyalists"—those who tend to use one particular carrier whatever the price differences among carriers might be—and a relatively smaller number of "switchers"—those who view rival carriers' offers as equivalent and choose on the basis of price. In markets with a strong correlation of shippers' preferences over rival carriers' offers, we would, by contrast, expect more switchers and fewer loyalists.

Horizontal differentiation is reflected in demand behavior in two related ways: the cross-price elasticities of demand between pairs of competing firms and the own-price elasticities of demand of individual firms. When horizontal differentiation is weak and most consumers see competing firms as offering very comparable service, cross-price elasticities of competitors will be positive and own-price elasticities will be highly negative. When horizontal differentiation is strong, cross-price elasticities will be close to zero and own-price elasticities will be small in absolute value. In the latter case, each firm will effectively have significant market power. When horizontal differentiation is weak, on the other hand, a firm enjoys very little market power, since even small increases in its price above the levels charged by rival firms would result in a large loss of volume.

One might expect that horizontal differentiation in freight rail markets would generally be quite weak. After all, purchasers are businesses that would have strong incentives to hold down their costs. These customers would be expected to be very knowledgeable about the prices charged by competing railroads, and they would be motivated to search for the carrier offering the lowest rate. That is, we might expect most freight rail customers to be switchers rather than loyalists.

As part of a study of the welfare effect of rail mergers Ivaldi and McCullough (2005) use U.S. data from 1986 to 2001 to estimate demand functions for three freight rail categories—bulk, intermodal, and general freight service—and their demand specification allows identification of the degree to which shippers preferences for individual railroads are correlated. They find a very high degree of preference correlation across rail firms in bulk and intermodal and more preference disagreement in general freight service. Bulk and intermodal service evidence weak horizontal differentiation, whereas general freight service in the United States appears to exhibit moderate horizontal differentiation.

What is interesting and important, is that the degree of horizontal differentiation in a restructured rail system will be endogenous to the choice of HS and VS. In its most ideal implementation, VS would be an arrangement in which every customer who could potentially use the rail system can purchase transportation services from every ROC who has rights to operate trains on the system. This is the way VS operates in the United Kingdom. Shippers send out requests for bids from some or all of the freight operating companies, who respond with quotations of price and service terms. In theory, this would suggest that VS should entail virtually no horizontal differentiation, as every customer is potentially a switcher. In practice, however, this is probably not the case. Some degree of "loyalty" among customers may exist due to switching costs. For example, in the United Kingdom, shipping contracts tend to be of long duration, often two or more years in length (OECD, 2013), so it is conceivable that nontrivial transactions costs exist. In addition, though business customers are likely to be oriented *primarily* toward price and service terms that could be easily matched by competitors, they may not be driven *entirely* by these considerations. In countries that have adopted VS, some ROCs have been around longer than others, and it is conceivable that this longevity could translate into a modicum of idiosyncratic brand loyalty that makes at least some customers loyalists rather than switchers. Perhaps more important, some ROC entrants into a vertically separated system may choose to occupy specialized niches, perhaps defined by geography or product type or both. For example, the account of Romania's experience with VS in freight railways by Pittman et al. (2007) points out that a number of new entrants were large shippers who backward integrated into rail transport, initially to haul their own freight but later serving others (e.g., Rompetrol Logistics began hauling its refinery output and later expanded into shipping both refinery outputs and inputs to and from ports). If a vertically separated system allocates portions of the network to ROCs on the basis of geography, we could simply have geographic-based horizontal differentiation in a different guise. Imperfect access regulation (or good regulation but with imperfect enforcement) could also give some ROCs under VS an advantage in serving certain customers, effectively creating more loyalists and fewer switchers. Thus, although there is a presumption that VS would be associated with a low degree of horizontal differentiation, there is no guarantee it will.

The interaction of HS and horizontal differentiation is potentially even more interesting. To the extent that horizontal differentiation in freight rail services is largely geography based, then the degree of horizontal differentiation under HS depends on how the system is designed. For example, consider the situation depicted in Figure 6.3. A country consisting of one large city, point $A$, and two smaller cities, $B$ and $C$, has a state-run monopoly rail system consisting of four main lines emanating from $A$. Two lines go northward, and two other lines go southward. If HS is implemented by creating two private firms that operate largely parallel systems, as in the left-hand panel, then most shippers will have a choice of railroads. We would expect a relatively small number of loyalists and a relatively high number of switchers. If, instead, HS was implemented regionally, with one private firm given the northern network and the other firm given the southern network as in the right-hand panel, then the number of loyalists would likely be larger. For example, a firm located at $C$ that ships freight to $A$ would have just a single choice, $VIS_2$. However, there

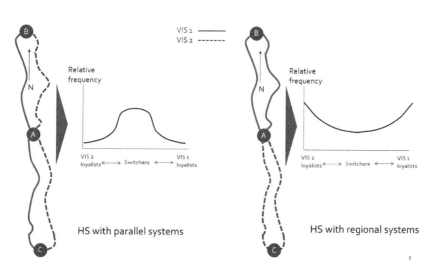

*Figure 6.3* Alternative Implementations of HS and Implications for Horizontal Differentiation

could still be switchers if source competition between the rail lines were possible. For example, some firms at *A* may have a choice between sourcing an input from *B* rather than *C*. Thus, even geographically separated implementations of HS could result in rail demand that characterized by less-than-perfect horizontal differentiation, depending on the distribution of economic activity around the country and the ultimate destinations of the goods and services shipped by rail.

### Horizontal Differentiation and Price Competition

Figure 6.4 illustrates how horizontal differentiation affects oligopolistic price competition. In the left-hand diagram, the curve $R_1$ shows the profit-maximizing price of one firm given the possible prices that could be charged by a competing firm; $R_2$ shows the profit-maximizing price for firm 2 given possible prices of firm 1. Each of these reaction functions is upward sloping. This reflects that if a firm's competitor charges a higher price, the firm has more "room" to raise its own price. The predicted equilibrium outcome is the point at which the two reaction functions cross. The middle diagram shows what happens when we keep all demand and cost fundamentals the same but weaken the degree of product differentiation. Each firm's reaction function becomes more sensitive to its rival's price, and the curves twist leftward and downward so that the equilibrium price falls. The right-hand diagram shows what happens when there is complete horizontal differentiation: the reaction functions become horizontal and vertical lines, indicating that each firm's profit-maximizing price is independent of the other firm's price. The absence of effective competition in this case enables each firm to charge its monopoly price.

These figures illustrate that, holding all else equal, the restructuring approach that results in a market with the weaker horizontal differentiation will have lower equilibrium prices, higher consumer surplus, and higher social welfare.

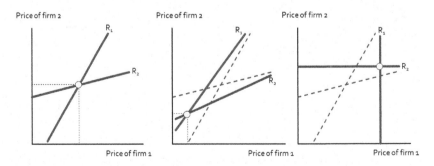

*Figure 6.4* Reaction Functions and Horizontal Differentiation

*Horizontal Differentiation, the Number of Competitors*
*under vs, and Intermodal Competition*

While a desire to exploit economies of network size, combined with geographic constraints, would be expected to limit the number of competing VISs under HS, under VS there could, in theory, be a large number of competing ROCs. In standard theories of oligopolistic competition with horizontally differentiated products (e.g., Besanko et al., 1990), an increase in the number of competitors has the same effect on price competition as weakening horizontal differentiation among a fixed number of firms. If an initial number of incumbent ROCs occupied market niches that give rise to horizontal differentiation, entry of additional ROCs would encroach upon some of these niches. Firm-level demand would, as a result, become more price elastic, intensifying price competition and lowering equilibrium prices. In addition to the lower prices brought about by more competitors, consumers also benefit from expanded service variety: with more ROCs, it is more likely that any given shipper can find an ROC whose offer matches the shipper's specific needs.

Intermodal competition would have the same directional effect on price competition as more competitors, but it would probably be more muted because rail and competing modes such as truck and barge would often be less perfect substitutes than two rail firms operating on the same network. But it does not necessarily follow that intermodal competition would confer an *advantage* on VS relative to HS because intermodal competition would also make price competition under HS more vigorous than it would be without such competition. We return to this point ahead.

### Cost Fundamentals

*Economies of Density in Freight Operations and Sunk*
*Entry Costs into Rail Transport Operations*

There is a large body of evidence from data spanning from the 1950s to the 1990s suggesting that railroad operations exhibit economies of density (e.g., Harris, 1977; Caves et al., 1981; Braeutigam et al., 1982; Wilson, 1997; Ivaldi and McCullough, 2001).[16] Economies of density in railroads are often thought to arise from the spreading out of volume-insensitive infrastructure costs over larger output. However, Ivaldi and McCullough (2001) present evidence of economies of density that are due not to high volume-insensitive costs of network operations but to total variable costs of transport operations that increase less than proportionately with volume. This suggests that economies of density could still arise in transport operations even if transportation operations and network operations are vertically separated.

As just discussed, an important potential source of advantage of VS over HS would be the ability of a vertically separated system to attract numerous ROCs into the downstream transport market. The presence of economies of density in freight train operations calls this source of advantage into question. Such economies would limit the number of competitors that could viably participate in the market under VS.

Of course, the presence of economies of density would not, *by itself*, preclude vigorous price competition under VS. After all, the market for freight transport could still be contestable, with the threat of entry of new ROCs serving to hold in check any effort by incumbent ROCs to exercise market power. However, the provision of transport operation almost certainly involves non-negligible sunk entry costs, weakening the threat of entry needed to discipline incumbent operators (Dyrhauge, 2013). It may seem surprising that ROCs would face sunk entry costs; after all, much of the equipment used by freight operators would seem to be general purpose and could presumably be redeployed if entry into a given market turned out to be unprofitable. However, in addition to the nontrivial legal and administrative costs involved in obtaining operating licenses and safety certifications, new ROC entrants would likely be faced with the need to make locomotives and rolling stock conform to the operating standards of the network firm. For example, operators may need to install automatic train control systems that are specific to the infrastructure. Moreover, the network may operate a track gauge that is incompatible with the gauges used in other geographies to which locomotives and freight cars could conceivably be redeployed if profitable operation proved to be elusive.

In practice, European countries that have adopted VS in freight transportation have struggled with ensuring sufficient numbers of ROCs. In the Netherlands, for example, though multiple ROCs offered service over ProRail's tracks infrastructure in the mid-2000s, one of these firms (DB Cargo) dominates the market, accounting for 60% of the market in the early 2010s (Scordamaglia and Katsarova, 2016). Part of the reason may be that because DB Cargo traces its roots to the freight division of the old state-run rail system, it may enjoy the benefits of loyalties that reside in long-standing relationships with customers. In addition, not every Dutch ROC serves the entire market; some choose to operate within specific niches. For example, KombiRail focuses on intermodal traffic between the port of Rotterdam and the Ruhr area in Germany.[17] The combination of brand loyalties and occupation of market niches would have the effect of increasing horizontal differentiation and softening price competition. Similar outcomes have occurred in other EU countries that have embraced VS. Figure 6.5, adapted from van de Velde et al. (2012), shows that in 2010, in 10 of 11 countries that had adopted VS, the market shares of new entrants in the freight rail market was less than 50%; only in Romania had new entrants managed to exceed more than half the market.

All of this suggests that neither a market structure with a large number of equally positioned competitors nor the threat of entry from identical potential entrants is likely to be a significant force in holding down prices

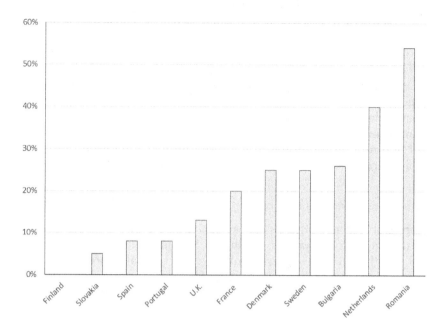

*Figure 6.5* Market Shares of New Entrants, Freight Markets, Selected Countries, 2010

Source: van de Velde et al. 2012

under VS.[18] Now this is not *necessarily* fatal. As Figure 6.4 illustrates, if horizontal differentiation is sufficiently weak, price competition between even two ROCs would be vigorous.

Still, this places a "heavy burden" on weak horizontal differentiation, and as argued earlier, there are reasons to worry that sufficiently weak horizontal differentiation would arise naturally. This, then, highlights that important policy choices under VS should be aimed at ensuring the offers of competing ROCs are seen by shippers as very close substitutes. At minimum, this requires that ROCs have nondiscriminatory access to the network. It may also require that regulators set standards of service that ensure that when there are just two or three ROCs, shippers view them as providing nearly identical offers. It also requires that the rail transport market be regularly monitored by competition authorities to ensure that incumbent firms do not engage in anticompetitive behavior.

But even if regulators are successful at engineering weak horizontal differentiation, if economies of density are strong enough, intense price competition between even two ROCs could result in each competitor failing to cover operating and capital costs. With non-negligible sunk entry costs, this would imply that the market would likely be dominated by a single firm. VS thus suffers from a problematic tension: intense competition in the market due to weak horizontal differentiation on the one hand, and economies of density on the other, may constitute a fundamentally incompatible package of conditions, which could make the promotion of sufficiently intense price competition among ROCs very difficult.

Under these conditions, intermodal competition might then become an important factor in making VS workable if it prevents a dominant ROC from exploiting its market power. In this respect, even though intermodal competition would not necessarily confer an advantage on VS relative to HS, it may serve to offset the disadvantage to VS that flows from the conjunction of economies of density and sunk entry costs.

## Economies of Vertical Integration

Empirical evidence suggests the presence of economies of vertical integration in railroad systems. Ivaldi and McCullough's (2008) study of U.S. freight railways suggests that a typical vertically integrated U.S. railroad over the period of their study (late 1970s to the early 2000s) would have had a 20% to 40% cost advantage over an otherwise identical vertically separated system. These economies are at least partly, if not largely, reflective of the coordination required between network operations and transport operations. For example, Pittman (2005) notes that although the point of contact between wheels and rails is only about the size of a dime, operating and maintenance decisions pertaining to rolling stock, such as the weight borne by freight car axles and the amount of lubrication received by wheels, has an enormous impact on the quality of the ride provided by the rails, and the condition of the rails has an impact on the wear and tear on the rolling stock. VS places any of these and other critical interfaces, such as capacity allocation, management of timetables, limits on train speeds and length, responsibility for security arrangements and emergency response, and investment planning, potentially up for negotiation. As Growitsch and Wetzel (2009) point out, these nexuses of coordination are information intensive, so it is not surprising that the transactions cost under VS would be quite large.

An interesting question is whether the cost advantage of a vertically integrated system not only takes the form of an advantage in *total costs* but also extends to an advantage in *marginal costs* of freight transport operations or network operations, or both. Ivaldi and McCullough's (2008) analysis suggests an affirmative answer; they found evidence of cost complementarities between infrastructure output and freight hauling output. This suggests that the sum of marginal transport cost and marginal network cost under HS would be lower than under VS. This would be a force working toward lower equilibrium prices under HS than VS, and, in turn, higher consumer surplus and social welfare under HS.

*Economies of Network Size*

Economies of network size (or, equivalently, increasing returns to scale) are present when a given percentage increase in both rail output and network size increase total costs by less than that percentage. *If* economies of network were present in freight rail systems, they would be a source of comparative advantage for VS for two reasons. First, holding constant total traffic volume and network size, the total cost of train operations and network management under VS would be less than the sum of the total costs of two VISs under HS.[19] Second, and perhaps more subtle, under empirically plausible conditions, the presence of economies of network size would make the *marginal* cost of improving the *quality* of the single network under VS less than the sum of the marginal costs of enhancing the qualities of each of the networks under HS.[20] The lower marginal cost of quality enhancement would be a force working to make equilibrium quality under VS higher than it would be under HS.

However, empirical work suggests that in railroad systems, economies of network size are slight or, if not, they are exhausted at a modest size compared with the scale of existing companies (Braeutigam, 1999; Savignat and Nash, 1999). For example, econometric evidence for U.S. railways suggests that the largest U.S. Class I railroads operate near the point at which they exhaust economies of network size (Bereskin, 2009). Thus, although economies of network size give VS a potential advantage over HS, at best that advantage is likely to be small.

*Cost Complementarities*

Cost complementarities are present when an increase in the volume of one type of rail service decreases the marginal cost of another. The presence of meaningful cost complementarities among freight services would be good news for VS, since it would suggest that it would be less likely ROCs would (in the absence of regulated service standards) occupy niches of the market by type of commodity, in turn eroding possible sources of horizontal differentiation between ROCs.

Early empirical studies found little evidence of cost complementarities in rail (see Braeutigam, 1999, for a summary). More recent studies have found evidence of positive cost complementarities. Ivaldi and McCullough (2001) report cost complementarities between general freight and intermodal service and between general freight and bulk service, but no significant cost complementarities between bulk and intermodal service.[21] Ivaldi and McCullough (2008) find cost complementarities between general freight and bulk service, where general freight includes intermodal service.

These complementarities seem to be rooted in general capabilities that railroads develop as they handle higher volumes of traffic of any type. If these capabilities are *not* bound up in the management of network infrastructure, the recent evidence would provide guarded optimism that VS would not be likely to result in ROCs that were specialized by commodity type (and perhaps, by extension, geography). But if these capabilities are tied to network operations such as scheduling or maintenance, then the associated cost complementarities might well disappear with a move from integration to separation. On balance, evidence about cost complementarities does not suggest a comparative disadvantage for VS, but it does not suggest an advantage either.

## Balance of Structural Incentives

Even if demand and cost fundamentals were identical under HS and VS, incentives for pricing and investment in network quality would not necessarily be the same. The two approaches to organizing a railway system differ in how key decision makers internalize the benefits and costs of improvements in infrastructure quality, which, in turn, affect the strength of incentives to invest in network quality. In addition, the vertically integrated systems under HS entail an implicit access charge equal to marginal network cost, whereas the variable access charge under VS will generally not equal marginal network cost, which could possibly exacerbate market power-based distortions in transport pricing or offset them. In what follows, we begin by discussing the three key differences between HS and VS in terms of investment incentives—the appropriability effect, the double marginalization on quality effect, and the coordination on quality effect. We then discuss how deviations of access prices from marginal network cost under VS might affect the performance of VS relative to HS with respect to consumer surplus and social welfare.

### The Appropriability Effect

Profit-maximizing network quality enhancement under VS occurs at the point at which the network firm's marginal benefit of quality enhancement equals the marginal cost of such enhancement. The condition is generically the same under HS, but because the VISs compete with each other, a firm's marginal benefit of quality enhancement also depends on rival firms' quality enhancements. Ignoring economies of network size that might lead to different marginal cost of quality schedules, differences in structural incentives for quality reside in differences in the marginal benefit schedules faced by the network firm and the VISs.

Better network quality has two potentially distinct effects: it could reduce the transport costs of freight operators (e.g., wear and tear on locomotives and rolling stock is reduced if higher quality materials are used to build roadbed and track), and it could increase the volume of transport demand at any price through the benefits higher quality confers on shippers (e.g., freight moves faster and safer on a network with sophisticated scheduling and congestion management capabilities). In this latter case—which will be our focus in the rest of this section—a key determinant of the extent to which firms can appropriate value from their investment is the margin between price and marginal cost.[22] This is because the additional volume stimulated by higher network quality increases the difference between revenue and total cost at a rate equal to the difference between price and marginal cost. The *appropriability effect* is the magnitude of the price-marginal cost margin.[23]

Under HS, the price-marginal cost margin is the difference between the price of freight transportation services charged by a VIS and the sum of its marginal transport and network costs, and it emerges from competition among the VISs. A system that creates parallel competition would have weaker horizontal differentiation, and thus lower price-marginal cost margins in equilibrium, than one that relies on more indirect source competition. In both cases, though, we would expect that price-marginal cost margins would be positive and perhaps even quite large.

Under VS, the price-marginal cost margin is the difference between the network firm's variable access charge and the marginal network cost, and it is determined through regulation of the access tariff. It is well understood that when a regulated monopolist faces a binding price ceiling, its profit-maximizing quality will be less than the socially efficient level and that setting the ceiling below the unregulated monopoly price would induce the monopolist to reduce its quality (Spence, 1975; Sappington, 2010). By increasing the variable access charge, the social welfare-maximizing regulator gives higher-power incentives for the network firm to invest in quality, ameliorating its tendency to underinvest.

But the regulator faces a trade-off because the variable access charge affects not only the network firm's investment incentives but also the equilibrium prices in the downstream transport market. To highlight this latter point, note that the first-best transport price (under either VS or HS) is the sum of marginal transport cost and marginal network cost. If the regulator under VS sets the variable access charge equal to the marginal network cost, then as the left-hand panel of Figure 6.6 illustrates, competition among horizontally differentiated ROCs would result in equilibrium transport prices that exceed first-best levels (because each ROC would charge a markup above the sum of its marginal transport cost and the variable access charge). Ignoring, for a moment, the use of access pricing to motivate the network firm to invest in infrastructure quality enhancement, the right-hand panel of Figure 6.6 shows that the regulator could increase social welfare by lowering the variable access charge just enough below marginal network cost so that the ROC's reaction functions intersect at the first-best prices.[24] Under this scenario, the regulator forces the network firm to subsidize network access in order to offset the deleterious effect of ROC market power.[25]

152   *David Besanko*

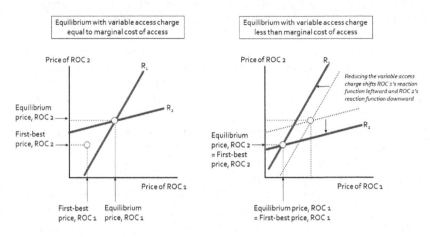

*Figure 6.6* By Setting Access Charges Less Than the Marginal Cost of Access,
the Regulator under VS Can Induce an Equilibrium in Which ROCs
Charge the First-Best Prices

The regulator's dilemma, then, is this: should it choose a low variable
access charge, which helps counteract market power in the downstream
freight transport market but does a poor job of motivating the network
firm to invest in a high-quality network? Or should it choose a high variable access charge, which worsens the impact of downstream market
power but motivates the network firm to invest in a high-quality network?

Whether this trade-off works to the advantage or disadvantage of VS
when it comes to investment in network quality depends on cost and
demand fundamentals. If the marginal cost of network quality enhancement rises rapidly with additional investment, the regulator would need
to set a very large variable access charge to motivate the network firm
to invest, but if it did so, it would likely face a large sacrifice of social
efficiency in the transport market due to high transport prices and low
volumes. This case might arise if the state-owned legacy network was
already of a very high quality (perhaps due to politically motivated "gold-
plating") so that further improvements in quality were extremely costly.

Horizontal differentiation between ROCs also affects this trade-off.
When horizontal differentiation is weak, there would be little downstream
market power for the regulator to counteract, and the regulator could
use the variable access charge almost exclusively to motivate the network
firm to invest in network quality. Weak horizontal differentiation helps
the appropriability effect work on behalf of higher network quality under
VS because it makes it "inexpensive" for the regulator to focus its access
pricing on creating higher-power incentives for the network firm to invest
in enhancing infrastructure quality.

In sum, the difference between HS and VS in terms of the appropriability effect is ambiguous. Depending on fundamentals, it is possible that the price-cost margin of the VISs that emerges in equilibrium under HS could be higher or lower than that which is induced by the regulator's choice of a variable access charge. On balance, though, the appropriability effect seems more likely to favor HS than VS. This is because the main circumstance under which the appropriability effect would favor VS would be when the horizontal differentiation between ROCs is minimal. But, as we have seen, with nontrivial economies of density in freight operations, vigorous price competition between a small number of ROCs might not be viable. Thus the best-case scenario for VS with respect to the appropriability effect is one that may not arise given plausible cost conditions.

### The Double Marginalization on Quality Effect

A second way in which incentives for network quality differ between HS and VS stems from an effect that is loosely analogous to double marginalization that arises in standard models of vertical relationships, what we call the *double marginalization on quality effect*. When enhanced network quality mainly serves to increase transport demand rather than reduce transport costs, this effect reduces the marginal benefit of quality enhancement perceived by the network firm under VS relative to that perceived by a VIS under HS.[26]

Under VS, the network firm's marginal benefit of quality is determined by the impact of quality on *network profits* not *system profits*. Higher network quality increases overall transport demand, thus increasing network profits if the variable access charge exceeds the marginal network cost. But this potentially beneficial impact on the network firm's profit is partly offset by a second impact shown in Figure 6.7: under plausible conditions, higher quality would increase the equilibrium prices charged by the ROCs.[27] This works to reduce the volume of transport demand, in turn working to decrease network profits (again assuming a variable access change that exceeds marginal network cost).[28]

This second impact reduces the network firm's marginal benefit of quality below what it would have been had it considered only the impact of quality on transport demand. In essence, under VS, the network firm exerts market power with respect to network quality enhancement, whereas the ROCs exert (some degree of) market power with respect to transport pricing. This double marginalization tends to suppress the network firm's marginal benefit of quality.

By contrast, under HS, a VIS's marginal benefit of quality is determined by the impact of quality investment on overall system *profit*. The marginal benefit of quality perceived by a typical VIS is shaped by the direct impact of quality enhancement on transport demand, but not its indirect consequences for the equilibrium transport prices. This is because the

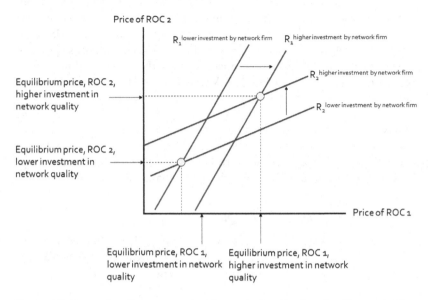

*Figure 6.7* Increasing Investment in Network Quality by the Network Firm Results in Higher Transport Prices in the Downstream Freight Hauling Market

positive impact of a higher transport price on *transport profit* offsets (to a first-order approximation) the deleterious impact of this higher price on *network profits*.[29]

The double marginalization on quality effect also operates when network quality enhancements decrease marginal transport costs. Under HS, reductions in transport costs due to enhancing the quality of the network would be fully internalized by the VISs, and the marginal benefit of investment would fully reflect the marginal profitability from lower transport costs. Under VS, by contrast, the network firm would internalize such investment benefits only to the extent that ROCs reduced their transport prices and generated higher volumes of traffic over the network. If this pass-through is imperfect—that is, the ROCs "bank" some of the reduction in marginal transport cost in the form of higher margins—the resulting increase in transport volumes under VS would fall short of those generated by the same increment to network quality under HS. In this case, the double marginalization on quality effect would tend to make network quality higher under HS than VS. Because pass-through rates in models of oligopoly competition could be 100% or greater (Weyl and Fabinger, 2013), the double marginalization on quality effect could, in theory, favor VS over HS. But this strikes us as an extreme possibility, especially when price competition between ROCs is soft. And even with 100% or greater pass-through, as the discussion of the appropriability effect stressed, the margin between the access charge and marginal network cost would need to be positive to motivate the network firm to invest at all.

### The Coordination on Quality Effect

A third way in which incentives for quality choice differ between HS and VS pertains to competition. When making its quality decision, each VIS takes into account the beneficial impact of increasing network quality on its own profit, but it does not internalize the (pecuniary) externality that arises because its increased quality reduces the transport demand on other VISs. Figure 6.8 depicts the equilibrium quality choices that arise under HS.[30] The network qualities chosen by competing VISs are greater than what they would have been had qualities been chosen collusively (represented by point C). The system-to-system competition under HS is thus a positive force for investments aimed at improving network quality.

By contrast, under VS, the ROCs do not choose network quality. This part of the offer to consumers is selected by the network firm. Because the ROCs operate over the same network, the network firm effectively chooses a common network quality for each ROC. In so doing, the pecuniary externality that VISs do not internalize is internalized by the network firm. Under VS, therefore, it is as if there was coordination on quality (hence our term, the *coordination on quality effect*) or, to put it

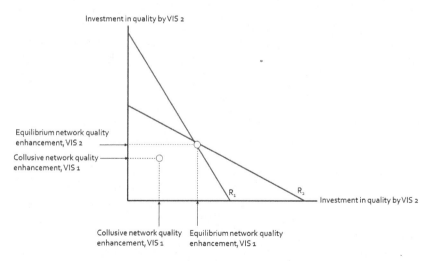

*Figure 6.8* Competition by VISs to Enhance Network Quality Results in Quality Levels That Exceed Collusive Levels

more bluntly, collusion. This works to reduce the level of network quality under VS relative to its level under HS.

To sum up, assuming that demand and cost fundamentals are the same under the two restructuring approaches, the double marginalization and coordination on quality effect make the marginal benefit of quality under HS higher than under VS, whereas the appropriability effect could favor either HS or VS. Still, there is an important caveat: the higher quality under HS due to the double marginalization and coordination on quality effect would work to make consumer surplus higher under HS than VS, but the impact of these incentives on social welfare is subtler. If competition among competing VISs is sufficiently intense, it is possible that equilibrium quality could be pushed beyond the level that maximizes social welfare (conditional on the prices and transport quantity that arises in equilibrium). That is, the equilibrium could reflect a sort of "arms race" in network quality. If this happens, then social welfare under HS could be lower than social welfare under VS, even though HS results in higher network quality. This is why workable competition under HS would most likely be preferable to cutthroat competition. Of course, if policymakers care more about infrastructure quality than social welfare, this arms race would be a feature not a bug.

### The Double Marginalization on Price Effect

A textbook rationale for vertical integration is the elimination of double marginalization that arises when an upstream supplier with market power sets the price of the upstream good in excess of its marginal cost. An analogous phenomenon in our framework becomes a potential advantage for HS with respect to consumer surplus and social welfare because the price of access under HS is effectively the marginal network cost, whereas under VS, the access price set by the social welfare maximizing regulator could exceed marginal network cost. That is, a factor that could lead HS to give rise to higher consumer surplus and social welfare is the *double marginalization on price effect*.

On the other hand, a social welfare-maximizing regulator might instead set the variable access price below the marginal network cost to counteract the downstream distortion in transport prices due to the market power of the ROCs. This effectively turns the double marginalization effect on its head, creating an advantage for VS with respect to consumer surplus and social welfare. (Though it also, as discussed, creates a disadvantage for VS with respect to network quality due to the appropriability effect.) Recall that an access price less than the marginal network cost is more likely when horizontal differentiation among the ROCs is strong (and price competition is thus soft) and when the marginal cost of network quality enhancement is high.

## Assessing the Comparative Advantages of Restructuring Approaches

Table 6.2, which is based on our discussion in the preceding sections, summarizes the sources of comparative advantage and disadvantage for HS and VS with respect to the direct and equilibrium effect of cost and demand fundamentals and the balance of structural incentives. Asterisks indicate that a source of advantage is contingent on policy choices. Advantages and disadvantages are classified as strong, weak, or without a modifier. Some potential sources of advantage, such as the appropriability effect and cost complementarities, are ambiguous because they depend on underlying fundamentals. One other factor—intermodal competition—offsets the potential disadvantages of VS due to economies of density and sunk entry costs.

Table 6.2 suggests seven conclusions:

**Conclusion 1:** *There are significant reasons to expect that HS will result more investment in network quality enhancement than VS.*

While the appropriability effect is ambiguous, the other structural incentives tend to favor higher network quality under HS under VS. Under those conditions in which the regulated access charge under VS is set at, or even below, the marginal cost of access, the appropriability would also create an advantage for HS with respect to network quality. The relative advantage that HS enjoys with respect to network quality would be further enhanced if policymakers designed horizontally separated systems that enabled ample opportunities for parallel or source competition, leading to rivalry between VISs not only on price but also on quality. The main advantage that VS would have over HS with respect to network quality would then be due to economies of network size that would lead to a lower marginal cost of quality enhancement under VS than under HS. This would tend to increase the quality-enhancing investments made by the network firm. But as noted earlier, the evidence of network size economies in freight rail is weak (hence our characterization, *"weak advantage"*).

In their theoretical comparison of HS and VS, Besanko and Cui (2016) computed equilibrium prices, network qualities, and (under VS) access charges for thousands of distinct combinations of parameter values in the model (including the degree of horizontal differentiation under VS and HS and the marginal transport and network costs). They tallied the percentage of parameterizations in which HS had a higher or lower equilibrium quality than VS. In a baseline specification in which there were no economies of vertical integration but strong economies of network size—"stacking the deck" heavily in favor of VS—they found HS to have

*Table 6.2* Assessing the Comparative Advantages and Disadvantages of VS and HS

| Source of Advantage or Disadvantage | Network Quality | Consumer Surplus | Social Welfare |
|---|---|---|---|
| *Direct Effects of Cost and Demand Fundamentals* | | | |
| Economies of vertical integration | | | strong advantage HS |
| Economies of network size | | | weak advantage VS |
| *Equilibrium Effects of Market Fundamentals* | | | |
| Economies of vertical integration | | strong advantage HS | strong advantage HS |
| Economies of network size | weak advantage VS | weak advantage VS | weak advantage VS |
| Economies of density and sunk entry costs | | weak disadvantage VS | weak disadvantage VS |
| Cost complementarities | | ambiguous | ambiguous |
| Workable parallel or source competition under HS* | advantage HS | advantage HS | advantage HS† |
| Weak horizontal differentiation between ROCs under VS* | | strong advantage VS | strong advantage VS |
| Intermodal competition | | offsets disadvantage of VS | offsets disadvantage of VS |
| *Equilibrium Effects of Structural Incentives* | | | |
| Appropriability effect* | ambiguous | ambiguous | ambiguous |
| Double marginalization on quality effect | advantage HS | advantage HS | advantage HS† |
| Coordination on quality effect | advantage HS | advantage HS | advantage HS† |
| Double marginalization on price effect* | ambiguous | ambiguous | ambiguous |
| Overall | advantage HS | weak advantage HS | weak advantage HS |

* Condition (and thus advantage and disadvantage) is partly contingent on public policy choices.
† Could be disadvantage for HS if quality competition is excessive.

the higher equilibrium network quality in over 80% of the parameter combinations.

Is Conclusion 1 supported by empirical evidence? While there has been a good amount of empirical work assessing the impact of vertical separation on productivity, efficiency, and costs in railroads—see the papers cited in the introduction or the comprehensive literature review by Abbot and Cohen (2017)—there is no empirical work, as far as we know, that directly compares network quality under otherwise identical systems organized as VS or HS. Several papers have examined the impact of service quality in vertically unbundled electricity markets. For example, Nillesen and Pollitt (2011) and Nepal et al. (2016), each studying New Zealand's experience with market restructuring, found that VS improved several dimensions of network quality, including a decrease in the incidence of service outages. However, this work does not speak directly to comparison we study in this chapter since it compares a setting with competition (vertical separation) to one without (previously vertically integrated monopoly systems). Our conclusion with respect to network quality, then, remains an open empirical question.

One other point can be made about the quality disadvantage of VS. Besanko and Cui (2016) show that a social welfare-maximizing regulator may set the variable access charge so low that the network firm would choose not to enhance network quality at all.[31] Besanko and Cui assume that the regulator imposes a minimum quality standard to prevent the network firm from reducing network quality below the status quo level. However, without such regulation, a sufficiently low variable access price could conceivably lead to a *reduction* in quality by the network firm. The need to design and enforce minimum network quality regulations in order to avoid such disinvestment is a potentially costly side effect of the structural incentives for quality arising under VS.

**Conclusion 2:** *The relative advantages and disadvantages of VS and HS with respect to consumer surplus are mixed but on balance suggest a weak advantage overall for HS.*

If the balance of structural incentives for network quality work to the advantage of HS with respect to network quality, they would also work to the advantage of HS with respect to consumer surplus as well because higher network quality ultimately benefits consumers. Potentially offsetting this are economies of network size that tend to favor higher quality under VS and thus would also tend to work toward a higher consumer surplus under VS. But because evidence on economies of network size is weak, this source of advantage may not be very powerful.

Economies of vertical integration would lower the marginal cost of freight transport operations under HS relative to VS and would lead to lower equilibrium prices and higher consumer surplus under HS. A potential offset to this advantage would be if policymakers were able to design a regime of access and service standards that resulted in multiple, nearly identical, ROCs engaged in intense price competition. The result would be equilibrium prices close to the marginal cost of transport and correspondingly high levels of consumer surplus. But this not only depends on good policy choices but also on the relative absence of economies of density, the presence of which could lead to a VS system with very few competitors and/or dominated by a single firm. If access or service standards enabled those few operators to occupy niches of the market that were relativity insulated from each other, we would not expect price competition under VS to be particularly strong. The result in that case would be equilibrium prices that significantly exceeded marginal cost, with consumer surplus not as high as would have been realized had competition been more intense and prices lower. In addition to all this, if policymakers could design an HS network with strong parallel or source competition, the potential advantage of VS when it comes to price competition might largely be nullified.

All in all, neither HS nor VS enjoys a clearly dominant advantage when it comes to consumer surplus, but if one accepts that economies of vertical integration are strong and that workable competition under HS is possible, HS should have a slight advantage.

> **Conclusion 3:** *The relative advantages and disadvantages of VS and HS with respect to social welfare parallel those with respect to consumer surplus, but with some additional wrinkles. On balance, they suggest a weak advantage overall for HS.*

The impact of market fundamentals on equilibrium outcomes, as well as the balance of structural incentives, create a pattern of advantages and disadvantages with respect to social welfare that are broadly similar to those with respect to consumer surplus. However, there are two additional considerations. First, economies of vertical integration confer a strong total cost advantage of HS over VS, an advantage that flows through directly to social welfare.

Second, it is conceivable that the incentives for network quality under HS could be so strong that they would lead to socially excessive levels of network quality enhancement, thus serving as a force to reduce social welfare under HS below that of VS.

> **Conclusion 4:** *The best-case scenario for VS with respect to consumer surplus and social welfare is one in which the freight transport market is characterized by weak horizontal differentiation. This scenario depends heavily on the choices of policymakers, but it may also be incompatible with cost fundamentals in freight markets.*

Weak horizontal differentiation leads to higher consumer surplus and social welfare under VS in two ways—by intensifying price competition and (indirectly) by making it more likely that the regulator sets a variable access above marginal network cost, giving the network firm sharper advantages to invest in network quality. To engineer a market with weak horizontal differentiation, the policy framework supporting VS should seek to minimize barriers to access, require price transparency (so as to make price salient to shippers), and impose service standards that prevent ROCs from "niche-ifying" and insulating themselves from price competition. To prevent "niche-ification," service standards could, for example, not only require ROCs to be common carriers but could also mandate that all ROCs stand ready to serve all geographies and all industries in the network so that ROCs are neither geographically specialized nor specialized by industry or commodity. In effect, an implementation of VS that realizes the highest level of consumer surplus and social welfare is one in which ROCs offers are nearly as uniform as possible, so that the only potential difference between them is the price they charge.

But the downside of this scenario is that in the face of economies of density, intense price competition may not enable the ROCs to cover their total costs, even if only a handful of ROCs compete in the market. This best-case scenario may therefore be a chimera.

**Conclusion 5:** *The best-case scenario for HS with respect to consumer surplus and social welfare is one in which there is workable, but not cutthroat, competition between VISs. Achieving this scenario depends to some extent on policy choices, but it could occur "naturally"—that is, as a result of fundamentals—even without much help from policymakers.*

Given the likely advantage of HS when it comes to network quality, and given the total and marginal cost advantages it enjoys due to economies of vertical integration, HS has strong "winds at its back." The main reasons why it could end up being inferior to VS with respect to consumer surplus and social welfare is if (1) price competition is exceedingly weak due to inadequate parallel or source competition or (2) quality competition is cutthroat due to extremely strong parallel or source competition. The best-case scenario for HS, then, is one where there are just enough shippers who could choose among competing VISs so that there is moderate price and quality competition. Though precise calibration of the appropriate amounts of price and non-price competition would appear to be beyond the capability of even the best policymaking institutions, it would not be too difficult for policymakers to devolve a state-owned system into two to four VISs that have some degree of geographical differentiation, while at the same time enabling the interchange of traffic in large geographic centers. Achieving this interchange would be aimed at giving most shippers at these large nodes a choice between at least two rail systems.

Still, a cautionary note is in order. If the services provided by VISs are perceived by potential shippers to be complements rather than substitutes, then it is possible we could get a (possibly weak) form of Cournot's complementary monopoly problem in which independent price setting by VIS results in higher total rates paid by shippers than would arise with a vertically integrated monopolist. Cournot's complementary monopoly problem could arise if a state-owned monopoly system was split into two geographically separate systems similar to those in the right-hand panel of Figure 6.3. If there was no or limited intermodal competition (e.g., so that a customer would be unable to bypass one of the VISs through use of truck or barges), then customers shipping from the far south of the country to the far north (or vice versa) would see the two VISs as complements rather than substitutes, since a shipper's freight would need to travel over the rails of both systems. Our analysis suggests that the geographic structure of the systems under HS should be designed, where possible, to avoid this possibility, either immediately or, better yet, as a future possibility from later mergers. Even if this extreme case does not arise, perceived complementarities of systems by shippers can arise when there are a large enough number of shippers who are captive to a particular railroad.[32] Thus, HS should be implemented to minimize the extent to which shippers are captive to a particular railroad.

> **Conclusion 6:** *Because effective realization of high levels of consumer surplus and social welfare under VS requires a more robust role of public policy than is the case under HS, the best chance for successful implementation of VS would be in countries with strong regulatory institutions. Successful implementation under HS is not as dependent on the presence of strong regulatory institutions. HS is, therefore, likely to be a more attractive choice in emerging or transition economies.*

As noted, the best-case scenario for VS requires robust price competition between ROCs. To achieve this, policymakers must be able to attract a large enough number of ROCs to the market, or if (as seems more likely) only a handful of firms enter the market, policymakers must be able to structure the market so that horizontal differentiation among ROCs is minimized. Mechanisms for achieving robust competition in the market include the processes by which operating concessions are awarded to ROCs, routes are assigned within the network, and timetables are established. These processes could be managed by the network firm or its regulator. Alternatively, they could be carried out by negotiation among the ROCs overseen by the network firm (as, for example, is the case the

Netherlands). Or they could take place through auction mechanisms overseen by the network regulator or the country's ministry of transport. In all cases, strong institutions would be required to prevent one or a handful of firms from engaging in anticompetitive activities or socially wasteful rent seeking aimed at dominating the rail transport market.

Even putting aside the need to ensure robust price competition, the regulatory and contractual environment required to implement VS is fairly complex. For example, ROCs will need, at minimum, to have operating licenses and safety certifications. Detailed divisions of responsibility between the network firm and each ROC will need to be specified with respect to rules of operation, availability of portions of the network, and the carriage of dangerous cargo. ROCs may be expected to adhere to weight limits and restrictions on train length, and they may face limits on availability of sidings, freight depots, and loading and unloading facilities. Further, as part of its efforts to upgrade network quality, the network firm may utilize technology such as automatic train control or automatic train stop, which requires some degree of adaptation of equipment by ROCs and certainly a healthy amount of operational coordination. Technical decisions about how the boundaries between network operations and train operations are drawn are consequential. As Beard et al. (2016) emphasize, "In the case of freight rail services, unbundling will not be a simple process. The consequences of poor freight rail system control are potentially catastrophic."

These policy and institutional demands would be challenging to meet even in the most advanced economies around the world. For example, in Europe, where restructuring around VS is now in its third decade, achieving robust levels of competition in all VS-adopting countries has proved elusive (recall Figure 6.5). Beard et al. (2016) draw parallels between proposed incremental moves toward vertical unbundling in the U.S. freight rail industry and the experience in implementing an ambitious plan of vertical unbundling in the U.S. telecom sector in the wake of the 1996 Telecommunications Act. That experience, they recount, was contentious and required protracted regulatory deliberations. And even after all this, "the network unbundling results under the Telecommunications Act of 1996 were decidedly mixed."

Like VS, successful implementation of HS would also require regulation. To achieve workable competition, clear rules on trackage access would be necessary. At minimum, one would want a regulation mandating that each rail system provides facilities for interchanging traffic so that the rail systems could negotiate trackage and haulage rights agreements with each other. Rules governing ownership of, and access to, terminal railroads may also be needed. Procedures for dealing with captive shippers might also be required. But because the intense competition that is vital for VS to generate high levels of consumer surplus and social welfare is not as critical under HS (and could even be counterproductive if it leads to excess competition on network quality), regulation under HS could likely proceed with a softer touch and would likely impose lighter burdens on regulatory institutions. In countries with less well-developed institutions, this could be a big advantage.

Conclusion 7: *The extent to which an approach realizes high levels of consumer surplus and social welfare depends in part on the nature of its legacy network.*

This conclusion may seem self-evident but is very important. As we have emphasized throughout, the intensity of competition between VISs (under HS) or ROCs (under VS) is a critical determinant of which structure best serves the interests of consumers and society, and this intensity, in turn, is shaped by the degree of horizontal differentiation between competing firms. Conclusions 4, 5, and 6 highlight how this differentiation is a function of policy decisions, but these policy decisions must themselves reflect the nature of a country's legacy network.

Mexico's experience in the late 1990s with privatizing its freight railway system, Ferrocarriles Nacionales de Mexico (FNM), provides an instructive example of this implication. At first glance, the legacy structure of FNM did not appear to have been well suited to HS. Though there were some opportunities for dividing up FNM's existing lines to create parallel competition between city pairs in Mexico, they were not abundant (see OECD, 2014, Figure 4.1 for a map of the system as it existed in 1995). Given the size of Mexico's network (12,000 miles in total, or roughly 60% of the size of France's system), new railway networks built to create parallel competition would probably have been less than the 5,000–10,000 mile threshold needed to fully achieve economies of network size (Pittman, 2007). Still, it was possible to make HS work in Mexico's legacy system by relying on source competition. Mexico divided FNM into three privately owned regional lines, each emanating from Mexico City where the presence of an open access terminal railroad (jointly owned by the three private firms and the government) allowed most shippers in the city to access any one of three railways.[33] Because a significant fraction of freight traffic in Mexico was bound for overseas, a shipper in Mexico City could often reach its ultimate destination over any one the regional lines, even though they went in different directions (Pittman, 2004). Similarly, shipments arriving from Asia could be shipped to one of several ports along Mexico's Pacific coast and then transported to Mexico City by the (single) railroad serving that port.

Mexico also considered VS as a model for freight privatization, but it rejected it partly out of concern that the quality of the legacy network infrastructure was too poor to safely dispatch multiple operators over the system and partly because (consistent with the insights of our framework) VS was expected to induce less investment in the network than would be the case under HS (OECD, 1997). In addition, in line with Conclusion 6, Mexico's institutions for regulating railways were just emerging and even today are considered in need of strengthening.[34] Though HS requires regulatory oversight on issues such as safety and trackage rights, VS would have almost certainly placed even more severe demands on regulatory capacity. All in all, Mexico provides an excellent example of how legacy network structure, institutional capacity, public policy, and economic incentives decisions interact to shape the trade-off between HS and VS.

We close this section by raising a question. In comparing VS with HS, this chapter has taken as given that VS would involve the traditional unbundling of "below-the-rails" and "above-the-rails" value chain activities. Is it conceivable, though, that a further unbundling of transport activities—such as separation of marketing and merchandising functions from freight train operations—could lead to more intense price competition under VS without sacrificing economies of density in transport operations? Perhaps "asset light" ROCs could compete for customers while responsibility for haulage operations could reside with a handful of freight train contracting companies or be auctioned off to a single firm through a concession contract that controls prices through a price cap mechanism.

Our tentative response is skepticism tempered with caution. Besanko and Cui (2016) showed that even when transport operations are subject to constant returns to scale, HS will often dominate VS when it comes to network quality, and it is more likely to perform better on all three metrics simultaneously. Our view is that differences in the incentives created by the two approaches are sufficiently powerful that it would be difficult to modify VS to make it a generically more robust approach. Still, technology is not static, and we should not rule out the possibility that VS might be well suited as model for rail system reorganization if technological progress or disruptions lead to major changes in demand or cost fundamentals.

## Implications for Railway Restructuring in China

With 127,000 km. of track, including more than 27,000 km. of high-speed rail lines as of 2017, rail transport in China enjoys a nontrivial share of the freight shipping market, accounting for about 19% of ton-kilometers of China's domestic freight traffic in 2015 and about 8% of total tonnage.[35] Table 6.3 shows the distribution of rail traffic by category of cargo in 2015. Coal shipments dominate China's freight traffic, accounting for about 41% of ton-kilometers and 53% of tonnage in 2015. More generally, bulk commodities together are far more important than manufactured merchandise, though container shipping has emerged as an important source of traffic in the last 15 years.

Although rail traffic has declined as a share of China's total freight traffic—as recently as the year 2000, rail accounted for 50% of domestic

*Table 6.3* China Freight Rail Traffic by Cargo Type, 2015

| Item | Ton-kilometers (million) | Share of Ton-kilometers | Tonnage (10,000 tons) | Share of Tons |
|---|---|---|---|---|
| Coal | 886,754 | 41.32% | 143,221 | 52.88% |
| Metal Ores | 175,184 | 8.16% | 32,841 | 12.13% |
| Containers | 169,203 | 7.88% | 9,464 | 3.49% |
| Steel, Iron, & Non-ferrous Metal | 166,688 | 7.77% | 16,063 | 5.93% |
| Petroleum | 105,667 | 4.92% | 12,553 | 4.64% |
| Grain | 101,254 | 4.72% | 5,590 | 2.06% |
| Coke | 76,028 | 3.54% | 7,553 | 2.79% |
| Mineral Building Materials | 35,649 | 1.66% | 10,438 | 3.85% |
| Nonmetal Ores | 31,957 | 1.49% | 5,670 | 2.09% |
| Less-than-truckload Freight | 26,711 | 1.24% | 2,410 | 0.89% |
| Phosphorous Ore | 16,359 | 0.76% | 1,494 | 0.55% |
| Timber | 15,911 | 0.74% | 1,883 | 0.70% |
| Cement | 9,083 | 0.42% | 2,447 | 0.91% |
| Other | 329,806 | 15.37% | 19,167 | 7.08% |
| Total | 2,146,254 | 100% | 270,794 | 100% |

Source: China Statistical Yearbook, 2016, Table 16–16, www.stats.gov.cn/tjsj/ndsj/2016/indexeh.htm (accessed May 1, 2018)

freight traffic and two-thirds of land-based traffic—freight rail is a key part of China's transportation future. For example, freight rail is an integral piece of China's Belt and Road initiative aimed at creating freight transport connectivity between China and Eurasia. Further, as a long as economic growth in China continues at rates between 6% and 8% per year, the rail system will be under constant pressure to upgrade network quality through enhancements to both capacity and sophistication.

At present, China's railway system is a vertically integrated, state-owned monopoly. China Railway Corporation (CRC), created as part of the restructuring undertaken in 2013, is responsible for the business functions of the rail system, including the design, construction, management, and maintenance of railway infrastructure (e.g., roadbed, track, freight and passenger stations, and communication systems) and the management and operation of passenger and freight service. These functions had previously been the responsibility of the Railway Ministry, which was disbanded in 2013.

The Railway Ministry was one of the oldest ministries of the People's Republic of China, with an extremely broad reach. At one time, the ministry included units that produced railroad rolling stock and railroad materials and operated railway hospitals and schools. At the time of the 2013 reorganization, though, the Railway Ministry had become focused on three core functions: the business operations that were devolved to the CRC, responsibility for setting technical railway standards and oversight of safety and service rules, and high-level responsibility for policymaking and system planning for China's railroads. The 2013 reorganization was aimed at separating the management of the railroad enterprise, the regulation of rail activities, and formulation of railroad policy. As such, the Railway Ministry's policymaking functions were shifted to the Ministry of Communications, and its standard-setting and regulatory functions were given to a new agency, the National Railway Administration.

CRC is organized into 18 regional railway bureaus, each operating a section of the national network, and three specialized subsidiaries, China Railway Container Transport Co. Ltd., China Railway Special Cargo Services Co. Ltd. and China Railway Express Co. Ltd. The bureaus are responsible for both conventional and high-speed rail within their geographies. The bureaus are significant enterprises in their own right. In 2000, the Beijing Railway Bureau accounted for 255.3 billion ton-km. of freight, more than Germany, France, United Kingdom, and Sweden combined in the same year (see Table 6.2 in Rong and Bouf, 2005). Historically, the Railway Ministry accounted for the profit of bureaus individually, but it did assign costs to bureaus, and it did not separate costs in any meaningful way between passenger and freight operations. As a result, bureau managers could be neither rewarded for superior profitability nor held accountable for poor profit performance. According to Rong and Bouf (2005), "The fact that nobody is really directly responsible for making a profit is considered to be one of the reasons for the decline of Chinese railways."

In 2017, the bureaus (as well as the specialized cargo subsidiaries) became limited liability companies, with boards of directors, boards of supervisors, senior management teams, and Communist Party committees. The bureaus were also "re-branded" through name changes that removed "bureau" from their titles (e.g., the Beijing Railway Bureau became CR Beijing Group). Though these renamed entities are still under control of the CRC, the 2017 restructuring could be argued to (perhaps ever-so slightly) open the door for further reforms currently under discussion. These include (1) continued efforts to attract private capital into the development of intermodal operations and facilities (Pittman, 2011 provides a number of such examples that began in the mid-2000s.); (2) further injection of private capital into China Railway Development Fund, an initiative that began in 2014 to attract financial capital for railway investment from lending institutions and other investors (To date, most of the funds raised have come from China's state-owned banks.); (3) expanded use of public-private partnerships for construction of new high-speed rail lines (China's first public-private partnership in high-speed rail was announced in 2017.); and (4) the opening up of CRC itself to infusions private capital so that it can eventually transition from a fully state-owned enterprise to one that is jointly owned by private investors and the state.[36]

Consistent with the intent of these reforms, China's railway system does appear to have become more somewhat market oriented in the last 15 years. For example, China's high-speed rail lines operate reliable, comfortable passenger service that is price- and time-competitive with other modes. Decisions to allow private investment in terminals and rail lines for containers reflects a sensible recognition of the need to rapidly build the capacity to support the intermodal traffic arising from China's position in the global economy. Further, there are promising trends in freight rail operations, with train speeds increasing from 32 km. per hour to 36 km. per hour and output per day per freight locomotive increasing from 994 gross ton-km. to 1,434 both over the period from 2000 to 2014 (World Bank, 2017, Figure 13).

Still, even if (1) more private capital flows to the CRC and its subsidiaries, (2) more sensible information and control systems are created to hold managers accountable on the basis of enterprise profitability, (3) political pressures for low rates or cross-subsidization can be eliminated in the transition from state-owned to partially private enterprise (this is a big *if*), it seems unlikely that China's rail system can advance to the ranks of those of rich countries as long as pricing and investment decisions are in the hands of a monopoly enterprise. In 2000, it seemed as if China were poised for serious consideration to begin a process toward introducing competition into its system through a plan embodying VS. The Minister of Railways submitted a plan that envisioned an infrastructure network company, three to five freight companies, and several specialty companies, but the plan was turned down in 2002. At the moment, restructuring the Chinese system toward competition is not currently on the horizon. Still, if the experiences of other rich and middle-class nations over the last 30 years is a guide, some form competition would be a natural end product of the reforms that accelerated in China in 2013.

There is no strong consensus in the academic literature on whether HS or VS is the better choice for China in restructuring its freight system. For example, Yuanyuan and Wen (2009) have advocated VS in China, and Rong and Bouf (2005) see some potential advantages of VS for China, even if the "above-the-rails" competition was between just two firms.[37] Zhao (2005) and Pittman (2004, 2011), on the other hand, argue that HS would be the better choice for China.

An important consideration for favoring HS over VS in China is that China's rapid growth implies that the rail system needs to remain ahead

*Figure 6.9* Possible Implementation of HS in China

of demand growth when it comes to network capacity, particularly for long-distance shipping of bulk commodities where capacity shortages have been most severe (Pittman, 2011). As we have argued, HS has the advantage over VS when it comes to network investment incentives.

In addition, a natural way to restructure China's freight rail network as a horizontally separated system would be to divide the existing national system into a number of regional systems. A first step might be to merge the railway bureaus into eight regional companies, corresponding to the regional units of the National Railway System. A more ambitious plan, depicted in Figure 6.9, would be to create a regional system with four independent rail corporations, one serving the northeast, one serving the northwest (including existing and planned lines that connect to Kazakhstan and points west to Europe), one serving the central region of the country, as well as the coast down to Shanghai, and one serving the south of China. Of China's 10 largest cities, nine would be served by two railroads under this restructuring. Coupled with the establishment of open access rules for terminal railroads in cities served by multiple carriers, the arrangement in Figure 6.9 would create many opportunities for source competition for shippers. For example, a system following this template should enable customers in Beijing to source coal from Shanxi province using the Central rail system or from Inner Mongolia using the Northwest system. The opportunities for source competition under this approach are further enhanced because four of China's six busiest ports—Shanghai, Shenzhen, Guangzhou, and Tianjin—would be served by two railroads under this restructuring template. Source competition is likely to engender the moderate amount of price competition that would move China close to the best-case scenario for HS.

But if one were worried that a regional system might induce insufficient price competition, there are other reorganizations that could give rise to parallel competition. Pittman (2011) proposes a structure involving for parallel competition between two independent rail lines within three north-south corridors: Beijing-Guangzhou, Beijing-Nanning, and Beijing-Harbin. At least two east-west corridors could be added to Pittman's proposal. One would include two roughly parallel routes serving Beijing, Baotou, and Lanzhou, which includes China's second and third highest traffic freight lines by tonnage.[38] The other would be in the south with two lines running from Shanghai to Kunming (the fifth highest volume rail corridor), one through Guangzhou and the other through Changsha.[39] Pittman's proposal would probably give rise to a greater degree of price competition than would arise in a regional system, but the competing lines in each corridor are geographically differentiated enough that they would not be seen as perfect substitutes, and thus price competition would be unlikely to be cutthroat.

On top of these advantages for HS, there is reason to believe that a potential advantage of VS—economies of network size—may not be especially relevant in the case of China. Given the econometric evidence cited earlier (e.g., Bereskin, 2009) it seems plausible that economies of network size would be exhausted in China well short of a national system.

Finally, a VS system that gives rise to the aggressive price competition needed to offset the potential network quality disadvantage of VS would require independent regulatory oversight to ensure nondiscriminatory access and closely matched service offerings by competing operators. The National Railway Administration would presumably serve as the primary regulator, but it is fair to say that its regulatory and oversight skills have yet to be tested by anything close to the complexity that would ensue if VS were adopted. Inadequate regulation, or even worse, regulatory capture, could not only lead to inferior market design under VS, but also create problems in the regulation of the network firm. We have presumed that VS is implemented through an access pricing regime that maximizes social welfare subject to the incentive constraints implied by the equilibrium behavior of the network firm and the ROCs. But if the regulator departs from welfare-maximizing choices, the disadvantages of VS would be magnified. If, for example, the variable access charge is set too low, the appropriability effect would compromise network quality even more than it does when the regulator maximizes social welfare. On the other hand, if the access charge is well in excess of the marginal network cost, the resulting double marginalization on price would work to decrease consumer surplus and social welfare. The same would occur if the network firm was unregulated and allowed to set the access charge at the monopoly level.

Of course, China's way forward with respect to railroad restructuring is still subject to many uncertainties. These include the future of coal traffic as China begins to take steps to reduce its carbon emissions, the mix of freight that will be carried by conventional versus high-speed trains, and the demand for long-distance shipments to west Asia and Europe by train. All of these will impinge on traffic patterns and will affect the best approach to restructuring. We believe, though, that even with these uncertainties, a persuasive case can be made for restructuring China's freight rail system around the principle of HS. It is likely to be workably competitive; it offers the prospect of inducing the investment in freight rail infrastructure China needs to support continued economic growth, and it places less strenuous demands on the country's regulatory capacity than VS would.

## Summary and Conclusions

This chapter develops a conceptual framework for evaluating two contending approaches to restructuring privatized rail systems: vertical separation (VS) and horizontal separation (HS). The framework isolates three distinct mechanisms by which a restructuring approach can affect network quality, consumer surplus, and social welfare: the direct effect of cost and demand fundamentals, the equilibrium effect of these fundamentals, and differences in structural incentives for investment in network quality. An example of a direct effect of a cost or demand fundamental is economies of vertical integration. Economies of vertical integration have the direct effect of making the total cost of production under HS lower than it would be under VS, which, in turn, tends to make social welfare under the former greater than under the latter. If vertical integration economies also lower the marginal cost of rail transport, then this fundamental would also have the equilibrium effect of lowering rail prices under HS relative to those under VS, which, in turn, would work to increase consumer and social welfare under HS relative to VS. An example of a structural incentive affecting quality choice is the double marginalization on quality effect. Under VS, the network firm's marginal benefit of quality is determined by the impact of quality on *network profit* not *system profits*. In essence, under VS, the network firm exerts market power with respect to network quality enhancement, whereas the ROCs exert (some degree of) market power with respect to transport pricing. This form of double marginalization works to reduce the network firm's marginal benefit of quality below that perceived by a VIS under HS, whose marginal benefit of quality reflects the impact of quality investment on overall system profit.

We argue that there is strong reason to believe that horizontal separation will do a better job promoting investments to enhance network quality. Either approach could conceivably result in higher levels of consumer surplus and social welfare, but the direct and equilibrium effect of cost and demand fundamentals give rise to, at the very least, a weak advantage for HS. Our analysis suggests that the best-case scenario for VS when it comes to consumer and social welfare is when price competition among ROCs is intense, which requires at least two (and ideally even more) ROCs, with weak or non-existent horizontal differentiation between them. To achieve this, the policy framework supporting VS should seek to minimize barriers to access, require price transparency so as to make price salient to shippers, and impose service standards that prevent ROCs from insulating themselves from price competition. This best-case scenario would probably place significant demands on a country's regulatory capacity. And it may be inconsistent with economies of density. The best-case scenario of HS, by contrast, involves workable, but not cutthroat, competition among the vertically integrated systems. This requires careful design choices when the state-owned system is restructured. The system would need to ensure some degree of parallel or source competition, and investment in terminal railway systems may be needed to allow customers to achieve the full benefits from competition. Overall, in emerging economies such as China, this best-case scenario seems more achievable than the best-case scenario for VS. Unless competition between vertically integrated systems is virtually impossible, our view is that HS should serve as the restructuring approach of choice for poorer or middle-class countries making the move from a state-run monopoly system to a system characterized by competition.

## Notes

1. There are three other vertically integrated Class I railroads that compete in the United States, but the amount of traffic they are responsible for is far less than these "big four."
2. The following discussion draws from Campos (2001).
3. In 2011, two of these firms merged, so there are now two major freight rail firms in Mexico.
4. Parallel competition (also known as end-to-end competition) refers to competition between two or more railroads that provide service between the same city pairs. Source competition between railroads (also known as geographic competition) arises when purchasers of a good that must be shipped by rail can purchase it from two or more different geographical sources and/or when suppliers of a rail-captive good can sell it in two or more geographic markets. For example, consider a purchaser of a commodity located in city $A$, and suppose there is a single railroad connecting $A$ and region $B$ and a different railroad connecting $A$ and region $C$. If purchasers at $A$ can source their products from either $B$ or $C$, the two railroads can become implicit competitors with one another: if one railroad attempts to raise rates, some buyers may shift their purchases to the other region, transferring traffic to the other railroad.

5. This paragraph draws from Mulder et al. (2005).
6. In practice, variable charges in access tariffs may vary by freight commodity as well as by time of day. In what follows, we ignore this complexity.
7. Throughout the chapter, we adopt a partial equilibrium approach and define social welfare to be the sum of the consumer surplus and producer surplus generated in relevant rail market.
8. In what follows, we discuss price competition as if the ROCs or VISs set a single price for one type of traffic. In reality, of course, rail firms provide transport services for many different types of commodities, possibly having very different price elasticities of demand. This is the reason they engage in differentiated pricing based on differences in price elasticities. However, this complication is not, in our view, an essential part of the key trade-offs that arise between VS and HS, so we will think of each rail firm as setting a uniform transport price to its customers. This uniform price can be interpreted as the weighted average price across a portfolio of different commodities. In this case, our framework pertains to a setting in which a railroad sets its overall price level in response to competitive conditions and then chooses individual commodity prices based on differences in price elasticities subject to attaining the chosen price level.
9. Empirical evidence discussed ahead suggests that economies of density in freight rail are non-negligible. However, for the purpose of this example, there is no loss of insight from assuming that they are absent.
10. We further assume $\gamma_V < 1$ and $\gamma_H < 1$ so that under either structure each firm would have a positive quantity demanded at prices equal to marginal cost and quality enhancements of zero.
11. Because competing firms are symmetric under each structure, under both VS and HS the two competing firms have the same equilibrium price, and under HS, each VIS has the same equilibrium network quality. Hence Table 1 does not distinguish outcomes between firms 1 and 2.
12. We explain in the section entitled "Balance of Structural Incentives" why this can arise.
13. For example, from the table, it is clear that it $X_H^* > X_V^*$, so $CS_H^* > CS_V^*$. It can also be verified that $SW_H^* = \dfrac{1,016}{289}(1 - \gamma_H)^2 > (1 - \gamma_L)^2 = SW_V^*$.
14. By "offer," we mean all of the non-price dimensions of a firm's good or service that might influence purchase decisions.
15. To simplify exposition, we use the term "shipper" to refer to the party initiating a freight shipment or the party receiving the shipment.
16. *See* Braeutigam (1999) and Ivaldi and McCullough (2001) for more evidence on economies of density in railroads.
17. "Railway Operators in the Netherlands," www.railfaneurope.net/list/netherlands.html#08 (accessed April 16, 2018).
18. To be sure, competition *for* the market, in the form of franchise bidding, could be a possible substitute for competition within the market. But for competition for the market to be able to keep transport rates low, countries would need to use an auction mechanism such as a Demsetz auction or a least present value revenue auction that directly determined rates or revenue requirements. Such auctions have not been used extensively in freight rail, and in practice they are subject to complications such as demand risk and opportunistic renegotiation.
19. This presumes no economies of vertical integration. If economies of vertical integration are strong enough, the inequality could go in the other direction.

20. To make this point more formally, suppose a railroad system's long-run total cost function (transport operations) is

$$TC(X, N, q) = c(X, q) + N^\alpha F(q),$$

where $X$ is traffic volume, $q$ is network quality, $N$ is network size, $c(X; q)$ is an increasing function of volume and a decreasing function of quality, $F(q)$ is a volume-insensitive cost of network operations that depends on network quality $q$, and $\alpha > 0$ is the elasticity of total cost with respect to network size. With this specification, we have economies of network size if and only

if $\dfrac{1}{\varepsilon + \alpha\theta} > 1$ where $\varepsilon = \dfrac{\dfrac{\partial c}{\partial X} X}{TC}$ is the cost elasticity of traffic volume (den-

sity), and $\theta = \dfrac{N^\alpha F(q)}{TC}$ is fixed infrastructure costs as a share of total costs.

Empirical estimates of $\varepsilon$ cluster between slightly more than 0.50 and 0.65 (Ivaldi and McCullough, 2001). Thus, a necessary condition for economies of network size would be $\alpha \leq \dfrac{0.35}{\theta}$. As long as the share of volume-insensitive infrastructure costs is 35 percent or more—a plausible estimate—the presence of economies of network size imply $\alpha < 1$.

Now, the marginal cost of network quality enhancement is $N^\alpha F'(q)$. Suppose that under HS, two VISs have networks of sizes $N_1$ and $N_2$, and under VS, the network is size $N_1 + N_2$. The marginal cost of quality enhancement given existing quality $q$ is $(N_1 + N_2)^\alpha F'(q)$, and the combined marginal cost of enhancing two systems' qualities under HS is $\left(N_1^\alpha + N_2^\alpha\right) F'(q)$. It is straight-forward to prove that when $0 < \alpha < 1$, $\left(N_1 + N_2\right)^\alpha < N_1^\alpha + N_2^\alpha$.

21. Ivaldi and McCullough (2008) find cost complementarities between general freight and bulk service, where general freight includes intermodal service.
22. To simplify the ensuing discussion, we assume that the marginal transport cost and the marginal network cost are independent of traffic volume.
23. Given this conceptualization, the appropriability effect pertains the case in which investment in network quality mainly enhances transport demand. The case in which network quality mainly reduces transport costs is relevant for other structural incentives discussed ahead.
24. Lowering the variable access charge shifts ROC 1's reaction function to the left in Figure 6.6 because ROC 1's effective marginal cost is marginal transport cost plus the variable access charge. With a lower marginal cost, it is willing to set a lower price for any price the ROC 2 charges. For an analogous reason, ROC 2's reaction function shifts downward.
25. The idea that the optimal variable access charge might be less than the marginal cost of infrastructure access is well understood in the regulatory economics literature. *See, e.g.,* Laffont and Tirole (2000).
26. We argue presently this is also likely to be the case when enhanced network quality reduces marginal transport cost.
27. The conditions are these: (1) higher network quality increases the quantity of transport services demanded from an ROC at any price it and rival ROCs charge (our maintained assumption throughout), and (2) an increase in network quality *does not* make each ROC's demand function more sensitive to its own price (i.e., the slope of the ROC's demand curve does not become

more negative). Conditions (1) and (2) can be shown to imply that an ROC's profit-maximizing price increases in network quality, holding the prices of other ROCs fixed. In Figure 6.7, this is reflected in ROC 1's reaction function shifting rightward and ROC 2's reaction function shifting downward.

28. Recall that if the variable access charge is less than or equal to the marginal network cost, there would be no investment in network quality enhancement under VS. In that case, the impact of higher equilibrium transport prices would be irrelevant.

29. To be complete, there is a subtlety that we should note. In our two-stage game structure, under HS, a VIS—say VIS 1—would anticipate that if it increases network quality, it will put rival systems at a competitive disadvantage, leading rival VISs to charge lower prices than otherwise, which, in turn, would adversely impact VIS 1's profits. This works to decrease each VIS's marginal benefit of quality a little bit. This effect is second order in comparison to the effect of double marginalization, which is why we ignore it in our discussion here.

30. In the Besanko and Cui (2016) model, the quality investments under HS can be shown to be strategic complements, and hence the reaction functions are downward sloping as shown in Figure 6.8. The coordination on quality effect would still arise if the quality investments were strategic complements.

31. And as discussed earlier, it is possible that the regulator would set the variable access charge less than marginal network cost to counteract oligopoly pricing distortions in the downstream rail transport market.

32. *See* Besanko and Cui (2016) for a discussion of this.

33. In 2011, two of these regional firms merged, so there are now two major freight rail firms in Mexico.

34. "A key part of the success of the other railways in North America is the existence of an economic regulator with a more clearly defined responsibility, adequate resources and expertise, and access to all necessary information needed to carry out its role. SCT [Secretaría de Comunicaciones y Transportes] in principle has a role vis-à-vis establishing the terms of the trackage rights but would need to develop its capabilities to be more effective in regulatory functions." (OECD, 2014, p. 25.)

35. Figures derived from Tables 16–8 and 16–9 China Statistical Year, 2016, www.stats.gov.cn/tjsj/ndsj/2016/indexeh.htm (accessed April 30, 2018). Domestic freight includes all traffic except for ocean shipping.

36. It is unlikely that CRC will, in the near and medium term, be fully divested to private investors. The likely end point is the Chinese government maintaining majority ownership of CRC but with a significant private presence (e.g., 51% state ownership to 49% private).

37. Rong and Bouf (2005) also identify some potential advantages of HS, but for passenger service.

38. Beijing to Baotou is the second heaviest volume line, accounting for more than 170 million tons in 2012, and Baotou to Langzhou is the third heaviest volume line, accounting for almost 90 million tons. *See* Chen and Haynes (2015), Table 1.11.

39. One line would run through Guangzhou and the other would run through Changsha.

# References

Abbott, M. and B. Cohen (2017) "Vertical integration, separation in the rail industry: A survey of empirical studies on efficiency," *European Journal of Transportation and Infrastructure*, Vol. 17, No. 2, pp. 207–224.

Beard, T.R., J.T. Macher, and C. Vickers (2016) "The time is different (?): Telecommunications unbundling and lessons for railroad regulation," *Review of Industrial Organization*, Vol. 49, pp. 289–310.

Bereskin, C.G. (2009) "Railroad economies of scale, scope, and density revisited," *Journal of the Transportation Research Forum*, Vol. 48, No. 2, pp. 23–38.

Besanko, D. and S. Cui (2016) "Railway restructuring and organizational choice: Network quality and welfare impacts," *Journal of Regulatory Economics*, Vol. 50, No. 2, pp. 164–206.

Besanko, D., M. Perry, and R. Spady (1990) "The logit model of monopolistic competition: Brand diversity," *The Journal of Industrial Economics*, Vol. 38, No. 4, pp. 397–415.

Bitzan, J.D. (2003) "Railroad costs and competition: The implications of introducing competition to railroad networks," *Journal of Transport Economics and Policy*, Vol. 37, pp. 201–225.

Braeutigam, R. (1999) "Learning about railroad costs," in *Essays in Transportation Economics and Policy: Essays in Honor of John R. Meyer*, Gomez-Ibanez, J., W. Tye, and C. Winston, eds. (Washington, DC: Brookings Institution Press).

Braeutigam, R., A. Daughety, and M. Turnquist (1982) "The estimation of a hybrid cost function for a railroad firm," *The Review of Economics and Statistics*, Vol. 64, No. 3, pp. 394–404.

Buehler, S., A. Schmutzler, and M.A. Benz (2004) "Infrastructure quality in deregulated industries: Is there an underinvestment problem?," *International Journal of Industrial Organization*, Vol. 22, No. 2, pp. 253–267.

Campos, J. (2001) "Lessons from railway reforms in Brazil and Mexico," *Transport Policy*, Vol. 8, pp. 85–95.

Caves, D., L. Christensen, and J. Swanson (1981) "Productivity growth, scale economies, and capacity utilization in U.S. railroads, 1955–74," *American Economic Review*, Vol. 71, No. 5, pp. 994–1002.

Chen, Z. and K. Haynes (2015) *Chinese Railways in the Era of High-Speed* (Bingley, UK: Emerald Press).

Drew, J. (2009) "The benefits for rail freight customers of vertical separation and open access," *Transport Reviews*, Vol. 29, No. 2, pp. 223–237.

Dyrhauge, H. (2013) *EU Railway Policy-Making: On Track?* (New York: Palgrave Macmillan).

European Commission (2013) "The performing rail infrastructure manager," http://ec.europa.eu/transport/media/publicthe-performing-rail-infrastructure-manager-lo-res.pdf (accessed July 7, 2016).

Gallamore, R. and J. Meyer (2014) *American Railroads: Decline and Renaissance* (Cambridge, MA: Harvard University Press).

Growitsch, C. and H. Wetzel (2009) "Testing for economies of scope in European railways: An efficiency analysis," *Journal of Transport Economics and Policy*, Vol. 43, No. 1, pp. 1–24.

Harris, R. (1977) "Economies of traffic density in the rail freight industry," *The Bell Journal of Economics*, Vol. 8, No. 2, pp. 556–564.

Haucap, J. and G.J. Klein (2012) "How regulation affects network and service quality in related markets," *Economics Letters*, Vol. 117, No. 2, pp. 521–524.

Ivaldi, M. and G. McCullough (2001) "Density and integration effect on class I U.S. freight railroads," *Journal of Regulatory Economics*, Vol. 19, pp. 161–182.

Ivaldi, M. and G. McCullough (2005) "Welfare trade-offs in U.S. rail mergers," *SSRN*, https://papers.ssrn.com/sol3/pap (accessed May 2, 2018).

Ivaldi, M. and G. McCullough (2008) "Subadditivity tests for network separation with an application to U.S. railroads," *Review of Network Economics*, Vol. 7, No. 1, pp. 159–171.

Laffont, J.-J. and J. Tirole (1993) *A Theory of Incentives in Procurement Regulation* (Cambridge, MA: MIT Press).

Laffont, J.-J. and J. Tirole (2000) *Competition in Telecommunications* (Cambridge, MA: MIT Press).

Mulder, M., M. Lijesen, G. Driessen, and D. van de Velde (2005) "Vertical separation and competition in the Dutch rail industry: A cost-benefit analysis," Working Paper (accessed December 6, 2017).

Nash, C.A. (2008) "Passenger railway reform in the last 20 years—European experience reconsidered," *Research in Transportation Economics*, Vol. 22, No. 1, pp. 61–70.

Nash, C.A., A.S. Smith, D. van de Velde, F. Mizutani, and S. Uranishi (2014) "Structural reforms in the railways: Incentive misalignment and cost implications," *Research in Transportation Economics*, Vol. 48, pp. 16–23.

National Audit Office (2015) "A short guide to network rail," www.nao.org.uk/wp-content/uploads/2015/08/rail-short-guide1.pdf (accessed December 6, 2017).

Nepal, R., A. Carvalho, and J. Foster (2016) "Revisiting electricity liberalization and quality of service: Empirical evidence from New Zealand," *Applied Economics*, Vol. 48, No. 25, pp. 2309–2320.

Nillesen, P. and M. Pollitt (2011) "Ownership unbundling in electricity distribution: Empirical evidence from New Zealand," *Review of Industrial Organization*, Vol. 38, pp. 61–93.

OECD (1997) "Railways: Structure, regulation and competition policy," www.oecd.org/regreform/sectors/1920239.pdf (accessed July 14, 2016).

OECD (2013) "Recent developments in rail transportation services," www.oecd.org/daf/competition/Rail-transportation-Services-2013.pdf (accessed May 19, 2016).

OECD, International Transport Forum (2014) "Freight railway development in Mexico," https://www.oecd-ilibrary.org/transport/freight-railway-development-in-mexico_5jlwvzjd60kb-en (accessed February 20, 2019).

Office of Rail and Roads (2013) "A guide to the rail programme for Network Rail 2014–19," http://orr.gov.uk/__data/a periodic-review-2013.pdf (accessed December 6, 2017).

Pittman, R. (2004) "Chinese railway reform and competition: Lessons from the experience in other countries," *Journal of Transport Economics and Policy*, Vol. 38, No. 2, pp. 309–332.

Pittman, R. (2005) "Structural separation to create competition? The case of freight railways," *Review of Network Economics*, Vol. 4, No. 3, pp. 181–196.

Pittman, R. (2007) "Options for restructuring the state-owned monopoly railway," *Railroad Economics: Research in Transportation Economics*, Vol. 20, Dennis, S. and W. Talley, eds. (Amsterdam: Elsevier), pp. 179–198.

Pittman, R. (2011) "Risk-averse restructuring of freight railways in China," *Utilities Policy*, Vol. 19, No. 3, pp. 152–160.

Pittman, R., O. Diaconu, E. Sip, A. Tomova, and J. Wronka (2007) "Competition in freight railways: 'Above-the-rail' operators in Central Europe and Russia," *Journal of Competition Law and Economics*, Vol. 3, No. 4, pp. 673–687.

Rong, Z. and D. Bouf (2005) "How can competition be introduced into Chinese railways?," *Transport Policy*, Vol. 12, No. 4, pp. 345–352.

Sánchez, P.C., J.M.P. Monsálvez, and L.S. Martínez (2008) "Vertical and horizontal separation in the European railway sector: Effects on productivity," Working Paper No. 12. Instituto Valenciano de Investigaciones Económicas, Fundación BBVA, https://www.fbbva.es/en/publicaciones/vertical-and-horizontal-separation-in-the-european-railway-sector-effects-on-productivity-2/ (accessed February 20, 2019).

Sappington, D. (2010) "Price cap regulation: What have we learned from 25 years of experience in the telecommunications industry," *Journal of Regulatory Economics*, Vol. 38, pp. 227–257.

Savignat, M.G. and C. Nash (1999) "The case for rail reform in Europe: Evidence from studies of production characteristics of the rail industry," *International Journal of Transport Economics*, Vol. 26, No. 2, pp. 201–217.

Scordamaglia, D. and Katsarova, I. (2016) "The fourth railway package: Another step towards a single European railway area," *European Parliamentary Research Service* (March), www.europarl.europa.eu/think (accessed April 17, 2018).

Spence, A.M. (1975) "Monopoly, quality, and regulation," *The Bell Journal of Economics*, Vol. 6, No. 2, pp. 417–429.

TERI (2009) "Competition issues in regulated industries: Case of the Indian transport sector: Railways and ports," The Energy and Resources Institute, New Delhi, www.cci.gov.in/sites/default/-les/ transport_20090723115524.pdf (accessed May 19, 2016).

van de Velde, D., C. Nash, A. Smith, F. Mizutani, M. Lijesen, and F. Zschoche (2012) "EVES rail economic effect of vertical separation in the railway sector," *CER Community of European Railway and Infrastructure Companies*, www.inno-v.nl/projecten/eves-rail-study-quantitativee/ects-on-vertical-separation/ (accessed April 17, 2018).

Vidaud, M. and G. de Tilière (2010) "Railway access charge systems in Europe," Conference Paper STRC 2010, 10th Swiss Transport Research Conference, www.strc.ch/2010/Vidaud.pdf (accessed June 22, 2018).

Weyl, E.G. and M. Fabinger (2013) "Pass-through as an economic tool: Principles of incidence under imperfect competition," *Journal of Political Economy*, Vol. 121, No. 3, pp. 528–583.

Wilson, W. (1997) "Cost savings and productivity in the railroad industry." *Journal of Regulatory Economics*, Vol. 11, pp. 21–40.

World Bank (2017) "China rail," in *Railway Reform: Toolkit for Improving Rail Sector Performance*, 2nd edition, (Washington, DC: World Bank Group), pp. 393–413.

Yuanyuan, J. and C. Wen (2009) "A study on the feasibility of vertical separation model in China's railway industry," *Industrial Economics Research* (in Chinese), Vol. 6, pp. 73–79.

Zhao, J. (2005) "Boundary problem of firm in restructuring China railways," *China Industrial Economics* (in Chinese), Vol. 1, pp. 63–70.

# 7 An Empirical Analysis of Economies of Scope in the U.S. Railroad Industry

*Azrina Abdullah Al-Hadi*
*and James Peoples*

## Introduction

Railroad service has traditionally been a common modal choice for transporting bulk products in the United States.[1] Products primarily transported by rail include coal, grain, lumber, and automobile parts. Given the economic importance of providing consumer access to these vital products, the federal government, since the passage of the 1887 Interstate Commerce Act (ICA), has regulated the operations of Class I rail carriers. Part of this regulation included requiring these large carriers to provide long-haul and short-haul service.[2] Achieving universal service for customers, especially agricultural firms in rural areas, explained part of the rationale for stipulating Class I carriers provide both freight services. While providing rail service to rural areas was key to agricultural producers having access to the U.S. transportation network, Class I carriers faced serious challenges making a profit on short-haul lines. Stepped-up competition from trucking starting in the early 20th century and a lack of traffic density on short-haul routes contributed to Class I carriers difficulties operating profitable short-haul service during the period of regulation by the Interstate Commerce Commission (ICC). These carriers also faced difficulties abandoning short-haul lines in part because abandonment approval from the ICC often meant contending with substantial delays and high cost associated with labor protection rules (Due, 1987). Furthermore, the ICC often considered the loss of business to shippers over the potential gain to rail carriers when ruling on route abandonment requests (Due, 1987).

Passage of the 1980 Staggers Act addressed the financial challenges facing Class I carriers by allowing them to abandon or sell costly lines. Following this Act, the application process for abandonment was streamlined and the burden of proof was transferred from the Class I carrier to the protestant (Due, 1987). Most of the abandoned lines provided short-haul services and were sold to short-line carriers who were better able to operate a profitable business. Short-line carriers employed a nonunion workforce compared with the near total unionization of the Class

I non-management workforce. Hence, short-line carriers operated with lower labor costs and less rigid work rules (Fischer et al., 2001). In addition, the slower speeds used to transport short-haul relative to the speeds used for long-distance routes allowed short-line operators to invest less in capital to maintain track and pay for expensive motive power (Due, 1984). Evidence of this change in business ownership is revealed by the increase of 157 short-line rail carriers in the seven years following the passage of the Staggers Act, compared with a total of 93 new short-line carriers for the preceding 50 years (Mielke, 1988). In contrast, the number of Class I carriers fell from 73 prior to regulatory reform to the current count of seven.

Even though the abandonment of short-haul service by Class I carriers accelerated following the passage of the Staggers Act, these carriers may still continue to provide the service if the line is economically viable. Given the fact that they provide multiple services such as short-haul and long-haul, an examination of economies of scope during the post-Staggers period allows for testing if Class I carriers have taken advantage of this abandonment provision to achieve cost efficiency by selling or abandoning cost inefficient lines and continuing to service cost efficient profitable short-haul lines. While data are not available that specifically identify information on Class I carriers providing short-line service, Class I annual reports (R-1 reports) do present information on the types of train service. These services are classified as unit, way, and through service. Unit train service is dedicated to the transportation of a single commodity for a specific originating-destination location pair (Bitzan, 1999; Growitsch and Wetzel, 2009). Way train service is characterized by the gathering of cars from differing originating locations and bringing them to a major freight terminal (Bitzan, 1999; Growitsch and Wetzel, 2009). Through train service transports goods between two or more major freight terminals (Bitzan, 1999; Growitsch and Wetzel, 2009). Of these three services, the operations of way service most often includes providing short-haul delivery (Bitzan, 1999). Indeed, 2011 information on average distance hauled by Class I carriers presented in Table 7.1 suggests that way train service is a good proxy for short-hauls. For instance, the average distance of a unit train is between three and 30 times longer than the average distance of a way train, and the average distance of a through train is between 4.67 and 14 times longer than the average distance of a way train. For purposes of this study, the significant observation gleaned from Table 7.1 is the fact that the share of freight hauled by way train service, based on number of cars loaded, is a nontrivial 29.49% and 21.48% of the freight hauled for carriers servicing the eastern and western part of the United States, respectively, by 2011. At issue is whether these carriers continue to provide this service in part because they benefit from economies of scope.

Table 7.1 Average Distance[3] of Unit Train Service (U), Way Train Service (W) and Through Train Service (T)

| Carrier (1) | Year (2) | Car Miles (U) (3) | Car Miles (W) (4) | Car Miles (T) (5) | Cars Loaded (U) (6) | Cars Loaded (W) (7) | Cars Loaded (T) (8) | Ave-U (9) | Ave-W (10) | Ave-T (11) |
|---|---|---|---|---|---|---|---|---|---|---|
| BN | 2011 | 6,385,717 | 177,053 | 4,828,145 | 4,262,000 | 2,634,000 | 5,935,000 | 1.50 | 0.07 | 0.81 |
| CN | 2011 | 229,186 | 141,624 | 875,531 | 1,184,000 | 2,313,000 | 318,0000 | 0.19 | 0.06 | 0.28 |
| CP | 2011 | 165,602 | 33,606 | 615,141 | 258,937 | 601,535 | 1,142,000 | 0.64 | 0.06 | 0.54 |
| CSXT | 2011 | 1,763,933 | 206,679 | 3,039,401 | 2,469,000 | 3,894,000 | 11,708,000 | 0.71 | 0.05 | 0.26 |
| EAST | 2011 | 3,143,290 | 660,597 | 6,819,335 | 6,128,000 | 11,288,000 | 20,858,000 | 0.51 | 0.06 | 0.33 |
| KCS | 2011 | 188,564 | 26,674 | 416,033 | 229,577 | 362,472 | 740,229 | 0.82 | 0.07 | 0.56 |
| NS | 2011 | 1,150,171 | 312,294 | 2,904,403 | 2,474,000 | 5,079,000 | 5,969,000 | 0.46 | 0.06 | 0.49 |
| UP | 2011 | 5,284,217 | 178,232 | 7,726,715 | 2,869,000 | 3,098,000 | 9,036,000 | 1.84 | 0.06 | 0.86 |
| WEST | 2011 | 12,024,100 | 415,565 | 13,586,034 | 7,620,000 | 6,697,000 | 16,854,000 | 1.58 | 0.06 | 0.81 |

Note: Data taken from www.stb.dot.gov/stb/industry/urcs.html

Key: In column 1, BN represents Burlington Northern, CN represents Canadian National, CP represents Canadian Pacific, CSXT represents CSX Transportation, EAST represents the east regional Class I carriers, KCS represents Kansas City Southern, NS represents Norfolk Southern, UP represents Union Pacific, and WEST represents the west regional Class I carriers. Columns 3, 4, and 5 represent the car miles for unit, way and through services, respectively. Columns 6, 7, and 8 represent the number of loaded cars for unit, way and through services, respectively. In columns 9, 10, and 11, the variables Ave-U, Ave-W, and Ave-T represent the average distance normalized by the number of loaded cars hauled for unit train, way train, and through train, respectively. Hence, the value of 1.50 for Burlington-Northern unit train service reported in column 9 does not indicate average distance. Rather, the value of 1.5 provides a normalized distance measure that can be used as a basis of comparison with the two other types of transport service. For instance, for Burlington Northern the normalized distance for unit trans service is 21.43 times that of way service and 1.85 times that of through service.

While several railroad studies examine economies of scale, there is a dearth of research examining economies of scope as an approach for analyzing cost efficiency in the post-Staggers era. Those that do examine economies of scope do not base their analysis exclusively on the type of freight services provided to shippers (Kim, 1987; Ivaldi and McCullough, 2004). Rail service considered by these studies represents the type of product hauled, whereas this study examines the type of services that hauls the product. Given the nontrivial freight transport share of way trains, a direct test of economies of scope associated with providing unit, way, and through train service is needed to examine why there has not been a total abandonment of short-haul services by of Class I carriers. This study contributes to our understanding of railroad operations by estimating a normalized quadratic cost equation to directly test for the existence of economies of scope by type of freight service.

## Economics of Scope and Rail Freight Service

An often-cited source of economies of scope is the presence of *public inputs* in the production process.[4] Baumol et al. (1982, pp. 75–76) explain that while these public inputs can be used to produce one good, they are available without additional cost for use in the production of other goods. As an example, these authors observe generating capacity of utility companies as a public input that can be used to provide energy services during peak and off-peak period without additional cost from using the capacity of the plant. Indeed, the cost of the plant itself is fixed. This thread of logic can be easily applied to rail, as Pepall et al. (1999, p. 93) reveal railroad tracks are fixed costs whose use does not vary if service is provided to haul freight or to haul passengers. In contrast, additional cost is incurred if two separate firms built their own tracks such that one company provided freight service and the other provided passenger service.

Early work by Kim (1987) empirically examines whether the U.S. railroad industry's operations satisfy the condition of economies of scope. He estimates a generalized translog form that includes freight service and passenger service as rail service output. The data used for that study comprise 56 Class I U.S. railroads in 1963. His findings suggest that "the cost of providing freight and passenger services separately would be 41% less than the cost of producing them jointly" (Kim, 1987, p. 738). He interprets these results to suggest that prior to deregulation in this industry, the cost structure of Class I carrier was consistent with diseconomics of scope, and cost savings were far from guaranteed when transporting different types of loads, even if shared track and terminals would seem to provide cost advantages of "public inputs." Indeed, industrial organization theory indicates that beyond the potential benefits associated with the existence of public inputs, a necessary condition for economies of scope is the existence of cost complementarity among outputs (Sharkey, 1982, p. 66). This condition requires that a decline in marginal or incremental costs of an output as the output or any other output increase.

More current research using post-deregulation data directly test the cost complementarity in the U.S. rail industry. For instance, Ivaldi and McCullough (2004) use regulatory reports filed by 22 major U.S. freight railroads for the period 1978–2001 to evaluate the technological feasibility of separating vertically integrated firms into an infrastructure company and competing operating firms. Making this separation allows for examining whether cost complementarity exists among infrastructure activities and operational activities. Estimating a multiproduct generalized McFadden cost function, these authors find statistically significant evidence of cost complementarities between infrastructure and operational services that consist of shipping bulk and general freight.

For the purposes of this study, the relevance of economies of scope as an approach for analyzing cost efficiency associated with rail abandonment is it allows for examining the cost effect of jointly providing unit, way, and through train service. Consistent with Pepall et al.'s (1999) observation, a contributing reason for economies of scope in unit, way, and through train service is sharing the existing railroad tracks. Another reason given by Growitsch and Wetzel (2009, p. 5) is the "potential transaction cost savings within an integrated organization since railroad services are characterized by a high level of technological and transactional interdependence between infrastructure and operations." Economies of scope can also arise from sharing "use of headquarters services such as management, marketing or communication services" (Growitsch and Wetzel, 2009, p. 2). There is also the possibility that joint production does contribute to higher cost when separate companies provide disjointed production of these transportation services. For example, Allen et al. (2002) indicate that following regulatory reform in the rail industry, Class I carriers emphasized operating a wholesale type of business requiring greater use of high-speed unit trains and intermodal trains for longer distances. Hence, the retail part of the business that provides service to smaller customers, such as rural farmers, required costly time intensive switching and slow speed operations, especially given the high-wage, highly unionized Class I workforce.[5] In contrast, the workforce of short-line carriers consists primarily of nonunion employees. Allen et al. (2002) also observe that short-line carriers enjoy a cost advantage focusing on short-haul (way) service because their operation requires less capital investment due to the low speeds associated with this service allows for less investment in track and motive power.

This study contributes to our understanding of economies of scope in the U.S. rail industry by directly testing whether economies of scope exist when jointly providing different types of hauling service. The significance for such an analysis is it allows for examining whether providing short-haul (way) service is cost efficient for those Class I carriers that continue to offer this service, even though evidence suggests that carriers specializing in short-haul service experience cost saving advantages relative to the Class I carriers.

The conceptual framework developed by (Sharkey, 1982) as depicted by equation (1) ahead is used to directly test whether economies of scope arises when providing different types of hauling services.

$$C(Y) + C(Y') \geq C(Y + Y') \tag{1}$$

Where $Y$ and $Y'$ are output vectors for N products $Y = (y_1, y_2, \ldots, y_n)$ and $Y' = (y'_1, y'_2, \ldots, y'_n)$ and these vectors consist of disjointed outputs such that when $y_{i,} > 0$, then $y'_{j,} = 0$. Within this theoretical framework of economies of scope for unit, way, and through train service is depicted as follows:

$$C(Y_U, 0, 0) + C(0, Y_W, 0) + C(0, 0, Y_T) > C(Y_U, Y_W, Y_T) \tag{2}$$

where $U$ is unit train service, $W$ is way train service, and $T$ is through train service. This study will refer to equation (2) as the basis for empirically testing the prevalence of economies of scope in the Class I railroad sector.

## Data and Empirical Approach

### Data

The empirical analysis of economies of scope in the U.S. railroad industry is achieved, in part, by using data from Class I annual reports (R-1 reports) from 1983 to 2008. Information on Class I rail carriers' total cost, price of factor inputs, outputs, and movement are taken from these reports. Input prices are provided for labor, fuel, equipment materials, and way and structures. Output levels are provided for unit train, way train, and through train freight service. Movement characteristics include miles of road hauled, average train speed, average length of haul, and percentage of train miles using a caboose. The description of the construction of these variables is presented in the appendix.

### Empirical Approach

The quadratic cost function is commonly used to analyze economies of scope. Baumol et al. (1982) suggested it as an appropriate specification to examine economies of scope since it allows for zero outputs in the estimation. The popular method of translog specification in estimating multiproduct cost function becomes a drawback when the objective is to obtain a direct estimate for economies of scope.[6] Substituting zero outputs will give undefined estimations for log values.[7] Further, the practice of using Box-Cox transformation for zero outputs are seen as inherently non-robust in examining economies of scope (Pulley and Humphrey,

1991). This robustness problem when using translog specification is due to its degenerate limiting behavior (Roller, 1990). To provide a direct test for economies of scope, a well-behaved cost function must be chosen and resolve the in-built interpolation problem (Pulley and Humphrey, 1993). To find a well-suited cost function in examining economies of scope, Pulley and Braunstein (1992) estimated a set of alternative functional forms.[8] They suggested the composite cost function as the chosen specification but admit that no attempt was done to impose regularity conditions. The composite cost function was selected on the basis of its highest log-likelihood value rather than satisfying regularity conditions, since 45% of observations violated concavity in prices. They argued that the regularity condition and statistical fit are most unlikely to be well-matched in selecting the right functional form. In addition, due to the nonlinear in parameters and meaningless interpretation for the coefficients, this form is less commonly used (Triebs et al., 2012).

While the quadratic cost function is widely used as direct estimation for economies of scope, it does not necessarily satisfy the condition of homogeneity in input prices (Lau, 1974; Baumol et al., 1982; Mayo, 1984a). Choosing the implementation of parametric constraints to impose homogeneity, however, sacrifices flexibility of the cost function's form (Caves et al., 1980).[9] Nonetheless, the violation of this regulatory condition can be overcome by normalizing the cost and factor input variable with one of the factor prices. Hence, this study uses the normalized quadratic cost function introduced by Diewert and Wales (1988).[10] The condition for linear homogeneity of this form is satisfied by construction. Besides being the simplest form of Taylor series expansion of second order, its Hessian matrix contains only constant numbers. Therefore, the normalized quadratic function has a distinctive feature whereby it can impose the desired curvature in a parsimonious way without sacrificing its flexibility (Diewert and Fox, 2009). It is common that most estimated flexible functional forms have a tendency of failing the curvature condition (Diewert and Wales, 1987). Since regularity conditions are important and should be satisfied by all observations in the estimation, this unique characteristic serves as a reason for this essay to use the normalized quadratic cost function as an approximation of the true underlying cost function.[11]

The cost structure introduced by Bitzan and Keeler (2003) is used to construct the normalized quadratic cost function. The total cost function[12] is specified as

$$C\left(w_i, y_k, a_m, t\right) \tag{3}$$

$$w_i = \left(w_L, w_E, w_F, w_M, w_{WS}\right)^{13}$$

$$y_k = \left(y_U, y_W, y_T\right)$$

$$a_m = \left(a_{miles}, a_{speed}, a_{haul}, a_{caboose}\right)$$

where $C$ is the total cost, $w_L$ is the labor price, $w_E$ is the equipment price, $w_F$ is the fuel price, $w_M$ is the material and supplies price, $w_{WS}$ is the way and structures price, $Y_U$ is the adjusted unit train gross ton-miles, $Y_W$ is the adjusted way train gross ton-miles, $Y_T$ is the adjusted through train gross ton-miles, $a_{miles}$ is the miles of road, $a_{speed}$ is the train miles per train hour, $a_{haul}$ is the average length of haul, $a_{caboose}$ is the fraction of train miles operated with caboose and $t$ represents time trend capturing the changes in technology. The previous cost function can be estimated by incorporating the second-order Taylor series expansion. Following the usual practice, the mean is used as base point for the approximation. The Taylor expansion is presented in the following equation:

$$C(w_i, y_k, a_m, t) = \frac{C(\bar{w}_i, \bar{y}_k, \bar{a}_m, t)}{0!}$$

$$+ \sum_i \frac{\partial C}{\partial w_i}(w_i - \bar{w}_i) + \sum_k \frac{\partial C}{\partial y_k}(y_k - \bar{y}_k) + \sum_m \frac{\partial C}{\partial a_m}(a_m - \bar{a}_m) + \frac{\partial C}{\partial t}(t - \bar{t})$$

$$+ \sum_i \sum_j \frac{\left(\frac{\partial^2 C}{\partial w_i \partial w_j}\right)}{2!}(w_i - \bar{w}_i)(w_j - \bar{w}_j) + \sum_i \sum_k \frac{\left(\frac{\partial^2 C}{\partial w_i \partial y_k}\right)}{2!}(w_i - \bar{w}_i)(y_k - \bar{y}_k)$$

$$+ \sum_i \sum_m \frac{\left(\frac{\partial^2 C}{\partial w_i \partial a_m}\right)}{2!}(w_i - \bar{w}_i)(a_m - \bar{a}_m) + \sum_i \frac{\left(\frac{\partial^2 C}{\partial w_i \partial t}\right)}{2!}(w_i - \bar{w}_i)(t - \bar{t})$$

$$+ \sum_k \sum_i \frac{\left(\frac{\partial^2 C}{\partial y_k \partial w_i}\right)}{2!}(y_k - \bar{y}_k)(w_i - \bar{w}_i) + \sum_k \sum_l \frac{\left(\frac{\partial^2 C}{\partial y_k \partial y_l}\right)}{2!}(y_k - \bar{y}_k)(y_l - \bar{y}_l)$$

$$+ \sum_k \sum_m \frac{\left(\frac{\partial^2 C}{\partial y_k \partial a_m}\right)}{2!}(y_k - \bar{y}_k)(a_m - \bar{a}_m) + \sum_k \frac{\left(\frac{\partial^2 C}{\partial y_k \partial t}\right)}{2!}(y_k - \bar{y}_k)(t - \bar{t})$$

$$+ \sum_m \sum_i \frac{\left(\frac{\partial^2 C}{\partial a_m \partial w_i}\right)}{2!}(a_m - \bar{a}_m)(w_i - \bar{w}_i)$$

$$+ \sum_m \sum_k \frac{\left(\frac{\partial^2 C}{\partial a_m \partial y_k}\right)}{2!}(a_m - \bar{a}_m)(y_k - \bar{y}_k)$$

$$+\sum_m \sum_n \frac{\left(\dfrac{\partial^2 C}{\partial a_m a_n}\right)}{2!}(a_m - \bar{a}_m)(a_n - \bar{a}_n) + \sum_m \frac{\left(\dfrac{\partial^2 C}{\partial a_m \partial t}\right)}{2!}(a_m - \bar{a}_m)(t - \bar{t})$$

$$+\sum_i \frac{\left(\dfrac{\partial^2 C}{\partial t \partial w_i}\right)}{2!}(t - \bar{t})(w_i - \bar{w}_i) + \sum_k \frac{\left(\dfrac{\partial^2 C}{\partial t \partial y_k}\right)}{2!}(t - \bar{t})(y_k - \bar{y}_k)$$

$$+\sum_m \frac{\left(\dfrac{\partial^2 C}{\partial t \partial a_m}\right)}{2!}(t - \bar{t})(a_m - \bar{a}_m) + \frac{\dfrac{\partial^2 C}{\partial t^2}}{2!}(t - \bar{t})^2 \tag{4}$$

The partial derivatives in equation (4) are replaced with parameters from the cost estimation as presented in equation (5). Applying the symmetry of second derivatives by Young's theorem,[14] simplifying and rearranging the terms, the resulting equation is the quadratic cost function as shown in the following equation:[15]

$$C = \alpha_0 + \sum_i \alpha_i (w_i - \bar{w}_i) + \sum_k \beta_k (y_k - \bar{y}_k) + \sum_m \sigma_m (a_m - \bar{a}_m) + \theta(t - \bar{t})$$

$$+ \frac{1}{2}\sum_i \sum_j \alpha_{ij}(w_i - \bar{w}_i)(w_j - \bar{w}_j) + \frac{1}{2}\sum_k \sum_l \beta_{kl}(y_k - \bar{y}_k)(y_l - \bar{y}_l)$$

$$+ \frac{1}{2}\sum_m \sum_n \sigma_{mn}(a_m - \bar{a}_m)(a_n - \bar{a}_n) + \frac{1}{2}\gamma(t - \bar{t})^2$$

$$+ \sum_i \sum_k \tau_{ik}(w_i - \bar{w}_i)(y_k - \bar{y}_k)$$

$$+ \sum_i \sum_m \vartheta_{im}(w_i - \bar{w}_i)(a_m - \bar{a}_m) + \sum_k \sum_m \varphi_{km}(a_m - \bar{a}_m)(y_k - \bar{y}_k),$$

$$+ \sum_i \partial_i (t - \bar{t})(w_i - \bar{w}_i) + \sum_k \pi_k (t - \bar{t})(y_k - \bar{y}_k)$$

$$+ \sum_m \mu_m (t - \bar{t})(a_m - \bar{a}_m) + \varepsilon \tag{5}$$

Tovar et al. (2007) identify two reasons why the variables deviation from the sample mean are commonly applied in research. It gives an immediate estimation of marginal costs and factor demand. Furthermore, it increases the variables' variations that avoid multicollinearity among linear, square, and cross terms. The properties of any cost function are monotonic in factor prices and outputs, homogenous of degree one in factor prices and concave in factor prices. Normalization is done by choosing one of the factor prices as the denominator when dividing the cost and all other factor prices. This allows estimation of relative prices and preserves linear homogeneity in factor prices

(Díaz-Hernández et al., 2005). In matrix form, this equation can be illustrated as follows:[16]

$$
C(W,Y,A,T) = \alpha_0 + \begin{bmatrix} \alpha_1 & \alpha_2 & \alpha_3 & \alpha_4 \end{bmatrix} \begin{bmatrix} w_L \\ w_E \\ w_F \\ w_{WS} \end{bmatrix} + \begin{bmatrix} \beta_1 & \beta_2 & \beta_3 \end{bmatrix} \begin{bmatrix} y_U \\ y_W \\ y_T \end{bmatrix}
$$

$$
+ \begin{bmatrix} \sigma_1 & \sigma_2 & \sigma_3 & \sigma_4 \end{bmatrix} \begin{bmatrix} a_M \\ a_S \\ a_H \\ a_C \end{bmatrix} + \theta[t] + \frac{1}{2} \begin{bmatrix} w_L & w_E & w_F & w_{WS} \end{bmatrix}
$$

$$
\begin{bmatrix} \alpha_{11} & \alpha_{12} & \alpha_{13} & \alpha_{14} \\ \alpha_{21} & \alpha_{22} & \alpha_{23} & \alpha_{24} \\ \alpha_{31} & \alpha_{32} & \alpha_{33} & \alpha_{34} \\ \alpha_{41} & \alpha_{42} & \alpha_{43} & \alpha_{44} \end{bmatrix} \begin{bmatrix} w_L \\ w_E \\ w_F \\ w_{WS} \end{bmatrix}
$$

$$
+ \frac{1}{2} \begin{bmatrix} y_U & y_W & y_T \end{bmatrix} \begin{bmatrix} \beta_{11} & \beta_{12} & \beta_{13} \\ \beta_{21} & \beta_{22} & \beta_{23} \\ \beta_{31} & \beta_{32} & \beta_{33} \end{bmatrix} \begin{bmatrix} y_U & y_W & y_T \end{bmatrix}
$$

$$
+ \frac{1}{2} \begin{bmatrix} a_M & a_S & a_H & a_C \end{bmatrix} \begin{bmatrix} \sigma_{11} & \sigma_{12} & \sigma_{13} & \sigma_{14} \\ \sigma_{21} & \sigma_{22} & \sigma_{23} & \sigma_{24} \\ \sigma_{31} & \sigma_{32} & \sigma_{33} & \sigma_{34} \\ \sigma_{41} & \sigma_{42} & \sigma_{43} & \sigma_{44} \end{bmatrix} \begin{bmatrix} a_M \\ a_S \\ a_H \\ a_C \end{bmatrix}
$$

$$
+ \frac{1}{2} \gamma[t][t] + \begin{bmatrix} w_L & w_E & w_F & w_{WS} \end{bmatrix} \begin{bmatrix} \tau_{11} & \tau_{12} & \tau_{13} \\ \tau_{21} & \tau_{22} & \tau_{23} \\ \tau_{31} & \tau_{32} & \tau_{33} \\ \tau_{41} & \tau_{42} & \tau_{43} \end{bmatrix} \begin{bmatrix} y_U \\ y_W \\ y_T \end{bmatrix}
$$

$$
+ \begin{bmatrix} w_L & w_E & w_F & w_{WS} \end{bmatrix} \begin{bmatrix} \vartheta_{11} & \vartheta_{12} & \vartheta_{13} & \vartheta_{14} \\ \vartheta_{21} & \vartheta_{22} & \vartheta_{23} & \vartheta_{24} \\ \vartheta_{31} & \vartheta_{32} & \vartheta_{33} & \vartheta_{34} \\ \vartheta_{41} & \vartheta_{42} & \vartheta_{43} & \vartheta_{44} \end{bmatrix} \begin{bmatrix} a_M \\ a_S \\ a_H \\ a_C \end{bmatrix}
$$

$$
+ \begin{bmatrix} a_M & a_S & a_H & a_C \end{bmatrix} \begin{bmatrix} \varphi_{11} & \varphi_{12} & \varphi_{13} \\ \varphi_{21} & \varphi_{22} & \varphi_{23} \\ \varphi_{31} & \varphi_{32} & \varphi_{33} \\ \varphi_{41} & \varphi_{42} & \varphi_{43} \end{bmatrix} \begin{bmatrix} y_U \\ y_W \\ y_T \end{bmatrix}
$$

$$+ [t][\delta_1 \quad \delta_2 \quad \delta_3 \quad \delta_4] \begin{bmatrix} w_L \\ w_E \\ w_F \\ w_{WS} \end{bmatrix} + [t][\pi_1 \quad \pi_2 \quad \pi_3] \begin{bmatrix} y_U \\ y_W \\ y_T \end{bmatrix}$$

$$+ [t][\mu_1 \quad \mu_2 \quad \mu_3 \quad \mu_4] \begin{bmatrix} a_M \\ a_S \\ a_H \\ a_C \end{bmatrix} \tag{6}$$

The previous equation can also be expressed as

$$C(W, Y, A, t) = \alpha_0 + (A * W') + (B * Y') + (C * Z') + (D * t)$$

$$+ \left(\frac{1}{2} * W * E * W'\right) + \left(\frac{1}{2} * Y * F * Y'\right) + \left(\frac{1}{2} * Z * G * Z'\right) + \left(\frac{1}{2} * t * H * t\right)$$

$$+ (W * I * Y') + (W * J * Z') + (Z * K * Y') + (t * L * W')$$
$$+ (t * M * Y') + (t * N * Z') \tag{7}$$

where

$$W = [w_L \quad w_E \quad w_F \quad w_{WS}]; \quad Y = [y_U \quad y_W \quad y_T]; \quad Z = [a_M \quad a_S \quad a_H \quad a_C]$$

$$A = [\alpha_1 \quad \alpha_2 \quad \alpha_3 \quad \alpha_4]; \quad B = [\beta_1 \quad \beta_2 \quad \beta_3]; \quad C = [\sigma_1 \quad \sigma_2 \quad \sigma_3 \quad \sigma_4]; \quad D = [\theta]$$

$$E = \begin{bmatrix} \alpha_{11} & \alpha_{12} & \alpha_{13} & \alpha_{14} \\ \alpha_{21} & \alpha_{22} & \alpha_{23} & \alpha_{24} \\ \alpha_{31} & \alpha_{32} & \alpha_{33} & \alpha_{34} \\ \alpha_{41} & \alpha_{42} & \alpha_{43} & \alpha_{44} \end{bmatrix}; \quad F = \begin{bmatrix} \beta_{11} & \beta_{12} & \beta_{13} \\ \beta_{21} & \beta_{22} & \beta_{23} \\ \beta_{31} & \beta_{32} & \beta_{33} \end{bmatrix}; \quad G = \begin{bmatrix} \sigma_{11} & \sigma_{12} & \sigma_{13} & \sigma_{14} \\ \sigma_{21} & \sigma_{22} & \sigma_{23} & \sigma_{24} \\ \sigma_{31} & \sigma_{32} & \sigma_{33} & \sigma_{34} \\ \sigma_{41} & \sigma_{42} & \sigma_{43} & \sigma_{44} \end{bmatrix}$$

$$H = [t]; \quad I = \begin{bmatrix} \tau_{11} & \tau_{12} & \tau_{13} \\ \tau_{21} & \tau_{22} & \tau_{23} \\ \tau_{31} & \tau_{32} & \tau_{33} \\ \tau_{41} & \tau_{42} & \tau_{43} \end{bmatrix}; \quad J = \begin{bmatrix} \vartheta_{11} & \vartheta_{12} & \vartheta_{13} & \vartheta_{14} \\ \vartheta_{21} & \vartheta_{22} & \vartheta_{23} & \vartheta_{24} \\ \vartheta_{31} & \vartheta_{32} & \vartheta_{33} & \vartheta_{34} \\ \vartheta_{41} & \vartheta_{42} & \vartheta_{43} & \vartheta_{44} \end{bmatrix};$$

$$K = \begin{bmatrix} \varphi_{11} & \varphi_{12} & \varphi_{13} \\ \varphi_{21} & \varphi_{22} & \varphi_{23} \\ \varphi_{31} & \varphi_{32} & \varphi_{33} \\ \varphi_{41} & \varphi_{42} & \varphi_{43} \end{bmatrix}$$

$$L = [\delta_1 \quad \delta_2 \quad \delta_3 \quad \delta_4]; \quad M = [\pi_1 \quad \pi_2 \quad \pi_3]; \quad N = [\mu_1 \quad \mu_2 \quad \mu_3 \quad \mu_4]$$

Furthermore, when expanding the brackets with matrices with $\alpha_{ij} = \alpha_{ji}$, $\beta_{kl} = \beta_{lk}$ and $\sigma_{mn} = \sigma_{nm}$, the cost function is illustrated in the following equation.

$$
\begin{aligned}
C(W,Y,A,t) = {} & \alpha_0 + \alpha_1 w_L + \alpha_2 w_E + \alpha_3 w_F + \alpha_4 w_{WS} + \beta_1 y_U + \beta_2 y_W + \beta_3 y_T \\
& + \sigma_1 a_M + \sigma_2 a_S + \sigma_3 a_H + \sigma_4 a_C + \theta t + \frac{1}{2}\alpha_{11} w_L^2 + \frac{1}{2}\alpha_{22} w_E^2 \\
& + \frac{1}{2}\alpha_{33} w_F^2 + \frac{1}{2}\alpha_{44} w_{WS}^2 + \frac{1}{2}\beta_{11} y_U^2 + \frac{1}{2}\beta_{22} y_W^2 + \frac{1}{2}\beta_{33} y_T^2 \\
& + \frac{1}{2}\sigma_{11} a_M^2 + \frac{1}{2}\sigma_{22} a_S^2 + \frac{1}{2}\sigma_{33} a_H^2 + \frac{1}{2}\sigma_{44} a_C^2 + \frac{1}{2}\gamma t^2 \\
& + \alpha_{12} w_L w_E + \alpha_{13} w_L w_F + \alpha_{14} w_L w_{WS} + \alpha_{23} w_E w_F \\
& + \alpha_{24} w_E w_{WS} + \alpha_{34} w_F w_{WS} + \beta_{12} y_U y_W + \beta_{13} y_U y_T + \beta_{23} y_W y_T \\
& + \sigma_{12} a_M a_S + \sigma_{13} a_M a_H + \sigma_{14} a_M a_C + \sigma_{23} a_S a_H + \sigma_{24} a_S a_C \\
& + \sigma_{34} a_H a_C + \tau_{11} w_L y_U + \tau_{12} w_L y_W + \tau_{13} w_L y_T + \tau_{21} w_E y_U \\
& + \tau_{22} w_E y_W + \tau_{23} w_E y_T + \tau_{31} w_F y_U + \tau_{32} w_F y_W + \tau_{33} w_F y_T \\
& + \tau_{41} w_{WS} y_U + \tau_{42} w_{WS} y_W + \tau_{43} w_{WS} y_T + \vartheta_{11} w_L a_M + \vartheta_{12} w_L a_S \\
& + \vartheta_{13} w_L a_H + \vartheta_{14} w_L a_C + \vartheta_{21} w_E a_M + \vartheta_{22} w_E a_S + \vartheta_{23} w_E a_H \\
& + \vartheta_{24} w_E a_C + \vartheta_{31} w_F a_M + \vartheta_{32} w_F a_S + \vartheta_{33} w_F a_H + \vartheta_{34} w_F a_C \\
& + \vartheta_{41} w_{WS} a_M + \vartheta_{42} w_{WS} a_S + \vartheta_{43} w_{WS} a_H + \vartheta_{44} w_{WS} a_C \\
& + \varphi_{11} a_M y_U + \varphi_{12} a_M y_W + \varphi_{13} a_M y_T + \varphi_{21} a_S y_U + \varphi_{22} a_S y_W \\
& + \varphi_{23} a_S y_T + \varphi_{31} a_H y_U + \varphi_{32} a_H y_W + \varphi_{33} a_H y_T + \varphi_{41} a_C y_U \\
& + \varphi_{42} a_C y_W + \varphi_{43} a_C y_T + \delta_1 w_L t + \delta_2 w_E t + \delta_3 w_F t + \delta_4 w_{WS} t \\
& + \pi_1 y_U t + \pi_2 y_W t + \pi_3 y_T t + \mu_1 a_M t + \mu_2 a_S t + \mu_3 a_H t \\
& + \mu_4 a_C t
\end{aligned}
\tag{8}
$$

Applying Shephard's Lemma obtains each factor demand equations. This is done by differentiating the cost function with respect to its price as follows:

$$
\frac{\partial C}{\partial w_i} = x_i = \alpha_i + \sum_j \alpha_{ij} w_j + \sum_k \tau_{ik} y_k + \sum_m \vartheta_{im} a_m + \gamma_i t
\tag{9}
$$

The factor demand equations together with the cost function are estimated in a seemingly unrelated regression system. In testing for the concavity, the Hessian matrix is used and since one of the factor prices is used for normalizing, the Hessian matrix consists of only four factor prices. To satisfy the condition of concavity in factor prices, the Hessian matrix which is matrix E, should be negative semi-definite.[17] For normalized quadratic cost function, its Hessian matrix consists of only scalars. The condition for concavity in input prices represents all observations in the sample in which global concavity is investigated rather than local concavity. This is different compared with translog cost function where each observation has its own calculated Hessian matrix. When global concavity is violated, curvature imposition can be achieved using the Cholesky decomposition technique. Curvature imposition can be carried out by rerunning the cost function, replacing the matrix of input prices parameters for the cost function. From the previous equation, to ensure a negative semi-definite Hessian, matrix E can be reparameterized by $E = -KK'$ where K is a lower triangular matrix K such that

$$
E = -KK' = -
\begin{bmatrix}
k_{11} & 0 & 0 & 0 \\
k_{21} & k_{22} & 0 & 0 \\
k_{31} & k_{32} & k_{33} & 0 \\
k_{41} & k_{42} & k_{43} & k_{44}
\end{bmatrix}
\begin{bmatrix}
k_{11} & k_{21} & k_{31} & k_{41} \\
0 & k_{22} & k_{32} & k_{42} \\
0 & 0 & k_{33} & k_{43} \\
0 & 0 & 0 & k_{44}
\end{bmatrix}
$$

$$
=
\begin{bmatrix}
-k_{11}^2 & -k_{11}k_{21} & -k_{11}k_{31} & -k_{11}k_{41} \\
-k_{11}k_{21} & -\left(k_{21}^2 + k_{22}^2\right) & -\left(k_{21}k_{31} + k_{22}k_{32}\right) & -\left(k_{21}k_{41} + k_{22}k_{42}\right) \\
-k_{11}k_{31} & -\left(k_{21}k_{31} + k_{22}k_{32}\right) & -\left(k_{31}^2 + k_{32}^2 + k_{33}^2\right) & -\left(k_{31}k_{41} + k_{32}k_{42} + k_{33}k_{43}\right) \\
-k_{11}k_{41} & -\left(k_{21}k_{41} + k_{22}k_{42}\right) & -\left(k_{31}k_{41} + k_{32}k_{42} + k_{33}k_{43}\right) & -\left(k_{41}^2 + k_{42}^2 + k_{43}^2 + k_{44}^2\right)
\end{bmatrix}
\quad (10)
$$

The elements of the previous matrix replaces the parameters in the cost function and factor demand equations which represents the curvature imposition. This actually made the system of equations no longer linear in parameters.

The use of normalized quadratic function enables testing the existence of economies of scope for the rail carriers since it allows evaluation at zero outputs. Following Baumol et al. (1982), the global economies of scope for the production of the three train services is shown in the following equation:[18]

$$
SCOPE = C\left(y_U, 0, 0\right) + C\left(0, y_W, 0\right) + C\left(0, 0, y_T\right) - C\left(y_U, y_W, y_T\right)
$$

$$
= 2*\left(\alpha_0 + \alpha_1 w_L + \alpha_2 w_E + \alpha_3 w_F + \alpha_4 w_{WS} + \sigma_1 a_M + \sigma_2 a_S + \sigma_3 a_H + \sigma_4 a_C + \theta t\right.
$$

$$
+ \frac{1}{2}\alpha_{11}w_L^2 + \frac{1}{2}\alpha_{22}w_E^2 + \frac{1}{2}\alpha_{33}w_F^2 + \frac{1}{2}\alpha_{44}w_{WS}^2 + \frac{1}{2}\sigma_{11}a_M^2 + \frac{1}{2}\sigma_{22}a_S^2 + \frac{1}{2}\sigma_{33}a_H^2
$$

$$
+ \frac{1}{2}\sigma_{44}a_C^2 + \frac{1}{2}\gamma t^2 + \alpha_{12}w_L w_E + \alpha_{13}w_L w_F + \alpha_{14}w_L w_{WS} + \alpha_{23}w_E w_F
$$

$$+ \alpha_{24} w_E w_{WS} + \alpha_{34} w_F w_{WS} + \sigma_{12} a_M a_S + \sigma_{13} a_M a_H + \sigma_{14} a_M a_C + \sigma_{23} a_S a_H$$

$$+ \sigma_{24} a_S a_C + \sigma_{34} a_H a_C + \vartheta_{11} w_L a_M + \vartheta_{12} w_L a_S + \vartheta_{13} w_L a_H + \vartheta_{14} w_L a_C + \vartheta_{21} w_E a_M$$

$$+ \vartheta_{22} w_E a_S + \vartheta_{23} w_E a_H + \vartheta_{24} w_E a_C + \vartheta_{31} w_F a_M + \vartheta_{32} w_F a_S + \vartheta_{33} w_F a_H$$

$$+ \vartheta_{34} w_F a_C + \vartheta_{41} w_{WS} a_M + \vartheta_{42} w_{WS} a_S + \vartheta_{43} w_{WS} a_H + \vartheta_{44} w_{WS} a_C + \delta_1 w_L t$$

$$+ \delta_2 w_E t + \delta_3 w_F t + \delta_4 w_{WS} t + \mu_1 a_M t + \mu_2 a_S t + \mu_3 a_H t + \mu_4 a_C t)$$

$$+ \beta_{12} y_U y_W + \beta_{13} y_U y_T + \beta_{23} y_W y_T \tag{11}$$

Farsi et al. (2007a) uses the following formula $(SC_m)$ to calculate the degree of product-specific economies of scope:

$$SC_m = \frac{C(y^m) + C(y^{-m}) - C(y)}{C(y)} \tag{12}$$

This measures the proportional increase in cost due to production of all outputs excluding the $m^{th}$ output. Fraquelli et al. (2004) defines it as cost advantage (disadvantage) of one particular "stand-alone" output in the production. In other words, it examines whether economies of scope still prevails when separating the production of $m^{th}$ output from the rest. Fraquelli et al. (2004) further use another measure for degree of product-specific economies of scope. It examines the proportional increase in cost due to production of certain combination of outputs where the other combinations exhibit zero output. Their measure is showed in the following equation:

$$SC_{mn} = \frac{C(y^m) + C(y^n) - C(y^{(m)}, y^{(n)})}{C(y^{(m)}, y^{(n)})} \tag{13}$$

Unfortunately, the contribution from research on economies of scope for multiple freight rail outputs is quite limited. This may be due in part to an absence of data providing information on the stand-alone cost of producing one of the outputs or any combinations of the three outputs. Information is not provided revealing the value of products shipped when Class I carriers provide only one or two of the freight train service.[19] Observations that have zero outputs for the unit train service are deleted from the sample as normally practiced by other researchers. Therefore, in this study, a hypothetical output vector is simulated and a direct approach is made by calculating the expected cost of every individual firm if it has produced specialized output or any combination of outputs. For example, one of the outputs is set at its actual value and the other outputs are given values equal to zero.[20] As a result, it permits tractable tests for economies of scope in the railroad industry.

Applying to the three train services, economies of scope can be tested by hypothetically simulating railroad firms producing zero outputs. Equation

(2) provides a direct test of test economies of scope for all three services. It gives the estimated cost of producing all the train services through one network. Specifically, equation (2) examines whether economies of scope exists if there is specialization in producing the train services. This analysis can be further extended in finding out whether economies of scope still exists when separating the production of one of the train services from the rest. This is shown from equation (14) to equation (16).

$$SCOPE-U: \quad C(y_U,0,0)+C(0,y_w,y_T) > C(y_U,y_W,y_T) \qquad (14)$$

$$SCOPE-W: \quad C(0,y_W,0)+C(y_U,0,y_T) > C(y_U,y_W,y_T) \qquad (15)$$

$$SCOPE-T: \quad C(0,0,y_T)+C(y_U,y_w,0) > C(y_U,y_W,y_T) \qquad (16)$$

SCOPE-U measures the proportional increase in cost due to production of all train services except unit train. SCOPE-W and SCOPE-T imply the same definition for way train and through train, respectively. Equation (17) through equation (19) are included for completeness in the analysis. These equations are used to test economies of scope for any combination of pairs of train services, which are between unit and way trains, between unit and through trains, and between way and through trains. The cost function exhibiting economies of scope for any two train services can be shown in the following:

$$SCOPE-U-W: \quad C(y_U,0,0)+C(0,y_W,0) > C(y_U,y_W,0) \qquad (17)$$

$$SCOPE-U-T: \quad C(y_U,0,0)+C(0,0,y_T) > C(y_U,0,y_T) \qquad (18)$$

$$SCOPE-W-T: \quad C(0,y_W,0)+C(0,0,y_T) > C(0,y_W,y_T) \qquad (19)$$

SCOPE-U-W investigates whether producing a combination of unit train and way train exhibits economies of scope. SCOPE-U-T and SCOPE-W-T examines whether economies of scope prevails when combination of unit-through train and way-through train are produced respectively while zero output for others. Baumol et al. (1982) mentioned that weak cost complementarities are considered as a sufficient condition of presence of economies of scope in contestable market. In the analysis, the economies of scope can be calculated for every firm from the cost function estimation. The predicted value for cost producing all outputs and individually is based on the estimates of the cost function. This is then substituted in the formula for economies of scope.

## Cost Results

The system of equations consisting of the cost function and factor demand equations is estimated using a seemingly unrelated regression technique first introduced by Zellner (1962). The variables in the system are deviations from the sample mean with the price of material as the normalizing factor.[21] The monotonicity condition for output and input prices is validated by looking at whether total cost increases as outputs increase $\left(\dfrac{\partial C}{\partial y_i} > 0\right)$[22] and also whether total cost increases as input prices increase $\left(\dfrac{\partial C}{\partial w_i} > 0\right)$.[23] The test shows that between 67% and 93% of observations fulfill the condition for monotonicity as shown in the following Table 7.2.

Another regularity condition to be satisfied by an estimated cost function is the condition for concavity in input prices. For normalized quadratic cost function, the concavity condition is not data dependent and therefore can be tested globally rather than locally. The Hessian matrix is negative semi-definite when all principal minors of the Hessian should alternate in signs starting with less than zero. Unfortunately, the estimated cost function does not satisfy the curvature conditions in input prices for all observations. Violation of concavity in input prices is often found in past studies and highlighted since it is a firm's rational behavior to minimize cost (Ogawa, 2011). Nonetheless, imposing global curvature can be done relatively easily[24] when estimating the normalized quadratic cost function. If the concavity in input prices is not imposed, the empirical model is not consistent with the economic theory and any linear combination in the price space can further minimize cost. In consideration of this problem, this chapter imposes concavity in the cost estimation by means of Cholesky decomposition discussed previously. The parameter estimates obtained from estimating the normalized quadratic cost function without imposing concavity becomes the initial values used for the nonlinear estimation.[25]

Table 7.3 shows the estimated coefficients for the equation systems before and after imposing concavity in input prices. The intercept depicts the total fixed cost that occurs at the sample mean. The second column

*Table 7.2* Summary of Monotonicity Condition for Outputs and Input Prices

| *Monotonicity Condition* | *Percentage* |
| --- | --- |
| $\partial C / \partial y_U > 0$ | 93% of observations |
| $\partial C / \partial y_W > 0$ | 67% of observations |
| $\partial C / \partial y_T > 0$ | 72% of observations |
| $\partial C / \partial w_L > 0$ | 71% of observations |
| $\partial C / \partial w_E > 0$ | 70% of observations |
| $\partial C / \partial w_F > 0$ | 75% of observations |
| $\partial C / \partial w_{WS} > 0$ | 85% of observations |

*Table 7.3* Parameter Estimates for the Normalized Quadratic Cost Function

| Variables | Without Concavity | | With Concavity | |
|---|---|---|---|---|
| | *Coefficient* | *s.e.* | *Coefficient* | *Approx s.e.* |
| Intercept | 59052.21*** | 3674.778 | 5209527** | 2445709 |
| $w_L$ | 19337425*** | 830899.7 | 35330212*** | 2845360 |
| $w_E$ | 1093.011*** | 268.007 | 9784.998*** | 1232.1 |
| $w_F$ | 4.00E+08*** | 31835309 | 2.98E+08 | 2.73E+09 |
| $w_{WS}$ | 12137.46*** | 199.9104 | 16557.98*** | 589.9 |
| $y_U$ | 0.000364*** | 0.000057 | 0.095018** | 0.0416 |
| $y_W$ | 0.003745*** | 0.000299 | 0.204913 | 0.2293 |
| $y_T$ | 0.000546*** | 0.000049 | 0.034689 | 0.0281 |
| $a_{miles}$ | −1.65865*** | 0.237675 | −432.175** | 173.1 |
| $a_{speed}$ | −249.267*** | 84.19541 | −83183.7 | 84037.5 |
| $a_{haul}$ | 24.42795*** | 7.312301 | 5454.166 | 6676 |
| $a_{caboose}$ | 522069 | 2559789 | −2.82E+08 | 2.25E+09 |
| $t$ | −2121.99*** | 178.884 | −315368** | 154310 |
| $0.5(y_U)^2$ | −2.99E-13 | 5.09E-13 | −5.63E-10* | 3.07E-10 |
| $0.5(y_W)^2$ | −1.24E-09*** | 4.65E-11 | −6.87E-08 | 4.29E-08 |
| $0.5(y_T)^2$ | 7.19E-12*** | 5.84E-13 | −2.39E-10 | 4.11E-10 |
| $0.5(W_L)^2$ | −4.20E+09*** | 1.94E+08 | −23914515.1 | ### |
| $0.5(W_E)^2$ | 48.54731*** | 4.279762 | −41.5190675 | ### |
| $0.5(W_F)^2$ | −6.88E+11*** | 4.45E+10 | −23991831.7 | ### |
| $0.5(W_{WS})^2$ | −76.382*** | 10.1424 | −81.4304148 | ### |
| $0.5(a_{miles})^2$ | 0.000595*** | 0.000041 | 0.05656** | 0.0244 |
| $0.5(a_{speed})^2$ | −33.5235*** | 6.097911 | −2377.71 | 7423.7 |
| $0.5(a_{haul})^2$ | −0.28017*** | 0.034789 | 23.27947 | 33.2802 |
| $0.5(a_{caboose})^2$ | −8.44E+09*** | 3.11E+09 | −6.17E+11 | 3.18E+12 |
| $0.5(t)^2$ | 68.04709*** | 13.3609 | 17465.62 | 10789.6 |
| $w_L * w_E$ | 798090.7*** | 46101.71 | −28769.7678 | ### |
| $w_L * w_F$ | −3.58E+10*** | 3.19E+09 | 23953114.14 | ### |
| $w_L * w_{WS}$ | −525085*** | 39094.04 | −9829.24964 | ### |
| $w_L * y_U$ | 0.139759*** | 0.011143 | −0.14232*** | 0.0245 |
| $w_L * y_W$ | −3.29477*** | 0.127369 | −0.40688 | 0.3871 |
| $w_L * y_T$ | 0.253375*** | 0.011565 | 0.076465** | 0.0341 |
| $w_L * a_{miles}$ | 337.9932*** | 81.88123 | 3486.44*** | 288.4 |
| $w_L * a_{speed}$ | 1000907*** | 57102.85 | 59734.72 | 196506 |
| $w_L * a_{haul}$ | 3009.409 | 3183.987 | −10478.7 | 8574.9 |
| $w_L * a_{caboose}$ | 9.35E+09*** | 1.14E+09 | 2.11E+09 | 3.07E+09 |
| $w_L * t$ | −709356*** | 74962.77 | −241409 | 261000 |
| $w_E * w_F$ | 4112048*** | 314702.7 | 28809.09453 | ### |

(Continued)

*Table 7.3* (Continued)

| Variables | Without Concavity | | With Concavity | |
| --- | --- | --- | --- | --- |
| | Coefficient | s.e. | Coefficient | Approx s.e. |
| $w_E * w_{WS}$ | 228.76*** | 7.244396 | 2.192292028 | ### |
| $w_E * y_U$ | −3.50E-06 | 3.75E-06 | −0.00004*** | 0.000014 |
| $w_E * y_W$ | −0.00037*** | 0.000045 | −0.0001 | 0.000211 |
| $w_E * y_T$ | 0.000047*** | 4.11E-06 | 0.000021 | 0.00002 |
| $w_E * a_{miles}$ | −0.08531*** | 0.023706 | 0.824577*** | 0.132 |
| $w_E * a_{speed}$ | 8.434251 | 15.43111 | −75.8357 | 72.6614 |
| $w_E * a_{haul}$ | 8.056295*** | 0.754206 | −11.6018*** | 4.2458 |
| $w_E * a_{caboose}$ | 3394215*** | 368263.9 | 2399180 | 1483523 |
| $w_E * t$ | 70.6142*** | 23.69644 | −106.02 | 97.1288 |
| $w_F * w_{WS}$ | −9282573*** | 332709.8 | 9908.487763 | ### |
| $w_F * y_U$ | −2.7989*** | 0.388153 | 3.744043 | 40.6422 |
| $w_F * y_W$ | −43.2156*** | 3.47669 | −53.744 | 568.5 |
| $w_F * Y_T$ | 13.57421*** | 0.396995 | 3.088161 | 40.2762 |
| $w_F * a_{miles}$ | −52675.6*** | 2738.005 | 25834.21 | 327255 |
| $w_F * a_{speed}$ | −2.01E+07*** | 1493029 | 24270326 | 1.53E+08 |
| $w_F * a_{haul}$ | −100275 | 103735.9 | −1712228 | 7168538 |
| $w_F * a_{caboose}$ | 1.32E+11*** | 3.32E+10 | 3.75E+11 | 3.15E+12 |
| $w_F * t$ | −1.96E+07*** | 2705368 | 12578500 | 2.44E+08 |
| $w_{WS} * y_U$ | 0.000033*** | 2.22E-06 | −0.00004*** | 6.75E-06 |
| $w_{WS} * y_W$ | −0.00067*** | 0.00003 | −4.92E-06 | 0.000114 |
| $w_{WS} * y_T$ | 0.000061*** | 2.47E-06 | 8.41E-06 | 7.11E-06 |
| $w_{WS} * a_{miles}$ | 0.62076*** | 0.018547 | 1.618261*** | 0.0816 |
| $w_{WS} * a_{speed}$ | 233.3992*** | 14.42347 | −22.6337 | 37.212 |
| $w_{WS} * a_{hual}$ | 7.050127*** | 0.727568 | −2.51739 | 1.774 |
| $w_{WS} * a_{caboose}$ | 599798.4** | 268094.8 | −1550330** | 675866 |
| $w_{WS} * t$ | −263.895*** | 17.89458 | −109.753** | 54.1955 |
| $y_U * y_W$ | −3.06E-11*** | 3.88E-12 | −2.98E-09 | 2.34E-09 |
| $y_U * y_T$ | −1.43E-12*** | 4.43E-13 | 1.48E-10 | 2.87E-10 |
| $y_U * y_{miles}$ | 2.27E-08*** | 4.67E-09 | −5.56E-06* | 2.94E-06 |
| $y_U * y_{speed}$ | 0.000029*** | 1.86E-06 | −0.00021 | 0.00134 |
| $y_U * a_{haul}$ | 1.48E-07 | 1.12E-07 | 0.000173* | 0.000091 |
| $y_U * a_{caboose}$ | 0.219255*** | 0.041383 | −23.361 | 31.6284 |
| $y_U * t$ | 2.00E-06 | 2.55E-06 | 0.002668 | 0.00166 |
| $y_W * y_T$ | 2.75E-11*** | 3.14E-12 | 6.21E-09*** | 2.22E-09 |
| $y_W * a_{miles}$ | 4.79E-07*** | 3.34E-08 | 2.55E-06 | 0.000023 |
| $y_W * a_{speed}$ | −0.00019*** | 0.00002 | −0.00055 | 0.0162 |
| $y_W * a_{haul}$ | −3.81E-06*** | 8.01E-07 | −0.00078 | 0.000664 |

| Variables | Without Concavity | | With Concavity | |
|---|---|---|---|---|
| | Coefficient | s.e. | Coefficient | Approx s.e. |
| $y_W * a_{caboose}$ | 2.826311*** | 0.412587 | 227.0504 | 307.3 |
| $y_W * t$ | −0.00021*** | 0.000025 | −0.00025 | 0.0172 |
| $y_T * a_{miles}$ | −9.33E-08*** | 4.29E-09 | −3.02E-06 | 2.53E-06 |
| $y_T * a_{speed}$ | −0.00003*** | 2.13E-06 | 0.002181 | 0.00139 |
| $y_T * a_{haul}$ | 1.01E-06*** | 1.34E-07 | −0.00011 | 0.000079 |
| $y_T * a_{caboose}$ | −0.32476*** | 0.045829 | 59.18539** | 27.4095 |
| $y_T * t$ | −0.00003*** | 3.02E-06 | 0.003372** | 0.00149 |
| $a_{miles} * a_{speed}$ | −0.01797 | 0.016516 | −25.4535** | 11.776 |
| $a_{miles} * a_{haul}$ | −0.00156** | 0.000776 | 0.134324 | 0.6032 |
| $a_{miles} * a_{caboose}$ | −430.326 | 260.7547 | −328421 | 204482 |
| $a_{miles} * t$ | 0.225063*** | 0.021707 | −42.1698** | 16.2978 |
| $a_{speed} * a_{haul}$ | 6.215739*** | 0.386726 | 3.687197 | 354.3 |
| $a_{speed} * a_{caboose}$ | 1198683*** | 120814.9 | 1.16E+08 | 1.17E+08 |
| $a_{speed} * t$ | −15.0218** | 6.626258 | 2568.9 | 6621.7 |
| $a_{haul} * a_{caboose}$ | 20183.95*** | 5399.54 | −3182217 | 5377594 |
| $a_{haul} * t$ | −0.70175 | 0.548849 | −651.032 | 433.7 |
| $a_{caboose} * t$ | −904903*** | 197655.3 | 1.04E+08 | 1.85E+08 |

Note: The variable $w_L$ is the labor price, $w_E$ is the equipment price, $w_F$ is the fuel price, $w_{WS}$ is the way and structures price, $y_U$ is the unit train gross ton-miles, $y_W$ is the way train gross ton-miles, $y_T$ is the through train gross ton-miles, $a_{miles}$ is the miles of road, $a_{speed}$ is the train miles per train hour, $a_{haul}$ is the average length of haul, $a_{caboose}$ is the fraction of train miles operated with *caboose* and $t$ for time. The notation *** indicates statistical significance at the 1% level, ** indicates statistical significance at the 5% level and * indicates statistical significance at the 10% level. The notation ### indicates P values exceed the level used to report standard errors.

represents the results before imposing concavity in input prices. The first-order output coefficients are positive and significant. The coefficients for input prices are also positive and significant. The coefficient for the price of material is not in the results since it is used as the numeraire in the estimation. The negative coefficient of the time trend suggests that cost decreases over time. This may be due to technology improvements over time and/or the adjustment of rail carriers to more efficient operations in the wake of the Staggers Act. Three variables show unexpected result: The estimated coefficient on the variables *milesroad* and *speed* are negative and statistically significant, the estimated coefficient on the variable *avehaul* is positive and statistically significant, and caboose shows a positive but not statistically significant coefficient. The third column shows the result after imposing concavity in input prices. The latter results vary where 34 coefficients show changes in signs and 58 coefficients become insignificant after impose concavity. All coefficients for input prices are positive and all are significant except fuel. That first-order output coefficients are positive with only unit train is significant. The time trend coefficient still suggests that cost decreases over time. All technological variables are found insignificant except for *milesroad*. However, the sign of *milesroad* is still not as expected.

A weak test for economies of scope examines the coefficient sign for the interaction variables between outputs. The presence of cost complementarities between outputs indicates the existence of economies of scope. Before concavity is imposed, the interaction terms between unit train and way train and also between unit train and through train show negative and statistically significant coefficients. The negative sign

$$\left( \frac{\partial^2 C}{\partial y_U \partial y_W} < 0 \, and \, \frac{\partial^2 C}{\partial y_U \partial y_T} < 0 \right)$$ indicates that these outputs are cost com-

plementarities[26] with each other. The presence of cost complementarity is one of the contributors for economies of scope.[27] However, the coefficient for interaction variable between way train and through train is

positive and significant implying cost discomplementarities $\left( \frac{\partial^2 C}{\partial y_W \partial y_T} > 0 \right)$

between these two train services. After concavity is imposed, the results do change somewhat. Parameter estimates on unit train and way train variables still suggest cost complementarities between these two transport services, whereas parameter estimation results for unit train and through train now lack statistical significance. Only the interaction term for way train and through train is positive and statistically significant which also suggest cost discomplementarites. The presence of cost complementarites between unit and way before and after concavity is imposed is consistent with the notion that unit train and way train share similar operations features. For instance, most origin-destination switches are used for unit and way train transport services (Tolliver et al., 2014). This may contribute to the jointly utilized inputs for both train services.[28] This evidence of cost complementarities warrants further examination of the possibility of economies of scope. This study test for this possibility by simulating hypothetical production of output combinations with and without imposing concavity.

Table 7.4 presents the percentage of firms exhibiting economies of scope and the expected cost savings when jointly providing the train services rather than having these same services provided by specialty firms. A positive value suggests a firm's operations exhibits economies of scope, and a negative value suggests the presence of diseconomies of scope. Without imposing concavity when estimating the cost function, 96% of the firms exhibit economies of scope, and when concavity is imposed,

*Table 7.4* Percentage of Firms Exhibiting Economies of Scope and Average Cost Savings[#]

|  | Scope | ScopeU | ScopeW | ScopeT | ScopeUW | ScopeUT | ScopeWT |
|---|---|---|---|---|---|---|---|
| Without Imposing Concavity (%) | 96.7 | 96.7 | 96.7 | 96.7 | 96.7 | 97.1 | 97.1 |
| Average Cost Savings ($1,000,000) | 162 | 94 | 75 | 77 | 85 | 87 | 68 |
| Imposing Concavity | 70.44 | 72.63 | 70.8 | 79.4 | 72.3 | 71.5 | 70.07 |
| Average Cost Savings ($1,000,000) | 185 | 96 | 91 | 87 | 98 | 94 | 88 |

[#] $Scope = C(y_U,0,0) + C(0,y_W,0) + C(0,0,y_T) - C(y_U,y_W,y_T)$

$ScopeU = C(y_U,0,0) + C(0,y_W,y_T) - C(y_U,y_W,y_T)$

$ScopeW = C(0,y_W,0) + C(y_U,0,y_T) - C(y_U,y_W,y_T)$

$ScopeT = C(0,0,y_T) + C(y_U,y_W,0) - C(y_U,y_W,y_T)$

$ScopeUW = C(y_U,0,0) + C(0,y_W,0) - C(y_U,y_W,0)$

$ScopeUT = C(y_U,0,0) + C(0,0,y_T) - C(y_U,0,y_T)$

$ScopeWT = C(0,y_W,0) + C(0,0,y_T) - C(y_U,0,y_T)$

more than 70% of firms exhibit economies of scope. Even though the percentage dropped by more than 20 percentage points compared with the cost findings without imposing input price concavity, it is reasonable to suggest that the percentage of firms exhibiting economies of scope is substantial.

Benefits associated with achieving economies of scope are quantified by calculating cost savings derived from Class I carriers providing all three services compared with providing each service separately or providing pairs of these services. For instance, results presented in the second row indicate cost savings ranging from $68 million to $162 million annually when providing all three services jointly. Similar results are found when using the concavity imposed cost results as the findings in the last row, indicating cost savings ranging from $88 million to $185 million annually. In addition, these findings suggest the cost associated with diseconomies when separately providing way train service closely resembles the cost of diseconomies associated with providing way and through service. The result provides significant insight into any future intention to unbundle the multiservice train. Since way train service is not the primary source for diseconomies of scope, any type of train services to be unbundled may also be equally likely to contribute to enhanced operating efficiency in an increasingly competitive transport industry.

## Discussion and Concluding Remarks

With the passage of the Staggers Act, some railroad Class I carriers took advantage of their ability to abandon unprofitable short-haul lines. Despite the post-deregulation trend of abandonment, there are many carriers still maintaining their short-haul line service. Way train service resembles the short-haul line; therefore, a question remains whether those carriers are still satisfying the condition of economies of scope in the industry. If carriers are exhibiting economies of scope, then multiservice train operation promotes cost advantages for the railroad carriers, whereas single-service train operation is at a cost disadvantage.

Due to non-availability of stand-alone cost data, testing directly the condition for economies of scope in the railroad industry for the three train services is not viable. Class I carriers are providing all three services for the entire observation period. Following common practice used when testing for in subadditivity this study constructs cost for hypothetical firms to simulate carriers producing a given combination of transport services. Two sets of results are presented depicting the expected cost savings from jointly producing three train services. The first set does not impose concavity in input prices, whereas the second set does using Cholesky decomposition. When concavity is not imposed, the condition for economies of scope is satisfied for over 95% of the simulations, and when input price concavity is imposed, more than 70% of simulation exhibit economies of scope. The difference in the results is not unexpected since the cost function may lose some flexibility when imposing concavity, and therefore caution should be exercised in interpreting those results (Chua et al., 2005).

Even though, following deregulation, Class I short-haul services (way train services) were recognized as unprofitable lines and most likely to be abandoned, a nontrivial share of such freight services is still provided by the seven Class I carriers. Findings from this study lend support for the maintenance of such service as a substantial percentage of cost simulations suggest economies of scope associated with providing short-haul (way) service and longer-haul (unit and through) service. Even when cost findings do reveal cost simulations that satisfy the condition of diseconomies of scope the cost disadvantage of providing multiple freight services are just as likely to occur when jointly providing short-haul and longer-haul service compared with jointly providing both types of longer-haul services. Nonetheless, evidence of a relatively small probability of diseconomies of scope supports Class I carriers taking advantage of the opportunity to outsource selective short-haul routes to short line rail carriers.

# Notes

1. Data on freight hauled in the United States indicate that in 2015, 33.15% of freight was moved by rail, which is nearly comparable to the 38.9% hauled by trucks. The share for these modes far exceeds that of the 9.32% share of barges, which is the next largest transporter of freight in the United States. Source: U.S. Bureau of Transportation Statistics www.bts.gov/content/us-ton-miles-freight.
2. U.S. Class I railroads are line haul freight railroads with $250 million or more in revenue adjusted for inflation. Currently, there are seven U.S. Class I rail carriers. Regional and short-line carriers depict the two remaining rail categories. Short-line operators are generally classified as operating less than 250 miles of track, and regional carriers typically operate more than 350 miles of track or generate more than $40 million in revenue adjusted for inflation since 1991. Often regional carriers are classified as short-haul carriers.
3. Average distance is calculated by dividing car miles by number of cars loaded.
4. The term "public input" is taken from Marshall (1925), as he identifies these inputs as factors that are readily shared by the processes used to produce several different outputs. He points to the use of sheep for wool and mutton, cows for the production of beef and hides, and grain for the production of wheat and straw.
5. Peoples (2013) reports unionization rates exceeding 75% in the rail industry as late as 2012.
6. Mayo (1984b) estimates a generalized version of the translog cost function that circumvents this drawback, but his method requires nonlinear estimation that can generate convergence challenges for parameter estimates.
7. Cowing and Holtmann (1983) examined the economies of scope for various groups of hospital outputs. Translog cost function was used where ln e = ln y when $y = 0$. The values of $e$ were 0.1, 0.01, and 0.001. However, they reported the results as instable and should be given limited considerations.
8. A general specification is developed which nested the translog cost function, generalized translog cost function, separable quadratic cost function, and composite cost function. Economies of scope in banking was examined for these five specifications using a sample of 205 banks in the year 1988.
9. A function is considered flexible if "there are no restrictions on its free parameters" (Diewert and Wales, 1988, p. 303).
10. Prior of using normalized quadratic cost function, this study also estimated a generalized translog cost function introduced by Caves et al. (1980) which accommodates zero output values through Box-Cox transformation. However, the results were disappointing when analyzing economies of scope. The values are unreliable, and Pulley and Humphrey (1991, p. 12) mentioned that "the difficulties with the translog cost behavior in the neighborhood of zero will remain." Furthermore, even when substituting a very small positive value for zero in a translog cost function, the form will still "badly behaved in a region around zero" (Pulley and Humphrey, 1993, p. 440).
11. It is common to impose global curvature rather impose monotonicity for normalized quadratic function (Barnett and Usui, 2006).
12. The total cost function is a long-run specification as it is reasonable to assume that the rail carriers are able to optimally adjust their capital stock to output changes.
13. The issue of endogeneity may arise when estimation includes input prices as cost determinants. This concern is highlighted by Levinsohn and Petrin (2003) when estimating the production function. They propose the use of intermediate inputs as proxy variables to overcome the endogeneity problem between

input levels and unobserved productivity shock. On the other hand, the vast literature on cost functions used to examine the transportation industry does not consider input prices as endogenous (Bitzan and Peoples, 2014; Bitzan and Keeler, 2014; Mizutani and Uranishi, 2013; Bereskin, 2009; Bitzan and Wilson, 2007; Farsi et al., 2007a; Ivaldi and McCullough, 2004; Bitzan and Keeler, 2003; Bitzan, 2003; Bitzan, 2000; Bitzan 1999; Kim, 1987). The absence of such analysis is due in part to the mechanism by which input prices such as labor are determined. Most transportation labor markets are unionized, and over 80% of rail workers are unionized. Among the major union rail workers are United Transportation Union (UTU), Brotherhood of Locomotive Engineers (BLE), Brotherhood of Maintenance of Way Employees (BMWE), and Transportation Communications International Union (TCU). Rail unions have used their negotiation leverage to heavily discount productivity as a determinant of wages. In addition, the concern regarding input price as an exogeneous variable has been highlighted by Bitzan and Keeler (2014). They argue that individual railroad firms purchase a relatively small percentage of factor inputs from the supply side, which makes it plausible to conclude that rail carriers might not influence input price movements, and therefore these companies are price takers of factor inputs. Handling factor input prices as exogenous when estimating the cost function has been universally accepted as the norm by other transportation research.

14. For example, $\dfrac{\partial^2 C}{\partial w_i \partial y_k} = \dfrac{\partial^2 C}{\partial y_k \partial w_i}$

15. This quadratic cost function with variables deviated from the means has been explained by Jara-Diaz (2000) as analogous with the translog form when the variables are in logs. He mentioned the quadratic and translog forms are flexible because no priori functions are assumed for technology or costs. Furthermore, the quadratic form can directly obtain the marginal costs valued at the sample mean. Farsi et al. (2007b) also used the procedure of demeaning all the explanatory variables from the sample mean in their cost function. They inferred the intercept as the production total cost at the sample mean.

16. The demeaning process is not shown in the matrix form for simplicity.

17. The Hessian matrix is negative semi-definite when every principal minor with odd order is $\leq 0$ and every principal with even order is $\geq 0$.

$$Hessian = \begin{bmatrix} \dfrac{\partial^2 c}{\partial w_1^2} & \dfrac{\partial^2 c}{\partial w_1 \partial w_2} & \dfrac{\partial^2 c}{\partial w_1 \partial w_3} & \dfrac{\partial^2 c}{\partial w_1 \partial w_4} \\[2ex] \dfrac{\partial^2 c}{\partial w_2 \partial w_1} & \dfrac{\partial^2 c}{\partial w_2^2} & \dfrac{\partial^2 c}{\partial w_2 \partial w_3} & \dfrac{\partial^2 c}{\partial w_2 \partial w_4} \\[2ex] \dfrac{\partial^2 c}{\partial w_3 \partial w_1} & \dfrac{\partial^2 c}{\partial w_3 \partial w_2} & \dfrac{\partial^2 c}{\partial w_3^2} & \dfrac{\partial^2 c}{\partial w_3 \partial w_4} \\[2ex] \dfrac{\partial^2 c}{\partial w_4 \partial w_1} & \dfrac{\partial^2 c}{\partial w_4 \partial w_2} & \dfrac{\partial^2 c}{\partial w_4 \partial w_3} & \dfrac{\partial^2 c}{\partial w_4^2} \end{bmatrix}$$

18. Pulley and Humphrey (1991) generalized the calculation for economies of scope in the case of $m$ firms as $SCOPE = [(m-1)\alpha_0 - \sum_{i=1 j>i}\sum \alpha_i q_i q_j] / h(q)$.

The former term in the right-hand side of the equation measures the fixed cost and the latter measures cost complementarity contributions to economies of scope.

19. Gabel and Kennet (1994) examined economies of scope in the local telephone exchange market without having observations producing a stand-alone output or combinations of them. An engineering optimization model is used that enables them to estimate the cost of stand-alone telecommunications networks. Simulation is done such that the optimization model chooses combination and placement of facilities that minimizes the production cost.

20. Bloch et al. (2001) used simulation for three different output paths in examining the ray-average cost in a given year. The ray-average cost is subject to the variables values and parameters estimated, and this cost behavior is observed through the simulation. An output or combination of outputs is scaled down to zero by increment of 0.1 while the remaining output are fixed at the actual level.

21. The sample mean is commonly used as the point of approximation. Martínez-Budría et al. (2003) used sample mean as point of approximation for their normalized quadratic cost function when apply to the electric sector in Spain.

22. For example, derivative of cost with respect to unit train service is shown as:

$$\frac{\partial C}{\partial y_U} = \beta_1 + \beta_{11} y_U + \beta_{12} y_W + \beta_{13} y_T + \tau_{11} w_L + \tau_{21} w_E + \tau_{31} w_F + \tau_{41} w_{WS}$$

$$+ \varphi_{11} a_M + \varphi_{21} a_S + \varphi_{31} a_H + \varphi_{41} a_C + \pi_1 t$$

23. For example, derivative of cost with respect to price of labor is shown as:

$$\frac{\partial C}{\partial w_L} = \alpha_1 + \alpha_{11} w_L + \alpha_{12} w_E + \alpha_{13} w_F + \alpha_{14} w_{WS} + \tau_{11} y_U + \tau_{12} y_W + \tau_{13} y_T$$

$$+ \vartheta_{11} a_M + \vartheta_{12} a_S + \vartheta_{13} a_H + \vartheta_{14} a_C + \delta_1 t$$

24. Featherstone and Moss (1994) carried out estimations with and without imposition of curvature. Comparing the two estimations their results for economies of scope did change when making this imposition.

25. Initially, non-converging result is expected since convergence highly depends on initial values. The specification consists of a large number of explanatory variables and hence an educated guess for the starting values from the functional form is not feasible. Many trials were made with defaults values and randomly chosen initial values with varying convergence criterion. Convergence is met when the parameters obtained without imposing concavity is chosen to be the appropriate and plausible initial values.

26. Any combination of train services is said to be cost complementarities (cost substitutabilities) if the marginal cost of one output decreases (increases) when there is an increase in the production of the other output.

27. Pulley and Humphrey (1991) mentioned two factors as contribution to economies of scope which are complementarily and fixed cost. The ability to spread the fixed cost over the broader mix of output may as well contribute to economies of scope.

28. The level of efficiency for three types of train services are known to be different. Tolliver et al. (2014) suggest that efficiency is mainly influenced by the type of train services. They consider way train and through train as 'non-unit train' since their movements are related and percentage of way train is very small compared with through train. Way train often stops to pick up and drop cars along the route. Through trains moving between yards, therefore, perform limited switching activities. Unit train operates in a cycling pattern

from origin to destination, least switching activities that suggest the most energy efficient train services. Bitzan (2000) explained the relationship of each train service with respect to efficiency. The unit train service is considered as the most efficient train service since it involves smaller switching requirement with high volume of shipments. The way train service involves high switching requirements, small volume, short distance, and slow speed, which makes it the most expensive service for railroad carrier. Through train is more efficient than way train but less than unit train even though it comprises the largest service in terms of gross ton-mile.

# References

Allen, W. Bruce, Michael Sussman, and Drew Miller. 2002. "Regional and Short Line Railroads in the United States." *Transportation Quarterly*, 56(4), pp: 77–113.

Barnett, William A., and Ikuyasu Usui. 2006. "The Theoretical Regularity Properties of the Normalized Quadratic Consumer Demand Model." *MPRA Paper 410*, University Library of Munich, Germany.

Baumol, William. J., John C. Panzar, and Robert D. Willig. 1982. *Contestable Markets and the Theory of Industry Structure*. New York: Harcourt, Brace Jovanovich, Inc.

Bereskin, C. Gregory. 2009. "Railroad Economies of Scale, Scope, and Density Revisited." *Journal of the Transportation Research Forum*, 48(2), pp: 23–38.

Bitzan, John D. 1999. "The Structure of Railroad Costs and the Benefits/Costs of Mergers." *Research in Transportation Economics*, 5, pp: 1–52.

Bitzan, John D. 2000. "Railroad Cost Conditions: Implications for Policy." Upper Great Plains Transportation Institute, North Dakota State University, Fargo, North Dakota.

Bitzan, John D. 2003. "Railroad Costs and Competition: The Implications of Introducing Competition to Railroad Networks." *Journal of Transport Economics and Policy*, 37(2), pp: 201–225.

Bitzan, John D., and Theodore E. Keeler. 2003. "Productivity Growth and Some of Its Determinants in the Deregulated US Railroad Industry." *Southern Economic Journal*, 70(2), pp: 232–253.

Bitzan, John D., and Theodore E. Keeler. 2014. "The Evolution of US Rail Freight Pricing in the Post-Deregulation Era: Revenues Versus Marginal Costs for Five Commodity Types." *Transportation*, 41(2), pp: 305–324.

Bitzan, John D., and James H. Peoples. 2014. "US Air Carriers and Work-Rule Constraints: Do Airlines Employ an Allocatively Efficient Mix of Inputs?" *Research in Transportation Economics*, 45, pp: 9–17.

Bitzan, John D., and Wesley W. Wilson. 2007. "A Hedonic Cost Function Approach to Estimating Railroad Costs." *Research in Transportation Economics*, 20, pp: 69–95.

Bloch, Harry, Gary Madden, and Scott J. Savage. 2001. Economies of Scale and Scope in Australian Telecommunications." *Review of Industrial Organization*, 18(2), pp: 219–227.

Caves, Douglas. W., Laurits R. Christensen, and Michael W. Tretheway. 1980. "Flexible Cost Functions for Multiproduct Firms." *The Review of Economics and Statistics*, 62(3), pp: 477–481.

Chua, Chew. L., Hsein Kew, H., and Jongsay Yong. 2005. "Airline Code-Share Alliances and Costs: Imposing Concavity on Translog Cost Function Estimation." *Review of Industrial Organization*, 26(4), pp: 461–487.

Cowing, Thomas G., and Alphonse G. Holtmann. 1983. "Multiproduct Short-Run Hospital Cost Functions: Empirical Evidence and Policy Implications from Cross-Section Data." *Southern Economic Journal*, 49(3), pp: 637–653.

Díaz-Hernández, Juan J., Eduardo Martinez-Budria, and Sergio R. Jara-Diaz. 2005. "Exact Allocative and Technical Inefficiency Using the Normalized Quadratic Cost System." *FEDEA Working Paper No. EEE 210*, Madrid, Spain.

Diewert, W. Erin, and Kevin J. Fox. 2009. "The Normalized Quadratic Expenditure Function." In Badi Baltagi and Efraim Sadka, eds. *Contributions to Economic Analysis*, 288, pp: 149–178.

Diewert, W. Erin, and Terrence J. Wales. 1987. "Flexible Functional Forms and Global Curvature Conditions." *Econometrica*, 55(1), pp: 43–68.

Diewert, W. Erin, and Terrence J. Wales. 1988. "Normalized Quadratic Systems of Consumer Demand Functions." *Journal of Business & Economic Statistics*, 6(3), pp: 303–312.

Due, John. F. 1984. "New Railroad Companies Formed to Take over Abandoned or Spun-off Lines." *Transportation Journal*, 24(1), pp: 30–50.

Due, John. F. 1987. "Abandonment of Rail Lines and the Smaller Railroad Alternative." *Logistics and Transportation Review*, 23(1), pp: 109–134.

Farsi, Mehdi, Aurellos Fetz, and Massimo Filippini. 2007a. "Economies of Scale and Scope in Local Public Transportation." *Journal of Transport Economics and Policy*, 41(3), pp: 345–361.

Farsi, Mehdi, Aurellos Fetz, and Massimo Filippini. 2007b. "Economies of Scale and Scope in the Swiss Multi-Utilities Sector." *Center for Energy Policy and Economics, Swiss Federal Institutes of Technology*, Working Paper 59, Zurich, Switzerland.

Featherstone, Allen. M., and Charles Moss. 1994. "Measuring Economies of Scale and Scope in Agricultural Banking." *American Journal of Agricultural Economics*, 76(3), pp: 655–661.

Fischer, Philip. A., John D. Bitzan, and Denver Tolliver. 2001. *Analysis of Economies of Size and Density for Short Line Railroads* (Master's Thesis, North Dakota State University). http://ntl.bts.gov/lib/13000/13100/13142/MPC01-128.html

Fraquelli, Giovanni, Massimiliano Piacenza, and Davide Vannoni. 2004. "Scope and Scale Economies in Multi-Utilities: Evidence from Gas, Water and Electricity Combinations." *Applied Economics*, 36(18), pp: 2045–2057.

Gabel, David, and D. Mark Kennet. 1994. Economies of Scope in the Local Telephone Exchange Market." *Journal of Regulatory Economics*, 6(4), pp: 381–398.

Growitsch, Christian, and Heike Wetzel. 2009. "Testing for Economies of Scope in European Railways: An Efficiency Analysis." *Journal of Transport Economics and Policy*, 43(1), pp: 1–24.

Ivaldi, Marc, and Gerald McCullough. 2004. "Subadditivity Tests for Network Separation with an Application to U.S. Railroads." *CEPR Discussion Paper No. 4392*, Centre for Economic Policy Research, London.

Jara-Diaz, Sergio R. 2000. "Transport Production and The Analysis of Industry Structure." In J. Polak and A. Heertje, eds. *Analytical Transport Economics:*

*An International Perspective.* Cheltenham, UK: Edward Elgar Publishing, pp: 27–50.

Kim, H. Youn. 1987. "Economies of Scale and Scope in Multiproduct Firms: Evidence from US Railroads." *Applied Economics, 19,* 733–741.

Lau, Lawrence J. 1974. "Application of Duality Theory: A Comment." In M.D. Intriligator and D.A. Kendrick, eds. *Frontiers in Quantitative Economics,* Vol. 2. Amsterdam: North-Holland Publishing Company, pp: 176–199.

Levinsohn, James, and Amil Petrin. 2003. "Estimating Production Functions Using Inputs to Control for Unobservables." *The Review of Economic Studies, 70(2),* pp: 317–341.

Marshall, Alfred. 1925. *Principles of Economics.* London and New York: Macmillan.

Martínez-Budría, Eduardo, Sergio Jara-Díaz, and Francis Javier Ramos-Real. 2003. "Adapting Productivity Theory to the Quadratic Cost Function: An Application to the Spanish Electric Sector." *Journal of Productivity Analysis, 20(2),* pp: 213–229.

Mayo, John W. 1984a. "The Technological Determinants of the U.S. Energy Industry Structure." *The Review of Economics and Statistics, 66(1),* pp: 51–58.

Mayo, John W. 1984b. "Multiproduct Monopoly, Regulation, and Firm Costs." *Southern Economic Journal, 51(1),* pp: 208–218.

Mielke, John. 1988. "Short Line Railroad Creations: Terms of Sale, Impacts on Viability and Public Policy Implications." *Journal of the Transportation Research Forum, 29(1),* pp: 138–148.

Mizutani, Fumitoshi, and Shuji Uranishi. 2013. "Does Vertical Separation Reduce Cost? An Empirical Analysis of the Rail Industry in European and East Asian OECD Countries." *Journal of Regulatory Economics, 43(1),* pp: 31–59.

Ogawa, Kazuo. 2011. "Why Are Concavity Conditions Not Satisfied in the Cost Function? The Case of Japanese Manufacturing Firms during the Bubble Period." *Oxford Bulletin of Economics and Statistics, 73(4),* pp: 556–580.

Peoples, James. 2013. "The Legacy of the Interstate Commerce Act and Labor: Legislation, Unionization, and Labor Earnings in Surface Transportation Services." *Review of Industrial Organization, 43(1–2),* pp: 63–84.

Pepall, Lynne, Dan Richards, and George Norman. 1999. *Industrial Organization: Contemporary Theory and Practice.* South-Western, Cincinnati, OH.

Pulley, Lawrence B., and Yale M. Braunstein. 1992. "A Composite Cost Function for Multiproduct Firms with an Application to Economies of Scope in Banking." *The Review of Economics and Statistics, 74(2),* pp: 221–230.

Pulley, Lawrence B., and David Humphrey. 1991. "Scope Economies: Fixed Costs, Complementarity, and Functional Form." *Federal Reserve Bank of Richmond Working Paper* (91–3), Richmond, VA.

Pulley, Lawrence B., and David Humphrey. 1993. "The Role of Fixed Costs and Cost Complementarities in Determining Scope Economies and the Cost of Narrow Banking." *The Journal of Business, 66(3),* pp: 437–462.

Roller, Lars-Hendrik. 1990. "Proper Quadratic Cost Functions with an Application to the Bell System." *The Review of Economics and Statistics, 74,* pp: 221–230.

Sharkey, William. W. 1982. *The Theory of Natural Monopoly.* Cambridge, UK: Cambridge Books.

Tolliver, Denver, Pan Lu, and Douglas Benson. 2014. "Railroad Energy Efficiency in the United States: Analytical and Statistical Analysis." *Journal of Transportation Engineering, 140*(1), pp: 23–30.

Tovar, Beatriz, Sergio Jara-Díaz, and Lourdes Trujillo. 2007. "Econometric Estimation of Scale and Scope Economies within the Port Sector: A Review." *Maritime Policy & Management, 34*(3), pp: 203–223.

Triebs, Thomas, David S. Saal, Pablo Arocena, and Subal C. Kumbhakar. 2012. *Estimating Economies of Scale and Scope with Flexible Technology* (No. 142). Ifo Working Paper, Munchen, Germany.

Zellner, Arnold. 1962. "An Efficient Method of Estimating Seemingly Unrelated Regressions and Tests for Aggregation Bias." *Journal of the American Statistical Association, 57*(298), pp: 348–368.

# Appendix
## Construction of Variables

---

*Variable Construction*

---

- **Real total cost = (opercost—capexp + roird + roilcm + roicrs)/gdppd**

opercost: railroad operating cost (schedule 410, line 620, column f)
capexp: capital expenditures classified as operating in r1 (schedule 410, lines 12–30, 101–9, column f)
roird: return on investment in road = (roadinv—accdepr) * costkap
roadinv: road investment (schedule 352b, line 31) + capexp from all previous years
accdepr: accumulated depreciation in road (schedule. 335, line 30, column g)
costkap: cost of capital (AAR railroad facts)
roilcm: =return on investment in locomotives = [(iboloco+locinvl)—(acdoloco + locacdl)] * costkap
iboloco: investment base in owned locomotives (schedule 415, line 5, column g)
locinvl: investment base in leased locomotives (schedule 415, line 5, column h)
acdoloco: accumulated depreciation of owned locomotives (schedule 415, line 5, column i)
locacdl: accumulated depreciation of leased locomotives (schedule 415, line 5, column j)
roicr: return on investment in cars = [(ibocars + carinvl)—(acdocars + caracdl)]*costkap
ibocars: investment base in owned cars (schedule 415, line 24, column g)
carinvl: investment base in leased cars (schedule 415, line 24, column h)
acdocars: accumulated depreciation of owned cars (schedule 415, line 24, column i)
caracdl: accumulated depreciation of leased locomotives (schedule 415, line 24, column j)
gdppd: gdp price deflator
Price of factor inputs

- **Price of labor = (swge + fringe—caplab)/lbhrs**

swge: total salary and wages (schedule 410, line 620, column b)
fringe: fringe benefits (schedule 410, lines 112–14, 205, 224, 309, 414, 430, 505, 512, 522, 611, column e)
caplab: labor portion of capital expenditure classification as operating in R1 (schedule 410, lines 12–30, 101–9, column b)
lbhrs: labor hours (Wage form A, line 700, column 4 + 6)

- Price of equipment = weighted average equipment price (schedule 415 and schedule 710)
- Price of fuel (schedule 750)
- Price of material = AAR materials and supply index
- Price of way and structure = (roird + anndeprd)/mot

anndeprd: annual depreciation of road (schedule 335, line 30, column c)
mot: miles of track (schedule 720, line 6, column b)
Factor input prices are divided by gdp price deflator
Outputs

- Utgtm: unit train gross ton-miles (schedule 755, line 99, column b)
- Wtgtm: way train gross ton-miles (schedule 755, line 100, column b)
- Ttgtm: through train gross ton-miles (schedule 755, line 101, column b)

adjustment factor multiplied by each output variable = rtm/(utgtm + wtgtm + ttgtm)
rtm: revenue ton-miles (schedule 755, line 110, column b)
Movement characteristics

- Miles of road: (schedule 700, line 57, column c)
- Speed = train miles per train hour in road service = trnmls/(trnhr-trnhs)

trnmls: total train miles (schedule 755, line 5, column b)
trnhr: train hours in road service—includes train switching hours (schedule 755, line 115, column b)
trnhs: train hours in train switching (schedule 755, line 116, column b)

- Average length of haul = rtm/revtons

revtons: revenue tons (schedule 755, line 105, column b)

- Caboose = fraction of train miles with cabooses = cabmiles/trnmls

cabmiles: caboose miles (schedule 755, line 89, column b)

Note: Adapted from "Productivity growth and some of its determinants in the deregulated US railroad industry" by Bitzan, J. D., & Keeler, T. E., 2003, *Southern Economic Journal*, pp. 250–251.

# Section IV
# Railroads and Post-Staggers Regulation

# 8 The Law and Economics of Revenue Adequacy

*Jeffrey T. Macher, John W. Mayo,
and Lee F. Pinkowitz**

## Introduction

With the benefits of nearly 40 years of economic analysis, it is well-established that the myriad of policy changes embedded in the Staggers Act of 1980 have been largely responsible for restoring an industry that was on the brink of utter failure in the 1970s.[1] Numerous economic studies have documented cost, pricing, quality, and productivity improvements attributable to Staggers. Little noticed in the Staggers-driven transition from a largely regulated to a largely deregulated environment, however, was "revenue adequacy" language first embedded in the 1976 Railroad Revitalization and Regulatory Reform (4R) Act and later retained with the Staggers Act. In particular, the "Adequate Revenue Levels" section (§205) charged the ICC with the task of developing "standards and procedures for the establishment of revenue levels adequate . . . to cover total operating expenses, including depreciation and obsolescence, plus a fair, reasonable, and economic profit or return (or both) on capital employed in the business."[2]

In the wake of this statutory language, the ICC and (later) the STB have dutifully provided annual quantitative measures of individual railroads' "revenue adequacy" based on STB-developed formulas that we describe ahead. STB calculations in most early years found Class I railroads were predominantly "revenue inadequate" (GAO, 1986). More recent STB calculations reveal that some railroads have achieved the STB's annual determination of "revenue adequacy."[3] Definitional questions remain, however, as to what achieving revenue adequacy over a relevant time period actually means. This upward trend in revenue adequacy and more generally the financial health of railroads have nevertheless provoked newfound economic and public policy attention and even calls for revisiting the railroad industry's governance structure created by the Staggers Act.

In light of both the passage of time and the newfound policy attention directed toward the emergent financial health of the railroad industry, this chapter examines revenue adequacy from a legal and economic perspective by addressing the following questions. First, what is the origin of revenue adequacy? Second, how have regulators chosen to measure revenue adequacy? Third, does revenue adequacy measure economic value, in either concept or practice? And fourth, as the railroad industry moves forward, what use, if any, might exist for revenue adequacy in policy oversight?

The rest of the chapter is organized as follows. The next section provides a discussion of the historical context and origins of revenue adequacy to generate insights into the motivations for and limits of this concept. The chapter then examines the measurement of revenue adequacy and the evolving uses to which it has been put. Next, the chapter discusses revenue adequacy in an economics context, with particular emphasis on what it is (i.e., what economic information it conveys) and what it is not (i.e., what economic information it does not convey). The chapter then undertakes an empirical benchmarking exercise, providing an assessment of revenue adequacy in the rail industry relative to both a narrowly defined set of comparable industries and a broader set of U.S. publicly traded and non-financial firms. Next, the chapter offers policy reflections on the revenue adequacy concept by adopting the taxonomy suggested by the classic spaghetti western movie *The Good, the Bad and the Ugly.* The chapter closes with some concluding remarks.

## The Origins of Revenue Adequacy

The origins of the current statutory language regarding revenue adequacy stem from the declining economic condition of the rail industry in the 1970s. As early as 1973, economists had identified a variety of underlying factors: (1) inflexible price and cost structures, (2) high fixed costs and high leverage, (3) excess capacity, (4) rigid labor and worker conditions, (5) negligible technological investments, and (6) antiquated management (Gaskins, 2008). While some of these factors—such as high fixed costs—are independent of the policy environment, other factors—such as inflexible prices and cost structures— were direct products of the pervasive regulatory constraints imposed. Hilton's (1966) analysis of the early governance structure of the railroad industry observed:

> An organization of the industry in which firms were free to quote prices, to enter or leave the industry, and to diversify, but not to collude, is diametrically opposite the present organization of the transportation industry.

Recognizing the troubled state of U.S. railroads, Congress passed the Regional Rail Reorganization (3R) Act in 1973. The stated purpose of the 3R Act was to reorganize railroads in the Midwest and Northeast regions into an "economically viable system capable of providing adequate and efficient rail service" by not only providing federal assistance to ailing railroads, but also establishing the United States Railway Association (USRA) and the Consolidated Rail Corporation (Conrail).[4] USRA was intended to take over some ICC powers by allowing bankrupt railroads to abandon unprofitable lines. Conrail was intended to take over bankrupt Northeast railroads—effectively nationalizing a portion of the rail industry and giving Congress a greater stake in the U.S. freight rail industry's long-term viability.

Despite the passage of the 3R Act and the creation of USRA and Conrail, railroad solvency problems remained. The public stake in Conrail and its own viability precipitated additional political pressure that further action was necessary. Congress subsequently passed the Railroad Revitalization and Regulatory Reform (4R) Act in 1976, which sought to directly take on the revitalization challenges:

> It is the purpose of the Congress in this Act to provide the means to rehabilitate and maintain the physical facilities, improve the operations and structure, and restore the financial stability of the railways system of the United States, and to promote the revitalization of such railway system, so that this mode of transportation will remain viable in the private sector of the economy and will be able to provide energy-efficient, ecologically compatible transportation services with greater efficiency, effectiveness, and economy.[5]

Prior to the 4R Act, rates had been set collectively in rate bureaus over a number of routes and divisions based on particular formulae. General rate increases by groups of carriers for large bodies of rates were considered in ICC Investigation & Suspension dockets in prolonged cases and proceedings. Relatively few individual rate cases were considered, as the ICC worried about discrimination vis-à-vis other shippers and routes. Rates were often justified on the basis of revenue necessary to cover the costs of the weakest carriers or the highest cost routes. In a break with decades of regulatory fiat that had previously guided the industry, the 4R Act began the deregulation process by permitting railroads in competitive markets to raise and lower rates without the express involvement of the ICC. Rates were not subject to regulation unless the ICC found the particular market railroad dominant, which entails a qualitative evaluation of competitive (e.g., intramodal, intermodal, product, and geographic competition) pressures (Wilson, 1996).

In its recognition of the need for financially healthy railroads, the 4R Act is where the revenue adequacy concept makes its first legislative appearance. Section 205 of the 4R Act tasks the ICC with developing and promulgating standards for determining adequate revenue levels that cover total operating expenses (including capital depreciation and replacement) as well as provide a fair economic profit or rate of return on railroad capital. The 4R Act specifically states:

> With respect to common carriers by railroad, the Commission shall . . . develop and promulgate . . . reasonable standards and procedures for the establishment of revenue levels adequate . . . to cover total operating expenses, including depreciation and obsolescence, plus a fair, reasonable, and economic profit or return (or both) on capital employed in the business.[6]

The 4R Act further indicates that the (adequate) revenues should be sufficient to:

> (a) provide a flow of net income plus depreciation adequate to support prudent capital outlays, assure the repayment of a reasonable level of debt, permit the raising of needed equity capital, and cover the effects of inflation[;] and (b) insure retention and attraction of capital in amounts adequate to provide a sound transportation system in the United States.[7]

The 4R Act also provided clear regulatory guidance in stating that "[t]he Commission shall make an adequate and continuing effort *to assist such carriers in attaining such revenue levels.*"[8] This language is consistent with the general thrust of the Carter administration and Congress at that time to eliminate unnecessary regulation and better position governmental resources to complement and enhance the productivity and performance of the transportation sector. It is clear in this context that revenue adequacy was not meant to be an extra arrow in the regulator's quiver, but instead was fashioned to be a metric by which to judge the railroad industry's progress in achieving financial stability and a method by which to gauge how regulatory policies were enabling or hindering that effort.

In the years following the 4R Act, the concept of revenue adequacy—or rather, revenue inadequacy of rail carriers at that time—became a central theme in congressional discussion of railroad policy. Congress held a symposium in 1977 that examined whether further legislation beyond the 4R Act was necessary as current regulations continued to hamper the railroad industry's ability to adjust rates, merge, and abandon obsolete services—all of which were seen as predicates to creating industry financial viability.[9] A symposium panelist described the ICC's implementation of the revenue adequacy portion of the 4R Act as follows:

> [I]t remains uncertain . . . whether it is as yet understood what it will take to achieve the desired revenue objectives. With much rail traffic having to move at less than fully adequate rates, rates on higher-rated traffic must contribute a return above the target rate

of return if, overall, railroads are prospectively to be allowed to bring their earnings and profits somewhat more in line with the goals of the 4-R Act.[10]

Issues with efficiency and reliability were also identified as major problems within the rail industry. Panelists noted that over 1970–1977, 10 railroad firms went bankrupt. In addition to the financial woes of rail carriers, shippers were suffering from less-than-adequate service. In the 12 years leading up to 1977, only between 55% and 72% of carloads were "on time" (i.e., arriving within one day before or one day after the scheduled delivery date) with late carloads arriving up to ten days late.[11]

In the years following the 1977 symposium, the railroad industry's financial woes continued. In 1979, 22% of the U.S. rail system was facing bankruptcy given continued returns on investment between 2% and 3%.[12] The ICC's assessment in 1978 (released December 1979) defined revenue adequacy as a rate-of-return on investment between 7.0% and 10.6%, yet by that standard, only 13 of the 36 Class I railroads submitted to the ICC's revenue adequacy test had reached these levels.[13]

Economists provided their concerns with the state of the railroad industry during this period, arguing that industry deregulation would result in a more efficient system for both railroads and shippers. For example, one analysis argued that railroad deregulation allowing for long-term contracts between shippers and railroads would increase industry efficiency on the whole and benefit both parties (Houston, 1979). Another quantitative analysis of the effect of mergers on intermodal freight ("piggybacking") suggested that "[r]egulation of railroad industry structure has prevented the rationalization of the rail network," and concluded that "the ICC is responsible for the structure of the industry and its consequences, including the failure of an obvious innovation to reach its potential in a quarter century of operation" (Ferguson, 1979).

Despite the passage of the 4R Act, there was widespread sentiment among industry participants, legislators, and economists that additional changes were still required for rail industry revitalization. While nominally granting pricing flexibility, some suggested that these rate-making freedoms were largely "emasculated" by the ICC and effectively retained many regulatory constraints of the pre-4R Act (Keeler, 1983). It was in this context that the Staggers Act garnered broad bipartisan support in both legislative bodies, passing in the House (337–20) and Senate (91–4) and becoming law in October 1980.[14] The Staggers Act's stated purpose was to "provide for the restoration, maintenance, and improvement of the physical facilities and financial stability of the rail system of the United States."[15]

The Staggers Act recognized that most rail service was subject to competition and that many government regulations affecting railroads had become unnecessary and inefficient. Consequently, the Act comprehensively reformed the industry governance structure by removing antitrust immunity for collective ratemaking, substantially removing pricing regulation, permitting private contracting between shippers and railroads, easing the path for abandoning unprofitable routes and for allowing mergers. Under the Staggers Act, shipments with rates less than 180% of a rail carrier's variable costs of providing the service are presumptively assumed reasonable and are precluded from regulatory challenge. Shipments with rates greater than 180% of the variable costs and where a railroad has "market dominance" must have "reasonable" rates.[16]

The overall goals of the Staggers Act were not altogether distinct from those of the 4R Act, but clearly reflected discussion since the 4R Act's passage. Reflecting its concern with the poor industry financial health, the Staggers Act provided a clear signal that revenues should be adequate to "promote a safe and efficient rail transportation system."[17] While leaving the concept of revenue adequacy unchanged from definitions established in the 4R Act, the Staggers Act pointed toward three applications of revenue adequacy on a forward-going basis. First, the Act directed the ICC to determine annually which rail carriers are earning adequate revenues. This application was a departure from the 4R Act's original handling of revenue adequacy determination, which required the ICC to develop, promulgate, and maintain revenue adequacy standards with no specific time frame for revisions. Second, the Act directed the ICC to "recognize" revenue adequacy when considering the reasonableness of rates. Specifically, the Staggers Act states:

> In determining whether a rate established by a rail carrier is reasonable for purposes of this section, the [Interstate Commerce] Commission shall recognize the policy of this title that rail carriers shall earn adequate revenues, as established by the Commission under section 10704(a)(2) of this title.[18]

Third, the Act forbids carriers earning adequate revenues from applying various surcharges to shippers, including joint-rate shipments and low-weight (less than 3mm. tons) shipments, and made rate changes within "zones of rail carrier rate flexibility" conditional on whether a carrier's revenues were deemed adequate.[19]

The primary provisions of the Staggers Act were designed to substantially free railroads from rate regulation, to end antitrust immunity for collective rate-making, and to ease line abandonments and corporate reorganizations. These provisions have not surprisingly received considerable attention. More subtle, but arguably of at least equal importance, the revenue adequacy language first introduced in the 4R Act and elaborated on in the Staggers Act became an important pillar of the policy governance of the freight rail industry.

## The Measurement and Uses of Revenue Adequacy

### Measurement

In the earliest determination of revenue adequacy in the wake of the 4R Act, the ICC sought to provide "a concrete interpretation of what is meant by the statutory concept of adequate revenue, and of what is not meant by that concept."[20] Several foundational findings emerged from that effort. First, the ICC made it clear that the objectives of the revenue adequacy provisions within the 4R Act were "to provide *guideposts* by which to evaluate progress in implementing the rate and service flexibility provisions of the Act."[21] The largely informative—as opposed to regulatory—role for revenue adequacy was underscored by the Commission which stated that "we do not expect to rely on the traditional form of earnings regulation employed for public utilities, where the objective is to equate the overall earnings level to a fair rate of return."[22] The ICC went on to note that its interpretation of the revenue adequacy concept would have "implications for policy toward maximum rates in individual markets, but does not itself specify limits directly applicable to individual rates."[23] Once established as a guidepost rather than a regulatory function, it was indicated that the revenue adequacy measurements would be "the very means by which the Commission would assist carriers in attaining adequate revenue levels."[24]

Second, the ICC provided its first, and as it turns out enduring, specification of the revenue adequacy metric. The Commission turned to the financial threshold concept of the "cost of capital" as the benchmark against which railroads would be judged revenue "adequate" or revenue "inadequate." In particular, if railroad $i$ had a return on investment ($ROI_i$) above the industry ($I$) cost of capital ($COC_I$) it would be labeled as "revenue adequate," whereas if $ROI_i$ fell below the industry $COC_I$, railroad $i$ would be labeled "revenue inadequate."[25]

Third, although revenue adequacy or revenue inadequacy was determined by the relationship between firm $ROI_i$ and industry $COC_I$, the ICC emphasized that measurement is "designed to compute a *minimum* adequate revenue level only for class I railroads,"[26] and that its methodology is "not necessarily appropriate for determination of the maximum fair revenue issues involved in individual rate proceedings."[27] Consistent with the pricing flexibility goals of the Staggers Act, the Commission also observed that the "[a]dded freedom for carriers to change rates and services should result in permitting the carriers in individual markets to undertake all potentially profitable investments (all those that could earn *at least* the current cost of capital)."[28]

This interpretation of the cost of capital as a *floor* for the ability of a firm to attract capital with which to invest is textbook economics. For instance, a standard valuation textbook indicates that:

> [t]he guiding principle of value creation is that companies create value
> by investing capital they raise from investors to generate future cash

flows at rates of return *exceeding* the cost of capital (the rates investors require to be paid for the use of their capital).

(Koller et al., 2010, emphasis added)

Similarly, a corporate finance textbook indicates that "[t]he cost of capital is the *minimum* risk-adjusted rate of return that a project must earn in order to be acceptable to shareholders" (Copeland and Weston, 1988, emphasis added). Yet another finance textbook (Higgins, 2011) states:

> When creditors and owners invest in a business, they incur opportunity costs equal to the returns they could have earned on alternative, similar-risk investments. Together these opportunity costs define the *minimum* rate of return the company must earn on existing assets to meet the expectations of its capital providers. This is the firm's cost of capital.
>
> (emphasis added)

In 1981, 1986, and 1988, the ICC reconsidered—and made subsequent minor refinements to—its measure of revenue adequacy.[29] The Commission returned in each instance to its basic proposition that the threshold is best proxied by the current cost of capital but continued to underscore that the measure constituted a floor for the prospect of industry re-capitalization and reinvigoration. For instance, the ICC observed that its standard "is widely agreed to be the *minimum necessary* to attract and maintain capital in the railroad, or any other industry."[30] It also noted that "[t]he minimum rate of return that will allow railroads to obtain investment funds is the cost of capital" and that "a financially sound firm must earn at a minimum a rate of return at least equal to the cost of capital."[31]

The current revenue adequacy measure remains essentially unchanged today—a largely "mechanical" procedure for assessing on an annual basis whether a railroad achieves a rate of return on net investment ($ROI_t$) at least equal to the current railroad industry cost of capital ($COC_t$), which we detail ahead.

### Uses of Revenue Adequacy

Apart from measurement and the "guidepost" function for which it was originally introduced, the STB has over time drawn upon the revenue adequacy concept for regulatory purposes. The first major instance of this use appears in the development of Constrained Market Pricing in the STB's Coal Rate Guidelines, which identifies a "revenue adequacy constraint."[32] The STB first notes in these guidelines that adequate revenues are "those which provide a rate of return on net investment equal to the current cost of capital."[33] This definition is consistent with the annual revenue adequacy calculations required by Section 205 of the Staggers

Act. The STB then departs significantly from—and seemingly outright ignores—its earlier determination that revenue adequacy calculations represent a guidepost rather than a regulatory tool:

> [o]ur revenue adequacy standard represents a reasonable level of profitability for a healthy carrier. . . . Carriers do not need any greater revenues than this standard permits, and we believe that, in a regulated setting, they are not entitled to any higher revenues.[34]

While statements such as this have led some to suggest that the STB may intervene if the railroad carrier is earning a rate of return greater than its cost of capital (Pittman, 2010), the practical importance of the STB Coal Rate Guidelines argument was tempered by two considerations. First, at the time of its formation, all railroads were revenue inadequate (GAO, 1986), which renders any such constraint nonbinding. Second, an alternative "stand-alone cost" (SAC) test for the reasonableness of specific rail shipments that are subject to regulatory oversight was adopted and implemented in the STB Coal Rate Guidelines.[35] The SAC test draws from modern microeconomic theory and is designed to ensure that rates for specific shipments are not so high as to generate cross-subsidies. In particular, rates for a multiproduct firm's offerings that lie above the marginal cost of that offering and below the SAC of that offering are deemed subsidy free and therefore "reasonable," whereas rates outside of these bounds embody subsidy flows and are deemed "unreasonable." In summary, although the immediate impact of the Coal Rate Guidelines' revenue adequacy constraint was muted, it is, nonetheless, clear that its introduction signaled a philosophical shift by the STB regarding the revenue adequacy concept.

The STB more recently has made additional connections between its calculation of revenue adequacy and regulated prices. In particular, an "RSAM Benchmark" was introduced in 1996 for determining the reasonableness of rates.[36] While not linking revenue adequacy determinations to price regulation directly, the RSAM Benchmark does so indirectly. RSAM is a measure of "the uniform markup above variable cost that would be needed from every shipper of potentially captive traffic (the >180 revenue-to-variable-cost traffic group) in order for the carrier to recover all of its . . . fixed costs."[37] As currently constructed, RSAM utilizes the following variables:

$REV_{>180}$ Total revenue from all traffic provided by a rail carrier which has a revenue-to-variable-cost ratio greater than 180.

$VC_{>180}$ Variable costs of all traffic provided by a rail carrier which has a revenue-to-variable-cost ratio greater than 180.

$REV_{shortage/overage}$ Total dollars by which a rail carrier either falls short of or exceeds revenue adequacy as determined by a four-year average of the annual revenue adequacy calculations.

A shortage represents the amount of additional revenue a revenue inadequate carrier would need to be revenue adequate and is added to the revenue actually received. An overage represents the amount of revenue a revenue adequate carrier receives in excess of the amount to be revenue adequate and is subtracted from the revenue actually received.

$$\text{RSAM is calculated as: } RSAM = \frac{REV_{>180} + REV_{shortage/overage}}{VC_{>180}}.$$

It is evident that with this RSAM formula, firm profitability (as proxied by revenue adequacy calculations) can trigger findings in which rates for a specific shipment or set of shipments are deemed unreasonable.

RSAM is calculated each year, but the STB averages RSAM values over the four most recent years to derive an RSAM factor that it uses in various price tests of profit regulation. One such test is the regulatory introduction of the so-called limit price approach.[38] First, the STB identifies a "limit price" which represents the highest price a railroad could charge for a shipment in question "without causing a significant amount of the issue traffic on a particular rail movement to be diverted to a competitive alternative."[39] This limit price is proxied as a practical matter by the "price of the transportation alternative" to the shipment in question. Second, the STB compares this limit price with the railroad carrier's variable cost of the identified shipment, referring to the ratio of the limit price over variable costs as the "Limit Price R/VC Ratio." Third, the STB compares the Limit Price R/VC Ratio with RSAM. In situations where the Limit Price R/VC Ratio exceeds RSAM, the STB infers that the alternative does not exert competitive pressure sufficient to constrain prices.[40] Because RSAM is determined on the basis of the STB's calculation of revenue adequacy, imposition of Limit Price to R/VC Ratio-based prices links regulated rates on specific rail shipments to the observed profitability of the railroad carrier.

Until recently, the prospect of revenue adequacy becoming an operational pricing constraint has been more hypothetical than likely. The reason is that, by the STB's own annual calculations, railroads have been largely deemed to be revenue inadequate over the years, with rate-of-return on investments consistently lower than the industry cost of capital. Three recent developments have, however, altered the heretofore largely hypothetical prospect of price regulation via the revenue adequacy standards established by the ICC/STB. First, in recent years, railroads have inched toward, and now some are exceeding, the "revenue adequate" thresholds that are published annually by the STB. For example, in its most recent release, four of the seven railroads that were examined by the STB were found to be revenue adequate.[41] This renewed financial health has predictably given rise to calls for regulators to establish regulations that would reduce prices for firms judged to be revenue adequate.

Second, observing that it had "not yet had an opportunity to address how the revenue adequacy constraint would work in practice in large rail rate cases,"[42] the STB in 2014 opened a proceeding to examine the role of revenue adequacy in the Board's determination of the reasonableness of rail freight rates. To date, this proceeding has received a host of evidence from the economics community indicating that price regulation based on revenue adequacy would be economically harmful in a variety of ways, and from shippers who have pressed their claims that revenues in excess of the cost of capital are "excessive" and should legitimately be used as the foundation for rate-reducing regulation. While the potential to either end or elevate the prospect for revenue adequacy regulation exists, the proceeding remains open at this point.

Third, after years without a contested regulatory proceeding involving the issue of revenue adequacy, an electric utility (Consumers Energy) in 2015 challenged the prices of coal shipments carried by a domestic railroad (CSXT) from Chicago, Illinois, to the utility's plant in West Olive, Michigan.[43] The Complaint by Consumers Energy was notable because it asserted that "CSXT's charges are excessive and unreasonable *both* under the Stand-Alone Cost Constraint and under the Revenue Adequacy Constraint of the Coal Rate Guidelines."[44] This complaint then became the first of its kind to challenge explicitly the reasonableness of railroad rates on the grounds the carrier was revenue adequate. In response, CSXT pointed out that the ICC/STB had found CSXT to be revenue inadequate for 28 years in a row and argued stridently that the revenue adequacy portion of the complaint be dismissed. Instead of dismissing this element of the case, however, the STB permitted evidence to be heard, including a variety of financial metrics beyond its own measure of revenue adequacy (viz., $ROI/COC_i$). After considering this host of financial evidence, the Board ultimately ruled that "Consumers has not demonstrated that CSXT is revenue adequate."[45]

While dismissing the complaint, the Board noted that "CSXT has recently made profound alterations to its operations, and presumably to its cost structure"[46] in an attempt to increase its profitability, and concluded that should CSXT become more profitable, Consumers could bring a new case against CSXT under the revenue adequacy standard. From an economic perspective, the possibility that CSXT's attempts to improve its profitability through cost reductions may be "rewarded" by a new, adverse rate case introduces the prospect of regulatorily induced highly perverse economic incentives. Specifically, should cost-reducing measures by CSXT or any railroad be met with enhanced regulation, firms are discouraged from engaging in this economically meritorious behavior. Collectively, these three recent developments create more salience and immediacy to the issue of how the statutory revenue adequacy language in the Staggers Act will be interpreted going forward.

## What Revenue Adequacy Measurement Is and Is Not

While the years following the regulatory reforms adopted in the 4R Act and the Staggers Act provoked discussion of the appropriate measurement of revenue adequacy (GAO, 1986), its measurement has remained essentially unchanged. This measure compares as a ratio railroad $i$'s return on investment $(ROI_i)$ with the industry cost of capital $(COC_I)$, and thus ranges from negative for firms with negative ROIs to positive for firms with positive ROIs. The ICC (and subsequently the STB) adopted the convention of declaring a firm "revenue adequate" if $\dfrac{ROI_i}{COC_I} > 1$ and "revenue inadequate" if $\dfrac{ROI_i}{COC_I} < 1$. The policy attraction to this threshold around a value of unity is natural, given that standard financial theory indicates firms with ROIs less than the cost of capital are financially constrained and intuitively "inadequate." It is less obvious how to interpret firms' financial standing when $\dfrac{ROI_i}{COC_I} > 1$. Two explanations prevail either implicitly or explicitly. First, among the financial community, it is uncontroversial that higher $\dfrac{ROI_i}{COC_I}$ ratios connote "better" economic performance. This is manifest by either cross-sectional comparisons or inter-temporal comparisons. Figure 8.1 provides an example whereby a

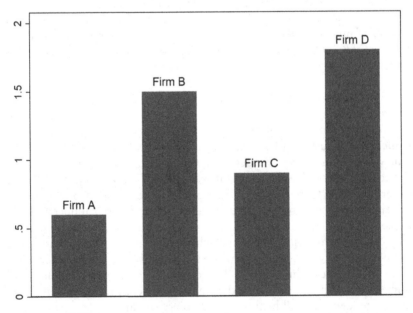

*Figure 8.1* $\dfrac{ROI_i}{COC_I}$ Intra-Industry Comparisons

hypothetical set of firms within a hypothetical industry produce a range of $\dfrac{ROI_i}{COC_I}$ ratios. Regardless of a particular regulatory benchmark for "revenue adequacy," a standard financial interpretation of the firms in Figure 8.1 would indicate that firm D is financially healthier than firms A through C, *ceteris paribus.*

Figure 8.2 similarly provides $\dfrac{ROI_i}{COC_I}$ ratios for a hypothetical firm over time, and again the standard financial interpretation would be that the financial health of the observed firm is improving over time. Whether viewed cross-sectionally or inter-temporally, standard financial interpretations of $\dfrac{ROI_i}{COC_I}$ thus provide a simple metric of the health of the observed firm or firms.

In many industries, there is little if any policy relevance of observed $\dfrac{ROI_i}{COC_I}$ values. In the railroad industry, however, the Staggers Act declares that it is U.S. policy "to promote a safe and efficient rail transportation system by allowing rail carriers to earn adequate revenues, as determined by the Interstate Commerce Commission."[47] Congress, in so doing, has

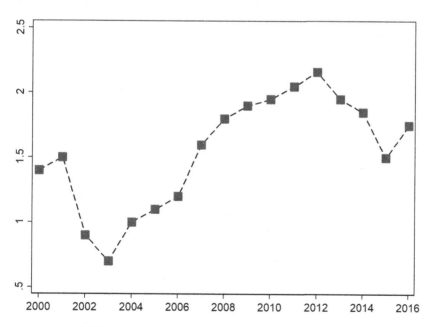

*Figure 8.2* $\dfrac{ROI_i}{COC_I}$ Temporal Comparisons

compelled regulators to consider the industry's financial health as proxied by revenue adequacy. Interpreted from a financial perspective, then,
higher $\dfrac{ROI_i}{COC_I}$ levels can be seen as indicators of regulators' success in
advancing the goals of the Staggers Act by fostering a policy environment
in which railroad firms are increasingly financially healthy.

Another interpretation of revenue adequacy arises implicitly or explicitly. In particular, some interpret $\dfrac{ROI_i}{COC_I} > 1$ as an indication of excess
economic or monopoly returns. This interpretation, in turn, may com-
pel calls for regulatory measures to restrict pricing flexibility of the firm
in question.[48] But while it is theoretically *possible* that observations of
$\dfrac{ROI_i}{COC_I} > 1$ are indications of monopoly returns, there are several reasons
why such an inference is in almost all instances incorrect.

These reasons begin with the observation that accounting returns—
such as those indicated by the revenue adequacy measure—are different
from economic returns. Economic returns are determined by the discount
rate that equates the present value of an expected cash flow stream to
the initial investment outlay. In this regard, "[i]t is an economic rate of
return (after risk adjustment) above the cost of capital that promotes
expansion under competition and is produced by output restriction under
monopoly" (Fisher and McGowan, 1983). In contrast, accounting returns
such as $\dfrac{ROI_i}{COC_I}$ are simply a measure of historical net income relative to
an accounting-depreciated asset base.

While conceptually different, even if accounting and economic returns
were congruent in practice, economic returns in excess of the cost of
capital may be generated by *either* "expansion under competition" or
"output restrictions under monopoly." It is, therefore, not possible to
infer the presence of excess or monopoly economic returns by observing
higher levels of accounting returns. That is, higher accounting returns may
be produced either from a variety of profit-enhancing pro-competitive
behavior—such as productivity enhancements, cost reductions, innovative management, and operating practices—or from monopolistic pricing.

The conceptual gulf between accounting profits and excessive or
monopoly economic profits is further widened for a variety of practical
reasons ranging from inflation effects; accounting and economic depreciation differences; alternative risk, cyclicality and (firm and industry) profitability measures; secular trends; and industry disequilibria (Schmalensee,
1981, 1985; Whittington, 1983; Stauffer, 1971; Bradburd and Caves,
1982). One examination of the misuse of accounting returns to infer the
existence of monopoly profits demonstrates that even under conditions
favorable to the potential for accounting returns to convey information

on economic returns, it is altogether possible that accounting returns may be *negatively* related to economic returns (Fisher and McGowan, 1983). Given the myriad ways in which accounting returns and economic returns differ, economists eschew inferences of monopolistic exploitation from the use of accounting returns.

Beyond the general inability for accounting returns to connote the presence of monopoly returns or monopolistic exploitation, there are several reasons why this admonition holds in relief for the rail industry. First, whereas excessive or monopolistic returns are a long-run phenomenon— at least from the perspective of public policy—the measurement of revenue adequacy is a calculation of annual firm performance.

Second, the STB measure of revenue adequacy compares a given railroad firm's return on investment ($ROI_i$) to the industry cost of capital ($COC_I$). A rail carrier could appear to be "revenue adequate" if its return on investment ($ROI_i$) exceeds the industry cost of capital ($COC_I$) although its cost of capital ($COC_i$) exceeds its ($ROI_i$). Conversely, a rail carrier could appear to be revenue inadequate because its $\dfrac{ROI_i}{COC_I}$ is less than unity, even though it may have a sufficiently low firm-specific cost of capital ($COC_i$) that exceeds its firm-specific return on investment ($ROI_i$).

Third, and arguably most profound, U.S. railroads typically provide a multitude of transportation services. These services vary by location (e.g., shipments from Kansas City to New Orleans are different from shipments from San Diego to Denver) and by shipment type (e.g., shipments of petro-chemicals differ from shipments of corn). It is widely acknowledged that since the Staggers Act, most transportation within the United States is competitive. Rail services in this context are principally, though not in every instance, provided subject to effective competition. A railroad firm's return in excess of its cost of capital is, therefore, as (or even more) likely to arise from competitive locations and commodities than noncompetitive locations and commodities. For example, to the extent that a railroad improves the value of its product offering for a competitive shipment, it may experience enhanced sales, increased accounting profitability, and corresponding increases in its revenue adequacy measurement. Similarly, to the extent that a railroad is able to reduce the costs of providing its competitive services, its profitability as reflected in the STB's measurement of its revenue adequacy will increase. And while demand enhancements or cost reductions from a railroad's competitive shipments will drive revenue adequacy in ways that have nothing to do with exploitation of market power, this same conclusion also holds true for railroad offerings in noncompetitive shipments. Profit-maximizing firms are naturally driven to create value from their entire product portfolio and have incentives to reduce cost and enhance demand in competitive and noncompetitive offerings. Even for noncompetitive shipments, competitive behaviors such as enhancing product quality or reducing cost elevate firm profitability and the consequent revenue adequacy measure reported by the STB.

Finally, railroads may affect profitability either through product-specific or firm-wide activities. Efforts to reduce fixed costs, to improve management or labor practices, or to provide company-wide innovative service offerings are all reflected in increases in the STB's revenue adequacy measures, yet these improvements are not reflective of excessive returns or monopolistic exploitation.

In short, although increases in $\dfrac{ROI_i}{COC_I}$ may arise from market power exploitation, it is clear that there are a host of alternative pro-competitive sources that give rise to revenue adequacy increases. As we argue ahead, changes in $\dfrac{ROI_i}{COC_I}$ suggest policies that condition or provoke regulatory intervention on the realization of revenue adequacy creates the substantial risk of punishing pro-competitive behaviors, rather than specifically testing for and targeting regulatory intervention indicative of market power exploitation. Indeed, as recently demonstrated by Mayo and Sappington (2016), either comprehensive earnings regulation (that is, regulate all rail carrier prices to equilibrate $ROIi$ and $COC_I$) or more focused earnings regulation (that is, limit rail carrier prices only on commodities judged to be producing excess earnings) would have devastating effects on firms' pro-competitive efforts to innovate and reduce costs. In summary, financial profitability measures—such as those reported by the STB's revenue adequacy measure—are particularly poor indicators of excessive returns that result from monopoly power. Increased financial profitability can and does routinely occur for firms as a result of cost savings, productivity gains, and value-enhancing services.

## Revenue Adequacy in an Empirical Perspective

Despite the general inability to interpret increased profitability as an indication of excessive or monopolistic returns, it is nonetheless instructive to benchmark rail industry returns with those from other comparable industries. To do so, we draw upon data from COMPUSTAT, a comprehensive financial information repository of nearly all U.S. publicly traded firms. For all nonfinancial firms in COMPUSTAT, we construct an estimate of each firm's ROI in a manner that comports as closely as possible to the methodology used by the STB in its revenue adequacy calculations.[49] Our total sample consists of 1,226 firms operating continuously for the 2000–2016 period.[50]

As ROIs typically vary within industries and over time, so too does the cost of capital, which determines the denominator in STB calculations of revenue adequacy. By combining modern cost of capital estimates with observed ROIs, we are able to further benchmark revenue adequacy of the rail industry over time and against other industries.[51]

As an initial comparison, we first examine $\dfrac{ROI_i}{COC_I}$ for the set of Class I railroads over 2000–2016 with a comparison set of industries used by the U.S. Government Accountability Office (GAO) in a benchmarking exercise conducted in 1986 (GAO, 1986).[52, 53] The GAO identified firms in the following "comparable" industries: trucking, electric utilities, natural gas pipelines, steel, industrial chemicals and synthetics, and oil and gas. We selected three-digit North American Industry Classification System (NAICS) industries with the same title used by GAO to identify firms in these industries.[54] This approach resulted in industry comparison groups of between eight firms (steel and natural gas pipelines) and 40 firms (oil and gas).

Figure 8.3 displays the annual median $\dfrac{ROI_i}{COC_I}$ in the rail industry and the comparable industries over 2001–2016. Two findings readily emerge. First, although generally improving over 2000–2016, rail industry revenue adequacy ratios are otherwise indistinguishable relative to the comparison set. In particular, the rail industry median $\dfrac{ROI_i}{COC_I}$ falls in the middle of other comparable industries' median $\dfrac{ROI_i}{COC_I}$ over 2000–2016. Second, although the rail industry median $\dfrac{ROI_i}{COC_I}$ has varied within the set of

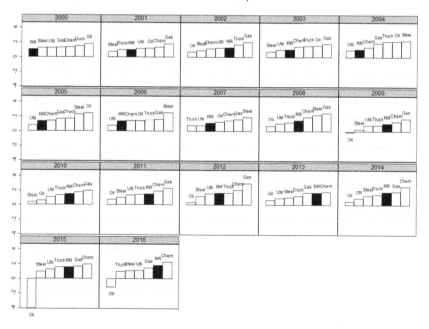

*Figure 8.3* Median $\dfrac{ROI_i}{COC_I}$ of Select Industries (with RRs indicated)

comparable industries, movements up or down among industries is entirely normal. For example, the oil and natural gas pipeline industries had the highest revenue adequacy ratios over 2000–2003; the steel industry in 2004 and again in 2006 and 2007; natural gas led from 2008–2012; and chemicals for 2013–2016.

Figure 8.4 displays the annual distribution of $\dfrac{ROI_i}{COC_I}$ ratios for 1,226 industrial firms over 2000–2016. The top and bottom of each box-year represent the 75th and 25th percentiles of revenue adequacy, respectively, and the line in the middle of each box-year indicates the median. The whiskers extending from the top and bottom of the bars show the range from the 90th percentile to the 10th percentile, respectively. This figure additionally shows revenue adequacy ratios for the five Class I railroads.[55]

Several observations readily emerge. First, firms realize $\dfrac{ROI_i}{COC_I}$ measures that range from "inadequate" to "adequate" every year. $\dfrac{ROI_i}{COC_I}$ equal to unity lies well within the 25th–75th percentile range of observed revenue adequacy realizations every year, with values both above and below the revenue adequacy threshold. Revenue adequate and revenue inadequate firms are thus an empirical regularity, and this mix appears economically normal. Second, across the set of all firm-year observations, median-value revenue adequacy measures are greater than unity. That is, median firms

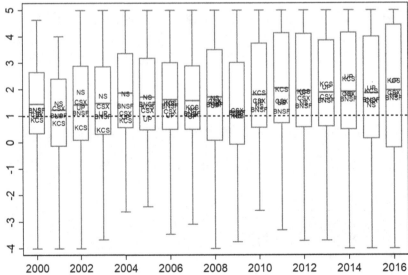

BNSF = Burlington Northern Santa Fe, CSX = CSX Railroad, KCS = Kansas City Southern, NS = Norfolk Southern, UP = Union Pacific
Top/Center/Bottom line of box is 75th/50th/25th percentile. Whiskers show 90th/10th percentile
ROI/COC is capped at 5 and -4

*Figure 8.4* Distribution of $\dfrac{ROI_i}{COC_I}$ for U.S. Nonfinancial Firms

across industries routinely and typically realize "revenue adequacy," and in some years, median-value observed $\dfrac{ROI_i}{COC_I}$ s approach two. Third, although there is an expected dispersion among realized revenue adequacy values across Class I railroads, these values fall well within the 25th–75th percentile range every year against the comparison set of U.S. publicly traded nonfinancial firms and are in no sense outliers. Finally, among this large class of publicly traded nonfinancial firms, railroad firms' adequacy is typically close to the median values. While revenue adequacy measures have improved for railroads in recent years, the position of railroads among the larger class of U.S. firms has remained relatively constant. In summary, if the revenue adequacy of the rail industry is put into a larger perspective and relative to the broader set of firms operating in the U.S. economy over the past dozen years, there is little to distinguish its performance. In the historical context of the industry's poor performance prior to deregulation, this analysis is encouraging and suggestive that the rail industry is operating as a more "normal" industry today. At the same time, the analysis provides no support for the proposition that rail industry's revenue adequacy realizations are unusual or excessive.

To provide additional perspective, we generate revenue adequacy measures for specific well-known firms operating in four different and generally competitive markets: Coca-Cola (soft drinks), Ford Motor (automobiles), Johnson & Johnson (J&J; consumer package goods), and

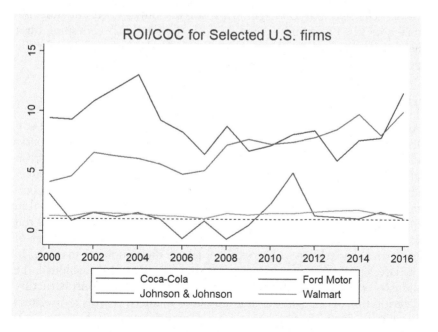

*Figure 8.5* $\dfrac{ROI_i}{COC_I}$ for Selected Large U.S. Firms

Walmart (retailing). These firms are among the largest and most well-recognized firms in the United States. Figure 8.5 shows the $\frac{ROI_i}{COC_I}$ ratio for each firm over 2000–2016. Coca-Cola and J&J have ratios that are significantly above unity (typically between five and 10) in each year of the sample. Relative to individual railroads, these $\frac{ROI_i}{COC_I}$ values are extremely high, but notably are of no immediate public policy concern. Walmart, one of the largest U.S. companies and a firm noted for bringing value to customers, has also been revenue adequate every year, with its ratio ranging between 1.07 and 1.83. Ford Motor, similar to the railroads, has exhibited greater variation over the years, with "inadequate" revenues in some years and adequate revenues in other years. Figure 8.5 thus indicates not only that variation in revenue adequacy metrics across companies and over time is normal, but also that firms operating in highly competitive market segments can realize revenue adequacy metrics above and below unity. In summary, whether assessed relative to firms in other comparable industries, the broad array of nonfinancial firms operating in the United States or leading firms operating in competitive markets, revenue adequacy measures of U.S. rail carriers are in every sense "normal."

## Policy Implications

In 1966, Clint Eastwood starred in a spaghetti western entitled, *The Good, The Bad and The Ugly*. This title not only evokes the indelible image of Mr. Eastwood draped in a Mexican poncho chomping on a half-smoked cigar, but also provides a particularly apt taxonomy for the policy prospects for revenue adequacy.

### The Good

As originally conceived, the concept of revenue adequacy had (and still has) the potential to provide two "good" functions. First, if properly measured and interpreted, the metric can convey useful information on an important economic dimension of the railroad industry. In particular, given the critical role of the industry for facilitating and promoting commerce, knowledge of the industry's financial health may prove useful in any policy discussions of the larger state of the economy. A healthy rail industry is likely to be a catalyst for economic growth in a number of industries that rely on rail services to deliver their goods to markets. In the late 1970s when the concept of revenue adequacy was fashioned, the industry was suffering from both physical and financial infrastructure deterioration. The result was not only poor financial returns to investors (leading to diminished ability to attract financial capital), but also poor service and safety performance that were well documented (GAO, 2007).

While not a cure-all, adequate revenues were then seen—and may still be usefully seen—to be the life-blood for enabling the industry to attract capital and to provide high-quality services.

Second, and related, should the metric of revenue adequacy indicate widespread shortfalls across a number of firms for a protracted period, policymakers may properly raise questions regarding the appropriateness of policy governance of the industry.[56] Given the clear consumer demand for high-quality rail services in the United States and the potential efficiencies of rail transport for a host of goods traveling to markets throughout the world, widespread and protracted indications of revenue inadequacy may provide a signaling value of a flawed governance structure for the industry. This certainly was the case for the rail industry in the 1970s. Aside from a variety of other indicators of economic failure, early ICC calculations revealed that revenue inadequacies were widespread.[57] This metric, together with other readily observable metrics of economic failure, provided a powerful message to Congress that the long-standing policy of granularly regulating rail rates was economically harmful and a more market-oriented system of directing railroad resources was warranted. Increases in the measures of revenue adequacy following the Staggers Act have been slow, but these improvements properly can be taken [together with other economic metrics] as signals to policymakers that the post-Staggers governance structure has proven successful.

### The Bad

The revenue adequacy concept was meant as a tool for informing regulators and the larger public about the financial health of the industry (and therefore the prospects of fulfilling the goals of the Staggers Act). The passage of time has permitted a (sometimes less than) subtle morphing of revenue adequacy from a measure capable of benchmarking railroad industry health into a backdoor regulatory tool, which creates the prospect of "bad" policy. This is not to say that regulatory oversight of the industry is *per se* bad. To be sure, although competition for rail shipments is widespread through intermodal and intramodal alternatives, particular circumstances require regulation to ensure captive shippers are not exploited. The necessity for this residual regulation should not be permitted to extend its reach beyond the minimal amount necessary to fulfill the Staggers Act's goals.

The morphing of revenue adequacy from an instructive metric to a regulatory tool, however, has proceeded over several years without serious notice or awareness of these potential consequences. As early as the introduction of the STB Coal Rate Guidelines "revenue adequacy constraint" in 1985, the possibility emerged that railroad profitability (as judged by the revenue adequacy measure) may be used as a trigger for determining the reasonableness of rates on particular rail shipments. While this potential regulatory constraint had relatively little practical effect when it was introduced because of the widespread "revenue inadequacies" at the time, the prospect for this construct to become binding is significantly more likely as railroads are increasingly deemed revenue adequate. More recently, STB introductions of regulatory mechanisms, such as RSAM and the R/VC Limit Price Test, exacerbate the potential linkage for specific regulatory constraints to turn directly upon the observed financial health of particular railroads.

If the STB were to explicitly allow the revenue adequacy concept to evolve from a primarily information-producing role into an active and ongoing regulatory constraint, it would represent a significant expansion of rail industry regulation. However, the linking of regulatory constraints to observed accounting profit measures, such as those captured in the revenue adequacy metric, lacks economic foundations. Even if $\dfrac{ROI_i}{COC_I} = 1$ is counterfactually assumed to represent a social ideal, moreover, history provides a clear indication that the imposition of such rates through regulatory fiat is extremely costly and laden with harmful side effects when applied in the rail industry. While it is tempting to pit an idealized notion of regulatory outcomes against observed market imperfections, the actual choice that policymakers must confront is rooted in the reality that *both* markets and regulation are imperfect governance structures (Mayo, 2013). From this perspective, policymakers should appropriately be wary of introducing expansive regulatory tools in situations where market-based governance is producing palatable economic outcomes. This perspective is especially true in industries such as railroads, in which the costs of poor regulatory design have been made so apparent.

### The Ugly

While an inadvertent morphing of the revenue adequacy concept from an information-producing role into a regulatory capacity creates the prospect for bad policy, a truly "ugly" prospect emerges from an examination of the evolution of rail industry regulation. The end aim of revenue adequacy has sometimes been interpreted as an explicit limitation on the ability of firms to earn economic profits. For instance, in the Coal Rate Guidelines, the STB declared a desire to use the concept of revenue adequacy as a regulatory vehicle to explicitly constrain the profits of railroads to be—as an upper bound—the industry-wide cost of capital:

> Carriers do not need greater revenues than . . . [the Revenue-Adequacy level which equals the industry-wide cost of capital] . . . and we believe that, in a regulated setting, they are not entitled to any higher revenues. Therefore, the logical first constraint on a carrier's pricing is that its rates not be designed to earn greater revenues than needed

to achieve and maintain this "revenue adequacy" level. Our concept is simply that a railroad not use differential pricing to consistently earn, over time, a return on investment above the cost of capital.[58]

This regulatory goal found its way into other rail commodities. In the 1996 Non-Coal Guidelines, the STB states:

> the statutory objective is for railroads to attain *only* the level of revenues that would be adequate . . . .[59]

Finally, similar calls for links between the regulatory governance structure and the financial profitability of railroad appears in other venues as well. A 2013 Senate Commerce Committee study on the financial state of Class I railroads indicated:

> [i]f the railroad industry is now proving to be financially viable for the near and long term, policymakers will need to consider whether regulatory changes are in order to make sure the industry does not enjoy unfair advantages.[60]

Our reading of the Staggers Act and its legislative history finds no such congressional intent to restrict railroads' earnings to be only those deemed adequate.[61] As noted, the cost of capital upon which the revenue adequacy concept is predicated serves in competitive markets as a minimal floor for successful firms. Firms operating in competitive markets routinely aspire for greater earnings; indeed, it is this aspiration that compels such firms to a number of salubrious behaviors including cost reductions, productivity enhancements, quality of service enhancements, and so on. As shown, firms across the United States —in a variety of industries and over extended periods of time—can and do generate adequate revenues without the need for profit-based regulation.

In contrast, were regulators to utilize the revenue adequacy provisions of the Staggers Act to constrain rates with the purpose of limiting railroads' profitability to be only equal to the industry cost of capital, profound economic incongruities and problems would arise. One of these problems is the creation of a knife-edge turning point between the clear congressional mandate for regulators to "assist" carriers in achieving adequate revenue levels and a regulatory policy to ensure that railroads are unable to earn anything more than exactly this level. Such an interpretation of revenue adequacy appears to be directly contrary to the aim of the Staggers Act to rely upon (1) competition and market forces to the maximum extent possible and (2) regulation to the corresponding minimum extent necessary to accomplish the goals of the Act. Aside from arguably "going off the tracks" laid out by Congress, such a policy is troubling from an economic perspective for several reasons.

First, such a policy ignores the economic reality that the vast majority of rail traffic faces competition with other railroads, other transportation service alternatives, and other geographic and product alternatives. As recognized by Congress—and widely embraced throughout the U.S. economy—such market-based allocation drives firms to reduce costs, innovate and, more generally, better serve the U.S. economy. Firms do not undertake these activities for altruistic reasons but for the pursuit of economic profits in excess of the firm's cost of capital. Regulatory policies that restrict firms to only earn the industry cost of capital effectively eliminate profit motives that drive innovative, cost-reducing, and value-enhancing activities. Regulatory policies that are more concerned with protecting competitors—rather than protecting competition—through notions of equity or fairness between carriers and between shippers and receivers have similar deleterious effects. Indeed, this is exactly the sort of regulatory regime that existed prior to the Staggers Act and which, in hindsight, is universally regarded as a principal source of the physical and financial deterioration of the industry in the 1970s.

The foundation of such a policy also errs in presuming that the source of returns in excess of adequate levels is differential pricing of dominant routes, when, in fact, such profits may arise from a variety of sources. This prospect creates the potential for regulation to substantially misalign incentives in the industry. Suppose a firm reduces its costs of providing service for a set of shipments that are not subject to regulatory review (because their prices are less than 180% of their variable costs). When a firm is at or near the revenue adequacy threshold, the consequence of this otherwise desirable cost reduction would be the prospect of an enhanced regulation of shipments that are within the regulators' purview. That is, efficiency enhancements would be "rewarded" by compensating increases in regulation. Similar "rewards" would emerge from innovations that enhance consumer demand, reduce product-specific or firm-wide fixed costs, or even reduce *any* shipment-related costs. In these instances, the regulatory structure creates perverse incentives to avoid such efficiency enhancements. For instance, consider the prospect of a firm-wide innovation that could be introduced immediately or, alternatively, introduced more slowly. With profit regulation operating as a binding constraint, the firm may benefit (though society will be harmed) by "slow-rolling" the introduction of the innovation.[62]

Finally, such a policy is neither efficiently targeted nor free of regulatory costs. That is, the regulatory tool of profit-based regulation applies a "dull axe" of firm-wide profit-triggered regulation to a far more specific issue of residual market power abuses on specific shipments. Apart from the perverse incentives created by such a policy, this profit-based regulation has proven to be sufficiently costly in a variety of industries to warrant substantial movement away from this tool over the past quarter century (Crew and Kleindorfer, 1996).

# Conclusion

Congress in 1980 declared that the goals of the Staggers Act were to (1) assist the railroads in rehabilitating the rail system; (2) reform federal regulatory policy to preserve a safe, adequate, economical, efficient, and financially stable rail system; (3) assist the rail system to remain viable in the private sector of the economy; (4) provide a regulatory process that balances the needs of carriers, shippers, and the public; and (5) assist in the rehabilitation and financing of the rail system. It is possible to state today that the governance structure established by the Staggers Act has been successful in accomplishing these goals. The rail industry is healthy, with benefits flowing to both rail carriers and shippers alike, as well as to the larger economy. With these benefits in hand, some industry observers have implicitly, if not explicitly, suggested that the industry's financial progress should presage policy reconsiderations, if not reformulations. This perspective essentially argues that the Staggers Act has been too successful, and that now, with a financially stable industry earning "adequate" revenues, it may be possible to use that "adequacy" as a trigger for enhanced regulation.

In this chapter, we examine the concept of revenue adequacy with an economic lens by exploring its origins, its evolution, its practical applications, and its prospects. We find that the concept was—in the first instance—well-motivated by the dire financial situation facing the rail industry and designed to serve as a benchmark for assessing the ability of the evolving regulatory structure in the post-Staggers industry to assist rail carriers in achieving financially secure footing (GAO, 2006). From this relatively straightforward beginning, revenue adequacy has subtly morphed from an informative concept into a regulatory tool. Beyond a deviation from the original legislative intent of the concept, we find that this transition is unwarranted on both conceptual and practical grounds. Moving forward, we argue that policymakers have the opportunity to use revenue adequacy as an instrument for good, bad, or ugly policy. Revenue adequacy calculations can provide "good" useful information on the financial health of the U.S. rail industry, a vital infrastructure industry supporting the larger economy. If permitted to drift in the direction of creating additional links between railroads' general profitability and regulatory stringency, however, the use of revenue adequacy will create the real prospect of "bad" or even outright "ugly" economic consequences.

# Notes

* This chapter draws upon and updates research previously published in Macher et al. (2014).
1. *See* Macher et al. (2014) and the studies cited therein. *See also* Burton (2015).
2. Railroad Revitalization and Regulatory Reform Act of 1976, 45 U.S.C. § 801 (1976).

3. *See* Railroad Revenue Adequacy—2016 Determination, S.T.B. Ex Parte No. 552 (Sub-No. 21) (September 6, 2017).
4. Regional Rail Reorganization Act of 1973, 45 U.S.C. § 741–797 (1973).
5. 45 U.S.C. § 801(a).
6. Railroad Revitalization and Regulatory Reform Act of 1976, Pub. L. No. 94–210, § 205, 90 Stat. 31, 41 (1976).
7. *Id.*
8. *Id.* Emphasis added.; *see also* U.S. Gov't Accountability Office, GAO/RCED-87–15BR, Railroad Revenues: Analysis of Alternative Methods to Measure Revenue Adequacy 8 (1986).
9. Staff of S. Comm. on Transp. & Commerce, 95th Cong., 1st Sess., Congressional Symposium, Railroads—1977 and Beyond: Problems and Promises VI (Comm. Print 1977).
10. *Id.* at 16 (statement of Richard J. Barber, President, Richard J. Barber Assocs., Inc.).
11. *Id.* at 5–7 (statement of William K. Smith, Acting Chairman of U.S. Railway Ass'n.).
12. *Staggers Rail Act Oversight Hearings Before the Subcomm. on Transportation., Tourism, and Hazardous Materials of the Comm. on Energy and Commerce of the House of Representatives*, 100th Cong. 13–14 (1987) (statement of Rep. Dan Schaefer, Member, H. Comm. on Energy and Com.).
13. Adequacy of Railroad Revenue (1978 Determination), 362 I.C.C. 199 (1979).
14. *Bill Summary & Status, 96th Congress, (1979–1980), S.1946, Major Congressional Actions,* THOMAS.gov,http://thomas.loc.gov/cgi-bin/bdquery/z?d096:SN01946:@@R (last visited July 5, 2018).
15. Staggers Rail Act of 1980, Pub L. No. 96–448, 94 Stat. 1985 (codified in scattered sections of 49 U.S.C.).
16. The 180% threshold was originally set at 160% and increased in five percentage point increments until reaching the current threshold in 1984. Market dominance is defined as an absence of effective competition from other rail carriers or modes of transportation for the transportation to which a rate applies. 49 U.S.C. § 10707(a); *see also* Wilson, *supra* note 22. The regulatory agency (then the ICC, now the STB) is charged with making the determination of whether a set of challenged rates is reasonable based on the threshold. The threshold represents the point at which the regulatory agency can begin to consider whether rates are unreasonable. That is, rates determined to be below the 180% threshold are conclusive that the rail carrier does not have market dominance. Rates determined to be above the 180% threshold do not necessarily establish a presumption of either market dominance or unreasonableness (or reasonableness). *See* Mayo and Sappington (2016) for a complete discussion of the residual price regulation authority retained post-Staggers and it implementation in practice.
17. *Id.* § 101(3).
18. Staggers Rail Act § 201(b)(3).
19. The Interstate Commerce Termination Act of 1995 eliminated the third set of revenue adequacy applications. *See* H.R. Rep. No. 104–311 *reprinted in* 1995 U.S.C.C.A.N. 793, 809 (regarding Joint Route Cancelation and Surcharge); H.R. Conf. Rep. No. 104–422 *reprinted in* 1995 U.S.C.C.A.N. 850, 859 (regarding ZORF).
20. Adequacy of Railroad Revenue (1978 Determination), 362 I.C.C. 199 (1979).
21. *Id.* Emphasis added.
22. *Id.*
23. *Id.*
24. *Id.*
25. *See id.* It is generally beyond the scope of this chapter to discuss how ROI and COC are calculated (e.g., historical versus replacement cost, definitions of long run).

26. *Id.* Emphasis in original.
27. *Id.*
28. *Id.* Emphasis added.
29. *See* Standards for Railroad Revenue Adequacy, 364 I.C.C. 803 (1981); Standards for Railroad Revenue Adequacy, 3 I.C.C. 2d 261 (1986); Supplemental Reporting of Consolidated Information for Revenue Adequacy Purposes, 5 I.C.C. 2d 65 (1988).
30. *Id.* at 809. Emphasis added.
31. *Id.* at 810, 816.
32. Coal Rate Guidelines, Nationwide, 1 I.C.C. 2d 520, 534–45 (1985).
33. *Id.* at 535.
34. *Id.*
35. *See* Coal Rate Guidelines, Nationwide, 1 I.C.C.2d 520, 6 (1985).
36. *See* Rate Guidelines—Non-Coal Proceedings, S.T.B. Ex Parte No. 347 (Sub-No. 2), 1 S.T.B. 1004, 1027 (Dec. 27, 1996).
37. *Id.*
38. *M&G Polymers USA, LLC v. CSX Transportation, Inc.*, S.T.B. No. NOR 42123, at 3–4 (decided Sept. 26, 2012, updated Dec. 7, 2012), *available at* www.stb.dot.gov/decisions/readingroom.nsf/UNID/64E3F8C385BA40A5 85257A8600483883/$file/41926.pdf.
39. *Id.* at 13.
40. *Id.*
41. See Surface Transportation Board, "Railroad Revenue Adequacy—2016 Determination," September 6, 2017.
42. Surface Transportation Board, Notice, Docket No. EP 722 "Revenue Adequacy," April 1, 2014.
43. Consumers Energy Company v CSX Transportation Company, Inc. "Original Complaint," Docket No. NOR 42142.
44. *Id.* at ¶18. Emphasis added.
45. *Consumers Energy Company v. CSX Transportation, Inc.*, Docket No. Nor 42142, Surface Transportation Board, March 14, 2018, p. 2.
46. *Id.* at 21.
47. Staggers Rail Act of 1980 § 101, Pub L. No. 96–448, 94 Stat. 1897 (codified as amended at 49 U.S.C. 10101(a)(3) (2014)).
48. *See* Mayo and Sappington (2016) for an evaluation of the likely economic impact of such regulation.
49. To do so, we begin with Schedule 250 "Consolidated Information for Revenue Adequacy Determination," which is filed by all Class I railroads as part of their annual R-1 filing. The computation of ROI (the numerator in revenue adequacy) is determined by dividing Adjusted Net Railway Operating Income (line 5 of Schedule 250) by the average Net Investment Base (line 13 on Schedule 250, average of beginning and ending year). We compare the information in Schedule 250 and the rest of the R-1 with the financial information provided in the annual 10-K, which public companies must file with the Securities and Exchange Commission (SEC). Using the information in the 10-K, we attempt to recreate the computation of ROI. The appendix to this chapter provides a detailed description of the process we employ.
50. Because we are examining the five Class I railroads which survived to the present, we compare them with other firms which were in existence over our sample period of 2000–2016. Our results are similar if we do not impose this survival restriction, although the distribution has many more firms with negative ROI. In the unbalanced panel, the annual number of firms varies between 1,969 and 3,004.
51. For industry cost of capital ($COC_i$), we use the data provided by Professor Aswath Damodaran on his website. The main site is http://pages.stern.nyu.

edu/~adamodar/. The current year industry cost of capital can be downloaded at www.stern.nyu.edu/~adamodar/pc/datasets/wacc.xls, and the historical measures can be found in his data archive. As cost of capital needs to be estimated, there are a plethora of assumptions involved in that estimation. The benefit of using the Damodaran data is that we can remain agnostic as to what assumptions to make across industries and remain as objective as possible. Using a single source for the entire time-series furthermore means that the assumptions are likely to remain consistent across time. While our *relative* revenue adequacies across firms are unaffected by any difference between the cost of capital estimated by Damodaran and that estimated by the STB, we are careful not to make too much of the levels. We compared the cost of capital estimates for railroads from Damodaran with those used by the STB. For the 2000–2016 period, the STB estimates were always higher than the Damodaran estimates, ranging from a low of 170 basis points to a high of 535 basis points. The mean difference is 319 basis points with a standard deviation of 95 basis points. To the extent that the STB would estimate a higher cost of capital than what we use, this would bias us toward finding higher levels of revenue adequacy than the STB would calculate. As such, our results would overstate the revenue adequacy of the railroad industry.

52. The Class I railroads we examine are BNSF Railway, CSX Transportation, Kansas City Southern, Norfolk Southern, and Union Pacific. We exclude two Class I railroads for lack of publicly available data. Grand Trunk Corporation is a subsidiary of Canadian National and Soo Line Corporation is a subsidiary of Canadian Pacific. We have data on the consolidated corporation only, which is primarily the Canadian operations; thus, we cannot examine the U.S. data separately.

53. The GAO study tested alternative revenue adequacy standards at the request of the House of Representatives' Subcommittee on Oversight and Investigations within the Committee on Energy and Commerce. The main finding is financial indicators indicate a "mixed picture" of railroads' financial health, with returns below the ICC-determined standard necessary to attract adequate capital but debt servicing levels showing improved financial health.

54. Railroads are defined as NAICS code 482. Trucking is 484, Utilities is 221, and Oil and Gas is 211. Note that Damodaran stopped classifying WACC for natural gas pipelines as of 2013, so in the later years, we drew upon the combined oil/gas distribution industry to provide continuity. For two industries, we used four-digit NAICS codes because the three-digit code was too broad. Steel is defined as 3311 or 3315 in order to examine only producers of steel rather than companies that manufacture products from purchased steel or companies that specialize in other metals. Chemicals is defined as 3251 so that we have only basic industrial chemicals and not pharmaceuticals or biotech companies, which are better classified as drug manufacturing. As a robustness check, we also used the three-digit categorization for all the comparable industries, with very similar conclusions to those we report here.

55. BNSF = BNSF Railway; CSX = CSX Corp.; KCS = Kansas City Southern; NS = Norfolk Southern Corp.; and UP = Union Pacific Corp.

56. At the outset of the determination of the concept of revenue adequacy, it was recognized that its "attainment depends upon enlightened government action in all areas that affect the health of the Nation's railroads." These governance tools were seen to include, for example, legislation, eliminating discriminatory taxation, requiring alternative transportation modes to bear an economic share of the highway and waterway costs which are incurred by the public for to support these modes, and reducing regulation "to the level that is genuinely necessary to protect the public interest." *See, e.g.,* Adequacy

of Railroad Revenue (1978 Determination), 362 I.C.C. 199 (1979); *ICC Ratemaking in Noncompetitive Markets—Oversight: Hearing Before the Subcomm. on Oversight & Investigations of the H. Comm. on Interstate & Foreign Commerce*, 96th Cong. 58, 68 (1980).
57. *ICC Ratemaking in Noncompetitive Markets—Oversight: Hearing Before the Subcomm. on Oversight & Investigations of the H. Comm. on Interstate & Foreign Commerce*, 96th Cong. 58, 69 (1980). The first assessment of revenue adequacy by the ICC found 23 Class I railroads faced inadequate revenues.
58. See Coal Rate Guidelines, Nationwide, 1 I.C.C.2d 520, 535–36 (1985).
59. Rate Guidelines—Non-Coal Proceedings, S.T.B. Ex Parte No. 347 (Sub-No. 2), 1 S.T.B. 1004, 1027 (Dec. 27, 1996).
60. See Staff of S. Comm. on Commerce, Sci., & Transp., 113th Cong., Update on the Financial State of the Class I Freight Rail Industry (Nov. 21, 2013).
61. See generally Staff of S. Comm. on Transp. & Commerce, 95th Cong., 1st Sess., Congressional Symposium, Railroads—1977 and Beyond: Problems and Promises III (Comm. Print 1977); Railroad Transportation Policy Act of 1979: Rep. on S.1946 to Reform the Economic Regulation of Railroads, and for Other Purposes, S. Rep. No. 96–470 (1979); Rail Act of 1980: Rep. on H.R. 7235 to Reform the Economic Regulation of Railroads, and for Other Purposes, H.R. Rep. No. 96–1035 (1980); Staggers Rail Act of 1980, Pub L. No. 96–448, 94 Stat. 1895 (1980) (codified in scattered sections of 49 U.S.C.).
62. See, e.g., George Sweeney (1981).

## References

Bradburd, Ralph M., and Richard E. Caves. 1982. "A Closer Look at the Effect of Market Growth on Industries' Profits." *The Review of Economics and Statistics* 64(4): 635–645.

Burton, Mark L. 2015. "Existing Railroad Oversight and Proposed Policy Change: An Application of 'Results-Based Regulation'." *Transportation Law Journal* 42(2): 153–192.

Copeland, Thomas E., and John F. Weston. 1988. *Financial Theory and Corporate Policy*. Reading, MA: Addison-Wesley.

Crew, Michael A., and Paul R. Kleindorfer. 1996. "Incentive Regulation in the United Kingdom and the United States: Some Lessons." *Journal of Regulatory Economics* 9(3): 211–225.

Ferguson, Lucy. 1979. "Regulation and Innovation: The Case of Piggybacking." *Eastern Economic Journal* 5(4): 453–462.

Fisher, Franklin M., and John J. McGowan. 1983. "On the Misuse of Accounting Rates of Return to Infer Monopoly Profits." *The American Economic Review* 73(1): 82–97.

Gaskins, Darius W. 2008. "Regulation of Freight Railroads in the Modern Era: 1970–2010." *Review of Network Economics* 7(4): 561–572.

Higgins, Robert C. 2011. *Analysis for Financial Management*, 10th edition. New York: McGraw-Hill/Irwin.

Hilton, George W. 1966. "The Consistency of the Interstate Commerce Act." *The Journal of Law and Economics* 9: 87–113.

Houston, Douglas A. 1979. "A Note on Railroad-Shipper Transactions: Appropriation, Private Contracts, and Regulation." *Transportation Journal* 19(2): 60–66.

Keeler, Theodore E. 1983. *Railroads, Freight and Public Policy*. Washington, DC: Brookings Institution Press.

Koller, Tim, Marc Goedhart, and David Wessels. 2010. *Valuation: Measuring and Managing the Value of Companies*, 5th edition. Hoboken, NJ: John Wiley & Sons.

Macher, Jeffrey T., John W. Mayo, and Lee F. Pinkowitz. 2014. "Revenue Adequacy: The Good, the Bad and the Ugly." *Transportation Law Journal* 41(2): 85–127.

Mayo, John W. 2013. "The Evolution of Regulation: Twentieth Century Lessons and Twenty-First Century Opportunities." *Federal Communications Law Journal* 65(2): 119–156.

Mayo, John W., and David E. M. Sappington. 2016. "Regulation in a 'Deregulated' Industry: Railroads in the Post-Staggers Era." *Review of Industrial Organization* 49(2): 203–227.

Pittman, Russell. 2010. "The Economics of Railroad 'Captive Shipper' Legislation." *Administrative Law Review* 62(3): 919–936.

Schmalensee, Richard. 1981. "Risk and Return on Long-Lived Tangible Assets." *Journal of Financial Economics* 9(2): 185–205.

Schmalensee, Richard. 1985. "Do Markets Differ Much?" *The American Economic Review* 75(3): 341–351.

Stauffer, Thomas R. 1971. "The Measurement of Corporate Rates of Return: A Generalized Formation." *The Bell Journal of Economics and Management Science* 2(2): 434–469.

Sweeney, George. 1981. "Adoption of Cost-Saving Innovations by a Regulated Firm." *American Economic Review* 71(3): 437–447.

U.S. Government Accountability Office. 1986. Railroad Revenues: Analysis of Alternative Methods to Measure Revenue Adequacy 8, GAO/RCED-87-15BR. Washington, DC. Accessed July 27, 2018. www.gao.gov/products/GAO/RCED-87-15BR.

U.S. Government Accountability Office. 2006. Freight Railroads: Industry Health has Improved, But Concerns about Competition and Capacity Should Be Addressed 1,7. GAO-07-94. Washington, DC. Accessed July 27, 2018. www.gao.gov/products/GAO-07-94.

U.S. Government Accountability Office. 2007. Freight Railroads: Updated Information on Rates and Other Industry Trends 4–5, GAO-08-218T. Washington, DC. Accessed July 27, 2018. www.ams.usda.gov/sites/default/files/media/RTIReportNotes.pdf.

Whittington, Geoffrey. 1983. *Inflation Accounting: An Introduction to the Debate*. Cambridge: Cambridge University Press.

Wilson, Wesley W. 1996. "Legislated Market Dominance in Railroad Markets." *Research in Transportation Economics* 4: 49–67.

# Appendix

## Calculating ROI With COMPUSTAT Data

For the STB, the computation of ROI (the numerator in revenue adequacy) is determined by dividing Adjusted Net Railway Operating Income (line 5 of Schedule 250) by the average Net Investment Base (line 13 on Schedule 250, average of beginning and ending year). Using COMPUSTAT (data codes are shown in italics), we attempt to estimate this calculation for a broad array of companies operating in the United States for 2001–2016. Our estimate of line 5, Adjusted Operating Income is earnings before interest and taxes less total taxes.

$$Adjusted\ Operating\ Income = EBIT - TXT$$

Our estimate of line 13, Net Investment Base, is Net property plant and equipment plus working capital minus deferred income tax credits (which are set to zero if missing). Working capital allowed needs to be calculated similarly to how it is calculated on line 28 of schedule 245. Working capital allowed is the minimum of [cash on hand, cash allowed], plus inventory. Minimum cash allowed is computed as days of working capital required multiplied by average daily expenses. The calculation using COMPUSTAT data codes follows:

$$Net\ Investment\ Base = PPENT + \text{minimum}\ (CHE, \text{allowed cash}) + INVT - TXDITC$$

$$\text{where allowed cash} = \left\{ \left[ \left( \frac{RECT}{SALE/360} + 15 \right) - \left( \frac{AP}{XOPR/360} \right) \right] \times XOPR/360 \right\}$$

Figure 8.A.1 shows how close our measure is to the STB calculation for each of BNSF Railway, Union Pacific Corp., and Norfolk Southern Corp, CSX Corp., and Kansas City Southern. Overall, our measure comes relatively close to matching the STB for BNSF Railway and Union Pacific Corp., where with the exception of a single year, our measure is always

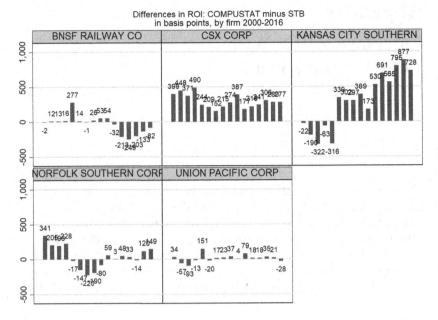

*Figure 8.A.1*   Differences in ROI: COMPUSTAT minus STB in Basis Points, by
Firm 2000–2016

off by less than one percentage point. The measure also works well for Norfolk Southern Corp. in the recent years, but less so in the early period. The methodology less closely produces a match to the STB methodology for CSX and Kansas City Southern. However, it is important to note that our calculation of ROI appears to be systematically higher than the STB. Thus, any bias this introduces would tend to make Class I railroads more profitable than the STB measure, and as such, our analyses would tend to overestimate the profitability of the railroad industry.

# 9 Open Access and Revenue Adequacy

*William Huneke*[1]

## Introduction

A primary aim of the Staggers Rail Act of 1980 was to substitute market-based competition for detailed regulatory oversight of the industry. In the wake of this transition, an ongoing concern has been whether the level of intramodal competition (between railroads) and intermodal competition (among railroads, trucks, and barges) is sufficient to ensure reasonable prices for freight rail services in the United States. To increase competition in the freight rail industry, some have argued for vertical separation of the industry. Specifically, vertical separation would mean separating ownership and control of train operations from the infrastructure, such as track and road beds. The economics of vertical separation are dealt with in detail in a companion chapter in this volume.[2] Another common proposal that has been championed as a source of enhanced competition, and which is the subject of this chapter, has been to adopt a policy of allowing access to an incumbent's rail trackage by other rail carriers. While specific proposals on how to design such access vary, these proposals collectively are referred to as "open access."

While these vertical separation and open access ideas have taken center stage in policy discussions in recent years, the merits or failings of these proposals have to date failed to account for a third important consideration in the evolution of freight rail policy. Specifically, with respect to open access, there has been inadequate consideration of how this proposal interacts with revenue adequacy. Revenue adequacy means the ability of a railroad company to earn sufficient compensation to remain an ongoing concern. These two regulatory concepts, open access and revenue adequacy, are usually discussed separately, but they interact with each other. In particular, allowing a competitor to use an incumbent's tracks to reach the incumbent's customers might reduce the incumbent's revenues. If so, this reduces the incumbent's ability to maintain or attain revenue adequacy.

Consideration of both concepts together—open access and revenue adequacy—complicates U.S. rail regulatory policy for the Surface

Transportation Board (STB). U.S. rail regulatory policy is supposed to balance shippers' need for reasonable rates with the railroads' need for adequate revenues. In fact, some Congressional staff who worked on the Staggers Act, which created the current statutory regime, have argued that Staggers did not aim to have open access act as a "backdoor" method of rate regulation and thus create a dilemma of competitive/reasonable rates or revenue adequate railroads.[3] STB's predecessor, the Interstate Commerce Commission (ICC), articulated a further regulatory principle: a shipper should not have to pay for facilities the shipper did not use.[4] However, if U.S. regulatory policy adopts open access and follows this principle (that shippers do not pay for facilities they do not use), this will have a detrimental impact on railroads' ability to maintain or achieve revenue adequacy.

This chapter will proceed in the following order. First, it will present the historical background of the economic structure of the industry, its pricing and regulation. It will then discuss the emergence of the current open access debate. The next discussion will review the interaction of revenue adequacy if the regulator opens Access more aggressively. Finally, it will discuss the regulatory dilemma that exists with the intersection of revenue adequacy and open access.

## Background

In atomistic, competitively structured industries, competition among various industry participants will produce a set of firm-level prices that are equal to the efficiently incurred marginal cost associated with producing the good or service. This result is, however, not possible in the production of rail services. In particular, railroading is not an industry marked by constant returns to scale, unlike firms in a competitive market. Railroading is a declining cost, and necessarily oligopolistic, industry. In particular, railroads have economies of scale, scope, and density.[5] These are defined as:

- Scale—The larger the operating plant or facility, the lower the average unit costs. For a railroad, the larger the network, that is, the more customers it reaches, and the more output moving on the network, the lower the average unit costs. Another way to think about this is that railroads have large fixed costs. As a railroad generates more volume, it is able to spread those fixed costs over more output: spreading the overhead.
- Scope—The firm enjoys lower average unit costs if it can use the same facilities to provide multiple services. Railroads can use the same track and locomotives to move grain, coal, or intermodal traffic.
- Density—The more intensely the firm uses a particular facility or production factor, the lower the average unit cost. The more traffic a railroad can push over a particular track segment, the lower is the per-unit cost of that track segment.

Because railroads provide multiple services using the same facilities, many of their costs are shared among these various services. Economists describe these shared costs as common costs. This makes estimating railroad costs problematic, but a more fundamental conundrum is how railroads price their services. A firm with high fixed costs, like a railroad, cannot simply price all its output at marginal cost like a firm in an industry with low fixed costs and minimal or no scale economies. Railroads' high fixed costs require railroad pricing above short-run marginal cost to achieve adequate revenues.

To tackle the need to generate revenues through pricing, 19th century railroads became proficient in charging different prices based on demand characteristics, cost characteristics, and market conditions. Railroads based rates on value of service. Price differences resulted from buyer location and railroads' leverage over customers. While aiding those consumers with ample competitive alternatives, this practice also created a set of disfavored, unhappy customers who sought political redress. The seeming arbitrariness of railroad rates fed an urge for regulation. Ultimately, this led Congress to enact the Interstate Commerce Act, which created the first federal regulatory in the United States, the Interstate Commerce Commission, in 1887.[6]

Compounding the irritant effects of substantial price differentials across consumers, another pricing issue also emerged. In particular, in a recession, with traffic falling, railroads have low variable costs and could stay in business while charging very low rates. This led to accusations of cutthroat or ruinous competition and ultimate bankruptcy. U.S. rail regulators received powers to block this by banning minimum rates and approving new construction in the Transportation Act of 1920.[7]

At the turn of the 20th century, railroads had limited competition from other modes of transportation. That competition came from water carriers, inland, and inter-coastal. However, the high fixed cost nature of railroads made them susceptible to volatile profit swings with the normal churn of the business cycle. This led leading industry executives and investors such as James J. Hill, Edward Harriman, and J. P. Morgan to search for ways to restructure the industry to remove the profit volatility through merger and common control.

But these efforts at restructuring got the attention of President Theodore Roosevelt, who drove his Justice Department to block such combinations, most notably Northern Securities. At the same time, Progressives like Roosevelt applied political pressure to the ICC to curb the market power of the railroads reflected in their rate structures.[8] The ICC was set on a course to limit rail rates below compensatory levels.

Railroads, tightly confined by regulation, could not respond when intermodal competition arrived with highway carriers. Truckers started siphoning off profitable traffic in the 1930s and 1940s, but the Interstate Highway System brought the railroads to an existential crisis in the 1950s and 1960s into the 1970s. Inland water carriers added to the railroads' troubles. Barge lines were exempt from regulation for bulk commodities where three or fewer different commodities were carried in the same tow. ICC regulation limited the railroads' ability to respond, through either rate changes or productivity innovations.

Southern Railway's Big John hopper car is a cogent example of ICC impedances on railroads' ability to grab market opportunities through productivity innovation. Bill Brosnan, the president of Southern Railroad in the early 1960s, decided to seek more grain hauling market share by introducing new equipment and lowering rates. Southern's existing equipment was dilapidated box cars. Southern replaced them with new aluminum hopper cars, but when it introduced the new service, barge line and the Tennessee Valley Authority, which had responsibility for an inland water system, protested to the ICC.

> Brosnan's new rates, slashing old tariffs in half, were to take effect 10 August 1961. The ICC suspended these rates 9 August and set hearings for January 1962. Brosnan was the first witness as the ICC opened the longest rate case in its history, a case in which witnesses were to leave almost 16,000 pages of testimony and 765 exhibits on the record over a period of thirty weeks—and in the end was to drag on for four years, to be heard thirteen times in Federal appellate courts, and twice by the Supreme Court.[9]

The Big John episode was symptomatic of a regulatory regime that stifled railroad innovation, competitiveness, and earnings.

With the entry of highway carriers and inland water carriers, the railroad industry no longer needed to be as large as it was before this intermodal entry. Yet ICC processes inhibited any railroad industry effort to restructure. The ICC approved industry mergers, which would be one route to industry restructuring, but the ICC was too slow, as was evident in the travails of Union Pacific's attempted takeover of the bankrupt Rock Island.[10] With dreadful financial returns and large segments in bankruptcy, the railroad industry was on the brink of bankruptcy. Nationalization seemed possible.

By the 1970s, it was clear that rail regulatory policy had to change dramatically. Large parts of the industry were in bankruptcy, most notably Penn Central in 1970. Additionally, beginning in 1967, and continuing for much of the decade of the 1970s, notable railroads failing financially included Central of New Jersey (1967), Boston & Maine and Lehigh Valley (1970), Reading (1971), Erie Lackawanna (1972), Lehigh & Hudson River (1972), Ann Arbor (1973), Chicago, Rock Island & Pacific (1975), and Chicago, Milwaukee, St. Paul & Pacific (1977).

Congress responded with the Regional Rail Reorganization (3R) Act of 1973, the Railroad Revitalization and Regulatory Reform Act (4R) of 1976, and the Staggers Act. In the 3R Act, Congress sought to solve the railroad crisis in the Northeast and Midwest by creating economically viable railroads at lowest taxpayer expense. This act created the United States Railway Association (USRA) to plan the new system and established the Consolidated Rail Corporation (Conrail) to take over many of the troubled railroads.[11] USRA created the Final System Plan (FSP) that identified all the rail properties Conrail acquired by the time it started operating on April 1, 1976.

The 4R Act enacted the FSP, offered taxpayer assistance to troubled railroads, and provided some regulatory reform. The regulatory reform notably included provisions that limited the ICC's powers such as railroads were freed to raise rates to variable cost and could lower rates to variable cost: both of these the ICC had prevented. The act also removed the ICC's rate jurisdiction if the railroad did not have "market dominance" (i.e., monopoly power).[12]

The Carter Administration's Department of Transportation (DOT) did not think the 4R Act had gone far enough in deregulating the railroads and giving them opportunity to succeed. DOT began to draft legislation to take regulatory reform further. These reformers sought to dramatically limit ICC's rate jurisdiction while providing a regulatory backstop against rate gouging and support the railroads ability to attain adequate revenues, revenues that would permit the railroads financial sustainability. Working with Congress, the Carter Administration enacted the Staggers Act in October 1980.[13]

In the wake of the pricing flexibility granted by the Staggers Act, railroads began to charge different customers different prices. Those customers with other purchasing options received lower prices than those with limited or no options.[14] In U.S. rail regulatory practice, this practice is known as differential pricing. One aspect of partial deregulation was the explicit policy acceptance of such differential pricing. The ICC recognized that with their fixed costs and common costs, railroads could not financially survive without differential pricing.[15] The theoretical basis for this approach stems from Ramsey (1927), and such differential pricing is routinely referred to as Ramsey pricing. Ramsey's goal was to develop the optimal pricing rule for situations where an entity could not cover its costs by marginal cost pricing. In these situations, Ramsey showed that the optimal pricing rule was based on setting prices marked up by the inverse of consumers' demand elasticities. In other words, the entity would charge higher prices to customers who placed higher values on the service, maybe because they did not have good alternatives.

The partial deregulation springing from Staggers allowed a rail industry recovery.[16] Railroad profits improved enough to permit the industry to escape the clutches of bankruptcy. With liberalized work rules, railroads could improve productivity. For the first two decades of deregulation, these productivity gains were translated into lower rates. However, after a two-decade decline, rates started to increase.[17] Rate increases and increased rail profits brought a public policy spotlight to rail regulatory policy.

## The Emergence of the Open Access Debate

After partial deregulation, the ICC issued new maximum rate case rules; the Coal Rate Guidelines, which created a rate case methodology known as stand-alone cost (SAC) in 1985.[18] As the title suggests, the ICC aimed this methodology at coal rates, rates railroads charged for unit train service from mines to utility power plants. For the following 20 years, ICC and STB litigation largely involved coal rates. In the first decade of the 21st century, chemical shippers filed a series of rate cases, but chemical shippers were dissatisfied with the results.[19] Grain shippers have not filed a rate case during the existence of the STB.

Frustrated by the lack of results at STB, particularly for any traffic not involving coal, in 2011, shippers coalesced behind a National Industrial Traffic League (NITL) petition for more open access.[20] In the petition, NITL argued that the railroad industry had changed significantly in the 30 years since partial deregulation. NITL took particular aim at the existing rules on open access, which required the petitioner show competitive harm prior to requiring railroads to share trackage. This reflected a view that the Board, and ICC before it, were loath to grant open access outside the context of a merger. Moreover, shippers did not petition to gain access using the existing rules. Instead, NITL's petition was requesting access in the form of reciprocal switching. Reciprocal switching is an interchange of inbound and outbound carload freight among railroads in which the cars are switched by one railroad to or from the siding of another under a regular switching charge that is usually absorbed by the carrier receiving the line-haul.

The NITL petition declared:

> This Petition proposes specific changes to the Board's existing rules on reciprocal switching, in order to implement a new competitive switching regime. It provides the Board with not just a concept, but an actual proposal, including regulatory language that would replace the rules currently set forth at 49 C.F.R. Part 1144 for reciprocal switching. In developing this proposal, the League has attempted to create a balanced system, one that would take into account both the needs of shippers who currently lack competitive transportation alternatives, as well as the needs of carriers to continue to earn adequate revenues. The objective of the League's proposal is also to establish clear rules that may be implemented in a straightforward manner and that reduce the need for complex and expensive litigation in many cases. The proposed competitive switching regime also does not overreach, since it would not apply to shippers who already have effective transportation alternatives.[21]

NITL's goal to get lower rates by introducing competition was based on the assumption that shippers suffer from a lack of competition, competition that could be enhanced by the development of open access rules and which would lower prices. This proposal was comprehensive with a set of presumptions to reduce litigation time and expense. To limit litigation regarding the effectiveness of inter or intramodal competition, NITL proposed that the STB presume such competition ineffective if traffic moved at a revenue to variable cost of more than 240% and the railroad had a market share of greater than 75%. To limit litigation regarding what constituted a working interchange within a reasonable distance of the shipper's facilities, NITL proposed these two presumptions: "a working interchange exists if the shipper's facilities are within the boundaries of an existing or future terminal" or the non-incumbent railroad is "within a 30-mile radius of the shipper's facilities."[22]

NITL's proposal would require a fundamental reordering of the regulatory regime that Staggers codified and ICC and STB have implemented. According to Woodman and Starke (1988), who worked on Staggers as Congressional staff, the balance between reasonable rates and revenue adequacy was determined by rate regulation.[23] They wrote that Staggers access provisions were

> more in the nature of "housekeeping" tools available for improving service to shippers and preserving competition. It is simply inconsistent with the overall statutory scheme of the Staggers Act and its legislative history to utilize these access provisions as a "backdoor" means for regulation of rail rates.[24]

In a July 2016 ruling, STB declined to adopt NITL's proposal. The STB recognized that the rail industry had changed since ICC's access rules had been put in place, but the agency believed it was better to enact a more limited, case-by-case approach. Instead of adopting the NITL proposal, the STB initiated a rulemaking and sought comments.[25]

> The Board proposes three criteria that shippers must satisfy to demonstrate that reciprocal switching is practicable and in the public interest: (1) that the facilities of the shipper(s) and/or receiver(s) for whom such switching is sought are served by Class I rail carrier(s); (2) that there is or can be a working interchange between the Class I carrier servicing the party seeking switching and another Class I rail carrier within a reasonable distance of the facilities of the party seeking switching; and (3) that the potential benefits from the proposed switching arrangement outweigh the potential detriments. . . . The second prong under which a party could obtain a reciprocal switching prescription is by showing that the proposed switching is necessary to provide competitive rail service. Again, the Board proposes three criteria that shippers must satisfy: (1) that the facilities of the shipper(s) and/or receiver(s) for whom such switching is sought are served by a single Class I rail carrier; (2) intermodal and intramodal competition

is not effective with respect to the movements of the shipper(s) and/or receivers(s) for whom switching is sought; and (3) there is or can be a working interchange between the Class I carrier servicing the party seeking switching and another Class I rail carrier within a reasonable distance of the facilities of the party seeking switching.[26]

Subsequently, the STB has held a series of *ex parte* meetings with various stakeholders and posted reports of each on the STB website, but this rulemaking remains open and unresolved.

A key feature of any open access regime is the price of access. Open access requires compensating the incumbent railroad that would be providing reciprocal switching or access to its facilities. Setting that access price too high could make it uneconomic for another railroad to take advantage of the proffered access. On the other hand, setting the price too low could mean the incumbent railroad is not compensated sufficiently to maintain the facilities. Too meager access compensation, if aggregated across much of a railroad's system, could have severe impacts on the railroad's ongoing financial health and its ability to be revenue adequate. By promulgating more open access, the STB could put itself into a dilemma of revenue adequacy versus price of access. A dilemma that Staggers may not have intended.

The ICC and STB have developed access pricing, also known as trackage rights, in the context of either mergers, abandonments, or offers of financial assistance (OFA).[27] These are different situations than what NITL had been seeking. In the case of mergers, the ICC/STB has been concerned with maintaining existing competition. The merger applicants negotiate with various interested parties to find an array of trackage rights that the regulator will deem sufficient to allay concerns about competition diminishment. In this case, if the regulatory agency finds the proposals insufficient and imposes a scheme that the merger applicants find too onerous, the applicants can withdraw their application. The NITL proposal or the STB's proposed rule, if enacted, would not have this opt-out feature.

Abandonments and OFAs are even more different from the situation contemplated by the NITL proposal or the STB's proposed rule. In an abandonment or OFA, the goal is to maintain service. These are situations where the health of the service provider is a paramount concern.

Modern ICC/STB precedents for trackage rights fees start with the Compensation Hearings,[28] a situation that evolved from the Union Pacific-Missouri Pacific-Western Pacific merger and the trackage rights imposed by ICC in that merger. The STB (and the ICC before it) holds that trackage rights fees have three components:

1. Variable cost—These are the incremental costs imposed on the landlord/incumbent railroad from the entrant's use of the open access facilities. Examples include switching costs and train operations.[29]

2.  Maintenance and operating expense—Although similar to variable costs, these are costs imposed on the landlord/incumbent that are not directly attributable. Examples include property taxes and track maintenance.
3.  Interest rental component—This represents a return on the landlord/incumbent's capital invested in the line.

The first two components (i.e., variable cost, maintenance and operating expense) have not been controversial, but the interest rental component has been a source of considerable controversy and litigation. Indeed, the ICC/STB has offered five methods for calculating this cost component.[30]

In contrast to the breadth of methods with which to determine the interest rental component, the ICC/STB's trackage litigation and analysis has considered only the costs for the operations and facilities directly involved in the proposed access. This litigation and analysis has not considered the costs or revenue loss imposed on other parts of the rail network. The existing rules provide only for the incumbent to receive a fee for the specific track at issue and neglects to include any profit the railroad might have earned for the rest of its system on the traffic now captured by the entrant. In particular, consideration of an open access regime must take into account the revenue and cost impacts on the landlord/incumbent's overall network if the incumbent's revenue adequacy is not to be negatively impacted. The STB has also faced various service crises in its 20-year history: for example, the Houston meltdown after the Union Pacific-Southern Pacific merger,[31] the fallout after Norfolk Southern and CSX acquisition of Conrail,[32] and the BNSF and Canadian Pacific winter miseries a few years ago.[33] The STB is familiar with how service impacts in one part of the rail network can ripple through the network. However, revenue losses imposed by an open access regime would be new territory for the STB. This leads to a consideration of revenue adequacy.

## The Role of Revenue Adequacy

Congress created revenue adequacy as a term to describe the financial fitness of the railroad industry. In the 1970s, Congress and the Carter Administration were concerned that the dire financial plight of the railroad industry might make much of the industry wards of the state. After all, at that time, the government was in the process of absorbing many bankrupt northeastern railroads into Conrail, a government entity.[34]

In a comprehensive assessment of revenue adequacy, Macher et al. (2014) have pointed out that the concept has evolved along two distinct paths: one that is purely informational and one that might become a regulatory tool. On the informational path, Congress directed the ICC to create an annual measure to gauge the rail industry's financial health. This has become the STB's annual revenue adequacy determination, in which the Board compares each carrier's return on investment with the industry's cost of capital. If a carrier's return on investment exceeds the industry cost of capital, the agency declares that railroad "revenue adequate" for the year in question.[35] Quite apart from the informational foundations of the revenue adequacy concept, the ICC/STB created the potential for revenue adequacy to become a regulatory tool in the language it adopted in its Coal Rate Guidelines. In that decision, the ICC created a regulatory path indicating that adequate revenues are those that provide a rate of return on net investment equal to the current cost of capital. The ICC goes on to state that this standard represents a reasonable level of profitability, that rail carriers do not need any greater revenues than this standard permits, and that in a regulated setting, they are not entitled to any higher revenues.[36]

The ICC/STB has never invoked revenue adequacy in its second form, as a regulatory tool. Indeed, no revenue adequacy complaint had been litigated to an agency decision until the *Consumers Energy v. CSXT* case.[37] In that case, Consumers Energy challenged the reasonableness of the rate it was being charged to transport coal from an interexchange near Chicago to Consumers' electric generating station located near West Olive, Michigan. Consumers sought rate relief from the STB both on the grounds that the focal railroad (i.e., CSX) was revenue adequate and under the more traditional stand-alone cost (SAC) test.[38] While a complete description of that case is beyond the scope of the present chapter,[39] a key result from that case is salient here. Specifically, in its decision, the STB reaffirmed its methodology for determining revenue adequacy: comparing the railroad's return on investment to the industry's cost of capital.[40] The STB was not persuaded by the complainant's evidence— using other financial measures rather the STB's standard of the railroad's return on investment compared to the industry's cost of capita—that the railroad in question was revenue adequate.

The result of this case was to reject the claim of revenue adequacy on the grounds that the financial data do not indicate that CSX was revenue adequate. The Board left open the potential, however, that with stronger financials, a railroad could be deemed revenue adequate and provide the basis for regulatory rate relief in the future.[41] Given the centrality of revenue adequacy in the freight rail industry, it is important to understand the linkages between the potential adoption of open access and revenue adequacy, that is, the financial health of the railroad industry.

To understand how open access could impact revenue adequacy, it is necessary to review the methodologies proposed to set access prices. In the literature, this usually means establishing a regulated price for rail bottlenecks, which occur when one carrier has a monopoly at the origin or termination of a shipment. For example, if a shipment originates at a location with competitive rail service but terminates at a destination with a monopoly rail carrier, the terminating segment is considered a bottleneck.

Similarly, if the situation is reversed and the monopoly is at the origin, the origin monopoly segment is considered a bottleneck. Because proposals for open access center on such monopoly segments and, in particular, on the pricing of access to such monopoly segments, it is important to consider the alternative methodologies that have been proffered for the pricing of access.

To explore these methodologies, the Federal Railroad Administration commissioned an independent report Beshers (2000) to review key questions surrounding the pricing of rail access. That reports considered a model of competitive originations at a coal mine with a bottleneck for delivery to a coal burning power plant. The study evaluates two rail bottleneck pricing rules:

1. Efficient component pricing (ECP)
2. Total element long-run incremental cost (TELRIC)

The report states that ECP

> sets a price for access to a bottleneck that depends on two factors: the contribution to fixed costs common with other traffic (surplus above incremental cost) that the incumbent now earns on the traffic in question and the incremental cost to the incumbent of allowing the entrant to operate over the bottleneck segment (or of providing haulage over the bottleneck). ECP defines the price as the sum of the contribution and the incremental bottleneck cost to the incumbent. With ECP, the incumbent preserves the contribution to common fixed costs it was getting (and must get somewhere) and recovers any cost the entrant imposes on its system.[42]

In contrast, TELRIC considers

> discrete elements and facilities of which the network is made up and to establish a price for use of each such element based on its long-run incremental cost (LRIC). These costs are "forward looking." That means they are based, not on the existing network, but on the facilities that would be put in place by an investor using "the most efficient technology for reasonably foreseeable capacity requirements." In other words, it is necessary to forecast future demand and decide what the network would consist of, and what it would cost, if it were built today with the "most efficient technology." Those costs are then used as the basis for setting prices for use of the existing elements.[43]

Because TELRIC prices elements [facilities] at their LRIC, it does not allow the incumbent/landlord to recover shared fixed costs. TELRIC's creator, the Federal Communications Commission (FCC), suggested that incumbents could recover common fixed costs through a uniform percentage markup. The FCC explicitly rejected Ramsey (differential) pricing as a method for recovering common fixed costs. The report argues, "TELRIC embodies inefficient pricing principles and could not work in the current framework of railroad regulation or anything close to it."[44] On the other hand the report finds ECP to fit within the STB's regulatory mandate. ECP means the incumbent/landlord sets a bottleneck price that incorporates a contribution for the non-bottleneck facilities.[45]

It should not be surprising that the FCC and the STB/ICC have taken different approaches to bottleneck pricing. Congress directed the ICC/STB to encourage industry revenue adequacy, whereas Congress directed FCC to encourage competition. Railroad deregulation emerged from a time of financial peril while telecommunication deregulation came against backdrop of financial strength and opportunity. Also remember that telecommunications has more technology dynamism than rail. So it should not be surprising that the two agencies adopted different regulatory methodologies, that is, SAC versus TELRIC.

In merger or abandonment cases, cases where the regulatory agency has applied its current trackage rights fee methodologies, the agency would develop the fees solely on the basis of the bottleneck. In other words, any compensation that the incumbent made from originating and carrying the traffic to the bottleneck would not be part of the formula for developing the access charge. That makes perfect sense for abandonments, where the goal is to maintain service, or a merger, where the goal to maintain *existing* competition. *These are significantly different goals from an access pricing regime designed to introduce new competition. These methodologies provide no consideration for what the incumbent's existing traffic diverted to the new entrant might contribute to the non-bottleneck segment of the incumbent's system.*

To understand the potential impacts this would entail for revenue adequacy, we need to review Beshers's algebra for setting bottleneck access. Before discussing the algebra, we should review some costing terminology.

We will define this set of economic cost concepts: fixed cost, variable cost, marginal cost, and incremental cost. To distinguish between fixed and variable cost, economists posit a time period they call short run, in which some productive factor or factors cannot be changed, added to, or reduced. This compares with the long run, in which all productive factors can be varied. These standard cost definitions are as follows:

- Fixed cost—A cost that does not change during the time period considered. An example might be an equipment lease. Economists often consider most capital costs as fixed. These often represent investments in plant and equipment.
- Variable cost—A cost that changes with the amount of output during the period considered. An example might be locomotive fuel.

- Marginal cost—This is the additional cost of producing the last unit of output. For the mathematically inclined, it is the first derivative of the cost function with respect to output.
- Incremental cost—This represents the additional cost incurred by implementing a specific management decision, for example, a new marketing program. It is similar to marginal cost except that it is not concerned with the last unit of output per se but with what might be several units of output as part of a management decision. Incremental cost is also related to variable cost except that the managerial decision may be extend beyond the short run.

Returning now to the bottleneck analysis and incorporating Beshers's discussion: for both the incumbent and potential entrant,

> we need to make a separation between the incremental costs either would incur in carrying the [traffic on bottleneck and non-bottleneck segments] and certain incremental costs on the bottleneck segment . . . that would be costs to [the incumbent/landlord] in any case. We refer to the former as "competitive costs," because it is the comparison between these costs that shows which firm is the more efficient carrier of [this] traffic. We refer to the latter as bottleneck costs; they will be the same in either case as they are costs only to [incumbent/landlord]. The competitive costs for [incumbent/landlord] are the costs it avoids if [the entrant] carries [this] traffic. For [the entrant], competitive costs are those it adds if it carries [this] traffic. Competitive incremental costs comprise: above-the-rail operating cost for [this] coal traffic plus wear and tear on rails, maintenance costs, and other variable costs on the [non-bottleneck segment] attributable to [this] coal traffic plus any fixed costs on the [non-bottleneck segment] that are solely attributable to [this] coal traffic. Bottleneck incremental costs are all incremental costs of [this] traffic on the [bottleneck] segment, except above-the-rail costs.[46]

Following Beshers (2000), we can now define relevant terms:

> "IC = Average incremental competitive cost
> IB = Average incremental bottleneck cost (costs on [the bottleneck], excluding above-the-rail costs)
> C = Average contribution to common costs, i.e., any surplus above incremental cost
> PF = Final price (to customer) for [this traffic]
> PB = Access price to [the entrant] for use of bottleneck."[47]

This would be the relationship between price and costs if the incumbent/landlord carries the traffic:

$$PF(I) = IC(I) + IB + C(I)$$

For the entrant, this would be the relationship if it carried the traffic:

$$PF(E) = IC(E) + PB + C(E)$$

If the incumbent/landlord carries this traffic, its incremental costs are $IC(I) + IB$. If, instead, the entrant carries the traffic, then the incumbent/landlord avoids $IC(I)$. $C(I)$ represents its surplus above incremental cost from carrying the traffic. For the entrant, the incremental cost is $IC(E) + PB$.

ECP's goal is to keep the incumbent/landlord whole despite the loss of traffic to the entrant. To do this, ECP sets the bottleneck access price as:

$$PB = PF(I) - IC(I) \text{ or}$$
$$PB = IB + C(I)$$

The second version provides a more intuitive starting point, particularly regarding keeping the landlord/incumbent whole after entry. In the second version, the landlord/incumbent receives compensation for the costs it incurs from the entrant's use of the bottleneck plus for lost contribution to the incumbent/landlord's non-bottleneck facilities.

A distinctly positive attribute of an ECP access price is that it permits the more efficient carrier to move the traffic.[48] Consider:

$$PF(I) > PF(E) \text{ means}$$
$$PF(I) > IC(E) + IB + C(I) + C(E) \text{ means}$$
$$IC(I) + IB + C(I) > IC(E) + IB + C(I) + C(E) \text{ means}$$
$$IC(I) > IC(E) + C(E)$$

If the entrant has lower costs than the incumbent, the entrant can undercut the incumbent/landlord and make a contribution to overhead, however infinitesimal. In other words, if the entrant is more efficient, it captures the traffic.

The incumbent/landlord's potential lost contribution, $C(I)$, is critical in a revenue adequacy context. Consider a revenue inadequate carrier that is subject to open access entry. If it is compensated only for IB, its bottleneck incremental costs, it takes a direct profit hit and moves farther away from revenue adequacy. If the STB uses its traditional trackage rights fee methods, it will ignore $C(I)$. In merger cases and abandonments, STB considers only the track at issue, that is, the bottleneck. This approach will constrain railroads' ability to be revenue adequate.

To ensure that ECP provides an economically efficient outcome, there must be some constraint on the incumbent's price prior to institution of an open access regime. Otherwise, as Economides and White (1995) have shown, ECP will embed a monopoly profit.[49] This puts a spotlight on the STB's rate regulatory methodologies, particularly SAC. Economides and White admit that ECP prevents the incumbent/landlord from preventing the entry of a more efficient competitor. However, they argue that the gain in productive efficiency can be offset by a loss in allocative efficiency, that is, the existence of monopoly profits embedded in the access price.

Economides and White's concern would be moot if the incumbent/landlord faced a regulatory constraint that eliminated monopoly profit, eliminating allocative efficiency losses. Shipper dissatisfaction with SAC might suggest that procedural difficulties and litigation expense make the STB's current SAC methodology incapable of eliminating monopoly profits.[50] Evidence of this dissatisfaction manifested when Congress significantly shrank SAC processing timelines in the 2015 STB reauthorization legislation.[51] The question is how SAC problems might matter from a revenue adequacy standpoint.

First, consider an incumbent/landlord railroad that is revenue inadequate. In this case, a robust SAC methodology that found the incumbent's rates unreasonable, would drive that railroad farther from revenue adequacy. Remember, U.S. rail regulation is a balance between the shippers' requirement for reasonable rates and the railroads' need for adequate revenues. This could be a situation that requires long-term disinvestment, making a bottleneck access moot.

On the other hand, consider an incumbent/landlord that is revenue adequate. To ensure that the access price did not embed a monopoly profit would require implementation of the SAC test. In particular, the STB would need to apply a SAC test that identified monopoly profits. But SAC has received a lot of shipper criticism for being too expensive and time consuming. That is not the only problem with SAC. SAC, which aims to simulate an efficient railroad, may have gone beyond simulating efficient railroad operations. In the recent *Consumers Energy* case, the stand-alone railroad had an operating ratio[52] of 47.6%;[53] that is far below what even the most efficient Class I can achieve today. This suggests that STB's current version of SAC identifies monopoly profits that only a hyper-efficient railroad could achieve.

But another problem with SAC cuts the other way: SAC overestimates the asset base railroads require a return on. In 2008, the Association of American Railroads (AAR) petitioned the STB to adopt replacement costs for revenue adequacy determinations. This petition estimated the replacement cost value of BNSF at $80 billion.[54] This contrasts with what Warren Buffett paid for BNSF when he acquired it in 2010. Buffett paid $34.5 billion, of which $14 billion was allocated to goodwill.[55] This means there is a $59.4 billion difference between what AAR estimated BNSF's replacement cost in 2008 and the value paid for it in an actual 2010 transaction. The discrepancy between the 2010 BNSF book value and the purchase value was only $8 billion, which was the asset markup from the transaction. AAR's replacement cost was nearly four times higher than the transaction value, whereas the book value was off only by about a third.

AAR's petition used simplified stand-alone cost values, which were based on actual SAC cases. This may suggest that Road Property Investment values in SAC cases are much higher than what an investor might pay for them in a market transaction—going back to what AAR estimated the value of BNSF was versus what Buffett actually paid for it. To determine if a monopoly profit is embedded in an access price, the STB will need to improve SAC or replace it with something more reliable at identifying actual monopoly profits.

## Conclusion: The Dilemma in Rail Regulatory Policy With SAC, Open Access, and Revenue Adequacy

One of the principles of Constrained Market Pricing is that shippers should not pay for facilities they do not use.[56] An ECP rule would violate that principle. The ECP's rate would incorporate a return on the incumbent's non-bottleneck facilities and these facilities would not be in use if the shipper uses the entrant.

However, as already discussed, not employing an ECP rule means the incumbent/landlord moves away from revenue adequacy, which is another policy goal. The STB has a dilemma when it considers open access: revenue adequacy and having shippers pay for facilities they do not use or less revenue adequacy and shippers do not pay for facilities they do not use.

If the STB moves forward with open access, it will need to confront how access pricing affects revenue adequacy. It will also need to confront that its existing access pricing precedents are based on situations that are merger related or abandonment related rather injecting new competition. The existing rules provide only for the incumbent to receive a fee for the bottleneck and neglects to include any profit the railroad might have earned for the non-bottleneck portion of its system on the traffic now captured by the entrant. This requires a much broader perspective than has been brought to the EP 711 (NITL petition for reciprocal switching) discussion so far. And it may be a fundamental change to the regulatory regime Staggers created.

## Notes

1. Dr. Huneke is a consulting economist. For 11 years, he was the chief economist at the Surface Transportation Board. The author would like to thank Ray Atkins, Eric Beshers, Bill Mullins, John Pertino, and Frank Wilner for reviewing the paper and commenting. John W. Mayo and Jeff Macher have been extremely helpful in preparing the manuscript for publication. Any remaining errors remain the author's responsibility.
2. Besanko (2018).
3. Woodman and Starke (1988).
4. Interstate Commerce Commission (1985).

5. To review some of the econometric literature on railroad economies of scale, scope, and density, *see* Bitzan (2000), Bitzan and Wilson (2006), R. Braeutigam (1999), Ivaldi and McCullough (2001), and Ivaldi and McCullough (2008).
6. D. Philip Locklin (1966), pp. 197–206 and Hoogeboom and Hoogeboom (1976), pp. 3–6.
7. Hoogeboom and Hoogeboom (1976), p. 96.
8. Martin (1971).
9. Davis (1985), p. 234.
10. Sanders (2001), pp. 153–155.
11. Gallamore and Meyer (2014), pp. 165–171 and Saunders (2003), pp. 87–94.
12. Gallamore and Meyer (2014), pp. 183–184, 227–228 and Saunders (2003), pp. 108–111.
13. Gallamore and Meyer (2014), pp. 227–241 and Saunders (2003), pp. 187–188.
14. In other contexts, economists label this practice price discrimination. It is worth noting that price discrimination may either increase or decrease economic welfare, depending on the particular circumstances. *See* Kahn (1970) pp. 137–150 and Scherer (1980), pp. 319–321.
15. Coal Rate Guidelines, Nationwide, 1 I.C.C.2d 520 (1985), aff'd sub nom. *Consolidated Rail Corp v. United States*, 812 F.2d 1444 (3d Cir. 1987).
16. For a discussion of the process by which rates may continue to be regulated, *see* Mayo and Sappington (2016).
17. Surface Transportation Board, Office of Economics, Rate Study (1985–2007).
18. Coal Rate Guidelines.
19. Surface Transportation Board (2014–1, 2014–2), 2016–2).
20. National Industrial Traffic League (2011).
21. NITL petition, July 7, 2011, p. 6.
22. NITL petition, July 7, 2011, pp. 46–52, 55–57.
23. *See* Woodman and Starke (1988).
24. *Ibid.*, pp. 272–273.
25. Surface Transportation Board (2016–1).
26. *Ibid.*, pp. 18–19.
27. An offer of financial assistance is a proposal from an interested party (often government) to provide a subsidy to maintain rail service rather than having a rail line abandoned.
28. Interstate Commerce Commission (1984, 1987, 1989, 1991).
29. Interstate Commerce Commission (1990), p. 623.
30. Interstate Commerce Commission (1995, 1990, 1991).
31. Gallamore and Meyer (2014), pp. 289–295.
32. *Ibid.*, pp. 297–301.
33. www.startribune.com/canadian-pacific-and-bnsf-get-poor-marks-for-service/283557941/; To see how the STB responded to the 2014 service crisis, see the decisions under Ex Parte 724, United States Rail Service Issues. For example: https://www.stb.gov/Decisions/readingroom.nsf/WEBUNID/646EB 423D1B5C90585257CAD0066F109?OpenDocument
34. Macher et al. (2014) and Huneke (2017).
35. Macher et al. (2014).
36. For a complete discussion, see the discussion in Macher et al. (2014), p. 99.
37. Surface Transportation Board (2018).
38. For a discussion of the SAC test, *see* Interstate Commerce Commission (1985) and InterVISTAS (2016).
39. *See* Macher et al. (2019), Chapter 8 in this volume, for a complete discussion.

40. It also found that as a practical matter, the focal railroad (viz., CSX) had not been deemed revenue adequate by the Board in its annual calculations.
41. Macher et al. (2014) offer a more fundamental critique, indicating that revenue adequacy is fundamentally flawed as a regulatory tool.
42. Beshers (2000), p. ii.
43. *Ibid.*, p. iii.
44. *Ibid.*, p. iv.
45. *Ibid.*, p. iii–iv.
46. *Ibid.*, p. 9.
47. *Ibid.*
48. *Ibid.*, pp. 9–12.
49. Economides and White (1995), p. 5.
50. Beshers (2000), pp. 18–19.
51. Surface Transportation Board Reauthorization Act of 2015 (P.L. 114–110).
52. Operating ratio divides railroad operating expenses by revenues.
53. Surface Transportation Board, *Consumers Energy v. CSXT* 2018, pp. 92, 94.
54. Baranowski (2008).
55. Surface Transportation Board (2011), pp. 1–3.
56. Interstate Commerce Commission (1985).

## Bibliography

Baranowski, Michael (2008). Workpaper in Ex Parte 679 Association of American Railroads: Petition Regarding Methodology for Determining Railroad Revenue Adequacy. https://www.stb.gov/Filings/all_2000s.nsf/d6ef3e0bc7fe3c6085256fe1004f61cb/85257ca7006c955b8525743d004af53c/$FILE/222251.PDF

Besanko, David (2019). "Restructuring rail systems: Implications for network quality and welfare," in *U.S. Freight Rail Economics and Policy: Are We on The Right Track?*, Macher, J. T. and J. W. Mayo, eds. Routledge Studies in Transport Analysis, New York.

Beshers, Eric (2000). "Efficient Access Pricing for Rail Bottlenecks," Prepared for Volpe National Transportation Systems Center, in Support of Federal Railroad Administration, US Department of Transportation. Washington, DC.

Bitzan, John D. (2000). *Railroad Cost Conditions: Implications for Policy.* U.S. Department of Transportation, Federal Railroad Administration, Washington, DC.

Bitzan, John D. and Wesley W. Wilson (2006). "Industry Costs and Consolidation: Efficiency Gains and Mergers in the Railroad Industry." *Review of Industrial Organization*, Vol. 30, No. 2, March, pp. 81–105.

Braeutigam, Ronald. (1999). "Learning about Railroad Costs," in *Essays in Transportation Economics and Policy: Essays in Honor of John R. Meyer*, Gomez-Ibanez, J., W. Tye, and C. Winston, eds. Brookings Institute Press. Washington, DC.

Davis, Burke (1985). *The Southern Railway, Road of Innovators.* University of North Carolina, Chapel Hill.

Economides, Nicolas. and Lawrence. J. White. (1995) "Access and Interconnection Pricing: How Efficient Is the 'Efficient Component Pricing Rule?'" *Antitrust Bulletin*, Vol. 40, No. 3, Fall, p. 5.

Gallamore, Robert E. and John R. Meyer (2014). *American Railroads: Decline and Renaissance in the Twentieth Century.* Harvard Press, Cambridge, MA.

Hoogeboom, Ari and Olive Hoogeboom (1976). *A History of the ICC: From Panacea to Palliative.* W. W. Norton & Co, New York.

Huneke, William (2017). "The Political Economy of Regulatory Costing: The Development of the Uniform Rail Costing System." *Association of Transportation Law Professionals Journal,* 84(2).

Interstate Commerce Commission (1984). St. Louis Southwestern Railway Company-Trackage Rights over Missouri Pacific Railroad Company-Kansas City to St. Louis-Trackage Rights Compensation, 1 ICC 2d 776. Washington, DC.

Interstate Commerce Commission (1985). Ex Parte 347, Coal Rate Guidelines-Nationwide. 1 ICC 2d 520. Washington, DC.

Interstate Commerce Commission (1987). St. Louis Southwestern Railway Company-Trackage Rights over Missouri Pacific Railroad Company-Kansas City to St. Louis-Trackage Rights Compensation, 4 ICC 2d 668. Washington, DC.

Interstate Commerce Commission (1989). St. Louis Southwestern Railway Company-Trackage Rights over Missouri Pacific Railroad Company-Kansas City to St. Louis-Trackage Rights Compensation 5 ICC 2d 525. Washington, DC.

Interstate Commerce Commission (1990). FD 31281 Arkansas and Missouri Railroad Co. v. Missouri Pacific Railroad Co. 6 ICC 2d 619. Washington, DC.

Interstate Commerce Commission (1991). St. Louis Southwestern Railway Company-Trackage Rights over Missouri Pacific Railroad Company-Kansas City to St. Louis-Trackage Rights Compensation 7 ICC 2d 164. Washington, DC.

Interstate Commerce Commission (1995). FD 32625 Dardenelle & Russellville Railroad Co.-Trackage Rights Compensation-Arkansas Midland Railroad Co. (Decided June 2). Washington, DC.

InterVISTAS (2016). "An Examination of the STB's Approach to Freight Rail Rate Regulation and Options for Simplification." www.stb.gov/stb/docs/IndependentStudy/Final/STB%20Rate%20Regulation%20Final%20Report.pdf

Ivaldi, Marc and Gerard McCullough (2001). "Density and Integration Effects on Class I U.S. Freight Railroads." *Journal of Regulatory Economics,* Vol. 19, pp. 161–182.

Ivaldi, Marc and Gerard McCullough (2008). "Subadditivity Tests for Network Separation with an Application to U.S. Railroads." *Review of Network Economics,* Vol. 7, No. 1, pp. 159–171.

Kahn, Alfred E. (1970). *The Economics of Regulation: Principles and Institutions.* Volume I. John Wiley & Sons, New York.

Locklin, D. Philip (1966). *Economics of Transportation.* Irwin, Homewood, IL.

Macher, Jeffrey T., John W. Mayo, and Lee F. Pinkowitz (2014). "The Good, the Bad, and the Ugly." *Transportation Law Journal,* Vol. 41, No. 2.

Macher, Jeffrey T., John W. Mayo and Lee F. Pinkowitz (2019). "The Law and Economics of Revenue Adequacy," in *U.S. Freight Rail Economics and Policy: Are We on The Right Track?,* Jeffrey T, M., and John W. Mayo, eds. Routledge Studies in Transport Analysis, New York.

Martin, Albro (1971). *Enterprise Denied, Origins of the Decline of American Railroads, 1897–1917.* Columbia, New York.

Mayo, John W. and David E. M. Sappington (2016). "Regulation in a 'Deregulated' Industry: Railroads in the Post-Staggers Era." *Review of Industrial Organization,* Vol. 49, September, pp. 203–227.

National Industrial Traffic League (2011). Ex Parte No. 711, Petition for Rule-making to Adopt Revised Competitive Switching Rules, July 7. https://www.stb.gov/Filings/all.nsf/WEBUNID/80EDC553B468F44B852578C60068783B?OpenDocument.

Ramsey, Frank P. (1927). "A Contribution to the Theory of Taxation." *The Economic Journal*, Vol. 37, pp. 47–61.

Saunders, Richard, Jr. (2001). *Main Lines, American Railroads 1900–1970*. Northeastern Illinois, DeKalb, IL.

Scherer, Frederic M. (1980). *Industrial Market Structure and Market Performance*. Rand McNally College Publishing, Chicago.

Surface Transportation Board (2011). FD 35506 Western Coal Traffic League: Petition for Declaratory Order, Served September 28. https://www.stb.gov/Decisions/readingroom.nsf/WEBUNID/88A1D33F3F9E5743852579180063616E?OpenDocument

Surface Transportation Board (2014–1). NOR 42125, E. I. DuPont de Nemours and Company v. Norfolk Southern Railway Company, March 24. https://www.stb.gov/Decisions/readingroom.nsf/WEBUNID/84F2B49D7BCC764B852580C0005EAF0D?OpenDocument

Surface Transportation Board (2014–2). NOR 42130, Sunbelt Chlor Alkali Partnership v. Norfolk Southern Railway Company, June 20. https://www.stb.gov/Decisions/readingroom.nsf/WEBUNID/DB7E86D79614762A85257CFD0050E589?OpenDocument

Surface Transportation Board (2016–1). Ex Parte 711, Reciprocal Switching, Served, July 27. https://www.stb.gov/Decisions/readingroom.nsf/WEBUNID/11DFF4D3703B81A885257FFD00475D63?OpenDocument.

Surface Transportation Board (2016–2). NOR 42121 Total Petrochemicals & Refining USA, Inc. v. CSX Transportation, Inc., September 12. https://www.stb.gov/Decisions/readingroom.nsf/WEBUNID/C1C437F9E2D6B4118525802E00407730?OpenDocument.

Surface Transportation Board (2018). Consumers Energy Company v. CSX Transportation, Inc., NOR. 42142, Served January 11. https://www.stb.gov/Decisions/readingroom.nsf/WEBUNID/06AECC5B958B8C748525821200795A5A?OpenDocument.

Surface Transportation Board, Office of Economics, Rate Study (1985–2007). www.stb.gov/stb/industry/1985-2007RailroadRateStudy.pdf

Woodman, G. Kent and Jane Sutter Starke (1988). "The Competitive Access Debate: A 'Backdoor' Approach to Rate Regulation." *Transportation Law Journal*, Vol. 16, pp. 263–290.

# 10 Regulation in a "Deregulated" Industry

## Railroads in the Post-Staggers Era*

*John W. Mayo and David E. M. Sappington*

## Introduction

The rail industry was in dire economic straits prior to the passage of the Staggers Rail Act of 1980.[1] Industry output, productivity, and investment were all relatively low, and rail carriers were suffering substantial financial losses. The losses arose despite the prevalence of extensive regulatory policy designed in part to promote carrier solvency.[2] In light of the limited success of nearly ubiquitous regulatory oversight, the Staggers Act took a different approach to enhancing industry performance. The Act afforded rail carriers expanded freedom to introduce new services and set reasonable prices for their services. For this reason, the Act is often referred to as "The Railroad Deregulation Act."[3]

The Staggers Act is widely regarded as a major triumph of deregulation. Numerous scholars have documented the many dimensions on which industry performance improved after the Act was enacted.[4] Industry output, productivity, investment, quality, and earnings all increased, whereas prices declined.[5]

Although the Staggers Act brought substantial deregulation to the rail industry, it did not eliminate regulatory oversight entirely. The legislation retained a variety of regulatory controls that were to be applied in settings where competition alone was judged incapable of imposing the requisite discipline on rates set by railroads. The Staggers Act also did not eliminate the mandate in the Railroad Revitalization and Regulatory Reform Act of 1976 to ensure that rail revenues are "adequate."[6] The precise meaning of this mandate is subject to considerable debate. However, if the mandate is interpreted to preclude railroads from earning revenues in excess of the level required to attract capital to the industry (as opposed to ensuring that revenues attain at least this level),[7] then the mandate introduces the prospect of explicit earnings regulation in the rail industry as industry revenues approach and exceed "adequate" levels.

The economic literature provides many useful insights regarding the effects of earnings regulation, both when it is applied to all services supplied by a regulated firm and when it is applied to only a portion of the firm's services. The literature also provides useful guidance regarding the use of cost allocation procedures in an attempt to measure the earnings derived from the provision of specific services. A primary purpose of this research is to review the key findings in the literature and assess their implications for regulation in the rail industry. A primary conclusion of this research is that explicit earnings regulation is likely to stifle innovation and limit economic efficiency in the rail industry. Thus, such regulation could reverse some of the well-documented successes that have arisen in the post-Staggers era freight rail industry.

Our chapter is organized as follows. The following section describes the pricing constraints that have been imposed in the rail industry since the passage of the Staggers Act, in the absence of explicit revenue adequacy regulation.[8] The discussion in this section emphasizes the fact that only a portion of the rates a rail carrier sets are subject to regulatory oversight. The next section reviews the key conclusions drawn in two related strands of the literature on regulatory economics: the literature that analyzes the partial regulation of multiproduct firms and the literature that assesses the merits and effects of earnings regulation. We then develop a stylized framework for assessing the economic implications of the introduction of explicit earnings regulation. Although this simple framework does not capture all relevant impacts of such regulation, the framework allows us to analyze several potentially concerning manifestations of the regulation, including reduced incentive for industry innovation. The concluding section discusses the implications of our analysis and identifies important questions that remain to be addressed.

## Rail Regulation in the Post-Staggers Era

### Cost Allocation and Price Ceilings

Regulation of the U.S. freight rail industry began in 1887 with the passage of the Interstate Commerce Act.[9] Rail rates were regulated extensively for nearly all of the ensuing 100 years.[10] However, in response to deteriorating conditions in the rail industry in the 1970s and a sense that overly intrusive regulation was a principal cause of the deterioration,[11] policymakers enacted the Staggers Rail Act in 1980.[12] The Staggers Act fundamentally altered the process for setting rates in the rail industry. Instead of relying primarily upon regulators to set rates, individual rail carriers were afforded substantial authority to establish rates, and shippers received expanded authority to challenge the established rates.

The Staggers Act promoted substantial gains on many fronts in the rail industry.[13] Rail carriers introduced new services and new pricing structures.[14] The implementation of new technologies and new production methods also was accelerated,[15] and substantial cost reductions and productivity gains were realized.[16]

The Staggers Act exempts many rail services from rate regulation. For example, the Act exempts from regulation rates that are established in privately negotiated contracts between railroads and shippers.[17,18] The Act also exempts from rate regulation rail traffic for which revenue ($R$) is less than 180% of the estimated variable cost ($VC$) of supplying the traffic ($R/VC < 180\%$). However, rail traffic traveling at rates above this level ($R/VC > 180\%$) is considered to be "potentially captive" and under the jurisdiction of regulators, who are obliged to ensure that these rates are reasonable.[19] In determining whether rates for which $R/VC > 180\%$ are reasonable, the Interstate Commerce Commission (ICC) and its successor, the Surface Transportation Board (STB), have considered (among other factors) whether the rail carrier faces effective competition for the traffic in question.[20]

The estimated VC that plays this central role in the Staggers Act does not reflect the standard definition of variable cost (which encompasses only costs that vary with the level of output of the service in question). In particular, the estimated VC employed to calculate the $R/VC$ ratios for a particular rail service includes substantial joint and common costs that are assigned to the service.[21,22] Therefore, the $R/VC$ ratio that is employed under the Staggers Act to provide an initial assessment of whether the rates established for rail services are reasonable is not a reliable measure of the extent to which the rate established for a service exceeds its marginal or incremental cost of production.[23]

Figure 10.1 reports the proportion of rail traffic that has traveled at rates above the 180% $R/VC$ threshold in recent years. Between 2002 and 2013, 30% to 40% of all U.S. freight rail traffic fell into this category. After eliminating traffic in this category that is explicitly exempted

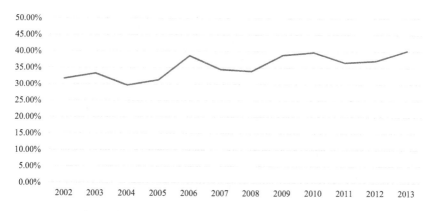

*Figure 10.1* Share of Freight Rail Shipments with $R/VC$ >180%

because of relevant product or transport mode characteristics, as much as 27% of rail traffic remains potentially subject to rate regulation.[24]

Some of this potentially captive traffic may be subject to effective competition from other rail carriers or other modes of transportation. If the regulator determines that such effective competition prevails, then prices are permitted to move freely, unconstrained by regulation. Alternatively, if such traffic is found to lack effective competition, then regulators must determine whether the prices that the rail carriers have set for the traffic are reasonable.

Figure 10.2 illustrates the post-Staggers rate rail regulation process. The figure emphasizes the fact that the prices of rail services are not regulated comprehensively. Regulation is restricted to a set of non-exempt and non-contract traffic for which R/VC > 180% is deemed to be "potentially captive." Within this set of potentially captive shipments, the authority to regulate prices is limited to traffic for which there is a lack of effective competition (i.e., for which market dominance prevails) and where the railroad is also determined to be charging unreasonable rates.[25]

The presence of substantial joint and common costs in the provision of rail services complicates the regulatory task of assessing whether the rate proposed for any individual service is reasonable. In its first attempt to deal with this challenge after the passage of the Staggers Act, the ICC allocated all joint and common costs across the services that a rail carrier supplies. The maximum reasonable rate for a service was set equal to the sum of the variable cost of supplying the service and the markup

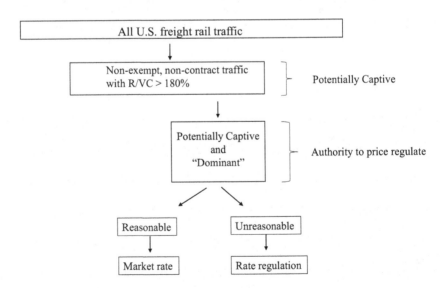

*Figure 10.2* U.S. Freight Regulation in the Post-Staggers Era

determined by the amount of joint and common costs allocated to the service. By 1985, however, the ICC rejected this approach, concluding that "a meaningful maximum rate policy could not be founded on a strictly cost-based approach."[26]

After rejecting fully allocated cost as the sole determinant of reasonable rates, the ICC implemented a "Constrained Market Pricing" policy, which features the stand-alone cost (SAC) test.[27] In its simplest form, the SAC test states that a price for a rail shipment that is below the SAC of providing the shipment is reasonable, whereas a price above the SAC is not reasonable. The SAC of a shipment (or group of shipments) is the minimum possible total cost of providing only the shipment in question, without supplying any other shipments.[28] To calculate the SAC of a shipment, one must estimate the cost that a hypothetical efficient rail carrier would incur if it constructed a new rail network to deliver the shipment in question.

In practice, the SAC test is somewhat more complex. The test also entails a calculation of the revenue that the efficient rail carrier could secure by carrying additional ("cross-over") traffic on its hypothetical rail network. The maximum amount that can be charged to the shipper in question is then the difference between the identified SAC of carrying the shipper's traffic and the revenue derived from carrying the relevant cross-over traffic. This adjustment effectively allows the shipper to benefit from the economies of scope associated with the provision of multiple services.[29]

After a decade of employing the SAC test as the primary measure of whether a proposed rail rate was reasonable, the STB determined that shippers should have access to simpler, less costly means to challenge rail rates.[30] In its 1996 Non-Coal Rate Guidelines, the STB introduced its Three-Benchmark methodology for assessing the reasonableness of rates. The first of these benchmarks is referred to as the Revenue Shortfall Allocation Method (RSAM).

The RSAM benchmark is "the uniform markup above variable cost that would be needed from every shipper of potentially captive traffic (the > 180 traffic group) in order for the carrier to recover all its . . . fixed costs."[31] The fixed costs in question are the joint and common costs that have not been recovered from revenues generated by "competitive traffic" (i.e., traffic transported at rates with an R/VC ratio below 180%). The Board emphasized that this benchmark was not to be used in isolation to determine if a rate is unreasonable. Nonetheless, the Board concluded that "the RSAM benchmark provides an appropriate framework for assessing the extent of a carrier's revenue needs that can and should be recovered through differential pricing."[32] Observe that the RSAM benchmark introduces a more central role for the cost allocation methodologies that the ICC abandoned in 1985 as the primary foundation for assessing the reasonableness of rates.

The second benchmark measure in the Three-Benchmark test, $R/VC_{COMP}$, is determined by calculating the markup over the estimated variable cost that a railroad secures on "traffic that involves similar commodities moving under similar transportation conditions."[33] This benchmark reflects the idea that, absent precise demand elasticity data, the benchmark can at least indicate whether the target traffic's rates are consistent with other traffic with similar demand characteristics.

The third benchmark, $R/VC_{>180}$, is the measure of the extent to which a carrier is marking up rates for its traffic above the 180 benchmark, on average. The purpose of this benchmark test is to "ensure that the complaining shipper's traffic is not bearing a disproportionate share of the carrier's revenue requirements *vis-à-vis* other relatively demand-inelastic traffic without good cause."[34] Although emphasizing that no single benchmark would be sufficient for determining the reasonableness or unreasonableness of a set of rates, the language developing the benchmarks is silent on exactly how regulators should aggregate individual benchmarks to reach such a determination.[35]

Despite the STB's attempt to streamline the procedures for challenging rates, no shipper challenged proposed rates using the Three-Benchmark test in the decade following their introduction.[36] To further afford shippers' less costly means to challenge proposed rates, in 2007, the Board altered both the pathways available to challenge rates and the standards for determining the reasonableness of rates. The Board determined that challenges involving requests for pronounced rate relief (greater than $5 million) should continue to employ the SAC test. The Board established a simplified SAC test for more moderate levels of proposed rate relief (between $1 million and $5 million).[37] The Board retained the use of the Three-Benchmark test for proposed rate relief below $1 million.[38]

The 2007 standards also clarify the application of the Three-Benchmark method. In particular, under the Three-Benchmark test, when a party challenges rates for a set of shipments, the Board first selects a comparison group for the $R/VC_{COMP}$ benchmark. Next, rates for the comparison group are scaled up (for revenue inadequate firms) or down (for revenue adequate firms).[39] Once scaled, the Board calculates the mean and the standard deviation for the prices in the comparison group. If the challenged rate falls above the 90 percentile of the distribution of the adjusted comparable rates, the Board will presume the challenged rate to be unreasonable, absent "other relevant factors."[40]

One additional element of the regulatory oversight process arose in 2012. Recall that rates are subject to regulatory oversight only if the traffic at issue is provided under conditions of market dominance. In 2012, the STB introduced the "limit price $R/VC$ ratio" test to determine whether a set of challenged traffic is subject to market dominance.[41] The test proceeds as follows. First, the Board estimates a "limit price," which is the highest price a carrier could charge a shipper without causing a significant amount of the traffic at issue to be diverted to a competitive alternative.[42] Next, the ratio of this limit price to the variable cost associated with the traffic is computed, yielding the "limit price R/VC ratio." Finally, this ratio is compared with the firm's RSAM (i.e., the uniform markup on all $R/VC > 180$ traffic that would allow the firm to break even). If the limit price R/VC ratio exceeds the RSAM markup, then the Board concludes that the traffic at issue lacks effective competition (i.e., is subject to market dominance).

The comparison of the limit price R/VC ratio to the RSAM figure to reach market dominance conclusions raises at least two concerns. First, recall that RSAM reflects the allocation of joint and common costs to the set of $R/VC > 180$ traffic. Consequently, the limit price R/VC test bases conclusions about market dominance on cost allocations, which are unavoidably arbitrary.[43] Second, the issue of market dominance has received considerable attention in the industrial organization literature.[44] No single formulaic approach for determining market dominance has emerged from this literature because numerous factors (including market structure, entry barriers, mobility conditions, and firm conduct) can interact in complex ways to determine the presence or absence of effective competition. This caveat notwithstanding, the STB's limit price R/VC formula seeks to determine whether a set of traffic is subject to market dominance simply by determining whether the estimated limit price exceeds the calculated RSAM.[45]

In sum, although the ICC deemed exclusive reliance of cost allocation methods to be arbitrary and unreliable in the early 1980s,[46] the STB presently relies upon a fully allocated cost benchmark (*viz.*, RSAM) in assessing both the extent of competition a set of traffic faces and the reasonableness of the rates associated with that traffic. Ironically, the introduction and application of RSAM and the limit price R/VC ratio threatens to bring full-circle the regulatory approach to the rail industry in the post-Staggers era. Specifically, the first attempt to determine the reasonableness of rates in the post-Staggers era emphasized the allocation of all joint and common costs to individual rail services. The more recent implementation of simplified procedures for assessing rate reasonableness and the adoption of RSAM as part of the market dominance determination has again made cost allocations central to the determination of the reasonableness of rates.

### Revenue Adequacy Regulation

The pricing principles described earlier have been formulated in the absence of any explicit attempt to limit rail carrier revenues to the level of capital costs. The Staggers Act calls for regulators to "*assist* rail carriers in attaining revenues that are 'adequate . . . to cover total operating expenses, including depreciation and obsolescence, plus a reasonable and economic profit or return (or both) on capital employed in the business.'"[47] Adequate revenues, in turn, are defined to be those that would provide a rate of return on net investment that was equal to the cost of capital.[48] The ICC has suggested such adequate revenues should serve as both a floor and a ceiling on appropriate revenues. Specifically, the ICC has stated that

> [o]ur revenue adequacy standard represents a reasonable level of profitability for a healthy carrier. Carriers do not need any greater revenues than this standard permits, and we believe that, in a regulated setting, they are not entitled to any higher revenues.[49]

Although this conclusion by the ICC nominally introduced a powerful new regulatory constraint to the rail industry in 1985, the practical impact of this constraint has been limited to date. This is the case because, until recently, the revenues that carriers have secured typically have been below capital costs. More recently, however, an increasing number of railroads are thought to be achieving revenue adequacy.[50] Figure 10.3 provides a historical comparison of revenues and capital costs in the rail industry.

The recent increase in the ratio of revenue to capital cost depicted in Figure 10.3, coupled with the ICC's comments in 1985, raise the possibility that explicit earnings regulation (that we sometimes refer to as

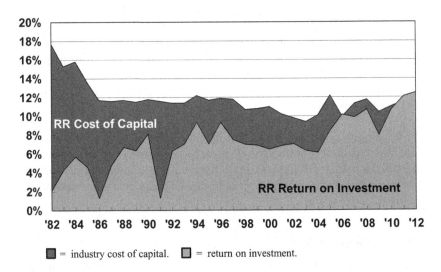

= industry cost of capital.   = return on investment.

*Figure 10.3* Class I Railroads' Cost of Capital vs. Return on Investment
Source. Surface Transportation Board.

The Surface Transportation Board changed the method by which it calculates the rail industry cost of capital in 2006.

"revenue adequacy regulation") might be imposed in the rail industry. The next section briefly summarizes the key conclusions from the economic literature that analyzes the imposition of explicit earnings regulation and associated cost allocation procedures.

## Related Literature

### Drawbacks to Cost Allocation

Fully distributed cost (FDC) allocation methodologies have been employed for many years in several regulated industries. Rigorous economic study of these methodologies began in the late 1970s. In an assessment of the merits of fully distributed costs in the rail industry, Owen and Braeutigam (1978) observe that fully distributed cost pricing "bears no direct relationship to economically efficient pricing since it attempts to set prices based on costs alone, with no considerations for demand schedules for the service" (p. 172).[51] In a more formal analysis, Braeutigam (1980) analyzes the economic consequences of three popular FDC allocation methods (*viz.*, the relative output method, the attributable cost method, and the gross revenues method), finding in each case that the resulting set of prices is inefficient and generally inconsistent with Ramsey prices.

Baumol and Willig (1983) offer a more pointed critique. They demonstrate that the application of fully allocated costs for establishing rate ceilings can fundamentally undermine not only the ability to achieve efficient pricing but also the financial viability of the regulated enterprise.[52] They also observe that the imposition of price ceilings that reflect FDC allocations can impair the incentives of railroads and shippers to negotiate mutually advantageous contracts. In the presence of FDC-based price ceilings, such contracts must not only recover the costs directly attributable to the contracted services but also compensate for the consequent reduction in the regulated ceiling rates. The reduction arises because any recovery of fixed costs from contract traffic reduces prices for non-contract traffic (because fewer fixed costs are allocated to such traffic). The authors conclude that "rate ceilings derived from fully distributed costs are inimical to the public interest" (p. 40).

Sweeney (1982) examines the performance of FDC methods in settings where only a portion of the firm's products are subject to regulation. He demonstrates that when the fraction of fixed costs allocated to a service increases with the output of the service, a partially regulated firm may implement prices that are strictly dominated.[53] That is, there are alternative prices that would secure both higher profit for the firm and lower prices for consumers. This outcome arises in the presence of earnings regulation because the firm has an incentive to shift costs to the regulated sector by reducing output in the unregulated sector (by charging higher prices for unregulated services). The resulting increased costs allocated to the regulated sector produce higher prices in that sector also.[54]

Brennan (1990) also explains how the combination of FDC allocation and earnings regulation can induce a regulated enterprise to shift costs from unregulated to regulated operations. Braeutigam and Panzar (1989) demonstrate that earnings regulation and FDC pricing can distort the incentives of a partially regulated firm to diversify into unregulated markets. In sum, the economic literature concludes that FDC allocation methods can induce inefficient pricing, distort market outputs, and alter incentives for efficient diversification.

### Drawbacks to Earnings Regulation

The economic literature has also identified many drawbacks to earnings regulation, primarily in the context of rate-of-return regulation. A survey of this literature concludes that these drawbacks include

> (1) limited incentives for innovation and cost reduction; (2) over-capitalisation; (3) high costs of regulation; (4) excessive risks imposed on customers; (5) cost shifting; (6) inappropriate levels of diversification and innovation; (7) inefficient choice of operating technology; and (8) insufficient pricing flexibility in the presence of competitive pressures.[55]

## A Stylized Model of Rail Regulation

To further assess the potential impact of explicit earnings regulation in the U.S. rail industry, we introduce a simple model that is designed to demonstrate formally some of the problems that earnings regulation can introduce. The model is highly stylized and does not capture every feature of the rail industry. However, the model permits a simple, straightforward illustration of the more general principle that stringent earnings regulation can stifle many different types of innovative effort. The model also demonstrates that the manner in which earnings regulation affects innovative effort varies with the manner in which the regulation is applied.

The rail industry benefited from many innovations after the passage of the Staggers Act, including superior engines, increased track durability, improved traffic control and scheduling capabilities, and enhanced railcar and container design.[56] These innovations reflect in part the diligent and creative efforts of rail carrier personnel. The streamlined model developed here is constructed to analyze the potential impact of stringent earnings regulation on such effort.

For simplicity, the model considers the activity of a single rail carrier (R) that supplies two services. One service (e.g., the transport of coal) is supplied in a regulated sector (sector 1). The other service (e.g., the transport of food products) is supplied in an unregulated sector (sector 2). The model posits particularly simple demand and cost structures. Specifically, the demand for R's service in the regulated sector is always $X_1$, regardless of the price charged for the service. R's total cost of producing $X_1$ units of the regulated service and $X_2$ units of the unregulated service is $C(X_1, X_2) = F + c_1 X_1 + c_2 X_2$. $F$ is a fixed cost of production that does not vary with the outputs that R supplies. $c_1$ is R's product-specific unit cost of production in sector $i \in \{1, 2\}$.[57]

For simplicity, provision of the unregulated service is assumed to be characterized by Bertrand price competition, where R is the least-cost supplier of the unregulated service. $p_2$ is the unit cost of production for the second-most efficient producer of this service. Consequently, in equilibrium, R supplies the entire demand for the unregulated service at price $p_2$.[58]

The central feature of the simple model we analyze is the cost-reducing effort that the rail carrier's workforce can supply if it is motivated to do so. The effort represents, for example, the diligence with which rail carrier personnel explore all possible means to reduce R's operating costs (e.g., by developing innovations like those noted earlier).

In practice, the diligence and creativity with which a firm's employees operate are inherently unobservable. To illustrate, although it is often possible to measure the number of hours that an employee is at work, it can be exceedingly difficult to assess the attention and effort the employee devotes to key tasks while at work. Attention and creative effort require time and energy that employees could otherwise devote to different matters (including personal matters that are unrelated to work). Consequently, creative effort is costly to supply and so must be motivated.

We model the critical task of motivating key personnel to labor diligently to improve the railroad's operations as follows. We assume that the rail carrier's workforce collectively can choose the amount of three types of cost-reducing effort to supply. The first type of effort ($e_1 \geq 0$) serves to reduce R's unit cost of production in the regulated sector. The second type of effort ($e_2 \geq 0$) serves to reduce R's unit cost of production in the unregulated sector. The third type of effort ($e_F \geq 0$) serves to reduce R's fixed cost of production, $F$. $E_i(e_i)$ denotes the (unmeasured) personal costs that rail carrier personnel collectively incur when they deliver cost-reducing effort $e_i$, $i \in \{1, 2, F\}$. These effort costs increase at a non-decreasing rate with the level of effort supplied.[59] Increased effort reduces production costs at a non-increasing rate.[60] Reflecting the practical difficulty of measuring the diligence with which an employee operates, the regulator is assumed to be unable to measure the innovative effort delivered by rail carrier personnel. Consequently, the regulator cannot reimburse R directly for the cost of the effort its personnel supply.[61]

The total resource costs—including effort costs—that R incurs in delivering outputs $X_1$ and $X_2$ are as follows:

$$F(e_F) + c_1(e_1)X_1 + c_2(e_2)X_2 + E_F(e_F) + E_1(e_1) + E_2(e_2). \tag{1}$$

$(e_1^*, e_2^*, e_F^*)$ denotes the efficient levels of $(e_1^*, e_2^*, e_F^*)$, that is, the levels that minimize the total resource costs identified in expression (1). Formally, $e_1^*$, $e_2^*$, and $e_F^*$ are determined by:

$$-F'(e_F^*) = E_F'(e_F^*) \quad \text{and} \quad -c_i'(e_i^*)X_i = E_i'(e_i^*) \quad \text{for} \quad i = 1, 2. \tag{2}$$

Expression (2) indicates that the efficient level of cost-reducing effort is the level that equates the marginal reduction in production costs with the marginal increase in effort cost.[62]

We explore some of the impacts of two forms of explicit earnings regulation (or "revenue adequacy regulation") in this simple setting. Under "comprehensive earnings regulation," the price in the regulated sector $(p_1)$ is set to eliminate R's aggregate measured profit in both sectors, given the price $(p_2)$ that R sets in the unregulated sector. Under "focused earnings regulation," $p_1$ is set to eliminate R's measured profit (only) in the regulated sector.

### Comprehensive Earnings Regulation (CER)

Formally, comprehensive earnings regulation (CER) requires the following:

$$[p_1 - c_1(e_1)]X_1 + [p_2 - c_2(e_2)]X_2 - F = 0. \tag{3}$$

Equation (3) implies that under CER, R secures exactly zero profit from all of its operations combined. This is the case regardless of the level of production costs that R secures. Under such a policy, if R were to undertake any cost-reducing effort, R would incur the associated expenditures but experience no corresponding financial benefit. Consequently, R will refrain from delivering any unmeasured cost-reducing effort under CER, as Conclusion 1 reports.

> **Conclusion 1:** *When it operates under CER, R will set* $e_1 = 0$, $e_2 = 0$, *and* $e_F = 0$.

*Proof.* When R operates under CER, its objective is to:

$$\underset{e_1, e_2, e_F}{Maximize}[p_1 - c_1(e_1)]X_1 + [p_2 - c_2(e_2)]X_2 - F - E_1(e_1)$$
$$- E_2(e_2) - E_F(e_F) \tag{4}$$

subject to equation (3). Expressions (3) and (4) imply that R's objective under CER is to:

$$\underset{e_1, e_2, e_F}{Maximize} - E_1(e_1) - E_2(e_2) - E_F(e_F).$$

Because R's objective function is strictly decreasing in $e_1$, $e_2$, and $e_F$, R will set each of these variables at its minimum feasible level (0). ∎

Conclusion 1 has two important implications for the application of CER to the rail industry. First, to the extent that shippers can observe rail carriers' earnings and can quickly contest established rates at low personal cost, a rail carrier will be precluded from earning more than its cost of capital. As soon as a carrier proposes rates that generate positive (extranormal) earnings, shippers will challenge the proposed rates for the regulated services, and thereby secure rate reductions that eliminate the carrier's earnings. Indeed, CER may introduce a race among shippers to be the first to challenge "excessive" rates (before other shippers secure rate reductions that eliminate the rail carrier's profit).

Second, like rate of return regulation (RORR), CER will limit incentives for innovation and cost reduction. In particular, cost reductions in either the regulated sector or the unregulated sector that result in earnings above the allowed threshold will generate offsetting reductions in regulated rates to ensure the rail carrier earns no extranormal profit. Consequently, CER will provide incentives for innovation only if there is a lag in translating observed cost reductions into offsetting price reductions.[63]

The distortions identified in Conclusion 1 are not the only distortions that CER can introduce. Potential additional distortions include the following three. First, CER regulation can curtail incentives for quality-enhancing innovation, just as it can limit incentives for cost-reducing innovation. CER limits the ability of a rail carrier to benefit financially from quality-enhancing innovation regardless of whether the innovation arises in the regulated or the unregulated sector. Consequently, CER is likely to stifle quality-enhancing innovation in both sectors, just as it can be expected to inhibit cost-reducing innovation in both sectors.

Second, cost reductions in the unregulated sector can reduce welfare in the rail industry by increasing the scope of regulation. This is the case because a reduction in the cost of supplying a service can increase the ratio of revenue to variable cost above the 180% threshold that triggers regulatory oversight. The rail carrier may not be harmed directly by the associated increased scope of regulation because CER limits the carrier's overall profit to zero, regardless of the number of regulated and unregulated services it offers. However, the carrier, the shippers, and the regulator alike may all incur higher costs due to the expanded scope of regulation. The expanded scope of regulation resulting from cost-reducing innovation can thereby reduce industry welfare.[64]

Third, CER can support, if not encourage, a rail carrier's efforts to maximize revenue or output, rather than earnings. The associated costs of inefficient output expansion (and potentially below-cost pricing) would be borne by "captive" shippers under CER, as regulated rates are adjusted to ensure zero profit for the rail carrier across all of its operations. Thus, CER can encourage a rail carrier to act particularly aggressively in the provision of "unregulated" services, conceivably displacing more efficient competitors.[65]

## Focused Earnings Regulation (FER)

Under focused earnings regulation (FER), the revenue adequacy constraint is applied to the rail carrier's earnings in the regulated sector rather than to its earnings in all sectors combined. Specifically, the firm's measured (extranormal) profit in the regulated sector is held to zero under FER. To calculate measured earnings in the regulated sector, one must allocate a portion of the firm's fixed costs ($F$) to the regulated sector. Let $f_1 \in [\,0, 1\,]$ denote this fraction. Then FER can be represented formally as:

$$[p_1 - c_1(e_1)]\, X_1 - f_1\, F = 0. \tag{5}$$

Conclusion 2 characterizes the cost-reducing effort the rail carrier (R) will deliver under FER.

> **Conclusion 2:** *When it operates under FER, R will set $e_2 = e_2^*$ and $e_1 = 0$. R will also set $e_F < e_F^*$ if $f_1 > 0$.*
>
> *Proof.* When it operates under FER, R seeks to maximize expression (4), subject to expression (5). Substituting expression (5) into expression (4) implies that R seeks to:
>
> $$\underset{e_1, e_2, e_F}{\text{Maximize}}\; f_1 F + [p_2 - c_2(e_2)]X_2 - F - E_1 - E_2(e_2) - E_F(e_F)$$
>
> which can be rewritten as:
>
> $$\underset{e_1, e_2, e_F}{\text{Maximize}}\; [p_2 - c_2(e_2)]X_2 - [1 - f_1]F(e_F) - E_1(e_1) - E_2(e_2) - E_F(e_F)$$
>
> The necessary conditions for an interior solution to this problem are given by:
>
> $$e_1: \; -E_i'(e_1) \leq 0; \qquad\qquad [-E_i'(e_1)]e_1 = 0; \tag{6}$$
>
> $$e_2: \; -c_2'(e_2)X_2 - E_2'(e_2) \leq 0; \qquad [-c_2'(e_2)X_2 - E_2'(e_2)]\, e_2 = 0; \tag{7}$$
>
> $$e_F: \; -[1 - f_1]F'(e_F) - E_F'(e_F) \leq 0; \quad [-(1 - f_1)F'(e_F) - E_F'(e_F)]e_F = 0. \tag{8}$$
>
> Expression (6) implies $e_1 = 0$. Expression (7) implies $e_2 = e_2^*$. Expression (8) implies $E_F'(e_F) = -F'(e_F) + f_1 F'(e_F)$. Consequently, if $f_1 > 0$, then $E_F'(e_F) < -F'(e_F) \Rightarrow e_F < e_F^*$. ∎

Conclusion 2 reports that R will deliver the efficient level of effort to reduce variable costs in the unregulated sector under FER. This is the case because R's earnings are not regulated in this sector. Consequently, R receives the full benefit of its cost-reducing effort directed toward its unregulated activities, and so will undertake the efficient level of cost-reducing effort in this sector.

In contrast, R will not pursue any cost-reducing effort in the regulated sector. This is the case because this effort is personally costly for R, and yet R receives no financial benefit from any cost reduction it secures in the regulated sector. R's measured profit is held to zero in this sector, regardless of the extent of the cost-reducing innovation that R implements. Thus, although FER can encourage cost-reducing effort in the unregulated sector, it stifles such effort in the regulated sector, just as CER does.

Conclusion 2 also reports that FER typically will induce R to deliver less than the efficient level of effort to reduce fixed costs. This is the case because R bears the full burden of the reducing fixed production costs but receives only a fraction $(1 - f_1)$ of the associated benefit under FER.[66]

Conclusions 1 and 2 together indicate that although the distortions created by CER can be particularly onerous and pervasive, FER is not without its flaws. Before considering alternatives to CER and FER, we briefly consider one additional distortion that can arise under FER. The foregoing analysis does not account for the fact that higher levels of fixed costs often can reduce variable production costs in practice.[67] We now consider whether FER will induce R to adopt the cost-minimizing mix of fixed and variable production costs. To do so most simply, we abstract from any cost-reducing effort that R might provide.

Suppose instead that R's only decision under FER is the choice of its fixed cost, $F$. Higher levels of $F$ reduce R's variable unit cost of production in both the regulated and the unregulated sector. Formally, $c_i'(F) < 0$ for $i = 1, 2$, where $c_i(F)$ is R's variable unit cost of production in sector $i$ when R installs fixed cost $F$.[68]

R's total cost of production when it implements fixed cost $F$ in this setting is $c_1(F) X_1 + c_2(F) X_2 + F$. Therefore, $F^*$, the efficient (cost-minimizing) level of $F$, is determined by:

$$c_1'(F^*)X_1 + c_2'(F^*)X_2 + 1 = 0. \tag{9}$$

Conclusion 3 considers the special case in which R's unit variable cost declines at precisely the same rate in the regulated and unregulated sectors as $F$ increases.

**Conclusion 3:** *Suppose R operates under FER and* $c_1'(F) = c_2'(F)$ *for all F. Then R will set* $F \gtreqless F^*$ *as* $f_1 \gtreqless \dfrac{X_1}{X_1 + X_2}$.[69]

*Proof.* When R operates under FER, its objective in the present setting is to:

$$\underset{F}{Maximize}[p_1 - c_1(F)]X_1 + [p_2 - c_2(F)]X_2 - F \tag{10}$$

subject to:

$$[p_1 - c_1(F)] X_1 - f_1 F = 0 \qquad (11)$$

Substituting expression (11) into expression (10) implies that R seeks to:

$$\underset{F}{Maximize} f_1 F + [p_2 - c_2(F)]X_2 - F$$

which can be rewritten as:

$$\underset{F}{Maximize} [p_2 - c_2(F)]X_2 - [1 - f_1]F.$$

The necessary condition for an interior solution to this problem is:[70]

$$-c_2'(F)X_2 - (1 - f_1) = 0 \Rightarrow c_2'(F)X_2 + 1 - f_1 = 0. \qquad (12)$$

Observe that $1 - f_1 \underset{>}{\overset{<}{\phantom{|}}} \frac{X_2}{X_1 + X_2}$ as $f_1 \underset{<}{\overset{>}{\phantom{|}}} \frac{X_1}{X_1 + X_2}$. Therefore, from expression (12):

$$0 = c_2'(F)X_2 + 1 - f_1 \underset{>}{\overset{<}{\phantom{|}}} c_2'(F)X_2 + \frac{X_2}{X_1 + X_2} \overset{s}{=} c_2'(F)[X_1 + X_2] + 1$$

$$= c_1'(F)X_1 + c_2'(F)X_2 + 1 \text{ as } f_1 \underset{<}{\overset{>}{\phantom{|}}} \frac{X_1}{X_1 + X_2} \qquad (13)$$

The last equality in expression (13) reflects the maintained assumption that $c_1'(F) = c_2'(F)$ for all $F$. The Conclusion follows from expression (13) because expression (9) implies:

$$F \underset{<}{\overset{>}{\phantom{|}}} F^* \text{ as } c_1'(F)X_1 + c_2'(F)X_2 + 1 \underset{<}{\overset{>}{\phantom{|}}} 0. \quad \blacksquare \qquad (14)$$

Conclusion 3 identifies a particular cost allocation rule (the "relative output rule," $f_1 = \frac{X_1}{X_1 + X_2}$) and a special technology ($c_1'(F) = c_2'(F)$) under which R will choose the cost-minimizing production technology under FER. To understand Conclusion 3, observe that R effectively pays $1 - f_1$ for each additional unit of $F$ it implements under FER. (R recovers the fraction $f_1$ of any increase in $F$ through higher rates in the regulated sector.) The only value R derives from this investment in $F$ is the associated reduction in its cost of producing $X_2$, which accounts for the fraction $\frac{X_2}{X_1 + X_2}$ of its total output. If increases in $F$ reduce $c_1(\cdot)$ and $c_2(\cdot)$ at precisely the same rate, then R will implement the level of $F$ that minimizes total production costs when $f_1 = \frac{X_1}{X_1 + X_2}$ and so $1 - f_1 = \frac{X_2}{X_1 + X_2}$ because in this case, the marginal return R anticipates from increasing $F$ is scaled down by the same amount that the cost it effectively incurs from increasing $F$ is scaled down.

More generally, FER typically will not induce R to implement the cost-minimizing level of $F$. Conclusion 3 illustrates this point when the fraction of common costs allocated to the regulated sector differs from $\frac{X_1}{X_1+X_2}$. Conclusion 4 further illustrates this point in the setting where, as is likely in practice, increases in R's fixed cost of production do not reduce variable costs symmetrically in all sectors. In this case, distortions arise even in the presence of the cost allocation rule $(f_1 = \frac{X_1}{X_1+X_2})$ that induces R to implement the efficient level of $F$ in the setting of Conclusion 3.

**Conclusion 4:** *Suppose R operates under FER and* $f_1 = \frac{X_1}{X_1+X_2}$ *Then R will set* $F \gtreqless F^*$ *as* $|c_2'(F)| \gtreqless |c_1(F)|$ *for all F.*

*Proof.* From expression (12), R's choice of $F$ is determined by:

$$c_2'(F)X_1 + c_2'(F)X_2 + 1 = 0$$

$$\Rightarrow c_1'(F)X_1 + c_2'(F)X_2 + 1 \gtreqless 0 \; when \; |c_2'(F)| \gtreqless |c_1'(F)| \, for \, all \, F. \qquad (15)$$

The conclusion follows from expressions (14) and (15). ■

To interpret Conclusion 4, consider the setting where increases in $F$ reduce R's variable unit cost in the unregulated sector more rapidly than they reduce R's unit variable cost in the regulated sector. Then, given the proportionate charge for $F$ that R effectively faces under the presumed form of FER, the marginal return R anticipates from increasing $F$ (i.e., the corresponding reduction in variable costs in the unregulated sector) is high relative to the associated effective cost. Consequently, R implements more than the cost-minimizing level of $F$.[71]

Taken together, Conclusions 3 and 4 indicate that attempts to allocate common costs across sectors in order to implement FER typically will induce R to adopt other than the cost-minimizing production technology. Of course, R has no strict incentive to adopt the cost-minimizing technology under CER either. Indeed, for the reasons explained earlier, R has no strict incentive to minimize any component of production costs under CER. Therefore, earnings regulation in any form has the potential to introduce serious distortions. These distortions can be particularly widespread if earnings regulation is imposed ubiquitously.

## Price Cap Regulation (PCR)

The preceding analysis demonstrates that comprehensive earnings regulation (CER) and focused earnings regulation (FER) both typically limit the incentives of a regulated enterprise to operate efficiently. Before concluding, we briefly consider an alternative to CER and FER. Many forms of "incentive regulation" have gained popularity in other industries in recent years.[72] Incentive regulation seeks to limit the detrimental effects of rate of return regulation by allowing firms that deliver exceptional performance to secure more than merely "adequate" earnings. Pure price cap regulation (PCR) is one relatively straightforward form of incentive regulation. In the context of the formal model analyzed in the section "Comprehensive Earnings Regulation (CER)," PCR replaces explicit earnings regulation with a ceiling $(p_1)$ on the price that R can set in the regulated sector. The distinguishing feature of this price ceiling is that its level is not linked to R's aggregate realized earnings or to R's realized earnings in the regulated sector.

Under PCR, R will choose the price in the regulated sector and its cost-reducing efforts to maximize its profit. Formally, the firm's problem is:

$$\underset{p_1 \leq \bar{p}_1, e_1, e_2, e_F}{Maximize} [p_1 - c_1(e_1)]X_1 + [p_2 - c_2(e_2)]X_2 - F(e_F) - E_1(e_1)$$

$$- E_1(e_1) - E_2(e_2) - E_F(e_F). \tag{16}$$

**Conclusion 5:** *When it operates under PCR, R will set* $p_1 = \bar{p}_1, e_1 = e_1^*, e_2 = e_2^*,$ *and* $e_F = e_F^*.$

*Proof.* Let $\lambda$ denote the Lagrange multiplier associated with the $p_1 \leq \bar{p}_1$ constraint. Then the necessary conditions for an interior solution to R's problem in expression (16) are:

$$-c_i'(e_1) - E_i'(e_1) = 0 \text{ for } i = 1,2; -F'(e_F) - E_F'(e_F) = 0; \text{ and } X_1 - \lambda = 0. \tag{17}$$

The first two equations in expression (17) imply that $e_1 = e_1^*$, $e_2 = e_2^*$, and $e_F = e_F^*$. The last equation in expression (17) implies that $\lambda > 0$ and so $p_1 = \bar{p}_1$.[73]

Conclusion 5 indicates that, in principle, price-based regulation can provide strong incentives for innovation and cost minimization. However, the implications of this theoretical conclusion for the rail industry must be tempered by actual experience with practice of price cap regulation.[74] In practice, the prices that are authorized for an upcoming price cap regulation regime often parallel the regulated firm's realized costs during the preceding regime. In some instances where the firm has secured unexpectedly high earnings, regulators have even increased the stringency of price controls before the scheduled review of the price cap regime.[75] Thus, in practice, regulators typically find it difficult to sever the link between authorized prices and realized costs for long periods of time and sometimes find it difficult to do so even for short periods of time. This experience supports the general critique that the theory underlying the standard analysis of PCR and other forms of incentive regulation "proceeds by ignoring an immutable institutional constraint, namely that neither commitment nor its associated information rents are reasonable assumptions."[76] This critique certainly applies to the simple model of PCR that underlies Conclusion 5, which abstracts from both the information asymmetries and the commitment difficulties that regulators typically face in practice.

## Conclusions

The Staggers Act of 1980 is widely ascribed to have deregulated the U.S. freight rail industry. Indeed, the majority of traffic in the post-Staggers era has traveled at prices and qualities that reflect the interaction of the supply and demand for rail services. The consequent economic benefits of this governance mechanism have been widely documented.

However, the Staggers Act did not fully deregulate the rail industry. The residual regulatory structure incorporates elements of older-era public utility regulation, including cost allocation and even the possibility of explicit earnings regulation.

We have reviewed the development of regulatory policy in the U.S. rail freight industry and drawn upon the cost allocation and earnings regulation literatures to highlight relevant economic lessons. We have also developed a stylized formal model of "revenue adequacy" regulation for rail shipments that are deemed to warrant direct regulatory intervention. In particular, we examined the potential impacts of comprehensive earnings regulation, focused earnings regulation, and price cap regulation. We found that earnings regulation in either a comprehensive or focused form introduces distortions that limit industry innovation. In principle, price regulation could conceivably eliminate this distortion. However, even under what is nominally introduced as price regulation, regulated prices typically are linked to realized earnings in practice, and so the associated distortion arises.[77]

"Pay for performance" is a central element of modern incentive regulation. Incentive regulation explicitly provides the potential for more than "adequate" earnings in order to motivate the regulated enterprise to deliver superior performance. Earnings above merely adequate levels is not necessarily a sign of regulatory failure. To the contrary, higher earnings can reflect regulatory success and corresponding benefits for consumers. Regulatory policies that rigidly preclude earnings above the minimum level required to attract capital to the industry generally are inconsistent with the tenets of modern incentive regulation.

In closing, we note that any potential gains an additional layer of regulation might engender in the rail industry should be weighed carefully against the associated costs. The relatively light-touch approach to regulation that followed the passage of the Staggers Act produced substantial gains in the rail industry. These gains can be quickly reversed by poorly designed regulation that eliminates the railroads' incentive for exceptional performance.

## Acknowledgments

We thank Richard Schmalensee, Wesley Wilson, two anonymous referees, and participants at the Georgetown Center for Business and Public Policy's June 2015 conference on "The Economics and Regulation of the Freight Rail Industry" for very helpful comments and suggestions.

## Notes

\* This chapter originally appeared under the same title in the September 2016 issue of the *Review of Industrial Organization*, pp. 203–227.

1. Public Law 96–448, 94 Stat. 1895, codified as amended at 49 U.S.C. §10101.
2. *See* Gallamore and Meyer (2014), for example.
3. *See, e.g.,* President Carter's speech when signing the bill into law (www. google.com/search?q=president+carter+signing+the+staggers+rail+act&ie=utf-8&oe=utf-8#q=president+carter+ signing +the+staggers+rail+act &tbm=vid).
4. Articles that review the economic consequences of deregulation are identified at http://cbpp.georgetown.edu/railroads/regulation-deregulation.
5. *See* Association of American Railroads (2015).
6. Railroad Revitalization and Regulatory Reform Act of 1976, Public Law 94–210, 90 Stat. 31, codified as amended at 45 U.S.C. §801.
7. It has been argued that a review of the legislative history suggests that this revenue adequacy language reflected a Congressional concern that the regulatory framework not *restrain* railroads from earning adequate revenues (Macher et al., 2014).
8. We review key pricing regulation. Beard et al. (2015) and Boyer (2016) discuss access regulation in the rail industry.
9. Interstate Commerce Act of 1887, Ch. 104, 24 Stat. 379. *See* Gilligan et al. (1989), Wilson (2013) and the companion papers in the August 2013 Special Issue of the *Review of Industrial Organization* for analyses of the origins and primary effects of the Interstate Commerce Act.
10. *See* MacDonald and Cavalluzzo (1996) and Gallamore and Meyer (2014), for example.
11. *See* Harris and Keeler (1981), for example.
12. When signing the Act, President Carter observed that "by stripping away needless and costly regulation in favor of marketplace forces wherever possible, this act will help assure a strong and healthy future for our Nation's railroads and the men and women who work for them. It will benefit shippers throughout the country by encouraging railroads to improve their equipment and better tailor their service to shipper needs. America's consumers will benefit, for rather than face the prospect of continuing deterioration of rail freight service, consumers can be assured of improved railroads delivering their goods with dispatch" (www.presidency.ucsb.edu/ws/?pid=45284).
13. The U.S. Senate Committee report on the legislation sunsetting the ICC in 1995 (and replacing it with the Surface Transportation Board) notes that "the Staggers Act is considered the most successful rail transportation legislation ever produced, resulting in the restoration of financial health to the rail industry" U.S. Senate (1995). *See also* Winston (2005) and Gallamore and Meyer (2014).
14. For example, in the wake of Staggers, rail carriers were able to set rates that significantly accelerated the growth of piggybacking, wherein truck trailers are transported on flatbed railcars.

15. For example, cabooses were rapidly replaced with more efficient end-of-train markers following the passage of the Staggers Act. In addition, mechanized track gangs replaced more labor intensive locally based track-maintenance methods.

16. Wilson (1997) estimates that costs were "up to 40 percent lower than they would have been under regulation." The productivity gains achieved in the rail industry substantially exceeded the corresponding gains achieved in other transportation industries (including trucking, which also was deregulated in 1980) and in the broader economy. *See* McFarland (1989) and Eakin and Schoech (2010), for example.

17. 49 U.S.C. §10709(c).

18. Although the Staggers Act substantially reduced regulatory control, some rail services were exempted from rate regulation even before the Act was passed. To illustrate, in light of significant intermodal competition for their transport, farm products (excluding grain, soybeans, and sunflower seeds) were exempted as early as 1979. The ICC also exempted intermodal shipments and boxcar traffic (which typically admits significant intermodal competition) from regulation in the immediate wake of Staggers.

19. 49 U.S.C. §10707(a).

20. The STB defines "effective competition" as present when there are "pressures on that firm to perform up to standards and at reasonable prices, or lose desirable business." See, M&G Polymers USA, LLC v. CSX Transport, Inc., Surface Transportation Board, September 27, 2012, updated - December 7, 2012, p. 2. For a more general discussion of the evolution of the term "effective competition," see Delp and Mayo (2016). For an early discussion set within the rail sector, see Wilson (1996).

21. *See* National Academy of Science (NAS) (2015, Chapter 3) and Wilson and Wolak (2016). Common costs are "those shared by two or more services in variable proportions, such as a terminal," whereas joint costs are "those shared by two (or more) services in fixed proportions, such as a front haul-back haul arrangement" (United States Surface Transportation Board. (1996). *Ex Parte 347 (Sub No.2) Rate Guidelines—Non-Coal Proceedings.* Washington, DC: Surface Transportation Board. [Hereafter Non-Coal Rate Guidelines (1996)], p. 3). The STB indicates that "inherent in the rail industry cost structure are large amounts of joint and common costs that cannot be directly attributed to particular traffic" (p. 3). Although it is difficult to determine the level of these costs precisely, if we assume that the industry secured a normal profit in 2013, STB reports suggest that nearly $25 billion of the industry's roughly $70 billion in costs are joint and common. (*See, e.g.,* Surface Transportation Board, 2013 Commodity Stratification Report.) Kahn (1970) provides a foundational discussion of joint and common costs in regulated industries.

22. Because the estimated VC includes joint and common costs, some R/VC ratios for rail services are less than 1. *See, e.g.,* "Commodity Revenue Stratification Report for 2013," Surface Transportation Board (www.stb.dot.gov/econdata.nsf/09a17a28a74b350d852573ae006d52cd?OpenView). Section 3 reviews the many potential drawbacks to cost allocation procedures like the one employed to determine the estimated VC of rail services.

23. The incremental cost of a service is the cost that would be avoided if the service were not supplied. National Academy of Science (2015, p. 103) characterizes the R/VC calculation as a "highly imperfect screen" for the reasonableness of established rail rates.

24. This 27% figure is an upper bound because revenue data on contract traffic, which is exempt by statute, are generally confidential and, therefore, unpublished.

25. The inquiry into whether a given set of rail movements is subject to effective competition or, alternatively, is subject to market dominance occurs in two steps. First, it is determined whether the rates of the target traffic exceed the ($R/VC > 180$) threshold. If not, the traffic is judged to be subject to effective competition. If so, the STB undertakes a "qualitative analysis" of whether there are "feasible transportation alternatives that are sufficient to constrain the railroad's rates to competitive levels." (*See, e.g., M&G Polymers USA, LLC v. CSX Transport, Inc.*, Surface Transportation Board, September 27, 2012, updated—December 7, 2012, p. 2.) For this set of traffic, regulators then determine whether the challenged rates are reasonable or unreasonable. In the latter case (only), regulators have the authority to exert rate regulation.

26. United States Interstate Commerce Commission, Section of Energy and Environment. (1985). Ex Parte No. 347 (Sub-No.1) Coal Rate Guidelines, Nationwide. Washington, DC: Interstate Commerce Commission. [Hereafter Coal Rate Guidelines (1985)], pp. 2–3 The reduced reliance on cost allocation did not extend to the regulatory determination of variable costs. *See* National Academy of Science (2015, Chapter 3).

27. *See* Coal Rate Guidelines (1985). In adopting Constrained Market Pricing, the ICC noted the theoretical appeal of the principles that underlie Ramsey pricing. These principles justify relatively pronounced increases in rates above marginal cost on those services for which demand is relatively insensitive to price. In relying on Ramsey principles, the ICC recognized that demand considerations can play an important role in determining appropriate rates. However, rather than apply the Ramsey inverse elasticity formula (which it deemed impractical), the ICC determined that prices below the SAC of providing a rail movement were reasonable, whereas prices in excess of SACs were not reasonable. Braeutigam (1989) and Baumol and Bradford (1970) discuss the implementation of Ramsey principles in public utility settings. Braeutigam (1979) and Baumol and Willig (1983) discuss the application of Ramsey principles in the rail industry.

28. A price above the SAC of providing a service, forces consumers of the service to pay more than they would pay if a competitive firm produced only the service in question. Conversely, if a price is less than the SAC of a service, then customers of the service "must not be harmed and may be benefiting from the fact that the supplier is serving other customers in addition to themselves" (Baumol, 1986, p. 121). The SAC test has been criticized on the grounds that (1) it is costly and cumbersome to implement, and (2) whereas the origins of the test lie in identifying prices that will preclude undesirable entry into the industry, such entry is not a practical concern in the rail industry (e.g., Pittman, 2010).

29. The Coal Rate Guidelines (1985, p. 544) state: "for ease of administration, we think it reasonable and practical to assume that the revenue contribution of other (i.e., non-complaining) shippers will be at the level of their current rates. However, this presumption is rebuttable and, if it can be shown that their rates are not at the Ramsey optimal level, then their revenue contribution to the hypothetical system may be adjusted accordingly."

30. A challenge to proposed rates that employs the SAC test can be expensive because it requires the shipper to demonstrate through comprehensive modeling of an efficient stand-alone rail network that the challenged rates exceed the cost an efficient rail carrier would incur to supply the service(s) in question.

31. Non-Coal Rate Guidelines, Surface Transportation Board, STB Ex Parte No. 347 (Sub-No. 2), 1996, p. 19. [Hereafter Non-Coal Rate Guidelines].

32. Non-Coal Rate Guidelines (1996, p. 21).

33. Non-Coal Rate Guidelines (1996, p. 25). Burton (2014) provides a discussion and critique of this process.
34. Non-Coal Rate Guidelines (1996, p. 28).
35. Non-Coal Rate Guidelines (1996, p. 30).
36. United States Surface Transportation Board. (2007). *Ex Parte 646 (Sub-No.1) Simplified Standards for Rail Rate Cases*. Washington, DC: Surface Transportation Board. [Hereafter, Simplified Standards for Rail Rate Cases (2007)], p. 4.
37. Principal among the changes embodied in the simplified test is that the assumption that the rail carrier's challenged traffic operates with fully utilized, efficiently deployed assets. This assumption avoids time consuming and contentious debates over managerial and productive efficiencies associated with the challenged traffic. For a complete description, *see* Simplified Standards for Rail Rate Cases (2007, pp. 13–15).
38. The Board estimated that with this set of methodologies in place, the Three-Benchmark test would be applicable to approximately 45% of the potentially captive traffic that may face shipper complaints. Simplified Standards for Rail Rate Cases (2007, p. 35).
39. The scaling mechanism is described in Simplified Standards for Rail Rate Cases (2007, pp. 19–22).
40. The Board does not specify these other relevant factors in detail but indicates that they should be sufficiently precise as to quantify their effects on the presumed maximum lawful rate.
41. *See, e.g., M&G Polymers USA, LLC v. CSX Transportation, Inc.*, Surface Transportation Board, Updated Decision—Public Version, December 7, 2012.
42. The mechanism for calculating this price is described in *M&G Polymers USA, LLC v. CSX Transportation, Inc.*, Surface Transportation Board, Updated Decision—Public Version, December 7, 2012, pp. 13–14.
43. The arbitrary nature of the cost allocations that generate RSAM is illustrated in part by the fact that these allocations differ from the allocations employed to estimate VC. *See* National Academy of Science (2015, Chapter 3).
44. *See* Bresnahan (1989) and Kahai et al. (1996), for example.
45. *See M&G Polymers USA, LLC v. CSX Transportation, Inc.*, Surface Transportation Board, Updated Decision—Public Version, December 7, 2012, pp. 3–4.
46. Coal Rate Guidelines (1985).
47. Coal Rate Guidelines (1985, p. 11). Emphasis added.
48. *See* Burton and Sims (2015) for an assessment of this process.
49. Coal Rate Guidelines (1985, p. 12).
50. This trend may not persist if declining coal shipments reduce rail revenues substantially.
51. Owen and Braeutigam (1978).
52. The authors show that the regulated firm reduces output of the service for which FDC pricing does not constrain pricing in order to allocate more cost to the FDC-constrained activities (thereby securing higher prices for the latter services). The allocations may improve the financial performance of the firm relative to the initial constrained situation but fail to permit the firm to fully recover its costs. Incentives for this inefficient output shifting persist even when the firm is financially viable under FDC pricing.
53. Rogerson (1992) develops a related model of a partially regulated defense firm that sells its outputs to the Department of Defense (DOD) and to commercial customers. The DOD imposes cost allocation rules that determine the price of services sold to the military. Rogerson shows that an FDC allocation

tied to direct labor costs will induce the firm to engage in pure waste and adopt inefficient combinations of inputs. This is the case because the labor-based allocation of costs creates an incentive for the firm to employ too much labor and to recover the associated costs in nominally "cost-based" contracts with the DOD.

54. Cavalluzzo et al. (1998) present empirical evidence that mandated FDC pricing of financial services promotes the allocation of overhead costs to less competitive services.

55. Sappington (2002, p. 240).

56. *See* Gallamore and Meyer (2014, Chapter 12) for additional detail.

57. In practice, of course, the demand for each rail service typically varies with the prevailing price of the service. Furthermore, variable production costs may increase more than proportionately as network capacity limits are approached. Similarly, the variable cost of supplying one service may vary with the level of the other service that is being supplied. In addition, the classification of a service as "regulated" or "unregulated" is not always clear-cut and can depend upon the price charged for the service. These more realistic features of the rail industry could be included in the model. However, their inclusion would complicate the formal analysis considerably without altering the key qualitative conclusions drawn ahead.

58. The assumption of Bertrand interaction among suppliers of a homogeneous service admits a simple representation of competition in the unregulated sector. In practice, railroads often compete with other transport suppliers on several dimensions, including the timeliness of a shipment and the special handling it is afforded (MacDonald, 1989). The key qualitative conclusions drawn ahead are not an artifact of our focus on price competition.

59. Formally, $E_i(0) = 0$, $E_i'(e_i) > 0$, and $E_i''(e_i) \geq 0$ for all $e_i > 0$.

60. Formally, $F'(e_F) < 0$, $F''(e_F) \geq 0$, $c_i'(e_i) < 0$, and $c_i''(e_i) \geq 0$ for $i = 1, 2$. We also assume that small levels of effort are very effective at reducing costs and are not very onerous for R. Formally, $\lim_{e_F \to 0} E_F'(e_F) = 0$, $\lim_{e_i \to 0} E_i'(e_i) = 0$, $\lim_{e_F \to 0} E'(e_F) = 0 - \infty$, and $\lim_{e_i \to 0} c_i'(e_i) = 0 - \infty$ for $i = 1, 2$.

61. The qualitative conclusions drawn ahead are unchanged if the regulator can observe some, but not all, of R's efforts to reduce its production costs.

62. In a multi-period counterpart to the present static model, the efficient level of cost-reducing effort would be the level that equates the marginal reduction in the present discounted value of future production costs with the marginal increase in effort cost.

63. Ironically, economic welfare may be enhanced in this situation by regulatory bureaucracy that introduces delays and/or by regulatory rules that limit the ability of shippers to rapidly secure rate reductions. Even with regulatory lag, though, RORR (and CER) are likely to diminish the pace of industry innovation (Sweeney, 1981).

64. CER is likely to entail considerable regulatory costs in part because the regulator may have to determine whether costs (in all sectors) have been incurred prudently. The prospect of such regulatory oversight introduces the possibility of "regulatory moral hazard," that is, a regulator may declare a prudent expense to have been incurred imprudently in order to increase the carrier's measured earnings and to thereby authorize lower prices for shippers.

65. Sappington and Sidak (2003) analyze the potential for corresponding behavior by state-owned enterprises.

66. R is permitted to recover through higher regulated rates the fraction $f_1$ of any realized increase in $F$. Therefore, R effectively secures a financial benefit of only $\$(1 - f_1)$ for each dollar by which it reduces $F$.

67. For example, investments in railroad signal equipment (which is largely invariant to the volume of rail traffic) can significantly reduce the variable costs that a railroad incurs by enabling the railroad to move traffic more expediently across its network.

68. We assume $c_i''(F) = 0$ for all $F$ 0, $\lim_{F \to 0} |c_i'(F)| = \infty$, and $\lim_{F \to \infty} |c_i'(F)| = 0$.

69. We assume $f_1$, the fraction of $F$ allocated to the regulated sector, is not affected by R's choice of $F$.

70. The maintained conditions ensure that $F > 0$ at the solution to this problem as long as $f_1 < 1$.

71. A corresponding argument explains why R implements less than the cost-minimizing level of $F$ when increases in $F$ reduce R's variable unit cost in the unregulated sector less rapidly than they reduce R's unit variable cost in the regulated sector.

72. For analyses of incentive regulation and additional references to the relevant literature, *see, inter alia,* Joskow and Schmalensee (1986), Laffont and Tirole (1993), Blackmon (1994), Lyon (1994), Crew and Kleindorfer (1996, 2002), Sappington (2002), and Sappington and Weisman (2010).

73. The inelastic demand for the regulated service ensures that the firm will set p1 at its upper bound, $\overline{p}_1$. More generally, the firm will set p1 equal to $\overline{p}_1$ as long as $\overline{p}_1$ does not exceed the price that an unregulated, profit-maximizing monopolist would charge for the service.

74. Sappington and Weisman (2010, p. 228) observe that, in practice, price cap regulation "can resemble ROR, affording little pricing discretion to the regulated firm and providing limited incentives for innovation and cost reduction." Armstrong et al. (1994, p. 172) note that, in practice, the distinction between price cap regulation and rate of return regulation "is one of degree rather than kind." Blank and Mayo (2009) provide a political economy model of regulation in which hybrid regulatory regimes arise in equilibrium despite the superior efficacy of pure price cap regulation.

75. *See* Armstrong et al. (1994), pp. 227–228).

76. Crew and Kleindorfer (2002, p. 13). Vickers and Yarrow (1988, pp. 427–428) note "it is difficult for governments to commit their successors to allow the regulated firm its fair share of the gains from successful investment and innovation, and hence dynamic efficiency may suffer. These concerns are greatest in industries with long asset lives and sunk costs."

77. For simplicity, the formal model we analyzed considered non-stochastic innovation processes. When innovation is stochastic, a firm that faces stringent earnings regulation may decline to pursue promising projects because the firm bears the cost of the project whether it succeeds or fails, and earnings regulation can limit the firm's financial reward when the project succeeds.

# References

Armstrong, M., Cowan, S., & Vickers, J. S. (1994). *Regulatory reform: Economic analysis and British experience.* Cambridge, MA: The MIT Press.

Association of American Railroads. (2015). *The impact of the Staggers Rail Act of 1980* (www.aar.org/BackgroundPapers/Impact%20of%20the%20Staggers%20Act.pdf).

Baumol, W. J. (1986). *Superfairness: Applications and theory.* Cambridge, MA: The MIT Press.

Baumol, W. J., & Bradford, D. F. (1970). Optimal departures from marginal cost pricing. *American Economic Review,* 60(3), 265–283.

Baumol, W. J., & Willig, R. D. (1983). Pricing issues in the deregulation of railroad rates. In J. Finsinger (Ed.), *Economic analysis of regulated markets* (pp. 11–47). New York: Palgrave Macmillan.

Beard, T. R., Macher, J. T., & Vickers, C. (2015). *This time is different? Lessons from unbundled access in telecommunications applied to railroad regulation.* Washington, DC: Georgetown University.

Blackmon, G. (1994). *Incentive regulation and the regulation of incentives.* Boston, MA: Kluwer Academic Publishers.

Blank, L. R., & Mayo, J. W. (2009). Endogenous regulatory constraints and the emergence of hybrid regulation. *Review of Industrial Organization*, 35(3), 233–255.

Boyer, K. (2016). Optimal pricing of traffic rights. *Review of Industrial Organization*, in press.

Braeutigam, R. R. (1979). Optimal pricing with intermodal competition. *American Economic Review*, 69(1), 38–49.

Braeutigam, R. R. (1980). An analysis of fully distributed cost pricing in regulated industries. *Bell Journal of Economics*, 11(1), 182–196.

Braeutigam, R. R. (1989). Optimal policies for natural monopolies. In R. Schmalensee & R. D. Willig (Eds.), *Handbook of industrial organization* (Vol. 2, pp. 1289–1346). Amsterdam: North Holland.

Braeutigam, R. R., & Panzar, J. C. (1989). Diversification incentives under "price-based" and "cost-based" regulation. *RAND Journal of Economics*, 20(3), 373–391.

Brennan, T. J. (1990). Cross-subsidization and cost misallocation by regulated monopolists. *Journal of Regulatory Economics*, 2(1), 37–51.

Bresnahan, T. F. (1989). Empirical studies of industries with market power. In R. Schmalensee & R. D. Willig (Eds.), *Handbook of industrial organization* (Vol. 2, pp. 1011–1057). Amsterdam: North Holland.

Burton, M. L. (2014). The economics of evolving rail rate oversight: Balancing theory, practice and objectives. *Journal of Transportation, Law, Logistics and Policy*, 81(4), 267–293.

Burton, M. L., & Sims, C. (2015). *Understanding railroad investment behaviors, regulatory processes and related implications for efficient oversight.* Knoxville, TN: The University of Tennessee (www.gcbpp.org/files/Railroad/Burton.SimsPaper.pdf).

Cavalluzzo, K. S., Ittner, C. D., & Larker, D. F. (1998). Competition, efficiency, and cost allocation in government agencies: Evidence on the Federal Reserve System. *Journal of Accounting Research*, 36(1), 1–32.

Crew, M., & Kleindorfer, P. (1996). Incentive regulation in the United Kingdom and the United States: Some lessons. *Journal of Regulatory Economics*, 9(3), 211–225.

Crew, M., & Kleindorfer, P. (2002). Regulatory economics: Twenty years of progress. *Journal of Regulatory Economics*, 21(1), 5–22.

Delp, A. B., & Mayo, J. W. (2016). The evolution of 'competition': Lessons for 21st century telecommunications policy. *Review of Industrial Organization*, 50(4), 393–416.

Eakin, B. K., & Schoech, P. E. (2010). *The distribution of the post-Staggers Act railroad productivity gains.* Madison, WI: Christensen Associates.

Eaton, J. A., & Center, J. A. (1985). A tale of two markets: The ICC's use of product and geographic competition in the assessment of rail market dominance. *Transportation Practitioners Journal*, 53(1), 16–35.

Gallamore, R. E., & Meyer, J. R. (2014). *American railroads: Decline and renaissance in the twentieth century.* Boston, MA: Harvard University Press.

Gilligan, T. W., Marshall, W. J., & Weingast, B. R. (1989). Regulation and the theory of legislative choice: The Interstate Commerce Act of 1887. *Journal of Law and Economics*, 32(1), 35–61.

Harris, R. G., & Keeler, T. E. (1981). Determinants of railroad profitability: An econometric study. In K. D. Boyer & W. G. Shepherd (Eds.), *Economic regulation: Essays in honor of James R. Nelson* (pp. 37–54). East Lansing, MI: Institute of Public Utilities, Michigan State University.

Joskow, P. R., & Schmalensee, R. (1986). Incentive regulation for electric utilities. *Yale Journal on Regulation*, 4(1), 1–50.

Kahai, S. K., Kaserman, D. L., & Mayo, J. W. (1996). Is the "dominant firm" dominant? An empirical analysis of AT&T's market power. *Journal of Law and Economics*, 39(2), 499–517.

Kahn, A. E. (1970). *The economics of regulation: Principles and institutions.* New York: John Wiley & Sons, Inc.

Laffont, J. J., & Tirole, J. (1993). *A theory of incentives in procurement and regulation.* Cambridge, MA: The MIT Press.

Lyon, T. P. (1994). Incentive regulation in theory and practice. In M. A. Crew (Ed.), *Incentive regulation for public utilities* (pp. 1–26). Boston, MA: Kluwer Academic Publishers.

MacDonald, J. M. (1989). Railroad deregulation, innovation, and competition: Effects of the Staggers Act on grain transportation. *Journal of Law and Economics*, 32(1), 63–95.

MacDonald, J. M., & Cavalluzzo, L. (1996). Railroad deregulation: Pricing reforms, shipper responses, and the effects on labor. *Industrial and Labor Relations Review*, 50(1), 80–91.

Macher, J. T., Mayo, J. W., & Pinkowitz, L. F. (2014). Revenue adequacy: The good, the bad and the ugly. *Transportation Law Journal*, 41(2), 86–127.

McFarland, H. (1989). The effects of United States railroad deregulation on shippers, labor, and capital. *Journal of Regulatory Economics*, 1(3), 259–270.

National Academy of Science. (2015). *Modernizing freight rail regulation*, Transportation Research Board Special Report 318 (www.nap.edu/21759).

Owen, B., & Braeutigam, R. (1978). *The regulation game: Strategic use of the administrative process.* Cambridge, MA: Ballinger Publishing Company.

Pittman, R. (2010). Against the stand-alone cost test in U.S. freight rail regulation. *Journal of Regulatory Economics*, 38(3), 313–326.

Rogerson, W. P. (1992). Overhead allocation and incentives for cost minimization in defense procurement. *Accounting Review*, 67(4), 671–690.

Sappington, D. E. M. (2002). Price regulation. In M. E. Cave, S. K. Majumdar, & I. Vogelsang (Eds.), *Handbook of telecommunications economics* (Vol. 1, pp. 225–293). Amsterdam: Elsevier.

Sappington, D. E. M., & Sidak, J. G. (2003). Incentives for anticompetitive behavior by public enterprises. *Review of Industrial Organization*, 22(3), 183–206.

Sappington, D. E. M., & Weisman, D. L. (2010). Price cap regulation: What have we learned from twenty-five years of experience in the telecommunications industry? *Journal of Regulatory Economics*, 38(3), 227–257.

Sweeney, G. (1981). Adoption of cost-saving innovations by a regulated firm. *American Economic Review*, 71(3), 437–447.

Sweeney, G. (1982). Welfare implications of fully distributed cost pricing applied to partially regulated firms. *Bell Journal of Economics*, 13(2), 525–533.

United States Senate. (1995). *Interstate Commerce Commission Sunset Act of 1995, report of the committee on commerce, science, and transportation,* Report 104–176. U.S. Government Printing Office, Washington, DC.

Vickers, J., & Yarrow, G. (1988). *Privatization: An economic analysis.* Cambridge, MA: The MIT Press.

Wilson, W. W. (1996). Legislated market dominance in railroad markets. *Research in Transportation Economics*, 4(1), 49–67.

Wilson, W. W. (1997). Cost savings and productivity in the railroad industry. *Journal of Regulatory Economics*, 11(1), 21–40.

Wilson, W. W. (2013). Introduction: The Interstate Commerce Act of 1887. *Review of Industrial Organization*, 43(1–2), 3–6.

Wilson, W. W., & Wolak, F. A. (2016). Rail costing and regulation: The uniform rail costing system. *Review of Industrial Organization*, in press.

Winston, C. (2005). *The success of the Staggers Rail Act of 1980*, Related Publication 05–24. Washington, DC, AEI-Brookings Joint Center for Regulatory Studies.

# Contributors

**Azrina Abdullah Al-Hadi** is a Senior Lecturer in the Centre of Global Business and Digital Economy at Faculty of Economics and Management, Universiti Kebangsaan Malaysia.

**David Austin** is a Principal Analyst in the Microeconomic Studies Division of the Congressional Budget Office (CBO) and an Adjunct Faculty member at Johns Hopkins University.

**David Besanko** is the IBM Professor of Regulation and Competitive Practices at the Kellogg School of Management at Northwestern University.

**Mark Burton** is a Research Associate Professor of Economics in the Haslam College of Business at the University of Tennessee (Knoxville).

**Ishay Hadash** is a former Research Associate in the Department of Applied Economics at the University of Minnesota and the co-founder and CEO of CoreTemp Technologies Inc.

**Paul Hitchcock** is a Senior Policy Advisor in the law offices of Holland & Knight and the former General Commerce Counsel at CSX Corporation.

**William Huneke** is a Consulting Economist and the former Director of the Office of Economics at the Surface Transportation Board (STB).

**Jeffrey T. Macher** is a Professor of Economics, Strategy, and Policy in the McDonough School of Business at Georgetown University.

**John W. Mayo** is the Elsa Carlson McDonough Professor of Business Administration and Professor of Economics, Business, and Public Policy at Georgetown University.

**Gerard J. McCullough** is an Associate Professor of Economics in the Department of Applied Economics at the University of Minnesota.

**Ferdinando Monte** is an Assistant Professor of Strategy and Economics in the McDonough School of Business at Georgetown University.

**James Peoples** is a Professor of Economics in the Department of Economics at the University of Wisconsin-Milwaukee.

**Lee F. Pinkowitz** is an Associate Professor of Finance in the McDonough School of Business at Georgetown University.

**David E. M. Sappington** is an Eminent Scholar in the Department of Economics and the Director of the Robert F. Lanzillotti Public Policy Research Center at the University of Florida.

**Robert D. Willig** is a Professor of Economics and Public Affairs (Emeritus) in the Woodrow Wilson School of Public and International Affairs at Princeton University.

# Index

Note: Page numbers in bold indicate a table and page numbers in italics indicate a figure on the corresponding page.

Printed in the United States
by Baker & Taylor Publisher Services